Market Integration, Regionalism and

Market Integration, Regionalism and the Global and the policy implication of changes in the global economy process of regional integration, conducted using the newest techniques of economic analysis. The principal message drawn from these analytical and policy insights is that in a world characterised by trade distortions and nonlinearities, regional integration may or may not foster global integration, and may or may not advance regional or global convergence. The key is good economic policy based on sound economic analysis. Part One of the volume covers three international trade policy issues: regionalism and multilateralism; the political economy of trade policy; and trade income inequality. Part Two focuses on three 'domestic' problems faced by regional groups: labour migration; exchange rate arrangements; and real convergence.

RICHARD E. BALDWIN is based at the Graduate Institute of International Studies in Geneva.

DANIEL COHEN is based at the Université de Paris.

ANDRE SAPIR is based at the Université Libre de Bruxelles.

ANTHONY VENABLES is based at the London School of Economics.

Centre for Economic Policy Research

The Centre for Economic Policy Research is a network of over 400 Research Fellows, based primarily in European universities. The Centre coordinates its Fellows' research activities and communicates their results to the public and private sectors. CEPR is an entrepreneur, developing research initiatives with the producers, consumers and sponsors of research. Established in 1983, CEPR is a European economics research organisation with uniquely wide-ranging scope and activities.

CEPR is a registered educational charity. Institutional (core) finance for the Centre is provided by major grants from the Economic and Social Research Council, under which an ESRC Resource Centre operates within CEPR; the Esmée Fairbairn Charitable Trust and the Bank of England. The Centre is also supported by the European Monetary Institute; the Bank for International settlements; 22 national central banks and 45 companies. None of these organisations gives prior review to the Centre's publications, nor do they necessarily endorse the views expressed therein.

The Centre is pluralist and non-partisan, bringing economic research to bear on the analysis of medium- and long-run questions. CEPR research may include views on policy, but the Executive Committee of the Centre does not give prior review to its publications, and the Centre takes no institutional policy positions. The opinions expressed in this report are those of the authors and not those of the Centre for Economic Policy Research.

Executive Committee

Chairman	Anthony Loehnis
Vice-Chairman	Guillermo de la Dehesa
Jan Krysztof Bielecki	Denis Gromb
Ronald Cohen	Philippe Lagayette
Diane Coyle	Peter Middleton
Jean-Pierre Danthine	Bridget Rosewell
Quentin Davies	Mario Sarcinelli
	Kermit Schoenholtz

Officers

President	Richard Portes
Chief Executive Officer	Stephen Yeo
Research Director	Mathias Dewatripont

90–98 Goswell Road
London EC1V 7RR
Tel: (44 171) 878 2900
Fax: (44 171) 878 2999
Email: cepr@cepr.org
Website: http://www.cepr.org

Instituto De Estudios Económicos de Galicia Pedro Barrié De La Maza

The Instituto de Estudios Económicos de Galicia, Pedro Barrié de la Maza (IEEG PBM) was established in 1994 as an affiliate of the Fundación Pedro Barrié de la Maza, under the patronage of this foundation and Banco Pastor. The aim pursued by the Fundación in forming the IEEG PBM is to create an instrument for the advancement and dissemination of economic knowledge and a locus of intellectual reference and debate on economic issues both for policy-makers and private sector interests in Galicia.

To attain its objectives of furthering the advancement and awareness of economic science in Galicia, the IEEG PBM undertakes research on matters of both scientific relevance and practical import to the Galician economy. Through this, the IEEG PBM intends to foster the development of highly qualified research economists in the universities of Galicia. This research, as well as other activities of the IEEG PBM, are made available to all interested scholars and the general public.

The IEEG PBM is an open and independent institution guided by the desire to advance knowledge. As with all other institutions appertaining to the Fundación Pedro Barrié de la Maza, it is not subject to any doctrine or dictate other than the scientific method and the understanding of the economic reality. Governance of the IEEG PBM is entrusted to a Board of Directors named jointly by the Fundación and Banco Pastor. The Board is chaired by Joaquın Arias y Dıaz de Rábago, Vice President of the Fundación. Its directors are Vicente Arias Moaquera and José Mara Arias Mosquera, designated by the Fundación, and Alfonso Porras del Corral and Guillermo de la Dehesa, Managing Director, designated by Banco Pastor. The Secretary is Higinio Guillamón.

The Board takes advice and delegates academic matters on a Commission of Scientific Coordinators, chosen mostly from university professors. Members of the Commission are: Antonio Erias, University of Corunna; Fernando González Laxe, University of Corunna; Antonio Grando, University of Corunna; Julio Sequeiros, University of Corunna; Luis Caramés, University of Santiago; Alberto Meixide, University of Santiago; Andrés Precedo, University of Santiago; José Mara da Rocha, University of Vigo; Jorge González Gurriarán, University of Vigo; and Manuel Varela, University of Vigo.

Market Integration, Regionalism and the Global Economy

Edited by

RICHARD BALDWIN

DANIEL COHEN,

ANDRE SAPIR

and

ANTHONY VENABLES

PUBLISHED BY THE PRESS SYNDICATE OF THE UNIVERSITY OF CAMBRIDGE
The Pitt Building, Trumpington Street, Cambridge CB2 1RP, United Kingdom

CAMBRIDGE UNIVERSITY PRESS
The Edinburgh Building, Cambridge, CB2 2RU, UK http://www.cup.cam.ac.uk
40 West 20th Street, New York, NY 10011–11, USA   http://www.cup.org
10 Stamford Road, Oakleigh, Melbourne 3166, Australia

© Centre for Economic Policy Research 1999

First published 1999

Printed in the United Kingdom at the University Press, Cambridge

Typeset in 10/12pt Times   [CE]

A catalogue record for this book is available from the British Library

Library of Congress cataloguing in publication data

Market integration, regionalism, and the global economy / edited by Richard Baldwin ... [et al.].
   p.   cm.
Includes index.
ISBN 0 521 64181 0 hb. – ISBN 0 521 64589 1 pb.
1. International economic integration.   2. Regionalism.
3. International economic relations.   4. Free Trade.
I. Baldwin, Richard E.
HF1418.5.M375   1999
337.1–dc21   98–11548   CIP

ISBN 0 521 64181 0 hardback
ISBN 0 521 64589 1 paperback

Contents

List of figures   *page* xi
List of tables   xiii
Preface   xv
Acknowledgements   xvii
List of conference participants   xviii

1   Introduction   1
Richard Baldwin, Daniel Cohen, André Sapir and
Anthony Venables

PART ONE: REGIONALISM AND THE GLOBAL ECONOMY   5

2   Regionalism vs. multilateralism   7
L. Alan Winters
1   Introduction   7
2   Definitions and classifications   8
3   Models of tariff regimes   11
4   What the evidence suggests   34
5   Finale   40
Appendix: and index of multilateralism?   42
Discussion   49
André Sapir

3   Preferential agreements and the multilateral trading system   53
Kyle Bagwell and Robert W. Staiger
1   Introduction   53
2   Reciprocity   56
3   Reciprocity and non-discrimination   65
4   Preferential agreements   71
5   Enforcement   72

6	Conclusions	76
	Discussion	**79**
	Raquel Fernández	

4   Politics and trade policy   **86**
Elhanan Helpman

1	Introduction	86
2	Political economy approaches	87
3	Double-edged diplomacy	103
	Discussion	**113**
	Thierry Verdier	

5   Globalisation and labour, or: if globalisation is a bowl of   **117**
cherries, why are there so many glum faces around the table?
Dani Rodrik

1	Introduction	117
2	Trade and wages	120
3	The consequences of increased international mobility by firms for the rent-sharing bargain	124
4	Trade and labour standards	128
5	Quantifying labour standards and their consequences	132
6	Trade, external risk and the role of government	141
7	Conclusions	146
	Discussion	**150**
	Alasdair Smith	

6   Openness and wage inequality in developing countries: the Latin   **153**
American challenge to East Asian conventional wisdom
Adrian Wood

1	Heckscher–Ohlin theory	153
2	Overview of empirical evidence	158
3	Differences between East Asia and Latin America	167
4	Differences between 1960s–1970s and 1980s–1990s	169
5	Summary and conclusions	175
	Discussion	**181**
	Riccardo Faini	
1	Greater international mobility of capital	182
2	Discriminatory trade liberalisation	183
3	Perverse trade-policy effects	183

PART TWO: MARKET INTEGRATION AND REGIONALISM   **185**

7   **Operationalising the theory of optimum currency areas**   **187**
    Tamim Bayoumi and Barry Eichengreen
    1   Introduction   187
    2   A review of theory and empirics   188
    3   New evidence: German unification and economic integration 198
    4   Conclusion   208
    Discussion   **216**
    Jean Pisani-Ferry
    1   Introduction   216
    2   Some shortcomings in the operationalisation of OCA theory 217
    3   Dynamic interactions between economic integration   222
        and monetary integration: are they already perverse?

8   **European migrants: an endangered species?**   **228**
    Riccardo Faini
    1   Introduction   228
    2   The fall in intra-European mobility   230
    3   Migration and migration intentions in Italy and Spain   235
    4   Job-search and job-mobility attitudes   243
    5   Economic integration and labour mobility   245
    6   Conclusions   247
    Discussion   **251**
    Richard Baldwin

9   **Geography and specialisation: industrial belts on a circular plain**   **254**
    Anthony J. Venables
    1   Introduction   254
    2   Overview of the model   256
    3   Centre vs. periphery   259
    4   Industries differing in trade costs   260
    5   Industrial linkages   262
    6   Alternative input–output structures   265
    7   Implications and conclusions   267
    Appendix: the model   **269**
    Discussion   **273**
    Alasdair Smith

10 **Convergence . . . an overview**   **275**
    Giuseppe Bertola
    1   Introduction   275

2   What the data say   276
3   Endogenous vs. exogenous growth theories   278
4   Relaxing neoclassical assumptions   281
5   Economic integration and income distribution   283
6   Conclusions   291
Discussion   **295**
Daniel Cohen

11   Convergence as distribution dynamics (with or without growth)   298
Danny T. Quah
1   Introduction   298
2   Theoretical models   300
3   Empirics   313
4   Conclusions   323
Discussion   **328**
Lucrezia Reichlin
1   Can we study convergence without addressing the distribution question?   328
2   The proposed empirical framework   329
3   What can we potentially learn?   330
4   Convergence   331
5   Inference   332
6   An alternative framework   333

Index   337

Figures

2A.1	Iso-multilateralism loci	*page*	43
3.1	Best-response conditions for good x		59
3.2	Nash and efficient iso-net tariff lines		65
D3.1	Trade policies and equilibrium		80
5.1	Incidence in the open economy		122
5.2	Volatility in the open economy		131
5.3	Partial correlation between openness and share of workforce in government employment		145
6.1	Effects of openness on relative wages: two traded goods		155
6.2	Effect of openness on relative wages: many traded goods		157
6.3	Entry of low-income Asia: two traded goods		171
6.4	Entry of low-income Asia: many traded goods		171
6.5	Price of developing-country manufactured exports relative to developed-country exports of machinery, transport equipment and services, 1975–95		172
6.6	Effects of openness and technology transfer		174
D7.1	Correlation of shocks and exchange rate flexibility		220
D7.2	Real exchange rate volatlity, 1970–90 and correlation of supply shocks		221
D7.3	Finger index of export structure similarity (*vis-à-vis* Germany), 1967–93		224
D7.4	Grubel–Lloyd indicator for intra-EC12 trade, all industries, 1980–94		225
8.1	Migration rates from Southern Europe, 1961–88		230
8.2	Income differentials, 1970–90		231
8.3	Real wage differentials, 1968–95		232
8.4	Unemployment differentials, 1969–92		232
8.5	The role of wage and amenities in the migration choice		234
8.6	Migration from Southern Italy, 1970–90		236
9.1	Centre and periphery		296

9.2	Differing trade costs	261
9.3	Industrial linkages	264
9.4	Upstream–downstream	266
10.1	'Classical' approach to convergence	280
11.1	Deterministic neoclassical convergence	303
11.2	Divergence towards non-degenerate steady-state invariant distribution	309
11.3	Stratification, polarisation and convergence clubs	312
11.4	Densities of normalised cross-country productivities: emerging twin peaks	315
11.5	Densities of normalised cross-country productivities: trade conditioning	319
11.6	Densities of normalised cross-country productivities: spatial conditioning	320
11.7	Stochastic kernel, normalised cross-country productivities: trade conditioning	321
11.8	Stochastic kernel, normalised cross-country productivities: spatial conditioning	321

Tables

2.1	The universalist argument: costs and benefits for a single country if the measure passes	*page* 33
5.1	Increasing instability in labour market outcomes, 1970–87	123
5.2	Correlation matrix	135
5.3	Labour standards and labour costs, 1985–8	136
5.4	Labour standards and comparative advantage	138
5.5	Labour standards and comparative advantage, excluding high- income countries	139
5.6	Labour standards and foreign investment, 1982–9	140
5.7	Openness and size of government, 1985–92	144
6.1	Skill intensity of trade in manufactures, 1966–73	159
6.2	Skill intensity of manufactured exports	160
6.3	Effects of increased openness in five Latin American countries, 1974–95	165
7.1	Correlation matrices of aggregate supply shocks, 1963–93	200
7.2	Correlation matrices of aggregate demand shocks, 1963–93	203
7.3	Coherence of aggregate supply disturbances, 1963–94	205
7.4	Trends in regional specialisation of production for the European Union and the United States, 1972–87	207
D7.1	Average standard deviation of GDP growth rates, 1964–94	223
8.1	Demographic evolution in Southern Europe, 1960–90	233
8.2	Unemployment rates in Italian regions, 1963–94	237
8.3	Mobility attitudes and job search	240
8.4	Econometric determinants of mobility attitudes	242
8.5	Mobility attitudes and job search	244
D11.1	Ergodic distributions	330

Preface

This volume contains the proceedings of a conference organised by the Centre for Economic Policy Research and held in La Coruña on 26 April 1996. The meeting was hosted by the Instituto de Estudios Económicos de Galicia, Pedro Barrié de la Maza. It was the final conference of the Centre for Economic Policy Research's programme 'Market Integration, Regionalism and Global Economy (MIRAGE)', which was funded by Grant Number 902–1265 from The Ford Foundation.

We are grateful to Julia Newcomb and Toni Orloff at CEPR and Higinio Guillemon Duch at Banco Pastor for logistical help with the conference and the volume, and to Barbara Docherty, who served as Production Editor. We are also grateful to Guillermo de la Dehesa, Richard Portes and Stephen Yeo for their support and encouragement for the conference. Fundación Pedro Barrié de la Maza provided excellent conference facilities and funding for the meeting. Finally, we should like to express our appreciation to the participants at the conference, whose contributions to the discussion and stimulating comments helped to make the conference and volume so interesting. The contributions to this volume demonstrate the richness of the MIRAGE research programme, whose objective was to analyse the process of regional integration accompanying changes in the global economy.

The Editors
October 1998

Acknowledgements

The editors and publishers wish to acknowledge with thanks permission from the following to reproduce copyright material.

World Bank Economic Review, for an earlier version of chapter 6.

Brookings Papers on Economic Activity, for data in table 5.1, from P. Gottschalk and R. Moffitt, 'The Growth of Earnings Instability in the US Labor Market' (1994).

University of Chicago Press, for data in table 6.1, from A. O. Krueger *et al.* (eds.), *Trade and Employment in Developing Countries: 1* (1981) and from A. O. Krueger, *Trade and Employment in Developing Countries: 3* (1983).

Journal of Development Studies, for data in table 6.2, from E. Londero and S. Teitel, 'Industrialisation and the Factor Content of Latin American Exports of Manufactures' (1996).

Harvard University, for data in table 6.3, from unpublished papers by D. Robbins (1995–6) and by D. Robbins, M. Gonzalez and A. Menendez (1995).

Lynne Reinner, for data in table 6.3, from D. Robbins and T. Grindling, 'Educational Expansion, Trade Liberalisation and Distribution in Costa Rica', in A. Berry (ed.), *Economic Reform and Income Distribution in Latin America* (1997).

OECD, for data in table D7.1.

ILO, for data in table 8.1.

ISTAT, for data in table 8.2.

European Commission/Kogan Page Earthscan, for Figure D7.1, from L. Fontagné *et al.*, *The Single Market Review*, Subseries IV, vol. 2 (1997).

Conference participants

Constantino Arosa Gómez, *Universidad de La Coruña*
Michael J. Artis, *European University Institute, Firenze, and CEPR*
Richard Baldwin, *Graduate Institute of International Studies, Geneva, and CEPR*
Robert Baldwin, *University of Wisconsin*
Pilar Barros Naveira, *Universidad de Santiago*
Tamim Bayoumi, *IMF and CEPR*
Giuseppe Bertola, *Università di Torino and CEPR*
Peter Bofinger, *Universität Würzburg and CEPR*
Jorge Braga de Macedo, *Universidade Nova de Lisboa and CEPR*
Daniel Cohen, *Université de Paris I, Ecole Normale Supérieure, Paris, and CEPR*
Manuel Conthe, *Ministry of Economy, Madrid*
Cristina Corado, *Universidade Nova de Lisboa*
Antonio Cortés, *Banco Central Hispano*
Guillermo de la Dehesa, *Banco Pastor and CEPR*
Antonio Erias Rey, *Universidad de La Coruña*
Andrés Faiña, *Universidad de La Coruña*
Riccardo Faini, *Università di Brescia and CEPR*
Raquel Fernández, *New York University*
Marta Fernández Redondo, *Universidad de La Coruña*
M. Jesús Freire, *Universidad de Vigo*
Juan Garca Cebro, *Universidad de La Coruña*
Jorge González Gurriarán, *Escuela Universitaria EE, Vigo*
Fernando González Laxe, *Universidad de La Coruña*
Higinio Guillamón, *Banco Pastor*
José Luis Malo de Molina, *Banco de España*
Carmela Martín, *Fundación FIES, Madrid*
Alberto Meixide Vecino, *Universidad de Santiago*
José Méndez Naya, *Universidad de La Coruña*

Volker Nitsch, *Bankgesellschaft Berlin*
Santiago Novoa Garca, *Universidad de Vigo*
Ramón Núnez Gamallo, *Universidad de La Coruña*
Tessa Ogden, *CEPR*
Toni Orloff, *CEPR*
José Luis Outes Ruso, *Universidad de Vigo*
Alfredo Pastor, *IESE, Barcelona*
Vicente López Perea, *Transportes Finisterre, La Coruña*
Roberto Pereira, *Universidad de Vigo*
Emilio Pérez Touriño, *Universidad de Santiago*
Jean Pisani-Ferry, *CEPII, Paris*
Andrés Precedo Ledo, *Xunta de Galicia*
Danny T. Quah, *London School of Economics and CEPR*
José Ramón Garca Menéndez, *Universidad de Santiago*
Lucrezia Reichlin, ECARE, *Université Libre de Bruxelles, and CEPR*
Jaime Requeijo, *CUNEF, Madrid*
Carlos Ricoy, *Universidad de Santiago*
Juan Rodriguez Yuste, *Xunta de Galicia*
Dani Rodrik, *Harvard University and CEPR*
André Sapir, ECARE, *Université Libre de Bruxelles, and CEPR*
Julio G. Sequeiros Tizón, *Universidad de La Coruña*
Alasdair Smith, *University of Sussex and CEPR*
Robert W. Staiger, *University of Wisconsin*
Juan Vázquez, *Universidad Internacional Menéndez Pelayo, Santander*
José Angel Vázquez Barquero, *Universidad de Vigo*
Anthony J. Venables, *London School of Economics and CEPR*
Ramón Varela Santamara, *Universidad de La Coruña*
Thierry Verdier, *DELTA, Paris, and CEPR*
L. Alan Winters, *World Bank and CEPR*
Adrian Wood, *Institute of Development Studies, University of Sussex*
Antonio Zalbalza Martí, *Universidad de Valencia*

1　Introduction

RICHARD BALDWIN, DANIEL COHEN,
ANDRE SAPIR AND ANTHONY VENABLES

The chapters in this volume are drawn from the final conference of the
CEPR's programme of research on 'Market Integration, Regionalism
and the Global Economy' (MIRAGE). The objective of this research
was to use new techniques of economic analysis to study changes in the
global economy in relationship to the process of regional integration,
and to draw out the policy implications of such changes. Chapters in
this volume are organised in two parts. Part One (chapters 2–6) covers
three international trade policy issues: regionalism and multilateralism;
the political economy of trade policy; and trade income inequality. Part
Two (chapters 7–11) focuses on three 'domestic' problems faced by
regional groups: labour migration; exchange rate arrangements; and real
convergence.

　Chapter 2, by Winters, surveys the burgeoning literature on regionalism
vs. multilateralism. Are regional integration schemes good or bad for the
multilateral trading system? In the seven years since Krugman's seminal
paper (1991) on the subject, the literature has progressed from analysing
external tariff setting by symmetric trading blocs, through to looking at
the process of bloc formation, the political economy of policy-making
and the role of internal institutional arrangements within blocs in
determining outcomes. Krugman's original result – that three blocs is the
pessimum number from the point of view of world welfare – has been
shown to be fragile, but what view of regionalism has taken its place?
Winters' answer is that 'we don't know yet'. Political economy analysis
suggests that regionalism may be more attractive to producer lobbies
than is multilateralism – because they get the benefits from trade
diversion. However, effective analysis of these issues requires that more
attention be devoted to analysis of institutional arrangements for
decision-taking within trading blocs.

　Bagwell and Staiger in chapter 3 also look at the relationship between
regional integration agreements and multilateral trading. They investigate

the incentives that governments have for pursuing reciprocal agreements rather than unilateral liberalisations, and whether the World Trade Organisation (WTO) serves countries' interests by allowing such agreements to violate the MFN principle.

One of the most important developments in recent policy analysis has been the increased attention now paid to the political process through which policy is formed. Helpman in chapter 4 provides an elegant survey and synthesis of different approaches in this new political economy literature. Authors have taken many different pathways: these include the direct-democracy approach, in which individuals vote directly over policy; the political support function approach, in which government seeks to maximize support from different interest groups; and models of lobbying, in which lobbies' expenditures determine policy outcomes, influence electoral competition, or shape the platforms on which parties stand. Helpman's chapter provides a unifying framework within which the common elements of these approaches, and the key differences which drive their results, are drawn out.

Chapters 5 and 6 are devoted to the interaction between trade and labour markets. Rodrik in chapter 5 reviews arguments as to why labour in developed countries often regards globalisation with hostility. He argues that the main impact of globalisation on the labour market may come not through a downward shift in the labour demand schedule, but through an increase in its elasiticity, as it becomes easier for firms to substitute foreign for domestic labour. He then turns to the role of government, arguing that the growth of trade enhances the role of government as a provider of insurance against external risk. This argument is supported by evidence showing that more open economies tend to have relatively larger governments than do less open countries. Globalisation creates a dilemma for this aspect of government activity, however. If globalisation curtails the role of government, this is another reason why labour – in particular immobile, unskilled labour – may feel threatened.

Wood in chapter 6 examines the impact of openness on wage inequality within developing countries, and challenges the conventional wisdom – based largely on East Asian experience in the 1960s and 1970s – that openness narrows the wage gap between skilled and unskilled workers. The experience of Latin America since the mid-1980s indicates that openness has increased wage differentials. Wood argues that the main reason for this lies not in differences between East Asia and Latin America, but instead in the later time period he studies. In particular, the entry of China into the world market, perhaps coupled with the technology bias of new techniques of production, means that a widening of skilled–unskilled wage gaps is also to be expected in other developing countries.

Whereas chapters 2–6 analyse regional integration in the global context, chapters 7–11 examine issues arising within regional groupings, especially core–periphery differences. Bayoumi and Eichengreen in chapter 7 turn from the design of trade policy and trade institutions to the exchange rate system, and look at empirical work assessing the extent to which the European Union meets the requirements of an optimum currency area. The standard approach is to look at the cross-country correlation of supply and demand disturbances, and research suggests that the European Union divides into a core region (countries with shocks highly correlated with Germany's) and a peripheral region. Bayoumi and Eichengreen extend the data period to include German reunification and find that the core–periphery distinction is still useful, although German disturbances are uncorrelated with other countries in the core from the early 1990s onwards.

As countries experience idiosyncratic shocks, so labour mobility may be an important adjustment mechanism for countries and regions – particularly if they form a monetary union. Faini in chapter 8 analyses migration flows in Europe. Massive pre-war overseas migrations were replaced in the post-war period by large-scale migrations within Europe, but these migration flows have now dropped to a fraction of their previous level. Faini reviews explanations for the decline in European labour mobility, and goes on to analyse the Spanish and Italian experience in greater detail. He argues that improved welfare systems together with family support networks reduce the 'push' factors behind migration, and that these combine with significant obstacles to intra-European labour mobility. He concludes that the prospects for resumption of a high level of labour mobility within Europe are not particularly bright.

Venables in chapter 9 turns from the labour market to investigation of the effects of economic integration on core–periphery differences in industrial structure and income levels. He argues that regions' industrial structures may be determined by their geographical location, and that economic integration may bring significant changes in the pattern of specialisation. Industries that were formerly located in central regions may relocate to the periphery, and regions may become more specialised. Some empirical work in the chapter suggests that a process of increasing regional specialisation is underway in Europe.

The final two chapters in the volume deal with regional and national convergence. Bertola in chapter 10 reviews both the empirical and the theoretical arguments addressing the question: does economic growth lead to convergence of *per capita* incomes across countries and/or regions? He concludes that the empirical evidence gives a (qualified) negative answer to this question. Theoretical work outlines many mechanisms through which growth will change inquality at all levels – from individual though regional to national. After reviewing this work, Bertola argues that more theoretical work on the relationship between openness and convergence is needed.

Quah in chapter 11 provides an overview of recent research that addresses the question: what determines the dynamics of cross-economy income distributions? He argues that economists should be studying the dynamics of the entire cross-section income distribution, and that standard analyses based on the 'representative economy' and the associated convergence regression analysis are quite inappropriate. Analysis of the full distribution dynamics reveals changes in the shapes of the distribution – for example, the 'twin-peaks' phenomenon of clustering in the income distribution – and indicates the probabilities that countries can change their relative positions.

In conclusion, this volume offers important analytical and policy insights in changes in the global economy occurring through the process of regional integration. The principal message is that in a world characterised by trade distortions and non-linearities regional integration may or may not foster global integration, and may or may not advance regional or global convergence. The key is good economic policy based on sound economic analysis.

REFERENCE

Krugman, P., 1991. 'Is Bilateralism Bad?', in E. Helpman and A. Razin (eds.), *International Trade and Trade Policy* (Cambridge, MA: MIT Press)

Part One
Regionalism and the global economy

2 Regionalism vs. multilateralism

L. ALAN WINTERS

1 Introduction

The literature on 'regionalism vs. multilateralism' is burgeoning as economists and a few political scientists grapple with the question of whether regional integration arrangements (RIAs) are good or bad for the multilateral system as a whole. Are RIAs 'building blocks or stumbling blocks', in Bhagwati's (1991) memorable phrase, or stepping stones towards multilateralism? As we worry about the ability of the WTO to maintain the GATT's unsteady yet distinct momentum towards liberalism, and as we contemplate the emergence of world-scale RIAs – the European Union, NAFTA, FTAA, APEC and, possibly, TAFTA – this question has never been more pressing.

'Regionalism vs. multilateralism' switches the focus of research from the immediate consequences of regionalism for the economic welfare of the integrating partners to the question of whether it sets up forces which encourage or discourage evolution towards globally freer trade. The answer is 'we don't know yet'. One can build models that suggest either conclusion, but to date these are sufficiently abstract that they should be viewed as parables rather than sources of testable predictions.

Moreover, even if we had testable predictions we have very little evidence. Arguably the European Union is the only RIA that is both big enough to affect the multilateral system and long-enough lived to have currently observable consequences. The European Union allows one convincingly to reject the hypothesis that one act of regionalism necessarily leads to the collapse of the multilateral system. But it is difficult to go further: the *anti-monde* to EU creation is unknown and one does not know to what extent the European Union is special. Thus any discussion of the evidence is necessarily judgemental. The majority view is, I think, that the advent of the European Union aided multilateralism. While I should like to believe this – especially now that US commitment to multilateralism is diluted by other 'lateralisms' (Summers, 1991) – more needs to be done before it can be considered proven beyond reasonable doubt.

This chapter has three substantive sections. Section 2 tries to define some terms, which turns out to be much more complicated than I expected: any reader who can define multilateralism simply can skip section 2.1 and let me know his or her definition. It also proposes an organisational classification for models of 'regionalism vs. multilateralism'. Section 3 discusses these models under five headings and Section 4 discusses some evidence. Section 5 offers some conclusions.

Survey articles are sometimes used to resolve issues of intellectual precedence. I have not sought to do this and would caution against using the dates of the papers included here as a means of doing so. In a field barely five years old, publication delays completely distort the time picture.

2   Definitions and classifications

2.1   Definitions

'Regionalism vs. multilateralism' is a much-discussed topic among trade economists, but one which is surprisingly short on precise measures. I shall define 'regionalism' loosely as any policy designed to reduce trade barriers between a subset of countries, regardless of whether those countries are actually contiguous or even close to each other. I shall not define 'multilateralism' precisely, however, because – to my surprise and regret – I find that I cannot easily do so.

Although multilateralism is a characteristic of the world economy or world economic system, it must ultimately reside in the behaviour of individual countries – the extent to which they behave in a multilateral fashion. For any one country, I shall treat the latter as a positive function of

(1) the degree to which discrimination is absent – perhaps the proportion of trade partners that receives identical treatment; and
(2) the extent to which the country's trading regime approximates free trade.

Strictly speaking criterion (1) would seem to be a sufficient definition of multilateralism. However, it is neither very interesting in the current context (any preferential trade arrangement with relatively few members will worsen multilateralism) nor, I infer from their writings, what most commentators have in mind when they debate the effects of regionalism on multilateralism. Criterion (2) attempts to add back the missing dimension.

The weights and functional form with which the two criteria enter the index of individual multilateralism are left vague. If, starting from a universal (MFN) tariff, a country abolished tariffs on one (small) partner, that would seem to decrease its multilateralism, but if it abolished them on all but one (small) partner that would seem to increase it.[1] Similarly, I cannot pin down precisely how to combine countries into a single global index of multilateralism. Thus we need to be cautious in comparing different views of 'regionalism vs. multilateralism' – maybe their bottom lines differ.

In assessing regionalism we need also to recognise another complication. Shifting one partner into a free trade area (FTA) has a direct impact on our measure of multilateralism but, far more importantly, it also potentially initiates a whole series of accommodating adjustments, as the integrating partners and countries in the rest of the world (RoW) adjust their policies to the new circumstances. We must consider multilateralism at the end of this process, not just at the beginning. Moreover, in some circumstances the final outcome will not be determinate; rather, regionalism might affect the probabilities with which different outcomes occur. Several of the models surveyed below examine whether regionalism makes it more or less likely that countries within and without the RIA can strike a deal to create or maintain world-wide free trade. Such models do not forecast particular outcomes, but nonetheless comment pertinently on the environment in which they might flourish.

The previous paragraph mentioned a 'process'. Multilateralism is sometimes referred to as a process whereby countries solve problems in an interactive and cooperative fashion (Yarbrough and Yarbrough, 1992). While such interactions could clearly be affected by regionalism, I do not use this definition here. It is a view far too closely associated with professional negotiators and international bureaucrats for my taste, and is far too vague on the question of what purpose a process serves if it is not to generate outcomes.

Other commentators might focus entirely on the final outcome – the pattern of international trade. If one could determine the perfectly multilateral volume and pattern of trade, one could then easily define the index of actual multilateralism by any of several distance measures between actual and 'perfect' trade. The problem is all too obvious, however: how do we determine perfectly multilateral trade? From a policy point of view I should also be uneasy about a definition that focused on outcomes rather than trade policy instruments, for such a definition might imply indifference between methods of achieving particular trade patterns. I recognise, however, that such unease should not influence us too much in the intellectual business of defining the phenomenon.

Finally, many economists explore the interactions between countries and the effects of regionalism on them by focusing on country welfare and, usually, world welfare. These contributions are not strictly about regionalism vs. multilateralism, for we surely cannot define multilateralism in terms of increasing welfare – even if, slightly less indefensibly, we sometimes equate them. Nonetheless, welfare is sufficiently basic to the business of economics that I include this class of studies in this survey.

2.2   A classification

To try to organise the rapidly growing model-based literature on 'regionalism vs. multilateralism', I have classified contributions according to four characteristics of their basic approach. These concern political objectives and organisation rather than economics *per se* for, in fact, most models adopt one of two main representations of the economy: the simple competitive homogeneous good model or the monopolistically competitive model. In each there is usually a one-to-one correspondence between goods and geographical entities – each entity having comparative advantage in one good – but in the latter several entities (say, provinces) accrete into one country. The four characteristics are:

(*A*) Is the objective function (1) national economic welfare or (2) some other criterion deriving from political considerations? Within the latter set, (2), does the analysis explicitly treat (i) one country, (ii) two (i.e. the partners) or (iii) three-plus (the partners and the RoW)?

(*B*) Is the model (1) symmetric or (2) asymmetric, the former entailing that the model deals only with circumstances in which all blocs are qualitatively identical? Within the latter set, I distinguish models which consider (i) only the integrating blocs, (ii) only the non-member countries (which are candidates for accession), or (iii) both.

(*C*) Is the interaction between countries (1) one-off or (2) repeated? The latter is operationalised (universally, I believe) in the form of trigger strategies.

(*D*) Is the aggregation of preferences or behaviour in the post-integration bloc (1) implicit – by far the more common assumption – or (2) explicit? While dimension (A_2) considers the roles of groups and interests as they affect each of the governments involved in the integration, this dimension (D_2) explicitly focuses on the interactions between pressure groups and between governments within the bloc when it comes to making post-integration decisions.

It is not possible to find examples of work in each of the 64 boxes that this classification defines. Equally, many authors offer examples in several boxes, and in a survey of this length one cannot enumerate all of these explicitly. Rather I locate studies according to their principal insights or those of the stream of literature to which they belong. Section 3 is based loosely on the classification. It starts with the conceptually simple symmetric welfare-maximising models (A_1, B_1, C_1, D_1) and then moves on to asymmetric models (A_1, B_2, C_1, D_1). Subsection 3.3 deals with models of negotiated tariffs (A_1, B_1 or B_2, C_2, D_1) and 3.4 with models of political economy (A_2). Finally, I consider models of the institutional structure of policy-making within an integrated bloc (D_2).

3   Models of tariff regimes

3.1   Symmetric models

While the consistency of regional trading arrangements with the multi-lateral trading system had attracted some debate previously and had, indeed, been modelled formally, the subject took off with a seminal article by Paul Krugman (1991a).[2] This considers a simple model of integration and trade policy in which there are N identical countries and B identical blocs. Each country produces one product; these are differentiated symmetrically from all others and all consumers consume all goods (Dixit–Stiglitz differentiation); there are no transport costs, but each country levies a tariff on imports from all non-partner countries. When $B = N$ each country is a bloc, but as B falls (with N/B taking integer values) the countries within each bloc offer each other free market access and levy a common tariff on all non-partners. Within each country some products are available tariff-free – domestic and partner supplies – while all others face an identical tariff, t. Tariffs are set to maximise bloc welfare given the tariffs charged elsewhere in the world – a traditional Nash optimum tariff game.

Krugman shows that as the number of blocs in the world decreases (that is, as integration occurs) each bloc's share in the other blocs' consumption rises, conferring more market power on each and raising the optimum tariff. Integration creates trade diversion but in this model it is exacerbated by raising the external tariff. Krugman (1993) shows that the effect of the latter on economic welfare is relatively weak, however, and that even if it is suppressed his main conclusion continues to hold. The latter is that the pessimum number of blocs in terms of welfare is very small – three for most of his examples.

Krugman (1993) disaggregates the causes of the welfare losses from regionalism and finds that they owe far more to trade diversion than to increases in the optimum tariff. That is, the first-order impact of what countries do to themselves through regionalism matters more than the second-order interactions between countries. This is a useful lesson when considering any trade policy, but it is particularly salutary for our discussion, reminding us that multilateralism is not the only dimension of relevance. According to the imperfect index developed above, region-alism with a fixed external tariff may or may not harm multilateralism *ceteris paribus* (see figure 2A.1, p. 43) but the act of raising the external tariff certainly does.

Krugman's work stimulated a storm of criticism and extension. The most pressing theoretical criticism was that his production structure contained no element of comparative advantage, and that this led him to over-emphasise trade diversion. Srinivasan (1993) offers one counter-example and Deardorff and Stern (1994) another; the latter have equal numbers of two kinds of country in the world and show that blocs containing equal numbers of each type realise the full benefits of free trade regardless of their external trade policies. Thus the latter become irrelevant.

A more sophisticated alternative is to be found in Bond and Syropoulos (1996a), who introduce comparative advantage in an elegant way. Each country has an equal endowment of all goods plus a supplementary amount (positive and negative) of one of them; the relative size of the supplement and the regular endowment represents the degree of comparative advantage. Working with a lower elasticity of substitution than Krugman, Bond and Syropoulos find that optimum tariffs can fall as bloc size increases symmetrically. The world welfare-minimising number of blocs is two if comparative advantage comprises having more of one good than others, but may be three or even higher if it comprises having less of only one. Thus the Krugman result – and, indeed, the effect of regionalism on multilateralism – is obviously sensitive to issues of comparative advantage.

Sinclair and Vines (1995) reproduce Bond and Syropoulos' result about the possibility of a falling optimum tariff as the number of blocs decreases, but in slightly more general circumstances – CES preferences (as in Krugman) rather than Cobb–Douglas. They also relate it to another important qualification. Krugman and most of his successors in this literature consider the creation of customs unions (CUs), which can increase tariffs above pre-integration levels because, by coordinating several countries' policies, they can exert more market power than any individual country. If the integration takes the form of FTAs, however, countries retain control of their own tariffs on the RoW and these will fall as regionalism proceeds. As more and more partners receive tariff-free access to one country's market the smaller becomes the set of goods subject to the tariff and thus the more distortionary the effect of a given tariff. Thus the incentive arises to cut the tariff in order to achieve better balance in the composition of imports –through what Sinclair and Vines call the 'optimal import-sourcing condition'.

The optimal import-sourcing condition also helps to explain why the optimal tariff for a CU might fall as the union enlarges. If countries have rather similar endowments,[3] they trade rather small proportions of their output and income and hence have rather little monopsony power over each other. Thus the optimal import allocation condition which promotes equal tariffs across partners (equal to zero if some tariffs are constrained by regional arrangements) can overcome the increased monopsony power arising from larger bloc size which tends to raise the tariff on the RoW. Krugman has wholly different endowments across countries, and hence for him the monopsony effect always dominates.

An important extension of Krugman's model is to recognise the role of transport costs. Krugman was the first to do this, in Krugman (1991b), but the issue has been most thoroughly taken up by Frankel, Stein and Wei in a series of papers.[4] Krugman (1991b) subdivided the world into continents and observed that if inter-continental trading costs were infinite – thus precluding inter-continental trade – a series of regional blocs each covering one continent would produce a first-best outcome equivalent to global free trade.[5] Krugman inferred a notion of 'natural blocs' from this – blocs for which low trade costs made regionalism a natural and beneficial policy.

Frankel, Stein and Wei (1995, 1996) and Frankel (1997) fill in the middle ground between the two Krugman views by allowing transport costs to be finite but non-zero. As might be expected they find that, as inter-continental transportation and business costs increase relative to intra-continental ones, regionalism becomes a better policy in welfare terms. For a particular parameter constellation (three continents each with two countries, tariffs of 30 per cent, an elasticity of substitution between varieties of four, and zero intra-continental trading costs) they find that if inter-continental costs absorb above 15 per cent of the gross value of an export, intra-continental regionalism is welfare-improving. This result is interesting, but not very robust. Frankel, Stein and Wei themselves quote contrary results and Nitsch (1996a) shows that just raising intra-continental costs to 5 per cent in the case above means that regional blocs are welfare-improving for all values of inter-continental costs. Inter-continental regionalism (i.e. blocs between countries in different continents) is always harmful for Frankel Stein and Wei, although as inter-continental costs rise it becomes less so because it affects less and less trade. This result has also been challenged by Nitsch (1996b) who gives examples with relatively low inter-continental transport costs in which 'unnatural' integration dominates 'natural' integration!

Frankel, Stein and Wei also consider preferential trading areas which merely reduce rather than abolish tariffs between partners. Preferential areas can always be constructed to be welfare improving – essentially because they ensure that the optimal import-sourcing condition is not too badly violated. In this sense Frankel, Stein and Wei argue that bloc formation is a stepping stone towards multilateral free trade, but since there is no mechanism through which the benign path is ensured or even encouraged this does not seem a particularly powerful characterisation. Merely referring to the welfare benefits is not sufficient, for one could equally well refer to the (greater) benefits of jumping straight to free trade.[6] I shall not pursue this (GATT-proscribed) analysis of preferential trading blocs further. It seems to me seriously flawed on the political economy grounds that it could completely undermine the MFN clause (which could easily prevent multilateral progress towards liberalisation) and encourages too much trade activism.

A further wrinkle on the Frankel model is provided by Spilimbergo and Stein (1996) who introduce trade based on comparative advantage in addition to Krugman's and Frankel's basic intra-industry variety. If inter-continental trading costs are very low Spilimbergo and Stein replicate the results above – i.e. Krugman's (1991a) 'anti-bloc' result if variety effects are strong, and welfare-increasing with the size of blocs (and thus their fewness) if these effects are weak. With moderate inter-continental costs, on the other hand, Spilimbergo and Stein replicate Frankel, Stein and Wei. This model is the current encompassing model for CUs – all the above discussion is, at least loosely speaking, a special case of Spilimbergo and Stein.

For completeness I mention one final symmetric welfare-maximising model which suggests that regionalism can provide stepping stones to multilateralism within a somewhat unconventional framework. Collie (1997) considers countries each with a constant returns to scale (CRS) sector and one differentiated good sector. The latter compete in a third market and receive export subsidies as in the traditional strategic trade policy story. Integration between these countries allows – and encourages – better coordination of export subsidies and hence reduces distortions and raises welfare. This effect continues as bloc size grows until all the (producing) countries are integrated. This is not a particularly persuasive model, however, for the CRS sectors do not change their level of integration, export subsidies are not the instrument of concern in regionalism and there is, in this model, no incentive for any country to join a bloc. For these reasons, Collie's is not a convincing refutation of the concerns that regionalism undermines multilateralism.

3.2   Asymmetric models

A feature of all the results discussed so far is that regionalism is always symmetric in the sense that as bloc size increases countries recombine into groups of equal size. This is a useful simplification for asking what the effects are of having bloc size B_1 in the world economy and how such effects compare with those of having bloc size B_2 in an otherwise identical world. But there is no sense of evolution or expansion in such a static setup and this severely limits the light it can shed on the issue of whether regionalism might *lead to* multilateralism. I turn now, therefore, to models in which blocs grow endogenously and thus which at some stage are asymmetric.

Bond and Syropoulos (1996a) make a start in the required direction by allowing their blocs to expand asymmetrically. Starting from a symmetric equilibrium, they show that a bloc would gain by admitting new members drawn equally from each of the other blocs. The terms of trade benefits of boosting demand for the bloc's comparative advantage goods would outweigh the trade diversionary effects in this model, even if the enlarged bloc did not increase its tariff on other countries. Second, Bond and Syropoulos ask what bloc size maximises member countries' welfare given that other countries levy optimum tariffs. The answer is large but not the whole world, for the benefits depend on terms of trade gains which are obviously missing if the bloc contains all countries.

Frankel (1997) also sheds a little light on this issue. In a world of four continents the countries of which initially practice MFN trade policy, he shows that a sequential Nash game leads to regionalism and lower welfare for all. (This does, of course, depend on parameter values.) Specifically, one continent (any one, since all are identical) can improve its welfare by creating an FTA, assuming that the other three keep their MFN tariffs. These three lose because, even absent the bloc increasing its tariff, their terms of trade decline. From here a second continent benefits itself by integrating, assuming unchanged policies elsewhere, and thence the third and fourth continents. In the end all are worse off than under MFN policies, but none has the incentive to undo the regionalism. Whether the process then continues to create two inter-continental blocs, however, Frankel does not say, but at least for a variety of parameter values this does not seem likely since inter-continental blocs have previously been shown not to be desirable.

Very similar results were derived by Goto and Hamada (1994, 1997) using a Krugman (1993)-type model with four countries.[7] They, too, found a scenario in which one regional bloc begat another but in which the two 'superblocs' then had an incentive to combine in order to achieve global free trade. More sinister, however, they also showed that once A and B had combined into a bloc it would pay them to pre-empt C and D's combining similarly, by bringing one of the latter into their own bloc. Of course, this would impose high costs on the country that was left out, but unless the other three acquiesced this country could do nothing about achieving freer trade. In detail this result just reflects an overly powerful terminal condition to an N-country game – the last country is always powerless. In more realistic circumstances the superbloc excludes more than one country and these countries would then have an incentive to create their own bloc. The insight that integrators may veto indefinite bloc expansion is real enough, however.

Nordström (1995) discusses these issues in a slightly more general framework, although at the cost of having to simulate his model rather than solve it analytically. Nordström starts with a model very similar to that of Frankel and his collaborators – with product differentiation and finite transport costs. He starts by considering just one bloc – a CU. Its creation and expansion harm excluded countries even at constant external tariffs; but in mitigation, these countries can always raise their welfare above free trade levels by joining the bloc and 'exploiting' further the remaining outsiders. As suggested by Goto and Hamada and by Bond and Syropoulos, however, this process does not lead to the so-called 'global coalition' (all countries within the CU), because existing members will eventually lose from further growth as the set of outsiders to exploit declines. Nordström suggests that after about half the countries are inside the CU, further growth will be vetoed from the inside.

Nordström observes that if the CU chooses an optimum tariff rather than a constant one, it will increase its tariff as it grows, hitting outsiders harder than in the previous example. Then, in the absence of retaliation, the optimum size of the union is about 60 per cent of the world economy. But, of course, the excluded countries might retaliate against such aggression. If they alter their MFN tariffs so that they are punishing each other as well as the CU, there is little they can do, but if they maintain tariffs against each other and coordinate their punishment tariff against the CU they can exercise significant market power. Such retaliation could reduce the CU's welfare below what it could achieve at a constant external tariff (and no retaliation) if it is smaller than about 75 per cent of countries.[8] A CU of more than 75 per cent of countries would win the tariff war even in the face of coordinated opposition.

The implication of all this for 'regionalism vs. multilateralism' is ambiguous. The assumed form of retaliation effectively transforms the excluded countries into a second CU, albeit one with non-zero internal tariffs. This raises the possibility that the two blocs could gain jointly from cooperation. However, in this model there is no identified way out of their prisoner's dilemma: the issue is not addressed. The threat of retaliation if the union raises its tariffs does nothing to prevent the creation of the union, it just limits its behaviour once formed.

Nordström explores inter-bloc issues more formally by breaking his world into two 'continents' – A and B – and allowing blocs in each, very similar to the approach taken by Frankel, Stein and Wei. Nordström finds that a CU on continent A hurts all excluded countries, but impinges much more heavily on those in A, which are the CU's 'natural' trading partners, than on those in B. The incentives are for both sets of countries to seek integration; as previously, the CU in A may close its doors, but nothing can stop a CU forming in B. However, if there is the prospect that after the formation of blocs on both continents an inter-bloc negotiation will take place, the blocs seem likely to include all the countries on their continents in order to maximise their power in this second round. Then, provided the continents are not of very disparate sizes, the subsequent negotiation of inter-bloc free trade would be mutually advantageous.

If one couples the previous paragraph with an argument that countries operating independently would not be able to negotiate global free trade, and if one is lucky with the relative sizes, Nordström's results are very favourable to regionalism. Starting from MFN tariffs a local CU forms; it is matched elsewhere in the world; both CUs expand to increase their bargaining power and then ultimately they negotiate global free trade.

Clearly there are many points at which this rosy scenario could break down. One, noted almost *en passant* by Perroni and Whalley (1994), arises because one can interpret the anxiety of small countries to join large neighbouring blocs as seeking insurance – a desire not to be left isolated if global trade war breaks out. Small countries pay for the privilege of belonging to a bloc by offering up their markets preferentially.[9] Insurance premia are higher the more uncertain the world and the costs of errors are lower if one is insured: in other words, the large powers may gain from sabre-rattling while small countries are deciding whether to join them, and after they have joined, the small countries will be less concerned to preserve a global system than previously. Since sabre-rattling is effective only if there is some chance of violence, this makes the *possibility* of regionalism look quite hostile to multilateralism.

Finally, again for completeness, I note an interesting model of a quite different nature in which regionalism is benign and welfare increases monotonically with bloc size. No country has any special characteristics, but the model is asymmetric in allowing for the formation of any coalition to block global free trade. In Kowalczyk and Sjostrom (1994) countries have monopolies in their own export goods and exploit each other by charging monopoly prices. The only policy variables in use are import price ceilings, although equivalent results would arise if import subsidies were used. Integration entails agreeing to use ceilings to force firms to price exports at marginal cost in partners' markets – i.e. it entails moving from free trade to intervention (!). The details of preferences and cost functions ensure that excluded countries are quite unaffected by such integration. In this world, identical or nearly identical countries that behaved rationally would find their way to global integration. If countries differed strongly, however, coalitions could arise that block this evolution, because they would find it more advantageous to exploit certain other countries. In these cases, however, a system of side-payments could be devised to achieve the first-best optimum. While Kowalczyk and Sjostrom's model is very stylised, it does suggest that regionalism may not lead to multilateralism and that this may be because global institutional structure cannot support mechanisms for side-payments.

A significant criticism of the work surveyed so far is that tariffs and other forms of protection are determined not by optimal tariff considerations but rather by domestic political processes mitigated by international negotiation. This is true, but the simple models are still useful in illustrating the spillovers and interactions between countries and in identifying threat points for various negotiating games. Moreover, the apparently related criticism – that GATT's Article XXIV prevents integrating countries from raising their tariffs – is not particularly powerful. Article XXIV has been notable for its weak enforcement so far; many trade policies have been unbound under the GATT and hence free of constraint; there are several GATT-consistent policies of protection – e.g. anti-dumping; and in a world of trend liberalisation, merely going more slowly than you otherwise would is essentially a form of increased protection. For these reasons I am not unhappy with models that take seriously the threat that blocs could raise barriers. On the other hand, the implications of strictly optimal tariffs (e.g. indifference to changes in trade volumes) are uncomfortable and generalisations would be welcome. The rest of this part of the chapter therefore considers a broader set of models, starting by recognising the importance of negotiations.

3.3 Negotiated tariffs

An early and elegant step in the direction of incorporating trade agreements into the analysis of regionalism is Bond and Syropoulos (1996b). Using the same basic model as Bond and Syropoulos (1996a), they consider trigger strategies such that initially there is inter-bloc free trade supported by the threat of perpetual trade war if any party breaks the agreement. They then ask what rate of discount just leaves blocs indifferent between defecting and continuing to cooperate. (The discount rate is critical because the decision balances current benefits to defection against future costs.) If the actual discount rate is above this value, blocs defect from free trade; thus, if integration (moving from smaller to larger blocs) reduces the critical discount rate, it makes cooperation less likely to be maintained.

Two countervailing forces exist as we consider larger blocs: the incentive to deviate is greater the larger are the blocs, but so too is the welfare loss in the resulting trade war. Bond and Syropoulos find that the former effect dominates, making it more difficult to maintain free trade in a bloc-ridden world. They also find that for any given discount rate the minimum supportable cooperative tariff rises as bloc size increases, also suggesting that integration increases the pressures for protectionism. Bagwell and Staiger (1997a, 1997b) reach a similar conclusion in a somewhat similar fashion, although only in the context of a temporary transition phase.

The discount rate is crucial to the assessment of trigger strategies because it trades off the immediate benefits of defection against the eventual costs of trade war. This raises the question of the time scale over which these games are played. In terms of individual tariffs and tariff wars – e.g. the occasional EC–US spats such as the Chicken War and the tussle over public procurement in early 1993 – the period required for retaliation is so short that there are hardly any gains to defection. Thus discipline seems virtually complete and the model suggests that nothing much affects the cooperative outcome. (This may change if finite rather than infinite periods of punishment were permitted, whereupon the main question would become what determines the punishment period.) If, on the other hand, we view this as a game in regimes, so that the GATT rounds represent the natural periodicity, and policies such as Super 301, the zeal with which anti-dumping policies are applied and the use of health and technical regulations become the weapons, the periods required to recognise defection and retaliate become much more meaningful. I find the latter interpretation more plausible: namely that the important effect of integration is not on the 'tactics' of trade policy, but on the 'strategy'; in some sense it tends to reduce the incentive to take a world view. In this regard I find the European Community's concern with the volume of intra-EC trade as an indicator of the success of integration disturbing – see, for example, Jacquemin and Sapir (1988).

Campa and Sorenson (1996) apply the repeated game model of tariff setting to something like Nordström's (1995) problem, and with similar results. In part they consider a hegemon facing a competitive fringe of small countries, and conclude that if the latter coordinate they might offset the former's market power and move the world towards freer trade. Of course, if the (ex-)fringe were too large it might become hegemonic in which case it would dominate the original one. In a second, symmetric, exercise they conclude that, as the number of blocs falls, the probability of free trade falls (i.e. the critical discount rate falls), but that equi-sized blocks are preferable (more likely to be liberal) than disparate-sized ones.

In a specifically EU application Bond, Syropoulos and Winters (1996) use the Bond and Syropoulos framework to consider explicitly the deepening of an existing regional arrangement. They consider a world of N symmetric provinces split initially into one large country (the United States) and two smaller ones (France and Germany); the latter have already combined into a bloc (the European Union) with a CET that is the result of a self-sustaining agreement between the European Union and the United States. They then allow the latter pair to integrate more deeply by reducing trade frictions between them and ask whether tariff cuts within the union affect the incentive-compatibility of agreements with the outside country. It turns out that the Kemp–Wan tariff reduction – the reduction in the union's external tariff that just leaves the outside country indifferent to the internal tariff reduction – is a useful benchmark for this.

For the outside country, the reduction in the union's internal tariffs reduces the attractiveness of an initial trade agreement because its trade with the union is reduced. The Kemp–Wan reduction in the union's external tariff, however, will just restore incentive compatibility for the outside country because it restores to their initial levels both its welfare under the agreement and its incentive to violate it. For the union, a Kemp–Wan adjustment generates two conflicting forces. First, the initial trade agreement becomes more attractive to union members because the expanded volume of intra-union trade raises the welfare of member countries at the initial level of the external tariff. This suggests that the union could 'live with' a lower tariff on the outside country. On the other hand, deviating from the agreement also becomes more attractive because the payoff to cheating also rises. This suggests that the external tariff needs to rise in order to keep the union in the agreement. (A higher tariff makes sticking to the agreement more attractive.) The first effect almost always dominates the second, so that incentive-compatibility is consistent with a fall in the union's external tariff.

To be more precise, the two forces on the union exactly offset each other if the share of union expenditure on union goods is invariant with respect to the external tariff. In that case, since the Kemp–Wan tariff reduction is incentive-compatible for both the union and the outside country, internal liberalisation plus a Kemp–Wan reduction will generate a new sustainable agreement. Of course, many other agreements will also be sustainable, so there is no guarantee that the Kemp–Wan reduction in the external tariff will actually be chosen, but at least for one simple representation of the negotiating process Bond, Syropoulos and Winters show that it will be.

If the share of union expenditure on union goods rises as the external tariff rises (heuristically, if demand is elastic) the Kemp–Wan tariff reduction is not incentive-compatible for the union: that is, if the original agreement was just sustainable, internal liberalisation plus a Kemp–Wan reduction will leave the union preferring to defect than to cooperate. As a result, the union, while likely to reduce its external tariff somewhat, will not be prepared to go as far as the Kemp–Wan reduction. Since the latter is necessary to keep the outside country at its initial level of welfare, the presumption is that, under these circumstances, the outside country will suffer from the union's internal liberalisation. This illustrates the dilemma of defining multilateralism starkly. By reducing all tariffs in the model we have presumably enhanced multilateralism, and yet the RoW – the intended beneficiary of multilateralism – suffers a decline in welfare.

Somewhat similarly to Bond, Syropoulos and Winters, Bagwell and Staiger (1996b) analyse a three-country model in a repeated game context. They assume two countries are patient (A and B) – and hence are happy with low tariff equilibria – while the third (C) is very impatient. Under MFN rules A and B offer C lower tariffs than it reciprocates with because they wish to have low tariffs on their mutual trade. How is this affected if they sign an FTA? Under such an eventuality the import-sourcing condition suggests further reducing A's and B's tariffs on C, but, pushing in the opposite direction, the same condition suggests that A and B are likely to impose less harsh punishment on C if it defects, and A's and B's mutual tariffs are no longer dependent on their tariff on C.

The net effect is ambiguous, but Bagwell and Staiger show that if C is very impatient and A and B very patient it could entail higher tariffs on C. This is more likely if A and B form a CU rather than an FTA because, being larger, a CU is less interested in freer trade.

Bagwell and Staiger's model is quite special because it assumes that, out of three goods, each country imports one from both partners while exporting both others, one to each partner. Its real significance, however, is to highlight the sensible proposition that if we ask 'how useful is regionalism?', part of the answer must be 'that depends on how well the MFN rule was doing initially'.

Bond and Syropoulos introduce regional blocs exogenously – e.g. for political reasons – and ask how they disturb an existing equilibrium. Ludema (1996) asks a more sophisticated question: how does the *possibility* of creating a regional bloc affect the conduct of multilateral negotiations aimed at achieving free trade? He uses welfare-maximisation as his objective function and considers a three-country multi-round two-step negotiation. In each negotiating round the first step is a multilateral offer, and if this is rejected a bilateral one may be made. If this is rejected, a new round is initiated. A very strong assumption is that international transfers of utility are feasible. This guarantees that negotiations will always eventually end up with global free trade – the only efficient solution – and because in these games (a) time is money (the discount rate is positive) and (b) information is complete, they actually get there straight away. Thus negotiation is *only* about distribution – every offer is 'global free trade plus some vector of transfers'.

In this context, Ludema does not help us much on 'regionalism vs. multilateralism', except to the extent that his results may condition attitudes towards whether to rewrite Article XXIV to ban regional arrangements. Ludema considers two questions. First, how would a pre-existing regional bloc affect a multilateral negotiation? If it is an FTA, not very much, because an FTA does not constrain the partners' negotiations with outside countries. If it is a CU, however, the effect is stronger because a CU precludes independent negotiation. However, this effect is weakened if the partners are asymmetric because the partners' ideal policies *vis-à-vis* outsiders would differ. Ludema's second question is: how does the possibility of regionalism affects negotiations? If only FTAs are possible the multilateral outcome resembles that of three separate bilateral negotiations, whereas if only CUs are permitted the first-mover advantage for the country that can first propose a CU allows it a disproportionate share of world income. In Ludema's model, this is randomly decided.

A model of negotiated tariffs in which the repeated game is only implicit is Bagwell and Staiger's chapter 3 in this volume. This starts from the position that countries gear trade policy to their own ends – be they political, economic, or whatever – and that trade agreements (and the GATT) exist to internalise the effects that A's policy has on B – specifically to internalise terms of trade effects. If MFN trade rules allow complete internalisation, then countries can reach the efficiency frontier (defined over their own objectives, not the economics community's) and regional arrangements have nothing to add. If, on the other hand, MFN tariffs cannot yield efficiency or, say, they pose enforcement problems, regional arrangements may have a role to play. In these cases regionalism is (potentially) optimal; there is no question of 'building blocs' or 'stumbling blocs' unless we wish to challenge governments' objectives. This brings us neatly to the next group of models, which recognise that governments are not always economic welfare-maximisers.

3.4   Pressure groups and voters

I now move on to what might loosely be called political economy models of integration – those in which governments are driven by economic considerations but not merely the (unweighted) maximisation of welfare/utility. In this section we take governments' objective functions as given and assume they are efficiently pursued. In the next we ask how the decision process itself – the institutions which determine government behaviour – affects the outcome. Many of the political economy models have a lot in common with the models I have already surveyed, but I collect them into one section because their focus on political economy is their main distinguishing characteristic.

Much of the political economy modelling derives from Grossman and Helpman (1994, 1995).[10] They argued persuasively that lobbying influences governments less in terms of determining which of the two polar policy stances wins an election than in terms of what policies an incumbent or newly elected government will pursue – the market for influence. In general, consumers find it hard to organise a lobby and so lobbying is dominated by producers, who organise along sectoral lines. This effectively gives profits additional weight in the government's objective function; they enter once in the traditional calculus of surpluses (consumer, producer and government revenue), and again as the source of lobbying funds which the government values in their own right. Thus moving into the realms of political economy effectively biases integration outcomes towards what producers desire.

Grossman and Helpman (1995) consider a negotiation between two governments that have suddenly been offered the chance of concluding an FTA. That is, they compare *staying* with MFN trade policy with creating mutual preferences. In certain circumstances they find that the latter is politically feasible (i.e. that it raises government 'welfare', which depends on consumer and producer surpluses but with unequal weights). The FTA is feasible either if it enhances consumer welfare while producers are unable to lobby against it, or if it enhances the profits of well organised producers who pass some of the benefit on to the government via lobbies. The latter possibility is malign, for it makes likely precisely those FTAs which generate most trade diversion. Trade creation is a mixed blessing for a negotiating government: it generates surpluses for consumers at home and for exporters in the partner country, but reduces them for domestic import-competing producers; trade diversion, on the other hand, generates no such reduction in profits, and although it correspondingly generates no (or fewer) consumer gains, that matters less to governments. If two such governments can swap trade-diverting concessions, trade diversion is good politics even if it is bad economics. Grossman and Helpman do not consider whether their process continues to create superblocs, although if it were driven by diversion alone it would have to stop before it achieved the global coalition, because the last step in that direction would generate only trade creation.

Krishna (1994) has an elegant stripped-down three-country version of Grossman and Helpman in which policy is determined solely by its effects on profits. He assumes imperfectly competitive markets that are segmented from each other. He replicates the Grossman–Helpman result that, considering two of the countries, the more trade-diverting an FTA between them, the stronger its backing and hence the more likely it is to come about. He then shows that the backing for further multilateral liberalisation with the third country is reduced. Included in this is the possibility that multilateral liberalisation that was feasible before the FTA would cease to be so afterwards – i.e. that, if the world attempted to achieve the multilateral free trade it desired via regionalism, progress would stop at the intermediate stage.

Very simply, let a sector's profits be π_1 under MFN tariffs, π_2 under the FTA and π_3 under global free trade. The gains from FTA ($\pi_2 - \pi_1$) may be sufficient to allow successful lobbying for the FTA; similarly, if it were the only option, the gains from global liberalisation ($\pi_3 - \pi_1$) might also permit successful lobbying; the gains from moving from an FTA to free trade ($\pi_3 - \pi_2$), however, might be insufficient to encourage lobbying for that step: they would certainly be smaller than ($\pi_3 - \pi_1$) because $\pi_2 > \pi_1$ if the FTA was formed, and they might actually be negative. Moreover, this 'suspended liberalisation' outcome is more likely the more trade-diverting was the initial FTA. Krishna shows that it may not even be possible for producers in the outside country to bribe those in the partner countries to adopt global free trade. This is because much of the benefit of the latter is 'wasted' on consumers.

Krishna's is a *very* simple model – which is one of its attractions – and clearly requires some generalisation. However, it is rather convincing that regionalism may hinder multilateralism – 'the good' preventing 'the best'!

The second extension of Grossman and Helpman is Baldwin (1995). This model of 'domino' regionalism has many countries each with a CRS (numeraire) sector and a differentiated product sector with capitalists who receive the rent. Government objectives are a convex combination of worker and capitalist welfare, the latter being enhanced by their ability to lobby. Baldwin assumes that a bloc already exists and that this situation is an equilibrium in the sense that countries on the outside wish to remain so because the economic benefits of joining do not outweigh the non-economic costs. He then shocks this world by deepening integration within the bloc – '1992' – or by allowing one country's desire for integration to increase – the United States in the 1980s. Each shock would increase the incentives for new members to join – starting with those that were previously just on the margin of joining – and as they do so the costs to others of remaining outside grow. This in turn attracts others, and so on.

Baldwin notes that the process of enlargement could stop as soon as all remaining non-members had high enough objections to joining. It could also, of course, do so when existing members shut the door. Baldwin deals, in fact, only with the demand for membership. As a parable for the absorption of the EFTA countries into the EC following '1992' – its intended purpose – Baldwin's explanation is admirable; however, its generalisation to other accessions looks less secure – think, for example, of Poland, Cyprus and Turkey. Given that deepening integration is bad for excluded countries (see above), Baldwin does not actually need political economy to generate his results, but it does help to explain some of the facts of political activity that surrounded the EFTA accession. Overall, however, the implications of all this for multilateralism are quite unclear.

An early contribution to the theory of endogenous protection and integration is Richardson (1993, 1995). Like Baldwin, Richardson's basic insight does not require a political economy dimension – welfare-maximisation would suffice. Suppose one country creates an FTA with a large partner (with a horizontal supply curve) and suppose that for certain imported goods the FTA is trade-diverting because $p_P < p_W$

$(1 + t)$ where p_P is the partner's price, p_W is the world price and t the MFN tariff. Domestic firms and consumers now face p_P instead of p_W $(1 + t)$, but the government loses tariff revenue. A rational government would now reduce its MFN tariff to just below t', where $p_W (1 + t') = p_P$. This would leave domestic residents unaffected relative to the FTA but generate tariff revenue. The main constraint on this behaviour is the reaction of the partner country which loses the rents it expected under the FTA. But if it is large and has other objectives in the integration, it might acquiesce. A reservation to this elegant model is the extent to which tariff revenues really motivate trade policy – the prevalence of VERs casts some doubt on this.

Political economy considerations support the rational outcome in Richardson's model. The initial reduction in the domestic price would probably reduce the size of the lobby for tariffs on the goods concerned,[11] and, besides, no one in the lobby has any interest in whether they are hurt by partner imports rather than non-partner imports. Richardson's results seem to require that partner and non-partner imports are perfect substitutes with fixed prices. If import supply curves slope upwards and/or the imports (and the home good) are imperfect substitutes in demand, then free access for the partner could well increase the demand for protection against non-members and this may outweigh the government's revenue concerns. The necessary condition for this to occur seems to be that imports are drawn from both sources after integration.

Two contributions offer significant generalisations of Richardson's work. Cadot, de Melo and Olarreaga (1996) have a three-country model with Grossman–Helpman lobbying for influence by the fixed factors in each of the three industries. They ask what A/B integration does to protection against C's exports and focus carefully on different types of integration. They find that if A and B create an FTA without rules of origin, protection is likely to fall, essentially for the reasons identified by Richardson. If there are rules of origin, however, the protective effects of the FTA are more complex and it is possible that either A or B will increase protection above either of the pair's pre-integration tariffs. Similar outcomes are also possible under a CU. The reason is that in this model tariffs on different goods are substitutes: if one is reduced (by FTA membership), others rise (on C). This is because the unprotected sector contracts, increasing the sizes and reducing the lobbying costs of the other sectors.[12] Cadot, de Melo and Olarreaga do not consider how C reacts to integration – it always offers free trade – but the propensity of the bloc members to raise their tariffs is likely to move us away from multilateralism.

The second generalisation of Richardson is Levy (1996b) who considers many countries in a model that also includes lobbying for influence and negotiated tariffs. He focuses on two major countries negotiating with each other and asks how this negotiation is affected if each acquires (exogenously) a fringe of FTA partners. Each country has effective lobbying in one import-competing ('sensitive') sector; export interests aim to reduce the other country's tariff in its 'sensitive' sector by inducing reductions in their own country's. The existence of the fringe affects the extent to which trade policy changes translate into increases in profits in the major powers. For example, suppose A's fringe can supply A's export good along a fairly elastic supply curve. A now has less interest in inducing B to reduce its tariff on these goods because part of the benefit spills over onto A's fringe's suppliers so that A's own producers get a smaller increase in price.[13] Levy shows that considering both countries' fringes, these effects could go in any direction, so that giving major negotiating powers FTA fringes could either increase or reduce tariffs on their mutual trade. Thus if it is the major powers that determine the progress of multinational negotiations (e.g. the United States and European Union in the Uruguay Round), Levy's model suggests we cannot necessarily be sanguine about the EU Association Agreements, APEC and NAFTA.

I turn now to models with slightly different pressure group technologies. Richardson and Desruelle (1997) use an analysis with features of both Krishna's and Baldwin's model to explain the height of EC countries' tariffs before and after integration: they have three countries and an economic specification like Baldwin's except that they explicitly consider the distribution of tariff revenues. In addition, they allow both workers and capitalists (now a single group) to lobby. Richardson and Desruelle compare Nash tariffs before and after the creation of a CU, assuming that the partners of the latter are identical.[14] Integration does not affect the relative weights of workers and capitalists in the formation of trade policy. The partners export the differentiated good both to each other and to the excluded country, while the latter exports the CRS good.

It turns out that integration could push the external tariff (on imports of the CRS good) either way in Richardson and Desruelle's model. Generally it will raise it: before integration each partner moderates its desire to tax the CRS good because doing so will increase its costs in the differentiated sector with a resultant loss of sales and rents to the other partner. A CU internalises this spillover, and hence allows a higher price. The counter-example occurs when workers determine the tariff but receive little of the revenue. Before integration they drive the tariff very high because they have no interest in the rents of the differentiated sector but do benefit from the Stolper–Samuelson effect on real wages. But this spills over to the other partners in terms of higher costs and prices of differentiated goods. Under the CU this spillover is recognised, and the tariff on the CRS good falls to the revenue-maximising level. Overall, Richardson and Desruelle's results seem to suggest that RIAs increase trade restriction, for the starting point of their counter-case – very high tariffs on the CRS good – does not accord very closely with reality.

Levy (1997) continues (implicitly) with labour and capital and explores the stepping-stones argument with a median voter model. He reaches similar conclusions to Krishna. The median voter's response to the offer of a trade policy change depends on his labour–capital ratio and the labour–capital ratio of the trading blocs to which he belongs before and after the change. An important restriction is that voters first consider autarky vs. a bilateral deal and then whatever they choose first vs. multilateralism. This allows Levy to show that in a simple Heckscher–Ohlin model one does not get stuck at the bilateral stage.

Suppose A and B consider forming a bloc and that $k^A < k^{AB} < k^B$ where k^i is the capital-labour ratio of country i and k^{AB} that of A and B combined. The median voter in A will agree to the FTA if increasing his economy's k is beneficial *to him* and the median voter in B will approve if he gains from a decrease. Suppose both approve and that we then pose the second question which would produce a world economy with ratio k^w. If $k^w > k^{AB}$ voter A will favour multilateralism. Voter B might also if k^w far exceeds k^{AB}, but more likely he will reject it, leaving the world stuck in bilateral mode. But voter A can foresee this and will therefore veto bilateralism at the first stage relying on the second ballot – which will then become autarky vs. multilateralism – to achieve his goals. Essentially no two countries that favoured multilateralism initially can create an FTA, so the world is safe!

Now Levy adds variety effects so that the median voter receives utility not just from his real income but also from increased variety. This can cause a breakdown at the intermediate stage. Suppose the median voter is only just in favour of multilateralism, balancing increased variety against disadvantageous price–wage effects. If the FTA offers disproportionate gains it could push the voter's utility above the multilateral level. For example, if A and B have identical capital–labour ratios $k^A = k^{AB} = k^B$ there are no price–wage effects but there are variety effects. These could leave the median voter better off and resisting the move to multilateralism, even though the latter would have been chosen relative to autarky. It is FTAs between similar countries that pose the greatest threats to multilateralism, those between dissimilar ones that pose the least. This suggests that the current rash of North–South arrangements, such as NAFTA and the EU Association Agreements, are not likely to be very harmful. However, subsequent work – Levy (1996b), see above – rebuts this presumption.

Frankel and Wei (1996) offer a counter-example to Levy's argument that bilateralism can never increase support for multilateralism. They do so in a Ricardian world with costs of adjustment for workers changing sectors. There are three countries (A, B and C) each with comparative advantage in one of three goods (a, b and c, respectively); in each of two potential partner countries (A and B) workers are spread over the three sectors such that none has a majority. If workers focus on the costs of adjustment a majority in A will oppose multilateral liberalisation (those in b and c), but favour bilateral liberalisation (those in a and c, who will benefit from the falling price of b). If the bilateral bloc is formed workers will have to move – perhaps all b workers move to a. Now there will be a majority in favour of opening up with C as well.

Frankel and Wei's argument relies either on workers not realising that the multilateral vote will follow the bilateral one (otherwise c workers would oppose bilateralism) or on voters believing that the following voting structure will be used regardless of outcomes: vote first on an A/B bloc and then, whatever the outcome, vote on opening up to C. In the latter case c workers cannot avoid liberalisation and so would go along with the A/B bloc. The latter seems implausible to me, but not the former given the uncertainties and glacial pace of trade diplomacy. It also seems fairly plausible that voters do focus on adjustment costs. Almost any discussion of trade liberalisation with policy-makers takes about ten minutes to get around to unemployment. Thus contrary to Levy's (1996a) comments on Frankel and Wei's paper, it seems to me a plausible counter-example, albeit one which is far from categorical, for the voting weights could easily generate alternative outcomes.

General conclusions from the political economy literature are elusive. One such conclusion is that the dominance of sector-based lobbies over economy-wide ones (factor-based or consumer) makes trade diversion more attractive to policy-makers, for trade diversion shifts rents and/or activity towards producers. While one cannot be categorical, this tendency seems likely to gravitate away from multilateralism, for trade diversion is possible only from preferential arrangements. The tendency is manifest first in the notion that integration beyond a trade-deflecting FTA may induce higher tariffs on the rest of the world and, second, in the more interesting observation that one might get stopped on a regional stepping stone before achieving free trade. While there are counter-examples, I find the broad thrust of this argument convincing.

3.5   *Institutional arrangements for regional blocs*

The discussion in subsection 3.4 presupposed that all the features of a regional bloc are fully determined at its onset – implicitly in the negotiation phase during which national governments, pressure groups and voter interests are identifiable and distinct. For FTAs this seems a reasonable assumption for, other than maintaining mutual free trade, governments are quite unconstrained by an FTA. Even for an FTA, however, it would be worth asking – rather along the lines of Levy (1996b) – how the existence of an FTA conditions governments' reactions to exogenous shocks. For example, if the price of a major exportable falls, will governments be more likely to resort to protection with or without an FTA? Bhagwati and Panagariya (1996) have suggested that being in NAFTA made the Mexican government's response to the 1994–5 crisis *less* liberal than if it had been unencumbered: the previous mid-1980s' crisis eventually led to thorough-going liberalisation whereas the mid-1990s' crisis produced tariff increases on some non-NAFTA imports. Most other commentators have argued that since the response in the mid-1980s was initially very protectionist, NAFTA appears to have constrained behaviour to be moderately liberal. While the literature surveyed so far sheds some light on these issues by asking whether an FTA increases propensities to protectionism, it does not address it directly because it does not really consider how FTA members take decisions.

If consideration of this issue is desirable for FTAs it is indispensable for CUs and deeper forms of integration. One might determine the initial CET in the negotiation phase, but thereafter one needs mechanisms for deciding how to change it either in multilateral negotiations or ad hoc via anti-dumping actions, etc. How one does this – how one aggregates preferences across members – is likely to be very important in determining the outcomes. This problem does not arise in models of welfare-maximising governments where members are symmetric, for one maximises the representative country's welfare. Thus it is essentially a problem of asymmetry and politics.

One interesting aspect of joint decision-making concerns how formerly national lobbies interact to bring pressure to bear on the CU authorities. The only formal analyses of this question all suggest that interest group pressure is diluted by the CU. The essential point is that it costs more to lobby for a 1 per cent increase in your tariff in a CU than in a constituent member country with the right to set its own tariffs: there is more opposition to overcome (Panagariya and Findlay, 1994; de Melo, Panagariya and Rodrik, 1993) or more representatives to influence

(Richardson, 1994). Given the lower returns, less lobbying occurs and the sum of the members' lobbying activity falls as a result of integration. This can equivalently be viewed as a public good problem, for a CET is a public good: the lobby from *A* does not wish to devote resources to lobbying for protection for producers in country *B*. Whether the resulting tariff is lower than that which would rule in *all* member countries in the absence of integration is unclear, however, and so one might be trading less protection in some members for more in others. Whether this enhances multilateralism clearly depends on precisely how you trade off breadth against depth in the external tariff.

All these models presuppose that lobbies in different member countries will oppose each other, but it is also possible that some of them have their power enhanced through integration (Winters, 1993). For example, anti-protectionist forces might also be diluted by the free-riding problem. Alternatively each member state might initially start with a lobbying game in which industry and agriculture more or less cancel each other out, but if integration lets the agriculture lobbies cooperate (because they produce the same things) while the industry lobbies compete (because they produce different things), the union may end up with high agricultural protection. Overall, therefore, while dilution effects will undoubtedly be present, it is not proven that they will always predominate.

I turn now to the organisation of government. Gatsios and Karp (1991, 1995) show that it might matter which member state 'leads' negotiations with the rest of the world on a particular issue. In their model, if a more aggressive member determines the union's position, the union is able to extract a more favourable deal from RoW than if the 'average' member does so. This is because the former is more credible in its threats to retaliate (with the whole of the union's resources). In this model, 'passive' members could benefit from delegating power for certain policies to aggressive ones because, although for any given RoW policy they would prefer a less aggressive union stance, the RoW is so much more accommodating under the delegation that they are better off overall. What about multilateralism? That depends on whether a more aggressive union can achieve a more liberal outcome with the RoW by virtue of its readiness to retaliate, or whether it actually needs to use its muscle. Gatsios and Karp's model deals with this essentially only by assumption.

The formal delegation of the power to settle negotiating positions is of limited relevance in real CUs, but informal and partial delegation clearly exists. It has commonly been observed (e.g. Winters, 1993) that the European Union allows countries disproportionate influence over policy in areas in which they claim vital interests, allowing them, *in extremis*, veto power. Given that for all the reasons noted above a country's 'interest' in a sector is commonly correlated with that sector's share of its GDP, it is easy to imagine this feature enhancing further the interests of producers. What effect this has on the union's trade policy depends on whether a sector's having a high share of a member's GDP reflects its comparative advantage or past policy distortions. If the former, one might expect relatively liberal stances,[15] whereas if the latter, protection will be more strongly favoured. One encouraging aspect of this is that since integration will tend to relocate union production in a sector towards relatively more efficient countries, over time this argument could lead to reduction in protectionist pressure.

Winters (1994, 1995) considers the institutional basis of decision-making more closely and, in an EU context, observes several features that could lead to protectionist biases in the aggregation of preferences. If the union is essentially inter-governmental, rather than democratic in its own right, policy will be made by groups of bureaucrats and, eventually, ministers representing their own governments. This can be protectionist, first because, as Messerlin (1983) notes, the incentives for bureaucrats tend towards protectionism and, second, because as Scharpf (1988) notes, adding layers of inter-governmental decision-making tends to swing influence away from voters and towards official preferences for administrative convenience and a quiet life. The secrecy that surrounds EU deliberations reinforces these tendencies because it confuses public perceptions of where the responsibility for trade policy outcomes actually lies.

Within the European Union, trade policy is essentially made by committee – the so-called '113 Committee' – the members of which represent particular constituencies (countries) and none of whom is publicly accountable for the final outcome. This gives rise to at least two (related) failures of aggregation. First, the 'restaurant bill' problem: suppose the benefits of a policy on product j to a country i are proportionate to the latter's share of union output (x_{ij}) and the costs to its share of GDP (g_i), and suppose that each country has a veto, or at least that consensus is valued very highly. If representatives sit down to decide a package of policies on $j = 1 \dots N$ products, each will press for inclusion of any good for which $x_{ij} > a\, g_i$, where $a > 1$ reflects the inefficiency of the conversion of costs into benefits. Since each is highly likely to have some j for which this is true and, provided the *perceived a* is not too large, the easiest package to construct will cover nearly all products even if, overall, each country would prefer no change to the final outcome.

The second failure is similar but operates in probability space – see

Table 2.1. *The universalist argument: costs and benefits for a single country if the measure passes*

Total number of countries voting 'for/in'	2	3
Cost	$-2(c+d)/3$	$-(c+d)$
This country votes 'in'		
Benefit	c	c
Probability of measure passing	0.5	0.25
This country votes 'out'		
Probability of measure passing	0.25	0

Shepsle and Weingast (1981), who christened the phenomenon 'universalism', Schattschneider (1935) on the Smoot–Hawley tariff, and Winters (1994) on the European Union. Imagine that protecting footwear is being discussed and that each of three member states is a producer of one type. If any one type is protected, the government in whose country it is produced perceives benefits of c (surplus to producers, political convenience, etc.) and each member bears cost of $-(c+d)/3$, where d (>0) is the deadweight cost of transferring c through protection. Net costs are zero if the measure is rejected. The issue is to be decided by simple majority, and each member must decide how to vote; each accepts that if it votes against the measure, its type of footwear will not be protected.

Table 2.1 reports the costs and benefits of the proposal passing according to whether a member votes 'for/in' or 'no/out'. It also reports the probability of the proposal passing, assuming that the other countries vote randomly with probability one-half each way. The expected value of voting 'for/in' is $0.5*[c-2(c+d)/3] + 0.25*[c-(c+d)]$ ($\geqslant 0$), while that of voting 'no/out' is $-0.25*2(c+d)/3$ (<0). Thus a government will vote 'for/in' if $4c > 5d$ – i.e. if its 'benefits' from the protection exceed the deadweight loss by 25 per cent or more – and even if it expects negative returns to doing so!

A more sophisticated view of voting for trade policy in the European Union is offered by Widgrén (1995a, 1995b) drawing on Hamilton (1991). Widgrén notes that small countries have disproportionate numbers of votes; he considers voting coalitions and calculates countries' voting power in terms of the frequency with which they might command a pivotal position in the European Union's qualified majority voting system. He argues that if we contrast liberals (the Netherlands, Luxembourg, Germany, Denmark, Belgium and the United Kingdom) with protectionists (Spain, Portugal, Italy and France) with Ireland and Greece as uncertain, no group has power in a deterministic sense (each has a blocking minority). The EFTA enlargement does not change this, and so changes to the status quo look unlikely. However, allowing for probabilistic voting, with the probabilities being the same for each member of each group but varying by group, change is possible most probably in a protectionist direction: the power of the two groups is roughly balanced over proposals covering the whole range of restrictiveness (as measured by the probability of receiving support from the liberals), but in the more protective range the protectionists appear to muster rather greater power and thus are more likely to get their way. Widgrén's work clearly depends on particular constitutional structure, but it illustrates how voting patterns may generate aggregation biases. Given that in the post-war period liberalism has required positive action, the EU system favouring the status quo is not particularly multilateral.

4   What the evidence suggests

This section briefly surveys the evidence on 'regionalism vs. multilateralism'. Regrettably it seems to be as ambiguous as the theory, at least so far as issues of current policy are concerned. As noted above, among current RIAs only the European Union is large enough and long-lived enough to have had identifiable consequences on the world trading system itself, and it is more or less impossible to sort out what is generic and what specific among the lessons it teaches. Perhaps the only unambiguous lesson is that the creation of one regional bloc does not necessarily lead to the immediate breakdown of the trading system.

Several fundamental problems confront the scholar in this area. Foremost is creating an *anti-monde* – how can we know what member countries' trade policy would have been in the absence of the RIA? Second, systems evolve over long periods of time; it is not inconceivable that while post-war RIAs have been liberal so far, they are sowing the seeds of destruction, for example by reducing the number of independent middle-sized states which have an interest in maintaining the world system. Third, as noted above, trade policy responds to shocks from other areas: RIAs may be benign under one set of circumstances, but not another. How, then, do we allocate responsibility over causes? Fourth, how do we define and measure multilateralism? Fifth, the rhetoric required to achieve a political objective does not necessarily reflect actual causes. Even if policy-makers say they are responding to an instance of regional integration – e.g. in raising a tariff or seeking a multilateral negotiation – how do we know this is the real cause?

One solution to these difficulties is to dispense with looking at the evidence altogether, on the grounds that nothing concrete can emerge. I prefer an alternative view: as long as we are frank about the degree of confidence we can have in various conclusions, it is better to consider actual cases than to ignore them.

4.1   Members' own trade policies

The evidence on whether the European Union has led to higher or lower tariffs and non-tariff barriers (NTBs) for member states' non-partner trade continues to defy simple conclusions. Hufbauer (1990) argues that it created the conditions for France and Italy to contemplate liberal-isation and that Germany would not have proceeded without its continental partners. Messerlin (1992) agrees that the EEC aided French liberalisation indirectly by creating the appropriate macroeconomic environment. *Prima facie* these views of France do seem plausible, for she has always appeared a reluctant liberalizer. On the other hand, crises and sudden perceptions that one is getting left behind can have dramatic effects: France's switch in the early 1980s from Keynesian expansionism to fiscal orthodoxy arose precisely because the former failed to work. A similar 'road to Damascus' could also have affected a highly protectionist France in a more liberal continent – consider Mexico in the mid-1980s, for example. Hufbauer, it seems to me, may well be wrong about Germany: in each of the two years prior to the creation of the EEC, Germany undertook tariff cuts of 25 per cent (Irwin, 1995). Thus not only did the tariff averaging attending the creation of the EEC raise German tariffs, it also possibly curtailed a liberalising momentum.

No one, I suspect, would argue that the EU has set external tariffs above the levels that would otherwise have ruled in at least one of its member countries, but this is quite different from arguing that it has not raised protection in some countries and sectors – e.g. footwear in Germany, agriculture in the United Kingdom and textiles and clothing in Sweden. The trade-off between the breadth and depth of protection is not well defined and so we cannot satisfactorily rule on whether these examples constitute increases or decreases in multilateralism.

Other recent evidence on countries' own trade is equally mixed. Following NAFTA, Canada reduced tariffs on 1,500 tariff items (mostly inputs) to help her industry compete with the United States where tariffs were lower (WTO, 1995). This looks similar to Richardson's tariff competition. On the other hand Mexico increased tariffs on 500 items – see above. In Mercosur, Argentina's tariffs on capital goods' imports will be raised to Brazilian levels.

Going back further in time, the 1960s' RIAs in Latin America were inward-looking and frequently maintained and even raised barriers against the RoW. The Central American Common Market, for example, generated huge growth in intra-trade behind such barriers (Nogues and Quintanilla, 1993). In all probability the import-substitution policy would have been less broad and/or foundered sooner if it had been restricted to small countries operating on an MFN basis. Even further back, in the 1930s, one also finds high external tariffs and burgeoning regionalism, but here the evidence is probably more favourable to regionalism (Oye, 1992; Irwin, 1993). Trade barriers were going up anyway and regional arrangements probably served to reduce the coverage of the increases by exempting some flows.

4.2   Other countries' policies

When one thinks of the effects of regionalism on the multilateral system one is obliged to deal with interactions between countries. How does an RIA cause other countries to respond? WTO (1995) suggests three classes of response: to seek to join an existing group; to create a new group; and to seek multilateral liberalisation.

The observation that regional arrangements have recently attracted new members is commonplace; one need not even list examples. However, whether this is good or bad for multilateralism is moot, for we are clearly far away from achieving a global coalition. Moreover, accretion is not inevitable and irreversible. Countries do leave groups – e.g. Chile and Peru effectively left the Andean Pact, although admittedly after it had become rather rigid. In both cases, multilateralism benefited from the defections.

The second option, of creating new RIAs, also looks popular according to the evidence. Regionalism has proceeded in waves – the 1960s and the later 1980s and 1990s – and policy-makers variously refer to demonstration effects, to the need to create their own market areas in case other blocs turn inwards, and the desire to create bargaining power. Examples include the establishment of EFTA, and recent discussions surrounding AFTA (the Asean Free Trade Area) and the CBI (the Cross-Border Initiative in Africa). Again, of course, it is moot whether this enhances or undermines multilateralism.

Finally, most directly relevant and most contentious, many commentators argue that excluded countries will seek multilateral liberalisations in response to RIAs. This occurs mainly in the realms of superpower trade diplomacy, because only superpowers can manipulate the multilateral system but even smaller powers may warm towards multilateral talks if they perceive a fragmenting world economy. Arguments of this sort have been made about each of the last four GATT Rounds, as well as in certain earlier instances.

Many commentators have argued that the creation of the EEC led directly to the Dillon and Kennedy Rounds as the United States sought to mitigate the former's trade-diversionary consequences – see, for example, Lawrence (1991), Sapir (1993) and WTO (1995). I have expressed some reservations about this linkage – Winters (1993, 1994). I do not deny some connection between these events, but I am still concerned that we have not established a necessary link between them, that any such link was benign, or that it is generalisable to other instances of integration.

First, it seems implausible to argue that multilateral progress would have stopped had the EEC not been created. After all, the benefits of liberalisation are not much affected by other countries' regionalism, it is just that, following the creation of an RIA, multilateral liberalisation may be necessary to avoid actual harm to excluded countries. The United States still had considerable hegemonic power in the late 1950s and early 1960s and so could probably have generated enough support for a Round whenever it wanted. It is not generally maintained that the EEC made the Europeans more willing to negotiate. Thus overall, I suspect that, at most, we are talking about the timing not the existence of the next Round.

Second, the Administration played the EEC card hard in public and in Congress. But whether they actually believed they *had to* respond to its creation and whether that creation was the major factor behind the push for talks is less clear. Recent debate in the United States about trade issues has sometimes demonstrated a disconnection between rhetoric and economic reality and so the EEC could just have been a convenient handle with which to manoeuvre US domestic interests and the EC nations into talks.

Third, since agriculture played such an important and delicate role in its formation, it is not surprising that the EEC resisted that sector's inclusion in the negotiations. But the fact that it got away with this (because the United States refused the '*montant de soutien*' offer) reinforced agricultural protectionism throughout the world and made it doubly difficult to negotiate in future rounds. Future agricultural disarmament may have been easier in the absence of the EEC.

Fourth, suppose it were true that the creation of the EEC forced the US Congress into trade talks. That would be tantamount to the aggressive unilateralism that many currently deplore in US trade policy. 'The Six' would have done something to harm their partners, at least in the partners' eyes, and then mitigated it in return for concessions. This is a dangerous game, even if a successful one, and might be playable only a few times. Indeed, if it were the case, it could explain why US policy has become more belligerent towards the latest enlargement and towards '1992'. However, in fact, the United States was generally sympathetic towards EC integration and actually encouraged it by allowing the Administration to offer deeper tariff cuts to a European CU than to the separate European nations (see Jackson, 1991).[16]

It has also been argued – although less frequently – that regionalism was behind the Tokyo Round. Winham (1986) reports both the first EEC enlargement (including free trade with EFTA) and the restrictiveness of the CAP as factors in the US view. The former observation seems no more compelling than those surrounding the creation of the EEC, while the latter is distinctly two-edged from our perspective: it requires, first, that the CAP induced negotiations and, second, that regionalism induced the CAP – i.e. that regionalism increased trade restrictions. Again, for this to be advantageous in its net effect on multilateralism requires a negotiating model in which might and countervailing power are the critical elements of liberalisation, quite contrary to the hegemonic views of, say, Keohane (1984). It has also been suggested to me that enlargement finally achieved a US goal by bringing the four biggest economies of Europe into one bloc and that this required a commensurate foreign policy response. Maybe, but why this response took the form of initiating a trade negotiation in the face of European opposition is unclear.

Finally, consider the Uruguay Round. Its initiation has not been related to regionalism, but its completion has. WTO (1995) says 'there is little doubt that ... the spread of regionalism [was a] major factor in eliciting the concessions needed to conclude' the Round. Bergsten's (1977) reports senior European policy-makers stating that the 1993 APEC meeting in Seattle was a major jolt to the European Union and the key which prompted it to reach settlement in the Round. On the WTO's general assertion there was a perception that the failure of the Round would lead to regional fragmentation, and this certainly encouraged the spread of defensive regionalism. How much pressure this put on the two major negotiating parties is not clear, however, for they would not have been the principal casualties of fragmentation. Bergsten's interlocutor seems to me (albeit from the outside) likely to have been confusing rhetoric and substance. The European Union had set up the conditions for settlement in the MacSharry farm reforms in 1991–2 and some insiders (e.g. Hathaway and Ingco, 1996) report that as early as 1990 EU negotiators recognised that they would complete the Round as soon as they had built an appropriate domestic coalition on agriculture.

A common theme runs through all these accounts of regionalism and GATT multilateral rounds: the threat of (or, worse, actual) violence and response. All the accounts report countries running back to the multi-lateral system to counter the damage that other countries' RIAs may do them. This may be an effective way forward but it clearly relies on rather fine judgement by both (all) protagonists that folding is better than fighting. Perhaps if regionalism has raised the average *de facto* level of multilateralism it has done so at the expense of increasing the chances of catastrophe.

Earlier evidence on regionalism is somewhat more positive, but in different circumstances. Irwin (1993) reports how the Cobden–Chavalier Treaty spawned a rash of MFN trade treaties and so created an era of significant liberalism (if not formal multilateralism). After about 1880, however, this began slowly to erode, not in a regional fashion but with MFN rates being increased. Nonetheless, the last quarter of the nine-teenth century remained a reasonably liberal period. In the inter-war period the multilateral trading system fell apart very rapidly following the imposition of the (MFN) Smoot–Hawley tariff. Both Oye (1992) and Irwin (1993) argue that whereas multilateral attempts to halt and reverse the collapse failed, regional attempts induced a measure of liberalism. Britain, France and Germany sought to protect their export markets by preferential arrangements, and in so doing did violence to US exports. This in turn induced the United States to turn to bilateral approaches in the Reciprocal Trade Agreements Act of 1934.

I draw two lessons from these historical analyses. First, regionalism–bilateralism, which entails much more obvious payoffs for exporters (internalisation) than multilateralism, can help to break down restrictive regimes. Whether it can lead all the way to multilateral liberalism is not proven, but it clearly has the ability to start the process off. This is consistent with the observation that difficult issues such as public procurement, standards and services feature more strongly in regional than in multilateral arrangements. The challenge for the policy-makers is to establish a means of switching to the multilateral horse once the race has started.

Second, building on Oye's analysis of 'shiftable externalities', poten-tially regionalised systems are likely to break down much more quickly than purely multilateral ones – cf. the late 1800s and the 1930s. 'Shiftable externalities' are externalities which an action creates but whose incidence can be moved between other agents according to their actions. Suppose I import equally from five partners and want to cut my total imports by 20 per cent. An MFN tariff increase might cut those from A, B, C, D and E each by 20 per cent. But suppose A offers me a concession to exempt itself from the cut. The others now have to bear a 25 per cent cut if I am to make the same target. Now suppose B wants to negotiate.

It has to offer a bigger concession because it has to claw back a bigger cut in exports. And so on. There is a clear incentive for any supplier to strike an exclusionary deal and as quickly as possible. The possibility of regionalism increases the speed of decay.

Perhaps the crucial question is 'where is the world economy now?' Fairly closed, so that regionalism is necessary (efficient) to crack open widespread barriers, or fairly open, so that the danger is that regionalism could precipitate a collapse if someone made a wrong call? Perhaps the answer differs by sector, so that while regional arrangements are important in new issues, they are a potential danger in areas such as goods trade.

5   Finale

This section collects together the principal lessons from this survey in terms both of conclusions and of directions for future research. Before doing so, however, it reports one final contribution to the literature that I have been unable to fit into the schema above.

5.1   Investment not trade

Many commentators argue that the recent crop of North–South RIAs – e.g. NAFTA and the Europe Agreements – have been aimed at locking in the southern partner's economic reforms and stimulating inflows of foreign direct investment (FDI). Ethier (1996) offers a brilliant formalisation of these ideas. Briefly, developing countries start in autarchy, and as the world grows and liberalises they start to think about opening up themselves. If they reform successfully and attract an inflow of FDI, they gain a step increase in productivity. Their problem is that if several of them reform simultaneously, none can guarantee that it will get the FDI – maybe the inflow will go to their rivals. Regionalism, by which an industrial country offers a particular developing country small preferences on its exports, overcomes this problem by ensuring that the industrial country will invest in its partner developing country rather than any other. (Since all industrial countries are assumed to be identical, as are all developing countries, the smallest preference on return exports stemming from an FDI flow is sufficient to create this link.) Thus regionalism ensures the success of reform, not only increasing the proportion of reforming developing countries that succeed, but also encouraging more to try. This is regionalism as coordination – it removes a source of uncertainty and thus encourages reform and openness.

Ethier's paper is original and important, but its model is very special. In particular, there are no conceivable costs to regionalism to the partners and, because countries are identical within their type-class, no dangers of inefficient regional arrangements growing up within the classes. Thus coordination comes essentially risk-free. Additionally, small changes to the model would allow the same coordination to be achieved multilaterally. For example, if each developing country considers coming out of the closet of autarchy at a unique time (because they all differ slightly from one another in dimensions that affect the timing of their reform decision), or if the supply of FDI for the industrial world is sufficiently large or the movements of factor prices in developing countries sufficiently strong, every developing country can be sure of getting some FDI if it opens up. Nonetheless the focus on FDI rather than trade is a powerful attraction of this approach, given the structure of and rhetoric surrounding current North–South regional arrangements.

5.2 *Conclusions and future research*

The issue of 'regionalism vs. multilateralism' is new analytically and deficient of empirical evidence. It is hardly surprising, therefore that this survey should conclude with more statements about research strategy than about the world we live in. Indeed, as I noted above, the only categorical statement that can be made in the last class is that one incident of regionalism is not sufficient to undermine a relatively multilateral system immediately.

My main conclusions from working on this fascinating literature include:

- Since we value 'multilateralism', we had better work out what it means and, if it means different things to different people, ensure that we identify the sense in which we are using the term when we do so.
- The symmetric models looking at the welfare effects of regionalism have served their purpose, and probably offer rather little return to future research. Their structure is not plausible and their results seems very fragile with respect to assumed parameter values. If completely new ways of thinking about regionalism emerge, it may be worth exploring them in a symmetric framework as a way of elucidating their properties, but this is not going to resolve the positive 'stepping-stones' question.
- Asymmetric models are more plausible, but it is important to model both the demand for and supply of bloc membership.
- Models of negotiated trade policy also take a significant step towards realism. However, it would be nice, in future, to try to move beyond the repeated game trigger strategies approach to model a richer set of objectives and disciplines. This, of course, is a challenge not only to

researchers on regionalism, but also to those working on the trading system in general.

- Sector-specific lobbies are a danger if regionalism is permitted. Trade diversion is good politics even if it is bad economics. I find the view that multilateral liberalism could stall because producers get most of what they seek from regional arrangements quite convincing.
- The direct effect of regionalism on multilateralism is important, but possibly more so is the indirect effect it has by changing the ways in which (groups of) countries interact and respond to shocks in the world economy. The way in which the existence of fringes of small partners affects relations between large players seems to be a fruitful avenue, as does the structure of post-integration institutions.
- It would be useful to embed the 'regionalism vs. multilateralism' question in a framework of general economic reform and/or economic growth to generate richer menus of potential benefits and chains of causation.
- Regionalism, by allowing stronger internalisation of the gains from trade liberalisation, seems likely to be able to facilitate freer trade in highly restrictive circumstances or sectors.
- The possibility of regionalism probably increases the risks of catastrophe in the trade system. The incentives established by the insurance motive for joining regional arrangements and Oye's (1992) analysis of 'shiftable externalities' both lead to such a conclusion. So, too, does the view that regionalism is a means to bring trade partners to the multilateral negotiating table, because it is essentially coercive. The latter may have been an effective strategy, but it is risky.

APPENDIX : AN INDEX OF MULTILATERALISM?

A country's multilateralism index is a positive function of:

(a) the absence of discrimination in its trade policy
(b) the closeness its trade regime is overall to free trade.

Assume that only one commodity is traded in the world and that our country imports it from every other country in an $(N + 1)$ country world. Assume also that initially all partners face the same (MFN) tariff at level t and that no other distortions exist. Suppose now that the country signs an FTA with some (n) partners. How do t and n enter the index of multilateralism (M)?

Figure 2A.1 plots contours of equal M in the space of the MFN tariff

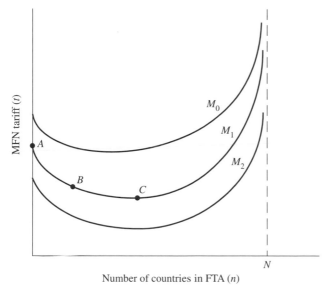

Figure 2A.1   Iso-multilateralism loci

(t) and the number of FTA partners (n). Starting at, say, A, with a positive t, assume we sign an FTA with one partner. This increases discrimination and so would require a decrease in t to keep M constant; similarly if another partner entered the FTA, t would need to fall further. Thus the iso-M curve would include a point like B. Eventually, however, say, at C, enough countries would be in the FTA that increasing n would, *ceteris paribus*, increase measured multilateralism, allowing an increase in t along the iso-M curve. Now imagine the far end of the curve. When the final country gets into the FTA, our country offers everyone free trade and the MFN tariff can be infinity.

For any n, n countries pay a tariff of zero, while ($N - n$) pay t. Since freer trade entails higher multilateralism, if, say, m countries are 'exceptional ($m < N/2$)', M will be higher if the majority ($N - m$) pay zero than if the minority (m) does. Looked at alternatively, for many values of the tariff (t), a given level of multilateralism ($\overline{M}$) could arise with two different values of n, say n_1 and n_2, $n_1 < n_2$. We require that $n_1 < (N - n_2)$, as in figure 2A.1. Figure 2A.1 presents three such iso-multilateralism loci, with the degree of multilateralism increasing the closer the locus is to the x-axis. In the limit the locus for perfect multilateralism runs along the x-axis and up the vertical from N.

Clearly this index is quite complex and will become even more so once we recognise that more than two trade regimes might exist (in this example partners pay either *t* or 0) and that regimes will actually vary across commodities. It becomes even worse once we recognise that we need to aggregate across countries.

The conclusions of this appendix are twofold. First, we actually need to think what we mean by 'multilateralism' if we think we are worried about it. Second, in the meantime our conclusions about 'regionalism vs. multilateralism' will remain a little fuzzy.

NOTES

I am grateful to Anju Kapur for research assistance, to conference participants and to Richard Baldwin, Will Martin, Pier Carlo Padoan and André Sapir for comments on an earlier draft, and to Audrey Kitson-Walters for logistical support. The views expressed here are the author's alone. They do not necessarily represent those of the World Bank or any of its member governments.
 1 The appendix (p. 42) offers a little more detail on such an index.
 2 Earlier contributions include Riezman (1985) and Kennan and Riezman (1990).
 3 Sinclair and Vines model the similarity somewhat differently from Bond and Syropoulos.
 4 They refer to their discussion as 'Krugman vs. Krugman', my nomination for title of the year.
 5 Deardorff and Stern (1994) effectively use the same approach but pairing countries by complementary comparative advantage rather than transportation costs. Arguably, however, their results gravitate away from continental blocs rather than towards them if comparative advantage varies more across continents than within them.
 6 Similar arguments surround the Kemp and Wan (1976) result that a CU can always find a common external tariff (CET) that renders it welfare-improving and thus that unions can beneficially expand and combine until they arrive at global free trade. 'Can', but there is no analysis of 'do'. This is not to criticise Kemp and Wan: their focus was not on stepping stones.
 7 That is, blocs do not raise their optimum tariffs as a result of integration.
 8 An alternative strategy would be for the union to *reduce* its tariff to keep non-member welfare constant – a so-called 'Kemp–Wan reduction'. The union would prefer this to trade war if it had below about 40 per cent of countries.
 9 As Perroni and Whalley observe, in strict trade policy terms Eastern Europe, the Mediterranean countries and Mexico gain little from their associations with larger blocs relative to unilateral MFN liberalisation.
10 See also Helpman (1997) for a summary.
11 This point is also made by McCulloch and Petri (1994).
12 Similar causal channels are found in Panagariya and Findlay (1994).
13 The analysis revolves around the elasticities with which the fringe demands and supplies sensitive products, not its excess supply *per se*. Presumably the latter would enter the decision to create the FTA in the first place. The link with Richardson (1993) is best seen on the import analogue of the argument in the text. If the fringe supply curve of the sensitive import is perfectly elastic, the lobbies in *A* lose all interest in maintaining a higher post-tariff price on *B*.

14 They still gain from integration because of the differentiated goods.
15 Such a sector may prefer high EU protection, so that it can reap high rents on EU sales, but at least it could survive with lower protection.
16 Maybe this reflected US fears of the EEC – i.e. that it felt obliged to offer and to seek bigger tariff reductions if the EEC completed its integration – but publishing the fact seems a clumsy negotiating ploy if that were the case.

REFERENCES

Bagwell, K. and Staiger, R. W., 1996a. 'Preferential Agreements and the Multilateral Trading System', mimeo
   1996b. 'Regionalism and Multilateralism Tariff Cooperation', paper prepared for the International Economics Association Round-Table Conference, International Trade Policy and the Pacific Rim (15–17 July)
   1997a. 'Multilateral Tariff Cooperation During the Formation of Regional Free Trade Areas', *International Economic Review*, **38**, 291–319
   1997b. 'Multilateral Tariff Cooperation During the Formation of Customs Unions', *Journal of International Economics*, **42**, 91–123
Baldwin, R.E., 1995. 'A Domino Theory of Regionalism', chapter 2 in Baldwin, Haaparanta and Kiander (eds.), 25–48
Baldwin, R.E., Haaparanta, P. and Kiander, J., 1995. *Expanding Membership in the European Union* (Cambridge: Cambridge University Press for the CEPR)
Bergsten, F., 1997. 'Open regionalism', *The World Economy*, **20**, 545–66
Bhagwati, J.N., 1991. *The World Trading System at Risk* (Princeton: Princeton University Press)
Bhagwati, J. N. and Panagariya, A., 1996. 'Preferential Trading Areas and Multilateralism: Strangers, Friends or Foes?', in J.N. Bhagwati and A. Panagariya (eds.), *Free Trade Areas or Free Trade? The Economics of Preferential Trading Agreements* (Washington, DC: AEI Press)
Bond, E.W. and Syropoulos, C., 1996a. 'The Size of Trading Blocs: Market Power and World Welfare Effects', *Journal of International Economics*, **40**, 411–37
   1996b. 'Trading Blocs and the Sustainability of Inter-regional Cooperation', in M. Canzoneri, W. Ethier and V. Grilli (eds.), *The New Transatlantic Economy* (Cambridge: Cambridge University Press)
Bond, E.W., Syropoulos, C. and Winters, L.A., 1996. 'Deepening of Regional Integration and External Trade Relations', *CEPR Discussion Paper*, **1317**
Cadot, O., De Melo, J. and Olarreaga, J., 1996. 'Regional Integration and Lobbying for Tariffs Against Non-Members', University of Geneva, mimeo
Campa, J.M. and Sorenson, T.L., 1996. 'Are Trade Blocs Condusive to Free Trade?', *Scandinavian Journal of Economics*, **98**, 263–73
Collie, D., 1997. 'Bilateralism is Good: Trade Blocs and Strategic Export Subsidies',*Oxford Economic Papers*, **49**, 504–20
Deardorff, A.W. and Stern, R.M., 1994. 'Multilateral Trade Negotiations and Preferential Trading Arrangements', in A.V. Deardorff and R.M. Stern, *Analytical and Negotiating Issues in the Global Trading System* (Ann Arbor: University of Michigan Press)

De Melo, J. and Panagariya, A. (eds.) 1993. *New Dimensions in Regional Integration* (Cambridge: Cambridge University Press for the CEPR)

De Melo, J. Panagariya, A. and Rodrik, D. (1993) 'The New Regionalism: A Country Perspective', in J. De Melo and A. Panagariya (eds.), *New Dimensions in Regional Integration* (Cambridge: Cambridge University Press for the CEPR)

Eichengreen B. (ed.), 1995. *Europe's Post-War Recovery* (Cambridge: Cambridge University Press)

Ethier, W.J., 1996. 'Regionalism in a Multilateral World', mimeo

Frankel, J.A., 1997. *Regional Trading Blocs* (Washington, DC: Institute for International Economics)

Frankel, J.A. and Wei, S.J., 1996. 'Regionalization of World Trade and Currencies: Economics and Politics', chapter 7 in J.A. Frankel (ed.), *The Regionalization of the World Economy* (Chicago: Chicago University Press)

Frankel, J.A., Stein, E. and Wei, S. J., 1995. 'Trading Blocs and the Americas: The Natural, the Unnatural, and the Super-Natural', *Journal of Development Economics,* **47**, 61–95.

   1996. 'Continental Trade Blocs: Are They Natural and Super-Natural?', chapter 4 in J.A. Frankel (ed.), *The Regionalization of the World Economy* (Chicago: Chicago University Press)

Gatsios, K. and Karp, L., 1991. 'Delegation Games in Customs Unions', *Review of Economic Studies,* **58**, 391–97

   1995. 'Delegation in a General Equilibrium Model of Customs Unions', *European Economic Review,* **39**, 319–33

Goto, J. and Hamada, K., 1994. 'Economic Integration and the Welfare of Those Who are Left Behind: An Asian Perspective', RIEB Kobe University, *Discussion Paper,* **47**

   1997. 'EU, NAFTA and Asian Responses: A Perspective from the Calculus of Participation', chapter 4 in T. Ito and A.O. Krueger (eds.), *Regionalism vs. Multilateral Trade Agreements* (Chicago: Chacago University Press), 91–110

Grossman, G. and Helpman, E., 1994. 'Protection for Sale', *American Economic Review,* **85**, 667–90

   1995. 'The Politics of Free-Trade Agreements', *American Economic Review,* **84**, 833–50

Hamilton, C.B., 1991. 'The Nordic EFTA Countries' Options: Community Membership or a Permanent EEA Accord', chapter 7 in *EFTA Countries in a Changing Europe* (Geneva: EFTA), 97–128

Hathaway, D.E. and Ingco, M.D., 1996. 'Agricultural Liberalization and the Uruguay Round', chapter 2 in W. Martin and L.A. Winters (eds.), *The Uruguay Round and the Developing Countries* (Cambridge: Cambridge University Press)

Helpman, E., 1997. 'Politics and Trade Policy', chapter 2 in D.M. Kreps and K.F. Wallis (eds.), *Advances in Economics and Econometrics: Theory and Application, vol. I* (Cambridge: Cambridge University Press)

Hufbauer, G.C., 1990. *Europe 1992: An American Perspective* (Washington, DC: Brookings)

Irwin, D.A., 1993. 'Multilateral and Bilateral Trade Policies in the World Trading System: A Historical Perspective', chapter 4 in De Melo and Panagariya (eds.), 90–119

1995. 'The GATT's Contribution to Economic Recovery in Post-war Western Europe', chapter 5 in Eichengreen (ed.), 127–50

Jackson, J.H., 1991. 'The European Community and World Trade: The Commercial Policy Dimension', Institute for Public Policy Studies, University of Michigan, Ann Arbor, *Discussion Paper*, **298**

Jacquemin, A. and Sapir, A., 1988. 'European Integration or World Integration?', *WeltwirtschaftlichesArchiv*, **124**, 127–39

Kemp, M.C. and Wan, H., Jr., 1976. 'An Elementary Proposition Concerning the Formation of Customs Unions', *Journal of International Economics*, **6**, 95–7

Kennan, J. and Riezman, R., 1990. 'Optimal Tariff Equilibria with Customs Unions', *Canadian Journal of Economics*, **23**, 70–83

Keohane, R.O., 1984. *After Hegemony: Cooperation and Discord in the World Political Economy* (Princeton: Princeton University Press)

Kowalczyk, C, and Sjostrom, T., 1992. 'Bringing GATT into the Core', *Economica*, **61**, 301–17

Krishna, P., 1994. 'Regionalism and Multilateralism: A Political Economy Approach', *Quarterly Journal of Economics*, forthcoming

Krugman P., 1991a. 'Is Bilateralism Bad?', in E. Helpman and A. Razin (eds.), *International Trade and Trade Policy* (Cambridge, MA: MIT Press)

1991b. 'The Move Towards Free Trade Zones', in 'Policy Implications of Trade and Currency Zones', a symposium sponsored by the Federal Reserve Bank of Kansas City, Jackson Hole, Wyoming (22–24 August)

1993. 'Regionalism versus Multilateralism: Analytical Notes', in J.De Melo and A.Panagariya (eds.), 58–78

Lawrence, R.Z., 1991. 'Emerging Regional Arrangements: Building Blocs or Stumbling Blocks?', in R. O'Brien (ed.), *Finance and the International Economy 5*, The AMEX Bank Review Prize Essays (New York: Oxford University Press), 23–35

Levy, P.I, 1997. 'A Political economic Analysis of Free Trade Agreements', *American Economic Review*, **87**, 506–19

1996a. 'Lobbying and International Cooperation in Tariff Setting', Yale University, mimeo

1996b. 'Comment on "Regionalization of World Trade and Currencies: Economics and Politics" ', chapter 7 in J.A. Frankel (ed.), *The Regionalization of the World Economy* (Chicago: Chicago University Press)

Ludema, R., 1996. 'On the Value of Preferential Trade Agreements in Multilateral Negotiations', Georgetown University, *Working Paper*, **97–22**

McCulloch, R. and Petri, P., 1994. 'Alternative Paths toward Global Markets', paper presented at a conference in honour of Robert Stern, University of Michigan (20 November)

Messerlin, P.A., 1983. 'Bureaucracies and the Political Economy of Protection: Reflections of a Continental European', *WeltwirtschaftlichesArchiv*, **117**, 468–96

1992. 'Trade Policies in France', in D. Salvatore (ed.), *National Trade Policies. Handbook of Comparative Economic Policies*. vol. 2 (Westport, CN and London: Greenwood Press)

Nitsch, V., 1996. 'Natural Trading Blocs: A Closer Look', paper prepared for the European Economic Association Meeting, Istanbul (August)

1996 'Do Three Trade Blocs Minimize World Welfare?', *Review of International Economics*, **4**, 355–63

Nogues, J. and Quintanilla, R., 1993. 'Latin America's Integration and the Multilateral Trading System', in De Melo and Panagariya (eds.), 278–313

Nordström. H., 1995. 'Customs Unions, Regional Trading Blocs and Welfare', chapter 3 in Baldwin, Haaparanta and Kiander (eds.), 54–78

Oye, K., 1992. *Economic Discrimination and Political Exchange: World Political Economy in the 1930s and 1980s* (Princeton: Princeton University Press)

Panagariya, A. and Findlay, R., 1994. 'A Political Economy Analysis of Free Trade Areas and Customs Unions', *Policy Research Working Paper*, **1261** (Washington, DC: World Bank)

Perroni, C. and Whalley, J., 1994. 'The New Regionalism: Trade Liberalization or Insurance?', *NBER Working Paper*, **4626**

Richardson, M., 1993. 'Endogenous Protection and Trade Diversion', *Journal of International Economics,* **34**, 309–24

1994. 'Why a Free Trade Area? The Tariff Also Rises', *Economics and Politics*, **6**, 79–96

1995. 'Tariff Revenue Competition in a Free Trade Area', *European Economic Review*, **39**, 1429–37

Richardson, M. and Desruelle, D., 1997. 'Fortress Europe: Jericho or Château d'If?', *Review of International Economics*, **5**, 32–46

Riezman, R., 1985. 'Customs Unions and the Core', *Journal of International Economics*, **19**, 355–65

Sapir, A., 1993. 'Discussion of chapter 7', in De Melo and Panagariya (eds.), 230–3

Scharpf, F., 1998. 'Joint Decision Trap: Lessons from German Federalism and European Integration', *Public Administration*, **66**, 239–78

Schattschneider, E.E., 1935. *Politics, Pressures and the Tariff* (New York: Prentice-Hall)

Shepsle, K.A. and Weingast, B.R., 1981. 'Political Preferences for the Pork Barrel: A Generalisation', *American Journal of Political Science*, **25**, 96–111

Sinclair, P. and Vines, D., 1995. 'Bigger Trade Blocs Need not Entail More Protection', University of Birmingham, mimeo

Spilimbergo, A. and Stein, E., 1996. 'The Welfare Implications of Trading Blocs among Countries with Different Endowments', chapter 5 in J.A. Frankel (ed.), *The Regionalization of the World Economy* (Chicago: Chicago University Press)

Srinivasan, T.N., 1993. 'Regionalism vs. Multilateralism: Analytical Notes: Discussion', in De Melo and Panagariya (eds.), 84–9

Summers, L., 1991. 'Regionalism and the World Trading System', in 'Policy Implications of Trade and Currency Zones', a symposium sponsored by the Federal Reserve Bank of Kansas City, Jackson Hole, Wyoming, 295–302

Widgrén, M., 1995a. 'Voting Power and Control in the EU: The Impact of EFTA Entrants', chapter 5 in Baldwin, Haaparanta and Kiander (eds.), 113–42

1995b. 'Probabilistic Voting Power in the EU Council: The Cases of Trade Policy and Social Regulation', *Scandinavian Journal of Economics*, **97**, 345–56

Winham, G.R., 1986. *International Trade and the Tokyo Round Negotiation* (Princeton: Princeton University Press)

Winters, L.A., 1993. 'The European Community: A Case of Successful Integration', *CEPR Discussion Paper*, **755**

1994. 'The EC and Protection: The Political Economy', *European Economic Review*, **38**, 596–603

1995. 'Who Should Run Eastern European Trade Policy and How', chapter 2 in L.A. Winters (ed.), *Foundations of an Open Economy: Trade Laws and Institutions for Eastern Europe* (London: Cambridge University for the CEPR), 19–39

World Trade Organization (WTO), 1995. *Regionalism and the World Trading System* (Geneva: WTO) (April)

Yarbrough, B.V. and Yarbrough, R.M., 1992. *Cooperation and Governance in International Trade: The Strategic Organizational Approach* (Princeton: Princeton University Press)

Discussion

ANDRE SAPIR

The modern literature on 'regionalism versus multilateralism' was born in 1991, of two exceptional parents. One, Bhagwati (1991), asked the key question: are regional trade arrangements (RTAs) 'building blocks' or 'stumbling blocks' toward multilateral trade liberalisation? The other, Krugman (1991), offered a formal model for investigating the consistency of RTAs with the multilateral trading system.

Alan Winters in chapter 2 provides a survey of the recent theoretical and empirical literature, seeking to answer Bhagwati's original question.

He focuses mainly on theoretical contributions, which he summarises remarkably. He also reviews some empirical evidence, dealing primarily with the European Community.

The seminal piece by Krugman showed that global welfare is maximised when the number of trading blocs is either equal to one (global free trade) or very large (each bloc behaving like a 'small country' and adopting unilateral free trade). The worst situation for global welfare is obtained when the number of blocs is three, an ominous result in view of predictions that the world might be evolving toward blocs centred on the European Community, the United States and Japan.

Krugman's result is based on a number of economic assumptions regarding the structure of production, consumption and trade. In particular, the following assumptions are made with respect to trade: (1) the world is divided into blocs of equal size; (2) blocs play a one-shot Nash game in tariffs; and (3) each bloc sets its tariff so as to maximise social welfare. The recent literature has attempted to relax all three assumptions.

Several authors have examined situations where the world is divided into blocs of different size, with the possibility that some countries do not belong to any bloc. The questions raised are whether blocs end up encompassing all countries in a single bloc (global free trade) or whether large blocs prefer to exclude some countries. The literature contains contributions on both sides of the fence.

Economists have also analysed situations where countries or blocs play repeated games. The question raised is whether cooperation or non-cooperation is the more likely strategy, depending on bloc size. Two opposing effects operate in situations with large blocs: each bloc has a short-term incentive to adopt high tariffs, but loses in the long run from trade wars. The crucial parameter in these models is therefore the discount rate: the higher the discount rate, the greater the incentive for non-cooperation. Winters notes correctly that this raises the question of the time scale over which these games are played. The shorter the horizon, the greater the incentive for cooperation. In this respect, he worries that, being a 'game in regimes' (where GATT/WTO rounds represent the natural periodicity), regionalism may increase the incentive for non-cooperation.

Finally, the literature has considered political economy models of regionalism, where governments set tariffs in response to pressure groups rather than in the public interest. Some authors find that regionalism, by shifting the relative power of pressure groups in favour of export interests, leads to multilateral trade liberalisation. Others argue, instead, that the process of regional integration is bound to be captured by protectionist lobbies intent on increasing external trade barriers.

In short, the recent theoretical literature on 'regionalism versus multilateralism' is far from conclusive. This point is rightly emphasised by Winters, who summarises the shortcomings of each group of models in his concluding section 5. Perhaps he could have noted that the issue of 'regionalism versus multilateralism' eminently belongs to the realm of second-best, which precludes a clear-cut theoretical answer and requires, instead, an essentially empirical evaluation.

The chapter contains such empirical evaluation, but unfortunately it is largely limited to the EC experience. Even more regrettably, it focuses on 'EC integration', whereas the main issue should be about 'EC regionalism'. This distinction is starkly brought out by Bhagwati and Panagariya (1996, p.xvii) who approve of the EC as

> a group of countries that wishes to opt for truly deep integration, both economic and political, with dismantled barriers to capital and labor mobility and aiming at common political structures such as parliament and even uniform foreign policiestformat

but castigate it for seeking, like the United States, free trade areas with other countries.

Winters and I continue to disagree on whether the EC is a 'stumbling block' (Winters) or a 'building block' (Sapir) toward multilateral trade liberalisation (see Winters, 1993; Sapir, 1993). On the other hand, I suspect that we share some concern on the extension of EC regionalism to non-EC candidates. Sapir (1998) finds that, currently, preferential trade accounts for no more than 25 per cent of total EC trade. At the same time, he points out that EC regionalism stands at a crossroads with three possible options. One extreme (1) is to continue along the regional path, all the way down to the demise of the multilateral trading system. The other extreme (2) consists of promoting multilateral free trade. An intermediate option (3) is to combine elements of the two extreme solutions, seeking an harmonious coexistence between regionalism and multilateralism by reinforcing GATT/WTO rules. Both of us, I suppose, consider option (2) as the most desirable, but would settle for option (3), provided it seeks to minimise the discriminatory aspect of regional trade agreements.

REFERENCES

Bhagwati, J.N., 1991. *The World Trading System at Risk* (Princeton: Princeton University Press)
Bhagwati, J.N. and Panagariya, A. (eds.), 1996. *Free Trade Areas or Free Trade?*

The Economics of Preferential Trading Agreements (Washington, DC: AEI Press)

Krugman, P.R., 1991. 'Is Bilateralism Bad?', in E. Helpman and A. Razin (eds.), *International Trade and Trade Policy* (Cambridge, MA: MIT Press)

Sapir, A., 1993. 'Discussion of chapter 7', in J. de Melo and A. Panagariya (eds.), *New Dimensions in Regional Integration* (Cambridge: Cambridge University Press for the CEPR), 230–3

   1998. 'The Political Economy of EC Regionalism', *European Economic Review*, **42**

Winters, L.A., 1993. 'The European Community: A Case of Successful Integration?', chapter 7 in J. de Melo and A. Panagariya (eds.), *New Dimensions in Regional Integration* (Cambridge: Cambridge University Press for the CEPR), 202–8

3 Preferential agreements and the multilateral trading system

KYLE BAGWELL AND
ROBERT W. STAIGER

1 Introduction

Are preferential agreements at odds with the multilateral trading system? This is a question of fundamental importance to the design of the GATT–WTO system. And it is a question that has become increasingly pressing as more countries negotiate free trade agreements (FTAs) (in which member countries eliminate their internal barriers to trade) and Customs Unions (CUs) (in which member countries also set common external tariffs (CETs)) under the GATT's Article XXIV exception to the principle of non-discrimination.

An answer to this question requires an understanding of the key components of the multilateral trading system, and of the way that these components work to shape the trade agreements that can be implemented within the GATT–WTO. There are three components that serve as the cornerstones of the GATT system: the principles of *reciprocity* and *non-discrimination*, which are regularly singled out as the 'pillars' of the GATT architecture, and the *enforcement* mechanisms, which Dam (1970, p. 81) calls the 'heart' of the GATT system. In this chapter, we describe how preferential agreements interact with the multilateral system in light of its three principal components.

We find it analytically convenient to divide the question posed at the outset into two parts. We first ask: are preferential agreements at odds with a multilateral trading system that is based on the principles of reciprocity and non-discrimination? A remaining question is then: how do preferential agreements interact with the enforcement provisions of the GATT? An answer to the first question requires a framework within which the principles of reciprocity and non-discrimination can themselves be interpreted and understood. In this chapter, we describe such a framework (developed more fully in Bagwell and Staiger, 1997a) and, from this perspective, offer support for the view that preferential agreements pose a threat to the multilateral system. An answer to the second question requires an understanding of how GATT agreements are enforced. Arguing that these agreements must be *self-enforcing*, we review earlier work to conclude that preferential agreements can both enhance and detract from the performance of the GATT system through their impacts on enforcement at the multilateral level.

In order to construct a theory of the multilateral trading system within which the workings of reciprocity, non-discrimination and enforcement mechanisms can be understood, a most basic question must first be confronted: why have governments found reciprocal trade agreements to be appealing? We start from the observation that, while governments acting unilaterally may seek to achieve political, distributional or other domestic goals by altering national prices through tariff intervention, this by itself provides no reason for them to seek reciprocal trade agreements. The possibility of mutual gains from such agreements requires something more: the unilateral trade policy decisions of each government, when viewed together, must be inefficient in light of the governments' own objectives.

In Bagwell and Staiger (1996) we argue that the inefficiency created when governments pursue trade policies cognisant of their ability to affect world prices (the *terms of trade*) is the driving force behind the appeal of reciprocal trade agreements. There, we develop a general framework in which reciprocal trade agreements provide politically/distributionally-motivated governments with an escape from a terms of trade-driven prisoner's dilemma. The observation that the terms of trade effects of trade policy intervention *can* provide governments with a reason to seek reciprocal trade liberalisation is not new, and its formalisation dates back to Scitovszky (1942) and Johnson (1953–4). However, these arguments were developed in the context of national income-maximising governments who exploited their monopoly power in international markets with 'optimal tariffs', and a common view is that these arguments become secondary in explaining the appeal of reciprocal trade agreements once more realistic government objectives that include political and/or distributional concerns are acknowledged. In Bagwell and Staiger (1996) we show that more general government objectives *do not* overturn the view that trade agreements provide governments with an escape from a terms of trade-driven prisoner's dilemma. Moreover, in the leading formulations of political economy, and indeed *whenever* government objectives can be represented as a function of national prices and the terms of trade, this is *all* that trade agreements do: political and/or domestic distributional considerations play *no role* in explaining why governments seek reciprocal trade agreements.[1] This follows from our earlier observation that governments seek reciprocal trade agreements to correct inefficiencies that arise from unilateral trade policy decisions, and because the unilateral decisions of each government to seek a set of national prices for political/distributional reasons will be inefficient by the governments' own objectives only if these decisions are distorted by a country's ability to affect its terms of trade.

In this chapter we describe how our basic approach can be used to shed light on the questions posed above. We first consider how preferential agreements interact with a multilateral trading system that is based on the pillars of reciprocity and non-discrimination. With a minimal amount of technical apparatus, we offer an interpretation of the notion of reciprocity as embodied in the GATT, and we characterise the kinds of trade agreements that can be implemented in its presence.[2] We show in particular that a multilateral system built on the principle of reciprocity can implement an efficient agreement only if it also embraces the principle of non-discrimination. Hence, our framework provides a formal rationale for the linkage between reciprocity and non-discrimination as pillars of an efficient multilateral trading system. Armed with this framework, we then ask a specific question with regard to preferential agreements: can a multilateral system built on the principle of reciprocity implement an efficient agreement in the presence of FTAs or CUs? We find that (1) reciprocity cannot serve to implement an efficient agreement when free trade areas are present, and (2) reciprocity may implement an efficient agreement in the presence of a CU, but only if the union comprises similar countries. As these conditions are quite stringent, we offer only limited support for the hypothesis that the principle of reciprocity can deliver an efficient trade agreement in the presence of preferential trade agreements. Instead our results suggest that preferential agreements pose a threat to the existing multilateral system.

The intuition for these results rests on a crucial property of reciprocity that we establish below: an efficient multilateral trade agreement can be implemented under the GATT's principle of reciprocity provided the externalities associated with trade intervention are transmitted only through world price movements. Externalities are transmitted only through world price movements when tariffs are non-discriminatory, and so reciprocity accompanied by such a requirement can deliver an efficient multilateral trade agreement. However, the introduction of discriminatory tariffs complicates the transmission of externalities across countries, as governments are induced to care about bilateral trade volumes. In such circumstances, local price movements in each national market can directly exert external effects on trading partners, and so the externalities associated with trade intervention travel through both world and local price movements. This undermines the ability of reciprocity to implement efficient trade policies. Hence, a multilateral system built on reciprocity must eliminate discriminatory treatment of international trade if it is to deliver an efficient agreement. The only form of tariff discrimination that can be excepted from this statement is the case where independent countries join in complete political and economic union to become a 'single country' for the purposes of trade policy.

We next turn to the second question posed above, and consider how preferential agreements interact with the enforcement mechanisms of the multilateral trading system. In particular, we argue that enforcement issues at the multilateral level may preclude governments from elim- inating the terms of trade motivations from their trade policy choices if each government is restricted to a policy of non-discrimination. In such circumstances, permitting tariff discrimination for those country pairs that can enforce greater bilateral liberalisation could enhance the overall efficiency of the multilateral agreement. However, such preferential agreements can themselves affect the operation of enforcement mechan- isms at the multilateral level, and thereby either enhance or detract from the overall efficiency of the system. Here, we review some of the additional considerations for a multilateral agreement that arise once the implications of the preferential agreements for enforcement of the broader multilateral agreement are themselves taken into account.

The remainder of the chapter proceeds as follows. Section 2 presents our basic two-country model, identifies the inefficiency associated with unilateral tariff-setting that a trade agreement can correct, and explores the logic of reciprocity. Section 3 extends our two-country model to a many-country setting. Here we establish a link between reciprocity and non-discrimination. Our results on the implications of preferential agreements for a multilateral trading system built on the principle of reciprocity are contained in section 4. Section 5 discusses the implications of preferential agreements for enforcement at the multilateral level, and section 6 concludes.

2   Reciprocity

In this section, we describe a simple two-country partial equilibrium model of trade in two goods. The model identifies the inefficiency that confronts governments when they set trade policies unilaterally, and it offers an interpretation of reciprocity as a negotiation principle that implements efficient trade policies. A more complete analysis is presented in Bagwell and Staiger (1997a).

2.1   Government welfare functions

We consider a world economy in which two countries, home (no *) and foreign (*), trade two goods, x and y.[3] The local prices of goods x and y in the home country are given as p_x and p_y, and the foreign local prices are similarly defined as p_x^* and p_y^*. For simplicity, we assume that the demand functions found in the two countries are symmetric: each good is demanded in each country according to a common and decreasing demand function, D. Thus, for example, the demand for good x in the home country is given as $D(p_x)$, and likewise the demand for good x in the foreign country is represented as $D(p_x^*)$.

We create a basis for trade between the two countries with the assumption that the supply functions differ across the two countries. The domestic supply functions arise from competitive markets and are represented as $Q_x(p_x)$ and $Q_y(p_y)$. The foreign supply functions may be expressed analogously. We assume these functions are increasing and satisfy $Q_x(p) = Q_y^*(p) < Q_y(p) = Q_x^*(p)$. Thus, holding fixed price across goods and countries, the domestic (foreign) supply of good x (y) is small relative to the domestic (foreign) supply of good y (x). Given the assumed symmetry in demand, it follows that x is the natural import of the home country and y is the natural import of the foreign country.

Local prices are determined in the following manner. Let $\tau_x(\tau_y)$ denote the import tariff (export subsidy) selected by the domestic government, and let $\tau_y^*(\tau_x^*)$ represent the import tariff (export subsidy) chosen by the foreign government. Assuming that trade taxes do not prohibit all trade, the local prices must obey an arbitrage condition, given by $p_i = p_i^* + \tau_i \tau_i^*$, for $i = x,y$, and also a market-clearing condition, given by $Q_i(p_i) + Q_i^*(p_i^*) = D(p_i) + D(p_i^*)$, for $i = x, y$. These conditions determine the market-clearing prices as functions of the corresponding net tariffs, $\tau_x \tau_x^*$ and $\tau_y^* \tau_y$. As would be expected, a higher net tariff raises the local price in the importing country (i.e. $p_x(\tau_x \tau_x^*)$ and $p_y^*(\tau_y^* \tau_y)$ are increasing) and lowers the local price in the exporting country (i.e. $p_y(\tau_y^* \tau_y)$ and $p_x^*(\tau_x \tau_x^*)$ are decreasing).

We may also define the world (i.e. offshore) prices of goods x and y. These prices are denoted as p_x^w and p_y^w, respectively, and they are defined by $p_i \equiv p_i^w + \tau_i$, for $i = x, y$. With the market-clearing local prices determined as above, we may represent the market-clearing world prices as $p_x^w(\tau_x, \tau_x^*)$ and $p_x^w(\tau_x, \tau_x^*)$. The world price is decreasing in each argument, as it falls when either the import tariff or the export subsidy is increased. We can also express local prices as explicit functions of world prices: $\hat{p}_i(\tau_i, p_i^w(\tau_i, \tau_i^*)) \equiv p_i^w(\tau_i, \tau_i^*) + \tau_i$ and $\hat{p}_i^*(\tau_i^*, p_i^w(\tau_i, \tau_i^*)) \equiv p_i^w(\tau_i, \tau_i^*) + \tau_i^*$.

We complete the description of the market environment by defining the market-clearing import and export volumes. For the domestic country, these are $M(\hat{p}_x) \equiv D(\hat{p}_x)Q_x(\hat{p}_x)$ and $E(\hat{p}_y) \equiv Q_y(\hat{p}_y)D(\hat{p}_y)$, respectively. Likewise, the foreign import and export volumes are $M^*(\hat{p}_y^*) \equiv D(\hat{p}_y^*)Q_y^*(\hat{p}_y^*)$ and $E^*(\hat{p}_x^*) \equiv Q_x^*(\hat{p}_x^*)D(\hat{p}_x^*)$, respectively. The market-clearing requirement ensures that $M(\hat{p}_x) = E^*(\hat{p}_x^*)$ and $M^*(\hat{p}_y^*) = E(\hat{p}_y)$. Finally, we assume throughout that governments do not choose tariffs that prohibit trade.

We are now prepared to define the government welfare functions. We assume that governments value consumer surplus, producer surplus and tariff revenue. As Baldwin (1987) has suggested (and as Grossman and Helpman, 1994, have confirmed in an explicit lobbying model), political economy influences can be captured with the assumption that governments weigh producer surplus move heavily than tariff revenue or consumer surplus. We thus let γ_m (γ_e) denote the weight the government attaches to the producer surplus of import-competing (exporting) firms.

For the domestic government, the welfare received on its import and export goods are:

$$W_x(\hat{p}_x, p_x^w) \equiv \int_{p_x}^1 D(p_x)d\,p_x + \gamma_m\Pi_x(\hat{p}_x) + [\hat{p}_x p_x^w]M\hat{p}_x);$$

$$W_y(\hat{p}_y, p_y^w) \equiv \int_{p_y}^1 D(p_y)d\,p_y + \gamma_e\Pi_y(\hat{p}_y) + [\hat{p}_y p_y^w]E(\hat{p}_y).$$

The objective of the domestic government is thus to maximise its total welfare function, given as $W(\hat{p}_x, \hat{p}_y, p_x^w, p_y^w) \equiv W_x(\hat{p}_x, p_x^w) + W_y(\hat{p}_y, p_y^w)$. The foreign government's import and export welfare functions take analogous forms:

$$W_y^*(\hat{p}_y^*, p_y^w) \equiv \int_{p_y^*}^1 D(p_y^*)d\,p_y^* + \gamma_m\Pi_y^*(\hat{p}_y^*) + [\hat{p}_y^* p_y^w]M^*(\hat{p}_y^*)$$

$$W_x^*(\hat{p}_x^*, p_x^w) \equiv \int_{p_x^*}^1 D(p_x^*)d\,p_x^* + \gamma_e\Pi_x^*(\hat{p}_x^*) + [\hat{p}_x^* p_x^w]E^*(\hat{p}_x^*)$$

so that $W^*(\hat{p}_x^*, \hat{p}_y^*, p_x^w, p_y^w) \equiv W_y^*(\hat{p}_y^*, p_y^w) + W_x^*(\hat{p}_x^*, p_x^w)$ defines the foreign welfare function.

2.2   Unilateral trade policies

We consider first the unilateral trade policies that arise when governments interact non-cooperatively. This situation can be described as a

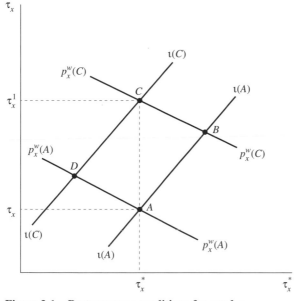

Figure 3.1   Best-response conditions for good x

static tariff game, in which the domestic government chooses (τ_x, τ_y) to maximise W at the same time that the foreign government chooses (τ_y^*, τ_x^*) to maximise W^*. We present in this subsection a brief interpretation of the unilateral or Nash trade policies.

The best-response tariffs for the domestic and foreign governments are defined implicitly by:

$$Home : W_{p_x} + \lambda_x W_{p_x^w} = 0; \ W_{p_y} + \lambda_y W_{p_y^w} = 0$$

$$Foreign : W_{p_y^*}^* + \lambda_y^* W_{p_y^w}^* = 0; \ W_{p_x^*}^* + \lambda_x^* W_{p_x^*}^* = 0 \qquad (1)$$

where $\lambda_x = \lambda_y^* < 0$ and $\lambda_y = \lambda_x^* < 0$. These parameters measure the ratio of world to local price movements, when import tariff and export subsidies are raised, respectively.

The best-response conditions can be interpreted for the domestic import good x with reference to figure 3.1. The initial tariff pair for good x is given by point $A \equiv (\tau_x, \tau_x^*)$. This point is associated with an iso-local-price line (or equivalently, an iso-net-tariff line), denoted as $\iota(A) \to \iota(^*)$, and an iso-world price line, denoted as $p_x^w(A) \to p_x^w(A)$. The iso-local-price line is linear with unitary slope, whereas the iso-world-price line slopes downward. Taking the foreign export subsidy τ_x^* as fixed, if the domestic government were to increase its import tariff from the initial value τ_x to the higher value τ_x^1, then the new point $C \equiv (\tau_x^1, \tau_x^*)$ would be induced. This point rests on new iso-price lines, represented in figure 3.1 as $\iota(C) \to \iota(C)$ and $p_x^w(C) \to p_x^w(C)$, and at point C the local price is higher and the world price is lower than at the original point A.

In figure 3.1, we disentangle the overall movement from A to C into separate movements in the world and local prices, respectively. The movement from A to B isolates the induced reduction in the world price, and the welfare significance of this change for the domestic government is associated in (1) with the term $W_{p_x^w}$. Similarly, the movement from B to C isolates the local price change, and the welfare implication of this change for the domestic government is captured in (1) with the term W_{p_x}. The world-price movement from A to B illustrates the cost-shifting inefficiency that arises when policies are set unilaterally. If the domestic government seeks to achieve a local price corresponding to the iso-local-price line $\iota(C) \to \iota(C)$, then a unilateral increase in the domestic import tariff serves to pass some of the costs of this outcome to the foreign government, whose exports are now sold at a lower world price.

In our working paper (Bagwell and Staiger, 1997a), we develop these points more fully and explore some additional features of the Nash equilibrium tariff policies. Working with a linear model, we find that a unique Nash equilibrium exists in which trade volume is positive. The Nash import tariff is positive, since the political economy considerations that arise when $\gamma_m > 1$ only reinforce the traditional terms of trade argument that leads to a positive import tariff. The sign of the Nash export policy is more ambiguous: we find that the Nash export policy is an export tax if governments do not weigh exporter producer surplus too heavily, such as when governments maximise national income, but a Nash export subsidy occurs when governments give exporter producer surplus sufficient weight in the welfare function.

2.3   Efficient trade policies

An alternative possibility is that governments set their trade policies in a cooperative manner. If there are no enforcement problems that limit the extent of cooperation, then governments that cooperate would set efficient trade policies. In other words, cooperative governments would set tariffs that maximise joint welfare, $W + W^*$. In this subsection, we offer a brief description of efficient trade agreements.

We begin with a pair of observations. First, we observe that joint welfare is a function only of local prices and thus net tariffs. This can be seen directly from the definition of the welfare functions presented above. (Recall that market clearing requires $M(\hat{p}_x) = E^*(\hat{p}_x^*)$ and

$M(\hat{p}_y) = E^*(\hat{p}_y^*)$, and then observe that the sum of W and W^* is independent of world prices.) Intuitively, a change in world prices that holds local prices fixed simply amounts to a redistribution of tariff revenue across countries, and so it does not affect joint government welfare. Second, we observe that the symmetry between sectors x and y implies that the efficient net tariff for market x will be the same as that for market y. It is thus convenient to define $\iota \equiv \tau_x \tau_x^* \equiv \tau_y^* \tau_y$.

The efficient net tariff, ι^E, maximises joint welfare $W + W^*$. The first-order condition for efficiency can be written as:

$$W_{p_x} + W_{p_x^*}^*/\lambda_x^* = 0. \tag{2}$$

It is interesting to contrast the efficiency condition (2) with the best-response conditions (1) that characterise the Nash equilibrium: the terms of trade are relevant to government choices in (1) but not in (2). We thus find that Nash trade policies are not efficient.

We next say that tariff policies are *politically optimal* if they satisfy

$$W_{p_x} = 0; \ W_{p_y} = 0; \ W_{p_y^*}^* = 0; \ W_{p_x^*}^* = 0. \tag{3}$$

Comparing (3) with (1), we see that these are the tariffs that governments would choose were they to ignore the terms of trade consequences of their unilateral tariff choices. But it is clear from (1) and (2) that tariffs are efficient when the terms of trade motivations from each government's Nash trade polices are eliminated. We thus find that politically optimal tariffs are efficient.

Figure 3.1 illustrates. Suppose again that the domestic government considers inducing the local price associated with point C. Let us hypothesise first that the government is not motivated by the terms of trade implications of its tariff policy. Observe that no terms of trade externality arises if the higher domestic import tariff is balanced against a lower foreign export subsidy, so as to keep the world price unaltered; this experiment corresponds to the movement from A to D. Under the stated hypothesis, it follows that the domestic government prefers choosing a higher tariff and inducing point C instead of selecting a lower tariff and inducing point A if and only if it prefers point D to point A. If both governments were to choose tariffs in this way, then a resulting consistent set of tariffs would be politically optimal. The politically optimal tariffs are not influenced by cost-shifting motives, and as a result they are efficient.[4]

Consider next a second hypothesis, under which the domestic government chooses its import tariff mindful of its ability to alter the terms of trade (i.e. the movement from A to B). In this case, the domestic government is motivated by the fact that some of the costs of achieving the higher domestic local price are shifted to the foreign government when the world price is reduced. This naturally leads the domestic government to choose a higher import tariff than is jointly efficient. In other words, the domestic government may elect to raise its import tariff and induce point C, even if it prefers the original point A to point D. It follows that Nash trade policies are always inefficient. Pulling these findings together, we may conclude that an inefficiency arises when governments set trade policies unilaterally if and only if they are motivated by terms of trade considerations.

In our working paper (Bagwell and Staiger, 1997a), we develop these points more fully. We also report there some specific features of the Nash, efficient and politically optimal trade policies. Working with a linear model, we find that the Nash trade policy is inefficient, because it results in too little trade: the Nash net tariff is higher than the efficient net tariff. We also find that the politically optimal import tariff and export subsidy are non-negative. This reflects the welfare benefits associated with redistributive policies when governments value producer surplus more than consumer surplus and tariff revenue.

2.4   Reciprocity

With the basic framework now described, we are prepared to consider the principle of reciprocity. As mentioned above, this principle is a cornerstone of the GATT–WTO system. We argue in this subsection that this principle can be understood in simple economic terms, as a negotiation principle designed to 'undo' the inefficient restrictions in trade that arise as a consequence of governments' ability to affect the terms of trade.

To begin, it is useful to remark that the notion of 'reciprocity' has (at least) two meanings. First, reciprocity has a general meaning that refers to the *balance of concessions* that governments seek to obtain in trade negotiations. In this general sense, reciprocity describes the negotiation practice whereby one government offers to reduce its tariffs provided that its trading partner agrees to a commensurate reduction in its own tariffs. Within the economics profession, there are two views on this practice. A first view is that the practice of reciprocity is divorced from sound economic principles; instead, it reflects a mercantilist perspective that presumably derives from political forces.[5] A second view, which we develop here, is that the practice of reciprocity can be understood with economic principles, once it is accepted that governments' trade policies generate terms of trade externalities.[6]

From the perspective of this second view, the general notion of reciprocity has a rather direct economic interpretation. If governments have both political and economic motivations, then the trade policies that are efficient given the government objectives need not involve free trade. Nevertheless, in the Nash equilibrium, governments will trade less than is efficient given their preferences, and as a consequence there is a sound economic basis for a cooperative trade agreement in which each government makes reciprocal concessions (reducing tariffs below the best-response level) in order to expand the volume of trade to the efficient level. As we show formally in our working paper (Bagwell and Staiger, 1997a), when governments offer balanced concessions so that each country's import and export volumes increase in equal amounts, the associated expansion in trade volume results in higher welfare for governments.

We mentioned above that reciprocity has two meanings. In addition to the general meaning just discussed, the principle of reciprocity also has a specific meaning within the GATT. It is perhaps surprising that the GATT itself does not require reciprocity in the general sense during negotiation rounds (GATT, Article XXVIII; Jackson, 1989, p. 123). In fact, GATT places little structure on the negotiation process, and the reciprocal concessions that governments often demand instead come directly from government negotiators. The GATT does, however, impose a specific form of reciprocity that applies after the negotiations are concluded and the tariff bindings are agreed upon. In particular, if either government withdraws or modifies a previously negotiated concession (tariff binding), and a government is essentially free to do this at any time, then its trading partners are entitled to respond by withdrawing *substantially equivalent concessions* of their own (GATT, Article XXVIII; Jackson, 1989, p. 119; Dam, 1970, pp. 79–99)

While the GATT does not provide an exact definition of 'substantially equivalent concessions', we propose in our working paper (Bagwell and Staiger, 1997a) that the central requirement is usefully captured by the following definition: if a country proposes to increase a previously negotiated tariff, a proposed set of tariff increases by its trading partner will constitute a withdrawal of *substantially equivalent concessions* provided that, when valued at existing world prices, the proposed tariffs together bring about equal reductions in the volume of each country's imports and exports. After balanced trade requirements are imposed, it can be shown that the requirement of substantially equivalent concessions can be described in the following formal terms. Given a previously negotiated set of tariffs $\{\tau_x^1, \tau_y^1, \tau_x^{*1}, \tau_y^{*1}\}$, a proposed set of renegotiated tariffs $\{\tau_x^2, \tau_y^2, \tau_x^{*2}, \tau_y^{*2}\}$ will represent an initial tariff withdrawal by one country and a withdrawal of substantially equivalent concessions by its trading partner provided that

$$[p_x^w(\tau_x^0, \tau_x^{*0})p_x^w(\tau_x^1, \tau_x^{*1})]M_x(\iota_x^1) = [p_y^w(\tau_y^0, \tau_y^{*0})p_y^w(\tau_y^1, \tau_y^{*1})]M_y^*(\iota_y^1),$$

where we now simplify our notation and express import volumes directly as functions of net tariffs. This condition may be satisfied in two ways. First, any set of tariff increases that leaves the world prices unchanged clearly satisfies the condition. Second, the condition is also satisfied by any set of tariff increases that alters world prices in a way that keeps each government's total welfare unaffected by the world price changes. As governments have no added incentive to pursue tariff renegotiations of the latter variety, the specific notion of reciprocity imposed by GATT amounts to the following requirement: any renegotiation must be over the set of outcomes that are feasible given the world prices that were established in the original negotiations.

This discussion suggests that GATT negotiations for a given market occur in two broad phases. In the first phase, which corresponds to a negotiation 'round' under GATT's Article XXVIII, the governments select an initial set of tariffs, and these tariffs determine a world price. In the second phase, which corresponds to renegotiation under GATT's Article XXVIII, each government decides whether to alter its binding and select a more restrictive tariff. When making this decision, a government recognises that reciprocity applies: if it modifies its tariff binding, then the initial tariff of its trading partner will also be modified, and the trading partner will select a more restrictive tariff that preserves the world price determined in the first phase. An initial tariff pair can be 'implemented under reciprocity' if neither government proposes a more restrictive tariff in the second phase. The key question is now: what (if any) efficient tariff pairs can be implemented under reciprocity?

The main ideas are captured in figure 3.2. This figure illustrates the Nash and efficient iso-net tariff lines, denoted as $\iota^N \to \iota^N$ and $\iota^E \to \iota^E$, respectively. Along the latter line, the iso-welfare curves of the import and export governments are tangent. To begin, suppose that the governments select in the first phase the efficient tariff pair denoted as H. This tariff pair is not politically optimal, and so one government (in this case, the importing government) would prefer a more restrictive tariff pair that induces different local prices, holding the world price fixed. Thus, the point H cannot be implemented under reciprocity. A similar

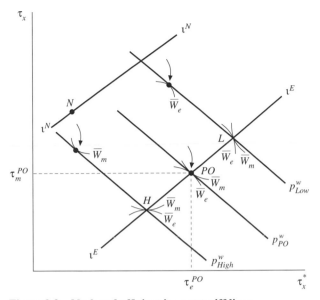

Figure 3.2   Nash and efficient iso-net tariff lines

argument indicates that the point L also cannot be implemented under reciprocity. Finally, if the governments select in the first phase the politically optimal tariffs (at the point PO), then neither government seeks a more restrictive tariff pair, given the politically optimal world price. We conclude that an efficient trade agreement can be implemented under reciprocity if and only if it is characterised by tariffs which are set at their politically optimal levels.

This conclusion establishes that the specific form of reciprocity found in the GATT also admits a simple economic interpretation. A cooperative trade agreement is sure to be efficient if it induces governments to negotiate the same tariffs that they would select unilaterally were they not motivated by terms of trade considerations. The specific principle of reciprocity can be understood in this context: an efficient agreement can be implemented under reciprocity exactly when the trade agreement specifies politically optimal tariffs.

3   Reciprocity and non-discrimination

We now sketch an extended model that serves to illustrate an efficiency link between the principles of reciprocity and non-discrimination, the latter embodied in the requirement that tariffs conform to the most favoured nation (MFN) principle. We describe here this link in general terms; the complete analysis is available in our working paper (Bagwell and Staiger, 1997a).

3.1   Government welfare functions

We begin with a description of the economic environment. There is a single home country (no*) and three foreign countries (*1, *2, *3). For simplicity, we focus only on good x; thus, the home country imports good x from three distinct foreign sources (we assume for simplicity that trade in x is precluded among the three foreign countries). Letting p denote the price of good x in the home country, we represent the home demand and supply functions as $D(p)$ and $Q(p)$. We assume that the foreign demand and supply functions are symmetric across countries. With p^{*j} denoting the price of good x in foreign country j, the corresponding demand and supply functions are represented as $D^{*j}(p^{*j})$ and $Q^{*j}(p^{*j})$, respectively. We define the export volume from foreign country j as $E^{*j}(p^{*j}) \equiv Q^{*j}(p^{*j}) - D^{*j}(p^{*j})$, and the (multilateral) import volume for the home country is represented as $M(p) \equiv D(p) - Q(p)$. We assume that demand (supply) functions are negatively (positively) sloped and that export and import volumes are always positive.

Prices are determined as follows. Let τ^j denote the import tariff selected by the home country, and let τ^{*j} represent the export subsidy offered by foreign country j. With p^{wj} representing the world price of good x between the home country and foreign country j, we have that the arbitrage conditions are given as $p = p^{wj} + \tau^j$ and $p^{*j} = p^{wj} + \tau^{*j}$ for $j = 1, 2, 3$. The market-clearing condition, $M(p) = \Sigma^{*i}(p^{*i})$, gives another relationship between prices. Solving these equations, we may express the market-clearing local prices as $p(Q^1, Q^2, Q^3)$ and $p^{*j}(Q^1, Q^2, Q^3)$, where $Q^j \equiv \tau^j - \tau^{*j}$ is the net tariff in the bilateral relationship between the home country and foreign country j. Market-clearing world prices can now be determined as $p^{wj}(\tau^j; Q^1, Q^2, Q^3)$, and it is convenient to represent local prices as $\hat{p}(\tau^j, p^{wj}(\tau^j; \iota^1, \iota^2, \iota^3)) = p^{wj}(\tau^j; \iota^1, \iota^2, \iota^3) + \tau^j$ and $\hat{p}^{*j}(\tau^{*j}, p^{wj}(\tau^j; \iota^1, \iota^2, \iota^3)) = p^{wj}(\tau^j; \iota^1, \iota^2, \iota^3) + \tau^{*j}$.

The model is constructed so that only the domestic government has the ability to apply discriminatory tariffs to the imports from its three trading partners. In what follows, a case of particular interest arises when the domestic government does not discriminate: This is the case of MFN tariffs, in which $\tau^1 = \tau^2 = \tau^3 \equiv \tau$. When the home country adopts MFN tariffs, the various bilateral trading relationships are all described by a single world price: $p^{w1} = p^{w2} = p^{w3} \equiv p^w$.

At this point, we are prepared to describe the government welfare functions. We continue to assume that governments maximise a weighted sum of consumer surplus, producer surplus and tariff revenue. As each foreign country trades only with a single partner (namely, the home country), the objectives of each foreign country can be written in familiar form as a function of its local price and the world price that arises between it and the home country:

$$W^{*j}(\hat{p}^{*j}, p^{wj}) \equiv \int_{p^{*j}}^{1} D(p^{*j})d\, p^{*j} + \gamma_e^j \Pi^{*j}(\hat{p}^{*j}) + [\hat{p}^{*j}p^{wj}]E^{*j}(\hat{p}^{*j}).$$

In this expression, $\Pi^{*j}(\hat{p}^{*j})$ represents the producer surplus in this country, which is weighed in the government objective at rate γ_e^j.

Consider next the welfare function of the home government. Defining $\Pi(\hat{p})$ and γ_m in the usual manner for the home-country import-competing sector, we represent the home government welfare function as:

$$W(\hat{p}, \hat{p}^{*1}, \hat{p}^{*2}, \hat{p}^{*3}, p^{w1}, p^{w2}, p^{w3}) \equiv$$
$$\int_{p}^{1} D(p)dp + \gamma_{mPI}(\hat{p}) + \sum_{j=1}^{3} [\hat{p}p^{wj}]E^{*j}(\hat{p}^{*j}).$$

In contrast to the two-country model presented above, the home-government welfare function now depends upon the home local price, the various world prices *and* the local foreign prices.

The externalities that are present in the home-government welfare function are novel and warrant special mention. As in the two-country model presented above, externalities pass between trading partners via the world price. In the multi-country model, however, externalities may also travel from the foreign countries to the home country through the foreign local price. Intuitively, for a fixed volume of imports (i.e. for a fixed home price), the home country benefits when a greater fraction of the import volume comes from the foreign country on whom it places the highest import tariff. This implies that foreign local prices, which determine foreign export flows, impart a separate externality on home welfare, even when the local home and world prices are held fixed. Importantly, this local-price externality is eliminated when the home country adopts MFN tariffs. In that case, the home-tariff revenue can be expressed as a function only of the home-local price and the single-world price, since home-tariff revenue is given as $[\hat{p}p^w]M(\hat{p})$.

We can also express the objectives of the home government as a function only of the home local price and a composite variable, $\hat{T}$, that represents the home country's multilateral terms of trade. To derive this representation, we define $\hat{T}(\hat{p}^{*1}, \hat{p}^{*2}, \hat{p}^{*3}, p^{w1}, p^{w2}, p^{w3})$, as a weighted average of the world prices that the home country faces:

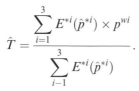

$$\hat{T} = \frac{\displaystyle\sum_{i=1}^{3} E^{*i}(\hat{p}^{*i}) \times p^{wi}}{\displaystyle\sum_{i-1}^{3} E^{*i}(\hat{p}^{*i})}.$$

It is now easy to confirm that home welfare may be expressed as:

$$W(\hat{p}, \hat{T}) \equiv \int_{p}^{1} D(p)dp + \gamma_m \Pi(\hat{p}) + [\hat{p}\hat{T}]M(\hat{p}).$$

With this representation in place, we see that the externalities associated with foreign tariffs travel through foreign local prices and world prices to the multilateral terms of trade, $\hat{T}$, and from this composite variable on to home government welfare. In the important case of MFN home tariffs, we have that $\hat{T} = p^w$, which confirms that in this case the world price is the only channel through which externalities flow.

3.2   Unilateral trade policies

We consider next the static tariff game, in which the domestic government selects a tariff policy (τ^1, τ^2, τ^3) so as to maximise W at the same time that each foreign government j chooses its tariff policy τ^{*j} to maximise W^{*j}. Maximising W with respect to τ^j and W^{*j} with respect to t^{*j} for $j = \{1,2,3\}$ defines implicitly the domestic and foreign government best-response tariffs:

> *Home* : $W_p + \tilde{\lambda}^j W_T = 0 \, for \, j = 1, 2, 3.$
> *Foreign* : $W_{p^{*j}}^{*j} + \tilde{\lambda}^{*j} W_{p^{wj}}^{*j} = 0, \, for \, j = 1, 2, 3,$

where $\tilde{\lambda}^j$ and $\tilde{\lambda}^{*j}$ measure the ratio of change in the terms of trade and the local price following a change in the corresponding tariff.

3.3   Efficient trade policies

We consider next the possibility that governments cooperate without limit and select the efficient trade policy that maximises joint welfare. To gain insight, we focus on the efficiency condition that pertains to the tariff that the home country places on imports from foreign country *1. This condition is given by:

$$W_p \frac{d\hat{p}}{d\tau^1} + W_T \frac{d\hat{T}}{d\tau^1} + \sum_{i=1}^{3} \{ W_{\hat{p}^{*i}}^{*i} \frac{d\hat{p}^{*i}}{d\tau^1} + W_{p^{wi}}^{*i} \frac{\partial p^{wi}}{\partial \tau^1} \} = 0.$$

This condition can be further interpreted as follows. First, recall that the home tariff affects the multilateral terms of trade through its effect on world prices and local foreign prices:

$$\frac{d\hat{T}}{d\tau^1} = \sum_{i=1}^{3} \{ \frac{\partial \hat{T}}{\partial \hat{p}^{*i}} \frac{d\hat{p}^{*i}}{d\tau^1} + \frac{\partial \hat{T}}{\partial p^{wi}} \frac{\partial p^{wi}}{\partial \tau^1} \}.$$

Second, using $W_T = M$, $\partial \hat{T}/\partial p^{wi} = E^{*i}/M$, and $W_{p^{wi}}^{*i} = E^{*i}$, we see that the efficiency condition can be written as:

$$W_p \frac{d\hat{p}}{d\tau^1} + W_T \sum_{i=1}^{3} \frac{\partial \hat{T}}{\partial \hat{p}^{*i}} \frac{d\hat{p}^{*i}}{d\tau^1} + \sum_{i=1}^{3} W_{p^{*i}}^{*i} \frac{d\hat{p}^{*i}}{d\tau^1}.$$

World price movements are again eliminated from the efficiency condition. As a consequence, we find once more that Nash tariffs are not efficient.

The novel feature of the multi-country model resides in the connection between the local foreign price and the home-country multilateral terms of trade. This local price externality corresponds to the second term in the final efficiency condition derived above. If home tariffs are discriminatory, then the multilateral terms of trade depends upon local foreign and world prices, and so the local price externality is non-zero. If instead home tariffs satisfy MFN, then the multilateral terms of trade is simply the (common) world price, and so this second term is zero. Reasoning in this fashion, we establish in our working paper (Bagwell and Staiger, 1997a) the following conclusion: a multilateral trade agreement is efficient if the terms of trade motivations from each government's Nash trade policy choices are eliminated *and* all tariffs conform to the principle of MFN. In other words, we find that an efficient agreement occurs when tariffs are politically optimal and satisfy MFN.

This finding may be understood in the following intuitive terms. Tariffs are politically optimal if the terms of trade motivations are eliminated from each government's Nash trade policy choices. Politically optimal tariffs are thus efficient if externalities are channelled across governments only via the world price. Now, if the home government selects discriminatory tariffs, then externalities travel through world and foreign local prices. In this case, when a foreign government sets its tariff at the politically optimal level, this will not be efficient, since the foreign government does not account for the externality that its local price has on the home government's tariff revenue. By contrast, if the home government adopts MFN tariffs, then externalities are channelled only through the world price, and so politically optimal tariffs are efficient.

3.4   Reciprocity and MFN

We next describe an efficiency link that arises between the two main principles of GATT: reciprocity and MFN. Drawing on definitions developed in section 2, we describe the link in an informal and intuitive manner. The link is formally explored in our working paper (Bagwell and Staiger, 1997a).

We regard the GATT negotiation process as embodying two phases. In the first phase, the various governments negotiate an initial set of tariffs. Next, in the second phase, each government considers whether to break its tariff binding and select a more restrictive trade policy. When making this decision, the government recognises that the GATT principle of reciprocity ensures that other governments will respond in a commensurate fashion: if a government increases a previously bound tariff, then other governments withdraw substantially equivalent concessions that serve to preserve the world prices that are associated with the initial set of tariffs. Our focus is again on the efficient tariffs that can be implemented under reciprocity.

To begin, it is useful to remark that there are many politically optimal tariffs. The requirement of political optimality corresponds to a set of four equations, with each of the four governments setting its trade policy so as to achieve its preferred local price. The number of tariffs–subsidies in the model, however, is six: the home government chooses three import tariffs, and each foreign government selects an export subsidy. Thus, in general, there will be many combinations of tariffs that are politically optimal. If we require further that the politically optimal tariffs must also satisfy MFN, then the number of tariffs–subsidies is reduced to four, as the home government now selects only one tariff, and so we can expect that there is a unique set of tariffs that is politically optimal and that satisfies MFN.

We now argue that efficient tariffs can be implemented under reciprocity if and only if the tariffs are politically optimal and conform to MFN. The main intuition can be described in two steps. Suppose first that efficient tariffs are implemented under reciprocity. Arguing as in section 2, we may expect that efficient tariffs can be implemented under reciprocity only if the tariffs are also politically optimal. Otherwise, some government would prefer a more restrictive tariff set, for the given world price. But we also know from subsection 3.3 that politically optimal tariffs are efficient only if they satisfy MFN. Thus, if efficient tariffs can be implemented under reciprocity, then the tariffs must be politically optimal and satisfy MFN.

Suppose second that a set of tariffs satisfies MFN and is politically optimal. Given that the tariffs satisfy MFN, it follows that all externalities travel through the world price. Using the arguments developed in subsection 3.3, we may thus conclude that the politically optimal tariffs are also efficient. Finally, expanding on the arguments presented in section 2, it is straightforward to establish that efficient and politically optimal tariffs can be implemented under reciprocity.

More broadly, this proposition establishes an efficiency link between reciprocity and MFN. Reciprocity works well as a negotiation principle with which to undo the terms of trade-driven restrictions in trade and achieve efficiency, provided that externalities travel through the world price. The principle of MFN thus complements the principle of reciprocity, since the former ensures that all externalities are indeed channelled through the world price.

4   Preferential agreements

We consider next the role of regional or preferential agreements in a multilateral trading system that is organised around the principle of reciprocity. GATT Article XXIV permits preferential agreements, provided that member countries go all the way to free trade on substantially all goods in a reasonable period of time. These agreements may take two main forms. In the context of our model, the home country forms a free trade area with foreign country i if $\tau^i = \tau^{*i} = 0$ and $\tau^j > 0$ for some $j \neq i$. The second possibility is that the members of a preferential agreement form a CU. When the home country forms a CU with foreign country i, the internal tariff between the two countries is again zero, but the external tariff of the home country is now set to maximise their joint welfare, $U^{*i} \equiv W + W^{*i}$.

We begin with free trade areas. Given the findings presented in subsection 3.4, it follows immediately that an efficient set of tariffs cannot be implemented under reciprocity when an FTA is present. Intuitively, an FTA violates MFN, and as a consequence externalities travel through both local and world prices. Given this situation, the principle of reciprocity cannot serve to implement an efficient trade agreement. The broader implication is the efficiency properties of a multilateral trade system that is founded on the principles of reciprocity and MFN is undermined when exceptions from the principle of MFN are granted for the formation of FTAs.

We consider next CUs. When the home country and foreign country i

form a CU, we cannot immediately conclude from the discussion in subsection 3.4 that the presence of a CU is incompatible with the pursuit of an efficient set of multilateral tariffs through the principle of reciprocity. The reason is that the formation of a CU corresponds to a 'new game', in which there are three participants instead of four, and so the conclusions derived above for the four-country setting cannot be directly applied. Nevertheless, the arguments presented above provide the essential intuition. In particular, if the two countries that form the CU are symmetric in the appropriate sense, then the union is analogous to a single country in the discussion above. This suggests that the principle of reciprocity can then deliver an efficient agreement in the presence of a CU if and only if all external tariffs satisfy MFN and are politically optimal.

In our working paper (Bagwell and Staiger, 1997a), we develop this idea and formalise the appropriate notion of symmetry. For the present discussion, the important point is that the form of symmetry that is required involves a particular relationship between the political economy parameters, γ_m and γ_e, which would render the two countries *natural integration partners*. Such countries must share common political objectives so that the removal of internal trade barriers is internally efficient. Generally, this relationship will fail, and CU will be like free trade areas: it is impossible to implement efficient tariffs under reciprocity when either type of preferential agreement is present. The case against CUs is slightly less severe, however, since it is possible to implement an efficient trade agreement with the principle of reciprocity in the presence of a CU between natural integration partners. As suggested above, in this special case, efficient tariffs can be implemented under reciprocity in the presence of a CU if and only if all external tariffs satisfy MFN and are politically optimal.

More generally, the discussion here suggests that a fundamental tension exists between the formation of preferential trading arrangements and a multilateral system that is based on the principle of reciprocity. We have argued that the principle of reciprocity is linked to the principle of MFN, in the sense that the former principle serves well to deliver efficient tariffs provided that tariffs also satisfy MFN. When preferential agreements are allowed, tariffs no longer satisfy MFN, and the presumption that a multilateral system based on reciprocity will deliver an efficient outcome is severely undermined.

5   Enforcement

Thus far we have compared efficient trading arrangements with non-cooperative outcomes, finding that the discrepancy is entirely attributable to terms of trade externalities and that the principles of reciprocity and MFN can serve to implement an efficient arrangement. In this setting, we have pointed out a basic tension between preferential agreements and the multilateral trading system. We have abstracted, however, from the process through which efficient (or at least more efficient) agreements might be enforced. In this section we turn our focus to issues of enforcement, and briefly consider how preferential agreements can affect the ability to enforce trade commitments at the multilateral level.

As there is no 'world jail', a trade agreement is credible only if it is self-enforcing (see, for example, Dam, 1970), and an agreement to open markets is in turn self-enforcing only if it also specifies credible retaliatory measures against any country that violates the agreement and places additional restraints on trade. From this perspective, GATT can be understood as an agreement that specifies cooperative trade policies as well as acceptable retaliatory measures. Building on this basic view, we may interpret the enforcement difficulties associated with a reciprocal trade agreement as reflecting a constant balance between (1) the short-term incentive to deviate unilaterally from the agreed-upon trade policy and experience the corresponding terms of trade benefits, and (2) the long-term cost of a consequent future loss of cooperation (i.e. a future 'trade war').[7] Viewed from this vantage point, it is clear that any event that alters the current incentive to cheat or the future value of cooperation can upset this balance, and thus that the enforceable level of cooperation may fluctuate with underlying market conditions.

A regional agreement is one possible source of 'imbalance'. While the results above indicate that regional agreements can undermine the efficiency properties of the principle of reciprocity, a different issue is whether such agreements might affect the level of multilateral cooperation that can be enforced. Papers that have considered various dimensions of the implications of allowing preferential agreements to form for the ability to enforce the multilateral agreement include Bagwell and Staiger (1997c, 1997d, 1998), Bond and Syropoulos (1996), and Bond, Syropoulos and Winters (1996). Here we review a number of the themes from this literature.

We first note that preferential agreements are typically formed over a lengthy *transition period* during which the trade policy changes associated with the agreement are being phased in. We begin by asking how emerging preferential agreements may affect the ability to enforce multilateral cooperation during this period of transition. Our analysis of this question is partly motivated by historical and current experiences with regard to regional trade agreements and multilateral tariff cooperation. The EC CU was formed in 1957, over a 12-year phase-in period, and was expanded to include Great Britain and other countries in 1973. As a WTO report concludes (WTO, 1995), both of these events heralded an improvement in multilateral tariff cooperation, as the successful GATT Kennedy Round took place in 1962–7 while the successful Tokyo Round occurred in 1973–9. More recently, important regional agreements include the 1988 US–Canada FTA (CUSTA) and its expansion to include Mexico in the NAFTA. The negotiation and implementation of these agreements, by contrast, appear to have taken place against a backdrop of strained multilateral cooperation.

Bagwell and Staiger (1997c, 1997d) present formal models consistent with these observations. To interpret the findings of these papers, it is helpful to keep in mind two principal effects of preferential agreements that are crucial in determining how they will affect enforcement at the multilateral level: a *trade diversion effect*, under which intra-member trade volumes rise at the expense of trade between member and non-member countries; and a *market power effect*, which occurs if the member countries adopt a common external tariff (CET) policy (i.e. form a CU) that enables them to impose higher (credible) tariffs on their multilateral trading partners should such punitive tariff action be desired.

With these two effects identified, the main ideas can be described in terms of a three-country setting. Consider first the transition to an FTA. When countries A and B are in the lengthy phasing-in process that culminates in an FTA, country C recognises that it is currently trading more with country A than it will in the future, since country A will divert more of its future trade to its free trade partner once the FTA is fully implemented. Thus, country C has a large current incentive to raise its tariffs and exploit its power over the terms of trade, owing to its large current volume of trade with country A, but country C is not especially fearful of a future trade war with country A, since it expects that it will in any case trade less with country A in the future. Incentives are thus thrown out of balance, and the trade policies that countries A and C can enforce will be less cooperative during the associated transition phase. It follows that the transition to an FTA will be characterised by heightened multilateral trade tensions, with these tensions being manifested in a proliferation of trade disputes and an inability to further lower multilateral tariffs. These predictions seem broadly compatible with recent experiences.

By contrast, when countries A and B are in the lengthy phasing-in process that culminates in a CU, country C perceives a new 'market power' effect: when a CU is formed, the union's CET enables it to exert great power over the terms of trade, and as a consequence the union will find high import tariffs tempting. This means that a trade war initiated in the transition phase might have heightened negative consequences for country C once the union is formed, since countries A and B will retaliate even more aggressively once they select a common tariff. As a consequence, country C's incentive to cheat in the transition phase is more than outweighed by its fear of the retaliation that a CU could later mete out. Country C's incentives are again out of balance, but in this case it will tolerate even more liberal multilateral tariffs before initiating a trade war. Hence, the transition to a CU involves an improvement in multilateral tariff cooperation, much as historical experience suggests.

Finally, let us turn from the transitional effects induced by the formation of preferential agreements and consider instead the steady-state effects associated with the presence of preferential agreements on the enforcement of multilateral cooperation. Bond and Syropoulos (1996) examine how the presence of CUs can affect the ability to enforce tariff cooperation at the multilateral level in a stationary world. They consider trading blocs of both symmetric and asymmetric size, and trace out how the 'market power' effect – which both increases the temptation of blocs to cheat on the multilateral agreement and augments their ability to punish cheaters – can lead to ambiguous implications of bloc formation for multilateral tariff cooperation.

Bagwell and Staiger (1998) consider the implications of allowing preferential agreements for multilateral cooperation in a three-country world in which two countries are better at cooperating than is the other. In particular, suppose that two countries, say A and B, are more patient, and thus more willing to embrace liberal trading policies, than is the other (impatient) country, say C. Within this setting, let us compare two trading regimes. First, when countries are constrained to abide by the principle of non-discrimination, the two patient countries A and B then cooperate best by acting as 'hegemons', extending tariff cuts to C that exceed the cuts that this country offers in return. In this case of non discrimination, the impatient country is therefore 'pooled in' with the patient countries, and it gets to free ride on their liberalisation efforts. Consider next a second trading regime, in which A and B form a preferential agreement and offer a tariff to C that differs from the zero tariff that they offer one another. In this case of discriminatory tariffs, the patient countries do not need to cooperate multilaterally in order to cooperate bilaterally, and so the impatient country loses its free-rider benefits.

The discriminatory tariff that is offered to the impatient country in this second trading regime will often exceed that which it would receive were the preferential agreement not allowed, and this implies an overall deterioration in multilateral tariff cooperation when the preferential agreement is formed. However, the opposite can also occur, as the discriminatory tariff offered to the impatient country may fall relative to that which it would receive were the preferential agreement not allowed. Which of these two outcomes occurs, and hence whether preferential agreements serve as 'stumbling blocks' or 'building blocks' for multilateral tariff cooperation, depends in this setting on how patient the two 'patient' countries are, which determines in turn how close the multilateral system can get to an efficient trade agreement in the absence of tariff discrimination. In particular, preferential agreements have their most desirable effects on the multilateral system in this setting precisely when multilateral enforcement mechanisms are ineffective and the multilateral system is working poorly.

More broadly, these results suggest that the impact of preferential agreements on the ability to enforce trade commitments at the multilateral level will depend critically on the period of analysis (i.e. transition or steady state), on the form that the preferential agreement takes (i.e. FTA or CU) and on the strength of the multilateral enforcement mechanism. While specific conclusions will depend on these factors, the results reviewed here, when combined with those of the previous sections, lend some support to the view that the efficiency of the multilateral trading system can be enhanced by the creation of preferential agreements if and only if multilateral enforcement mechanisms are sufficiently weak.

6   Conclusions

The findings presented above suggest that the multilateral trading system can be interpreted as a cooperative arrangement among governments that is designed to provide an escape from a terms of trade-driven prisoner's dilemma. From this perspective, and in the absence of enforcement difficulties, the principles of reciprocity and non-discrimination can be seen to work in tandem to implement an efficient outcome. As free FTAs violate the principle of non-discrimination, an immediate implication is that the principle of reciprocity cannot serve to implement an efficient agreement when FTAs are present. Reciprocity may implement an efficient agreement in the presence of a CU, but only if the union comprises similar countries. These conditions are quite stringent, and so our findings offer only limited support for the hypothesis that the principle of reciprocity can deliver an efficient trade agreement in the presence of preferential trade agreements. Instead, these findings support the conclusion that preferential agreements pose a threat to the existing multilateral system.

This conclusion may be tempered, however, when enforcement concerns are considered. Such concerns cannot be ignored, as the threat of future retaliation may not be sufficient to deliver a fully efficient multilateral agreement. As a consequence, changes in the trading environment, such as occurs with regional agreements, can influence the level of tariffs that can be enforced at the multilateral level. Predictions can then be drawn with respect to the impact of these changes for cooperative multilateral trade policies. At a broad level, these predictions appear consistent with historical experience. In any event, the results described above suggest that the impact of preferential agreements on the ability to enforce trade commitments at the multilateral level will depend critically on the period of analysis (i.e. transition or steady state), on the form that the preferential agreement takes (i.e. FTA or CU) and on the strength of the multilateral enforcement mechanism.

Finally, in regard to the question posed at the outset of the chapter, the results reviewed above, when taken together, lend some support to the view that the efficiency of the multilateral trading system can be enhanced by the creation of preferential agreements if and only if multilateral enforcement mechanisms are sufficiently weak. Put differently, successful efforts to strengthen the enforcement–dispute settlement procedures of the GATT–WTO should weaken the case for preferential agreements.

NOTES

We thank Raquel Fernández, Dick Baldwin and participants at the CEPR Conference on Regional Integration (La Coruña, 26–27 April 1996) for very helpful comments. This chapter was completed while Staiger was a Fellow at the Center for Advanced Study in the Behavioral Sciences. Staiger is also grateful for financial support provided by The National Science Foundation Grant No. SBR-9022192.
1 This statement presumes that governments do not seek trade agreements as a means of commitment relative to their own private sectors. For more on the distinction between these two possible roles of trade agreements, see Staiger (1995) and Bagwell and Staiger (1996). For a recent analysis stressing this latter role, see Maggi and Rodriguez (1996).
2 A more complete and technical analysis of these issues is contained in Bagwell and Staiger (1997a). Bagwell and Staiger (1997b) contains a general equilibrium treatment of these and related themes.
3 As is standard in partial equilibrium analysis, one can imagine a third (numeraire) good in the background that enters linearly into the utility of each agent. The assumption that this good is always consumed in positive amounts serves to eliminate income effects from the model, and thereby justifies the partial equilibrium analysis of each (non-numeraire) sector. Trade in the numeraire good is determined by the condition of overall trade balance.

4 The movement from point A to D gives rise to no terms of trade externality, but it does generate a change in the foreign local price. Provided that the foreign government also selects tariffs that are politically optimal, however, a small change in the foreign local price does not yield a first-order change in the level of foreign government welfare.

5 This argument has been made by many. See Krugman (1991) for an especially clear discussion of this position.

6 The extent to which countries are able to significantly affect the terms of trade is an issue of some debate. We mention the following points of support. First, at the level of theory, even ostensibly small countries have some power over the terms of trade, if the industry is monopolistically competitive (Gros, 1987). Second, with regard to empirical evidence, it is relevant to mention the large literature that documents imperfect pass-through in the face of exchange rate shocks. If symmetric empirical patterns arise when the cost increase is associated with a tariff increase, then the finding of imperfect pass-through would offer evidence of a reduction in the world price – i.e., a terms of trade externality (see Feenstra, 1989, for empirical support of the symmetric pass-through hypothesis). Finally, we note the study of GATT negotiations by Kreinin (1961, p. 314) who suggests that

> less than a third ... of the tariff concessions granted by the United States were passed on to the US consumer in the form of reduced import prices, while more than two thirds ... accrued to the foreign suppliers and improved the terms of trade of the exporting nations.

7 We draw a distinction between *unilateral deviations* from an agreed-upon trade policy which may go undetected for some time but which, once observed by trading partners, would trigger a retaliatory 'trade war', and the lawful *withdrawal or modification of a previously negotiated concession* under Article XXVIII, which must be pre-announced to trading partners who are then free to simultaneously withdraw substantially equivalent concessions under the procedures of Article XXVIII described in subsection 2.4 above.

REFERENCES

Bagwell, K. and Staiger, R.W., 1996. 'Reciprocal Trade Liberalisation', *NBER Working Paper*, **5488**
    1997a. 'Reciprocity, Non-discrimination and Preferential Agreements in the Multilateral Trading System', *NBER Working Paper*, **5932**
    1997b. 'An Economic Theory of GATT,' *NBER Working Paper*, **6049**
    1997c. 'Multilateral Tariff Cooperation During the Formation of Regional Free Trade Areas', *International Economic Review* (May)
    1997d. 'Multilateral Tariff Cooperation During the Formation of Customs Unions', *Journal of International Economics* (February)
    1998. 'Regionalism and Multilateral Tariff Cooperation', in J. Piggott and A. Woodland (eds.), *International Trade Policy and the Pacific Rim* (London: Macmillan)
Baldwin, R., 1987. 'Politically Realistic Objective Functions and Trade Policy', *Economic Letters*, **24**
Bond, E. W. and Syropoulos, C., 1996. 'Trading Blocs and the Sustainability of

Inter-regional Cooperation', in M. Canzoneri, W. Ethier and V. Grilli (eds.), *The New Transatlantic Economy* (Cambridge: Cambridge University Press)

Bond, E. W., Syropoulos, C. and Winters, L.A., 'Deepening of Regional Integration and External Trade Relations', *CEPR Discussion Paper*, **1317**

Dam, K. W., 1970. *The GATT: Law and International Economic Organization* (Chicago: University of Chicago Press)

Feenstra, R. C., 1989. 'Symmetric Pass-through of Tariffs and Exchange Rates under Imperfect Competition: An Empirical Test', *Journal of International Economics*, **27**, 25–45

Gros, D., 1987. 'A Note on the Optimal Tariff, Retaliation and the Welfare Loss from Tariff Wars in a Framework with Intra-Industry Trade', *Journal of International Economics*, **23**, 357–67

Grossman, G. and Helpman, E., 1994. 'Protection for Sale', *American Economic Review*, **84**, 667–90

Jackson, J. H., 1989. *The World Trading System* (Cambridge, MA: MIT Press)

Johnson, H. G., 1953–4. 'Optimum Tariffs and Retaliation', *Review of Economic Studies*, **21**, 142–53

Kreinin, M., 1961. 'Effect of Tariff Changes on the Prices and Volume of Imports', *American Economic Review*, **51**, 310–24

Krugman, P. R., 1991. 'The Move Toward Free Trade Zones', in 'Policy Implications of Trade and Currency Zones', a symposium sponsored by The Federal Reserve Bank of Kansas City, Jackson Hole, Wyoming 22–24 August)

Maggi, G. and Rodriguez-Clare, A., 1996. 'The Value of Trade Agreements in the Presence of Political Pressures, mimeo (May)

Scitovszky, T., 1942. 'A Reconsideration of the Theory of Tariffs', *Review of Economic Studies*, **9**,

Staiger, R. W., 1995. 'International Rules and Institutions for Trade Policy', in G. M. Grossman and K. Rogoff (eds.), *The Handbook of International Economics*, vol. 3 (Amsterdam: North-Holland)

World Trade Organisation (WTO), 1995. *Regionalism and the World Trading System* (Geneva: WTO) (April)

Discussion

RAQUEL FERNANDEZ

Bagwell and Staiger's chapter 3 reviews and consolidates a recent series of papers by the two authors. It is an excellent summary of their

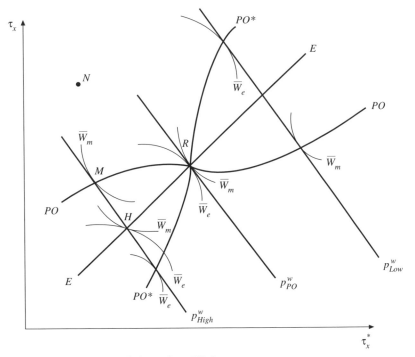

Figure D3.1   Trade policies and equilibrium

important work in this area, though at the cost of presenting perhaps too much material in too short a space.

The main argument made by the authors has several interlinking chains of logic. These can best be followed by making use of my figure D3.1.[1] The first thesis is on the face of it a rather obvious one: unilateral trade policies yield an inefficient equilibrium. Trade policies, in the absence of some other mechanism, are taken to be the Nash equilibrium of a simultaneous-move game in which governments choose tariffs to maximise their welfare function (W), taking those of all other governments as given. Countries, in pursuit of their objectives (which need not be national income-maximisation), exploit their market power in international markets, resulting in a terms of trade-driven prisoner's dilemma. This leaves them in an inefficient equilibrium illustrated, in a two-country world, by point N.

The second thesis is also familiar: the GATT/WTO, by coordinating policies, allows countries to escape this trap. The subtle and innovative part of this argument is the insistence that the GATT/WTO allows an efficient (given the governments' welfare functions) equilibrium to be reached. This conclusion is based on the assumption that all government objectives, including redistributive ones, can be represented as a function of local and world prices.[2] If this is the case, then it is easy to show that maximisation of joint welfare ($W + W^*$) is obtained if each government chooses tariffs so that they maximise its own welfare while ignoring the effects of changes in the world price on welfare (i.e. ignoring the terms of trade consequences of their own unilateral tariff choices). The *PO* schedule in figure D3.1 shows the tariff that would be chosen by the home country were it to take the foreign country's tariff (subsidy) as given and to ignore the welfare effects of induced world-price changes. Thus this curve joins all points of tangency between home-welfare indifference curves and world-price lines. *PO** is the equivalent schedule for the foreign country. Note that the intersection of these two curves yields an efficient equilibrium given by point *R*.

How does the GATT ensure that countries negotiate to an efficient equilibrium (that is, anywhere on the *EE* locus) and do not deviate from it once there? The answer to this constitutes the more interesting (and more controversial) thesis of the chapter. The authors maintain that efficiency is ensured by the principles of reciprocity and most favoured nation (MFN). Below we consider the contribution of each of these principles to ensuring efficiency.

As defined by the GATT, reciprocity entitles trading partners to respond to another government's modification of a previously negotiated concession by withdrawing 'substantially equivalent concessions of their own'. Bagwell and Staiger interpret this to mean that, when valued at existing world prices, the newly proposed tariffs together must bring about equal reductions in the volume of each country's imports and exports. In the symmetric two-country model depicted in figure D3.1, this implies that in response to, say, an increase in one country's tariff, the other country can decrease its subsidy of that good up to the point where the world price remains unchanged.

This imposition of reciprocity implies that a point such as *H* cannot be an equilibrium of the initial GATT negotiations.[3] Why? Note that if countries were to agree to the tariffs defined by *H*, then the home country could make itself better off by unilaterally increasing its tariff to the level implicitly defined by point *M*. It would know that the best that the foreign country could do in this case, and still respect the principle of reciprocity, is to reply by setting its tariff to the level implied by point *M*. This would still leave the home country better off than under *H*. Thus *H* cannot be an equilibrium. This logic reveals that the only equilibrium to a negotiation that thereafter must respect reciprocity would be a tariff pair such that both countries' indifference curves were tangent to the world price induced by the pair of tariffs (i.e. the intersection of the *PO* and *PO** schedules). These are the tariffs implicitly defined by point *R*.

This more innovative and interesting part of the chapter, however, is also somewhat problematic. Bagwell and Staiger could easily have ignored reciprocity, and concluded somewhat more vaguely that the bargaining process under the GATT must leave both countries somewhere on the efficiency frontier. The exact tariff pair would not be pinned down except for the requirement that each country's welfare must be at least as high as under the unilateral trade policy Nash equilibrium. By tying themselves down to a particular *ex post* negotiation principle (i.e. the respect of reciprocity), they make it very difficult to understand how the GATT would continue to guarantee efficiency in the face of, say, changing welfare functions on the part of governments, changes in the production function, or changes in endowments.

Suppose, for example, that the welfare function changes in such a way that importers receive greater weight than before (to keep matters simple, let us assume that this change happens across both countries). The equilibrium tariff pair implied by *R* will no longer be efficient given the governments' new welfare function. Furthermore, renegotiation that respects the principle of reciprocity at point *R* will not lead in general to an efficient equilibrium. Of course, it can always be maintained that governments will somehow renegotiate to a new efficient equilibrium (say, by ignoring reciprocity at *R* and establishing a new tariff pair over which reciprocity must be respected). In that case, however, it is not clear what the authors' interpretation of the principle of reciprocity offers over the usual belief that negotiation leads to an efficient outcome. Note that reciprocity is not an enforcement mechanism; it is simply a rule that governs changes in tariff levels once initial negotiations have been concluded.[4]

The authors' interpretation of the principle of MFN follows relatively straightforwardly from the intuition developed above (and is thus subject to the same caveats). Extending the framework to a more than two-country world, the MFN principle (whereby countries are prohibited from extending lower tariffs to one trading partner without offering it to all others) is understood as a way of preventing a government's welfare function from depending on foreign local prices. Note that otherwise, for a fixed home price for its import good (i.e. for a given volume of imports), the home country benefits more the greater is the fraction of the imports that originates from the country on which it has placed the highest import tariff. This implies that foreign local prices, which determine foreign export flows, impart a separate externality on home welfare in addition to those of world prices and its own local prices. This effect is eliminated, however, if a country must apply the same tariff rate (for a given import) across all its trading partners.

In the light of the above, it is easy to see why Bagwell and Staiger are in general not enthusiastic about regional trade agreements (RTAs). A free trade area (FTA) (which need not set a uniform tariff on non-member countries) violates MFN and hence reciprocity cannot guarantee that an efficient trade agreement will be negotiated.[5] But perhaps what is at fault here is Bagwell and Staiger's insistence that all externalities pass through domestic and world prices. This may be a rather narrow lens by which to analyse the possible costs and benefits of these arrangements. Below, I briefly explore several 'non-traditional' sources of possible gains from RTAs.[6]

One possible explanation is that a RTA may help with problems of time inconsistency. For example, unilateral liberalisation of a country's economy, even for a small country, is unlikely to be a time-consistent policy. A RTA, by making punishments after an agreed trade liberalisation large, makes temptations to deviate relatively smaller. The question that must be asked here, however, is: why can this commitment not be reached via some other mechanism, e.g. the GATT? The answer, it seems to me, must lie in the differing incentives for countries to punish a deviating member within the two organisations (or the ease with which they can do so). Within the GATT, the responsibility for singling out a culprit and, if the organisation delivers a guilty verdict, meting out the retaliation, lies with the country(ies) that have been hurt by the action. In a large organisation with a more diffuse trade structure (i.e. trade is presumably more diversified across trading partners than it would be under a RTA), this incentive is likely to be smaller and the process slower and the outcome less certain than within a regional organisation. Whether this conjecture is true, however, remains to be verified.[7]

Alternatively, RTAs may help with political time-inconsistency problems by providing countries with greater commitment to more abstract objectives such as democracy, human rights and peace than would be feasible with the GATT (since the externalities from these are more likely to be regional). Membership in the European Union, for example, has always been seen as a way of committing a country to 'Europe', by which is meant not only – and not even primarily – trade liberalisation within Europe, but membership in the European political system of liberal democracy. Mercosur and the Europe Agreements also have this as an explicit objective for their respective members.

There are several alternative candidate explanations for why regional agreements enhance efficiency. These include increased bargaining strength (in other multilateral arenas), insurance (of access to markets, for example), signalling (of government type or economic conditions) and coordination (over issues in different arenas). In each case for the argument to be persuasive, one would have to examine whether these agreements were self-enforcing, and whether existing arrangements such as the GATT could not provide the same (or superior) services. This is beyond the scope of this discussion and the interested reader is referred to Fernández (1998). Below, I simply provide an extremely brief discussion of these possibilities in light of NAFTA.

NAFTA (with varying degrees of success) can provide an example of several of these non-traditional gains from RTAs. NAFTA can be interpreted as ameliorating problems of time inconsistency by making it more difficult for future Mexican governments to move away from a substantially more liberalised economy. It can also serve as a signal to uncertain investors of the degree of commitment to trade and investment liberalisation (though here it would have to be argued that other types of governments would find signing NAFTA more costly than the type that is committed to a liberalised economy). On the insurance front, it may provide Mexico with some shelter from a regional bloc trade war and it most probably gave the impetus for the US government to help out in the face of the Tequila crisis. For the United States, NAFTA could serve as an impetus for other countries to increase the slow pace of negotiations under the GATT. Lastly, it could help coordinate Mexican concerns about a continued guaranteed access to US markets, and US concerns over illegal immigration and environment.

In conclusion, Bagwell and Staiger's work in this area constitutes an ambitious attempt to make rigorous economic sense of the GATT and its provisions. While I disagree with some of their analysis, and in particular consider their lens for viewing RTAs too narrow, I find their work consistently interesting and thought-provoking.

NOTES

1 Figure D3.1 is for the same model as used by Bagwell and Staiger. It introduces a new locus – the unilaterally politically optimal one – to their figure 3.2.
2 So, for example, concerns about foreign pollution levels (presumably a function of foreign local prices), are ruled out.
3 We are implicitly defining equilibrium here as a tariff pair that no country will have an incentive to renegotiate given the principle of reciprocity.
4 Enforcement of equilibrium follows the familiar repeated-game logic, which I will not review.
5 The case against customs unions (CUs) is more nuanced, but I will pass over it here.

6   The discussion below is based on Fernández (1998).
7   See Fernández (1998) for a fuller analysis of time inconsistency and RTAs.

REFERENCES

Fernández, R., 1998. 'Returns to Regionalism: An Evaluation of Non-Traditional Gains From RTAs', *World Bank Economic Review*

4 Politics and trade policy

ELHANAN HELPMAN

1 Introduction

Economists have devoted much effort to the study of *efficiency* properties of trade policies. These efforts have produced a coherent body of literature that describes how trade policy instruments – such as tariffs, export subsidies, quotas or voluntary export restraints (VERS) – affect economies that trade with each other. And they produced empirical models that have been extensively used to evaluate the efficiency losses from trade policies on the one hand and prospective gains from trade reforms on the other. Examples include quantitative studies of the Single Market programme in Europe (e.g. Flam, 1992) and of the NAFTA (e.g. Garber, 1993).

At the same time another strand of the literature has examined possible explanations for prevailing trade policies. Here efficiency considerations have not played centre stage. Many policies – such as quotas and VERS – impose large burdens on society. Researchers therefore looked for objectives of the policy-makers other than overall efficiency in order to explain them. This literature emphasises distributional considerations. It views trade policy as a device for income transfers to preferred groups in society. And it explains the desire of a policy-maker to engage in this sort of costly transfer by means of political arguments in her objective function (see Hillman, 1989, for a review).

Political economy explanations of trade policies are important, because they help us to understand the structure of protection as well as the major public policy debates. It would be impossible, in fact, to understand such debates without paying close attention to political considerations. Examples include the debate about the NAFTA in the United States, in which special interests – such as the sugar industry – were able to effectively voice their concerns in Congress, or the debate about the Uruguay Round in France, that brought farmers out into the streets.

Quite often countries design their trade policies in a way that yields to pressure from special interest groups, and trade negotiations at the international arena respond similarly.

As important as the political economy of trade policy seems to be, however, there exists no coherent theory to explain it. Models that underline some features of the policy-formation process have been designed by economists and political scientists. But they do not as yet add up to a coherent theory. One reason for this state of affairs is that there exists no agreed-upon theory of domestic politics. This partly reflects the fact that there are many channels through which residents convey their desire to policy-makers, and these ways differ across issues and across concerned groups in society. Moreover, political institutions vary across countries and they affect the ways in which influence works out through the system. As a result, there are potentially many modes of interaction that require close scrutiny. Special interest politics are prevalent, however, and economists need to understand these processes in order to better predict policy outcomes and to better design feasible policy options.

My purpose is to describe in this chapter a number of political economy approaches that have been developed to explain trade policies. I present these approaches in section 2, using a unified framework that helps to highlight the key differences among them. These comparisons revolve around tariff formulas that are predicted by the political equilibria. A typical formula explains cross-sectoral variations in rates of protection as well as differences in average rates of protection across countries. Section 3 then reviews a set of results that emerge from a new approach to the interaction of international economic relations with domestic politics. Importantly, there are two-way interactions in such systems, as pointed out by Putnam (1988). They link the formation of trade policies in the international arena with the activities of domestic special interest groups. The use of a framework of this sort is essential for a proper analysis of a host of important problems, such as negotiations about tariff levels or the formation of free trade areas (FTAs). Recent studies have developed suitable tools for this purpose, as I will argue in section 3.

2 Political economy approaches

I briefly describe in this section some of the leading political economy approaches to the formation of trade policies.

2.1   Direct democracy

Wolfgang Mayer (1984) proposed to view trade policy as the outcome of majority voting over tariff levels. There are, of course, very few countries in which direct democracy is applied to a broad range of issue, Switzerland being the prime example. Nevertheless, there exists a view that in representative democracies policy outcomes are reasonably close to what is supported by a majority of the voters. In such cases, the simple analysis of majority voting serves as a good approximation. There remain, of course, the difficulties involved in voting over multi-dimensional issues, that have not yet been resolved (see Shepsle, 1990). And these difficulties apply to trade policies, which are often multi-dimensional in character. Witness, for example, the various rounds of trade liberalisation under the auspices of the GATT (the Uruguay Round being the last), in which the removal of many tariffs and other trade barriers were negotiated simultaneously. Nevertheless, we may be able to learn something useful from the direct democracy approach.

The essence of Mayer's approach is quite simple. Suppose that a country has to decide the level of a particular tariff rate. We shall denote by τ_i one plus the tariff rate on product i.[1] Then we can derive a reduced-form indirect utility function for each voter j $\hat{v}_i(\tau_i, \gamma^j)$, where γ^j is a vector of the voter's characteristics. These characteristics may include his endowment (such as his skills, his ownership of shares in companies) or parameters describing his preference for consumption. Naturally, the shape of $\hat{v}_i(.)$ depends on various details of the economy's structure. If an individual j was asked to choose the tariff level that she preferred most, she would choose τ_i that maximises $\hat{v}_i(\tau_i, \gamma^j)$.[2] Let $\hat{\tau}_i(\gamma^j)$ describe the solution to this problem as a function of the individual's characteristics. The assumption that $\hat{\tau}_i(.)$ is a function means that individual preferences over tariff rates are single-peaked. Under these circumstances voting over pairs of alternative tariff rates leads to the adoption of τ_i^m, which is most preferred by the median voter. It is the tariff rate that has the property that the number of voters that prefer a higher rate equals the number of voters that prefer a lower rate. As a result no other tariff obtains more votes in a competition with τ_i^m.

Mayer studied properties of the equilibrium rate of protection τ_i^m in a Heckscher–Ohlin-type two-sector two-factor economy, in which all individuals have the same homothetic preferences, every sector produces a homogeneous product under constant returns to scale (CRS), and people differ in their relative endowment of the two factors. Taking labour and capital to be the two factors, γ^j represents the capital–labour ratio owned by individual j. Then, assuming that tariff revenue is redistributed to the public in proportion to income, he was able to derive the most preferred tariff rate of the median voter and to study its characteristics.

As an example of tariffs determined by direct voting, I now develop a model that will also be used for future purposes. Consider an economy with a continuum of individuals. Each individual has the utility function

$$u(c) = c_0 + \sum_{i=1}^{\nu_i} (c_i) \tag{1}$$

where c_i is consumption of product i and $u_i(.)$ is an increasing concave function. Population size equals one.

Let there be labour and a sector-specific input in each sector i. Aggregate labour supply is normalised to equal one. Individual j owns the fraction γ_L^j of labour.[3] The numeraire good, indexed 0, is produced only with labour, using one unit of labour per unit output. Each one of the remaining goods is produced with labour and the sector-specific input. We shall measure all prices in terms of the numeraire. Then the wage rate equals one and the reward to the sector-specific input in sector i, $\Pi_i(p_i)$, is an increasing function of the producer price of product i, p_i. Now normalise all foreign prices to equal one. Then $p_i = \tau_i$. Next let γ_i^j represent the fraction of the sector i-specific input owned by individual j.[4] Finally, suppose that the government redistributes tariff revenue in a lump-sum fashion and equally to every individual. It then follows that the reduced form indirect utility function is given by

$$\hat{v}(\tau, \gamma^j) = \gamma_L^j + \sum_{i=1}^{n} (\tau_i - 1) M_i(\tau_i) + \sum_{i=1}^{n} \gamma_i^j \Pi_i(\tau_i) + \sum_{i=1}^{n} S_i(\tau_i) \tag{2}$$

where $M_i(\tau_i)$ represents aggregate imports of product i.[5] The first term on the right-hand side represents labour income. The second term represents income from the government's transfer and the third term represents income from the ownership of sector-specific inputs. The last term represents consumer surplus.

It is evident from (2) that individual j's preference for the tariff rate in sector i depends only on his fraction of ownership of the sector-specific input in that sector. This preference function can be represented by $\hat{v}_i(\tau_i, \gamma_i^j) = (\tau_i - 1) M_i(\tau_i) + \gamma_i^j \Pi_i(\tau_i) + S_i(\tau_i)$.[6] As a result we have $\partial \hat{v}_i(\tau_i, \gamma_i^j)/\partial \tau_i = (\tau_i - 1) M_i'(\tau_i) + (\gamma_i^j - 1) X_i(\tau_i)$, where $X_i = \Pi_i'$ represents the output level in sector i. Since imports decline with the tariff, it follows that individuals with above-average ownership of the sector-specific input vote for a tariff while individuals with below-average ownership vote for an import subsidy.[7] And an individual's most preferred tariff rate is higher the larger his ownership share of the sector-specific input. It follows that voting on the tariff level in sector i leads to a tariff rate that is most preferred by the individual with the median value of γ_i^j. The larger this median value γ_i^m, the higher the resulting tariff rate. When the median voter's most preferred tariff rate is not on the boundary of the feasible set, it can be calculated from the condition $\partial\hat{v}_i(\tau_i, \gamma_i^m)/\partial\tau_i = 0$, which yields the following formula for the equilibrium tariff:[8]

$$\tau_i - 1 = \frac{(\gamma_i^m - 1)}{X_i(-M_i')}. \tag{3}$$

The tariff rate is higher when the median voter's share of ownership of the sector-specific input is higher, and it also is higher the larger the sector in terms of output and the smaller the slope of the import demand function. Larger output levels imply higher stakes for the industry, which makes it more profitable to have a high tariff (as long as γ_i^m is above average), while the less elastic the import demand function, the lower the excess burden of a tariff. Part of this excess burden is born by the median voter. Therefore he prefers a higher tariff rate the lower this marginal cost. This is, of course, a standard consideration in Ramsey pricing.

One last point should be noted concerning equilibrium tariff rates in a direct democracy. My discussion assumed that the ownership of the sector-specific inputs is thinly dispersed in the population. Occasionally (or perhaps even often) this is not the case. So consider the other extreme case, in which, say, the ownership of the sector-specific input in sector k is highly concentrated, up to the point that it is owned by a negligible fraction of the population. Under these circumstances a member of this minority group, who owns a finite amount of the sector-specific input, wants the tariff rate to be as high as possible. On the other hand, an individual who has no ownership of this input whatsoever wants an import subsidy. Since the latter type of people represent almost 100 per cent of the voters, the median voter most prefers to subsidise imports. More generally, it is clear from this example that under majority voting we should not observe tariffs but rather import subsidies in sectors with a highly concentrated ownership. If anything, the opposite seems to be true. As argued by Olsen (1965), however, in sectors with a highly concentrated ownership it is relatively easy to overcome the free-rider problem and to form pressure groups whose purpose it is to protect sector-specific incomes. Therefore we need to consider the role of such organisations in the shaping of trade policies, to which we will turn at a later stage.

2.2 Political-support function

An alternative approach was proposed by Hillman (1982). Borrowing from the theory of economic regulation, as developed by Stigler (1971) and Peltzman (1976), he suggested that we could view the choice of a tariff rate as the solution to an optimising problem in which the government trades off political support from industry interests against the dissatisfaction of consumers. Industry interests provide more support the higher the industry's profits, while the government gains more support from consumers the lower the consumer price. In the event, by raising domestic prices higher tariffs bring about more support from industry interests (whose profits rise) and less support from consumers (whose real income declines). And the government chooses a tariff level that maximises aggregate support.

Hillman postulated a reduced-form aggregate support function for a tariff in sector i, $P_i[\Pi_i(p_i) - \Pi_i(p_i^*), p_i - p_i^*]$, in which the first argument represents the gain in profits from a trade policy that raises the domestic price from the free-trade price p_i^* to p_i, while the second term represents the loss in consumer welfare that results from the same price increase. Political support rises in the first argument, and it declines in the second argument for $p_i^* < p_i$. Hillman used this approach to study the trade policy response to a declining foreign price. In particular, he showed that under mild assumptions a decline in the foreign price leads to higher domestic protection, but the resulting tariff increase does not fully compensate for the fall in the foreign price. As a result, the decline in the foreign price leads to a decline in the domestic price as well, but to a lesser degree.

I will now reformulate the political support function approach in order to derive a formula for equilibrium tariff rates that is comparable to (3). For this purpose suppose that the economic structure is the same as in subsection 2.1. In this event we can use (2) to calculate aggregate welfare, by integrating the individual welfare functions over the entire population. The result is

$$W(\tau) = 1 + \sum_{i=1}^{n}(\tau_i - 1)M_i(\tau_i) + \sum_{i=1}^{n}\Pi_i(\tau_i) + \sum_{i=1}^{n}S_i(\tau_i). \qquad (4)$$

Next, suppose that the government's political support for a policy is an increasing function of the income gains of sector-specific inputs and of the aggregate welfare gain. For simplicity assume that this function is linear,[9] i.e.

$$\hat{P}(\tau) = \sum_{i=1}^{n} \frac{1}{a_\pi} [\Pi_i(\tau_i) - \Pi_i(1)] + [W(\tau) - W(1, 1, \ldots, 1)]. \qquad (5)$$

The parameter a_π represents the marginal rate of substitution in the government's political support function between aggregate welfare and profits of special interests in sector i. These parameters are allowed to vary across sectors. The larger a_π, the more willing is the government to give up profits of sector-i interests in exchange for aggregate welfare. The government chooses rates of protection to maximise its political support, as measure by $\hat{P}(\tau)$. Using (4) and (5), an interior solution to this maximisation problem implies the following tariff rates:[10]

$$\tau_i - 1 = \frac{1}{a_\pi} \frac{X_i}{(-M_i')}. \qquad (6)$$

Comparing this formula with (3), we see that they are the same, except for the fact that the parameter $\frac{1}{a_\pi}$ replaces $(\gamma_i^m - 1)$. In both cases, the tariff is higher the larger the sector's output level and the flatter the import demand function. Importantly, however, while the political support function approach implies that each sector in which special interests count (i.e. in which a_π is finite) will be protected and no sector will be afforded negative protection, direct voting over tariff rates brings about positive protection in sectors with median ownership of sector-specific inputs larger than the average, but negative protection in sectors in which median ownership of sector-specific inputs falls short of the average. It follows that in a direct democracy the distribution of ownership has an important effect on the structure of protection, while in a representative democracy – in which the government evaluates a political support function in its design of trade policy – the political support function's marginal rates of substitution between the wellbeing of consumers and sectoral interests importantly affect the structure of protection. Evidently, building on the political support function approach, a better understanding of the forces that shape the structure of protection requires some insights on what determines the marginal rates of substitution between aggregate welfare and special interest profits. Unfortunately, the theory is not particularly helpful on this critical point.

2.3   Tariff-formation function

The political-support function summarises a trade-off between the support that a government obtains from special interests on the one hand, and the support of consumers on the other. Under this approach, a government designs its trade policy so as to balance the conflict between these opposing groups in a way that serves it best. Considerations of this sort are, of course, quite common in representative democracies, and even in totalitarian regimes rulers tend to listen to the concerns of the general public. But competition for preferential treatment very often takes on an active form, rather than the passive form envisioned in the political support-function approach. Lobbying for the protection of real incomes is prevalent, and many interest groups participate in this process.

To deal with the active seeking of protection of real incomes, Findlay and Wellisz (1982) proposed the use of tariff-formation functions. A function of this sort describes the level of protection afforded to an industry as depending on the amount of resources devoted to lobbying by a group of supporters of protection on the one hand, and by the lobbying efforts of opposers of protection on the other. According to this view, the level of protection reflects the outcome of a contest between interest groups on the opposing sides of the issue.[11] More precisely, let $T_i(C_i^S, C_i^O)$ describe the tariff-formation function in sector i, where C_i^S represents the lobbying expenditure of the pro-protectionist interest group and C_i^O represents the lobbying expenditure of the anti protectionist interest group. The resulting rate of protection is higher the larger the expenditure of the former group and the lower the expenditure of the latter. In the political equilibrium $\tau_i = T_i(C_i^S, C_i^O)$.

In order to derive the equilibrium level of protection, we need to describe the incentives of the various interest groups. So suppose that the benefits of the pro-protectionist lobby are given by the increasing function $W_i^S(\tau_i)$ while the benefits of the opposition are given by the declining function $W_i^O(\tau_i)$, both measured in terms of numeraire income. Then the lobbying expenditure levels are determined as the Nash equilibrium of a non-cooperative game in which each interest group chooses its lobbying expenditure so as to maximise net benefits, which are $W_i^S[T_i(C_i^S, C_i^O)] - C_i^S$ for the pro-protectionist lobby and $W_i^O[T_i(C_i^S, C_i^O)] - C_i^O$ for its rival. Findlay and Wellisz developed a two-sector specific-factor model, in which the owners of the specific factor in the import-competing industry lobby for import protection while the owners of the specific factor in the exporting industry oppose protection. As is well known, in an economy of this type the former group gains from protection while the latter group loses (see Jones, 1971), therefore they naturally take the opposite side of the protection issue. In this framework, Findlay and Wellisz have investigated the determinants of the equilibrium rate of protection. Given that the results depend on the shape of the tariff formation function, however, and the fact that their theory has little to say about this shape, they were unable to derive sharp predictions.

In order to relate this approach to my previous discussion, let us consider a somewhat different variant of the tariff-formation model. Suppose that the economy is the same as in subsection 2.1. Also suppose that the owners of the sector i-specific factor form an interest group that lobbies for protection. The purpose of the lobby is to maximise the individuals' joint welfare. Joint welfare-maximisation is suitable whenever the interest group can resolve its internal conflicts, such as ensuring the participation of all factor owners and the distribution of the burden of the lobbying expenses among them. If these owners constitute a fraction α_i of the population, then the joint welfare that they derive from sector i can be represented (see (2) by:[12]

$$W_i^S(\tau_i) = \Pi_i(\tau_i) + \alpha_i[(\tau_i - 1)M_i(\tau_i) + S_i(\tau_i)].$$

The first term on the right-hand side represents income of the sector-specific input while the second term describes the share of the lobby in the tariff rebate and in consumer surplus. So this describes the benefit function of the protectionist lobby. Marginal benefits of protection equal $W_i^{S'} = (1 - \alpha_i)X_i + \alpha_i(\tau_i - 1)M_i'$, which are positive for values of τ_i that are not too large.

Next suppose that there exists a lobby that opposes protection, which consists of all the other individuals in the economy.[13] The joint welfare that this group derives from a given tariff level equals

$$W_i^O(\tau_i) = (1 - \alpha_i)[(\tau_1 - 1)M_i(\tau_i) + S_i(\tau_i)].$$

They obtain a fraction $1 - \alpha_i$ of the tariff rebate and the same fraction of consumer surplus. To this group the marginal benefit of protection equals $W_i^{O'} = (1 - \alpha_i)[-X_i + (\tau_i - 1)M_i']$, which is negative for positive rates of protection (i.e. for $\tau_i > 1$).

Finally, consider an interior equilibrium to the non-cooperative game between the interest groups. The first-order conditions for the choice of lobbying expenditures that maximises net benefits are given by $[(1 - \alpha_i)X_i + \alpha_i(\tau_i - 1)M_i']T_{iS} = 1$ for the protectionist lobby and by $(1 - \alpha_i)[-X_i + (\tau_i - 1)M_i']T_{iO} = 1$ for its rival. T_{iS} and T_{iO} represent partial derivatives of the tariff-formation function with respect to the spending levels of the pro-protectionist lobby and the anti-protectionist lobby, respectively. In the first condition, the left-hand side represents the marginal benefit of an additional dollar spent to promote protection, which consists of the product of the marginal benefit of protection and the marginal gain in protection from a dollar of spending. The right-hand side represents the marginal cost. A pro-protectionist lobby chooses its spending level so as to balance costs and benefits at the margin. A similar interpretation can be given to the second condition, which applies to the interest group that opposes protection. Together these conditions yield

$$\tau_i - 1 = \frac{(1 - \alpha_i)(b_i - 1)}{\alpha_i b_i + (1 - \alpha_i)} \frac{X_i}{(-M_i')} \tag{7}$$

where $b_i = -T_{iS}/T_{iO} > 0$ represents the marginal rate of substitution between the spending levels on lobbying in the tariff-formation function.[14] When $b_i > 1$, a marginal dollar of spending on lobbying by the pro-protectionist interest group raises the tariff by more than it declines as a result of an extra dollar of spending on lobbying by the anti-protectionist interest group. We see from this equation that the sector is protected if and only if $b_i > 1$. And if a marginal lobbying dollar of one interest group is as effective as a marginal lobbying dollar of the other interest group, then there is free trade. Importantly, whenever the sector is protected, the rate of protection is higher the more effective is a lobbying dollar of the pro-protectionist interest group relative to a lobbying dollar of the anti-protectionist interest group, and the smaller the fraction of people that belong to the former group. The last result implies that the more highly concentrated is the ownership of a sector-specific factor, the higher will be the rate of protection afforded to this sector. This result – which is just the opposite of the prediction of the direct-voting model – stems from the fact that the fewer the owners of the sector-specific input, the less account does the lobby take of the excess burden produced by protection. In the extreme case, when the entire population has a stake in the sector, free trade prevails, because the lobby internalises all welfare considerations. Finally, as in the cases previously discussed, the rate of protection is higher the larger the output level and the flatter the import-demand function.

Equation (7) results partly from the assumption that the opposition to the pro-protectionist lobby consists of all the other individuals in the economy. This is obviously not the typical case. The important point is, however, that the welfare of at least some fraction of the general public counts in the design of a trade policy. Those members of society may be represented by an organised group or by the government itself. In the latter case the government's motivation may be the desire to do good or just cool political calculus. Indeed, Feenstra and Bhagwati (1982) have used a tariff-formation function with a government that cares about welfare of the general public. Under these circumstances, the desire to minimise excess burden plays an important role.

2.4   Electoral competition

Unlike most other approaches to the politics of trade policy, Magee, Brock and Young (1989) (hereafter MBY) advocate an emphasis on electoral competition.[15] According to this view interest groups give contributions to political parties and candidates in order to improve their chances for being elected. This contrasts with the tariff-formation function approach in which contributions influence policy choices. For this reason MBY construct a model in which two parties compete in an election. Each one commits to a policy *before* the choice of contributions by special interests. As a result, the choice of contributions does not affect policy choices and their only role is to improve the likelihood of one or the other party being elected. Anticipating the electoral motive in campaign-giving, however, the parties – which are interested in max-imising their electoral prospects at the polls – choose policies that correctly anticipate future campaign contributions.

Somewhat more formally, suppose that there are two political parties and two lobbies. Each lobby is aligned with one party. In MBY there is a pro-capital party with which the lobby of capital owners is aligned and a pro-labour party with which labour is aligned. Other alignments are of course possible, depending on context. For present purposes let us be agnostic about the precise interpretation of these allegiances, and let us have party A and party B, and lobby 1 and lobby 2. Lobby 1 is aligned with party A while lobby 2 is aligned with party B. Party A gets elected with probability $q\left(\sum_{i=1}^{2} C_i^A, \sum_{i=1}^{2} C_i^B, \tau^A, \tau^B\right)$, where C_{iK} stands for the contribution of lobby i to the political campaign of party K and τ^K is the trade policy of party K. This probability is higher the more contributions party A amasses, the less contributions party B amasses, the less distortive is the trade policy of party A and the more distortive is the trade policy of party B.

In the second stage of the game, after the parties have committed to their trade policies, the lobbies decide on campaign contributions. Let $W_i(\tau)$ be the benefit function of lobby i when the trade policy is τ. Then this lobby expects the benefit level $W_i(\tau^A)$ with probability q(.) and the benefit $W_i(\tau^B)$ with probability $1-$q(.). Lobbies choose their contribu-tions non-cooperatively. Therefore, contributions are a Nash equilibrium of the game in which each lobby maximises its expected net benefit. The best response of lobby i to the contribution levels of the other lobby is given by the solution to the following problem:

$$\max_{C_i^A \geq 0, C_i^B \geq 0} q\left(\sum_{i=1}^{2} C_i^A, \sum_{i=1}^{2} C_i^B, \tau^A, \tau^B\right) W_i(\tau^A)] +$$

$$\left[1 - q\left(\sum_{i=1}^{2} C_i^A, \sum_{i=1}^{2} C_i^B, \tau^A, \tau^B\right)\right] W_i(\tau^B) - \sum_{K=A,B} C_i^K.$$

In the resulting Nash equilibrium the contribution levels are functions of the tax policies. Substituting these functions into q(.) yields a reduced-form probability function that depends only on the trade policies, $\tilde{q}(\tau^A, \tau^B)$. The function $\tilde{q}(\cdot)$ anticipates the contribution game that will be played by the lobbies for each policy choice by the parties. In the first stage the parties play a non-cooperative game. Each one chooses its policy so as to maximise its probability of winning the election. Therefore party A chooses τ^A so as to maximise $\tilde{q}(\tau^A, \tau^B)$ while party B chooses τ^B so as to maximise $1 - \tilde{q}(\tau^A, \tau^B)$. The Nash equilibrium of this game identifies the equilibrium levels of the rates of protection.

Mayer and Li (1994) have re-examined the MBY analysis, using probabilistic voting theory as the micro foundations. Probabilistic voting allows for preferences of voters that depend on economic policies as well as on other attributes of political parties, such as their positions on social issues or political ideology. Preferences over non-economic issues are diverse and parties know only their distribution in the voting population (see Coughlin, 1992). Mayer and Li also assume that voters are not sure about the economic policy stance of the parties, and that each party can use campaign contributions in order to clarify their position. Each party chooses its policy so as to maximise the probability of being elected.

Their analysis supports some of MBY's conclusions, but not all. For example, it supports the result that a lobby will contribute to at most one political party – i.e. lobbies specialise in campaign-giving. Unfortunately, this result does not fare well on empirical grounds; it is quite common in parliamentary systems for lobbies to contribute to the two major political parties (e.g. Israel). On the other hand, Mayer and Li find that both lobbies may end up contributing to the same political party, while MBY *assumed* that each lobby is aligned with one party only. My conclusion from the Mayer–Li analysis is that it is indeed important to develop more detailed models in order to deal satisfactorily with the role of the electoral motive for campaign contributions in the political economy of trade policies; we will explore this further in subsection 2.5.

2.5   Influence-driven contributions

Political contributions that influence election outcomes are a desirable feature of trade policy models. They seem to emphasise, however, a motive for contributions that is at most secondary. To be sure, from the point of view of politicians and their political parties the total amount of contributions serves an important role in enhancing their chances of being elected or re-elected. But this does not mean that the individual contributors view the improved chance of a candidate as a major consideration in their giving. For one thing, there typically exist many contributors with the contribution of each one being small relative to the total. This is particularly true in countries with legal limits on contributions, but not only in countries of this type. As a result, each contribution has a marginal effect on the election outcome. Under these circumstances it is more likely that contributions are designed to influence the choice of policy than to influence election outcomes. Namely, having a choice between an emphasis on the electoral motive for contributions (as in MBY) and an influence motive, the latter seems to be more attractive on theoretical grounds. This point is made explicit in the detailed model of electoral competition and special interest politics by Grossman and Helpman (1996), in which they show that with a large number of organised interest groups the electoral motive for campaign contributions is negligible.[16]

At the same time the empirical literature also supports the view that the influence motive is more prominent. For example, Magelby and Nelson (1990) report: (1) Political action committees (PACs) in the United States gave more than three-quarters of their total contributions in the 1988 Congressional campaign to incumbent candidates. (2) Not counting elections for open seats, incumbents received over six times as much as challengers. (3) Over 60 per cent of the campaign contributions by PACs occurred in the early part of the election cycle, often before a challenger had even been identified. (4) PACs switch their contributions to the winner even if they supported the loser to begin with. In addition, in parliamentary democracies, interest groups often contribute simultaneously to more than one major political party.

Relying on these considerations, Grossman and Helpman (1994) have developed a theory that puts the influence motive at the heart of campaign contributions. According to this approach, interest groups move first, offering politicians campaign contributions that depend on their policy stance. Special interests seek to maximise the wellbeing of their members. Then the politicians choose policy stances, knowing how their contributions depend on the selected polices. Politicians seek to maximise a political objective function that depends on contributions and on the wellbeing of the general public.[17]

A political objective function that depends on contributions and the wellbeing of voters is consistent with electoral competition. Grossman and Helpman (1994) have shown that it emerges in a political system in which special interests design contributions in the way described above, and two parties compete for seats in Parliament.[18]

So suppose again that the economy is the same as in subsection 2.1, but that the policy-maker's objective function is $C + aW$, where C stands for campaign contributions that he amasses, W represents aggregate welfare (or *per capita* welfare), and a is a parameter that represents the marginal rate of substitution between welfare and contributions. The larger a, the more weight is placed on the wellbeing of voters relative to contributions.[19] Contributions depend on the policy choice and so does welfare, and the policy-maker maximises this political objective function.

Now consider the special interest groups. Suppose that in some subset of sectors, denoted by $L \subset \{1, 2, \ldots, n\}$, the owners of the sector-specific inputs form lobby groups. Let α_i represent (as before) the fraction of people who owns the input in sector i. Also assume that each person owns at most one type of sector-specific input. Then the aggregate wellbeing of the individuals that belong to lobby i is given by

$$W_i(\tau) = l_i + \Pi_i(\tau_i) + \alpha_i \sum_{j=1}^{n} \left[(\tau_j - 1) M_j(\tau_j) + S_j(\tau_j) \right]. \tag{8}$$

The first term on the right-hand side represents their share in labour supply, the second term represents their income from the sector-specific factor, and the last term represents their share in tariff rebates and in consumer surplus.[20] The lobby's purpose is to maximise $W_i(\tau) - C_i$, where $C_i \geq 0$ is the contribution of lobby i. How should the lobby design its contributions?

Interest group i takes the contribution functions $C_j(\tau)$ of all the other interest groups $j \neq i$ as given. Therefore it knows that if it does not lobby, the policy-maker will attain the political welfare $G_{-i} = \max_\tau \left[\sum_{j \neq i} C_j(\tau) + aW(\tau) \right]$; i.e. the policy-maker will choose a policy vector τ that maximises its objective function, disregarding lobby i's preferences.[21] It follows that if lobby i wishes to affect the policy outcome, it needs to offer a contribution function that induces a policy change and provides the policy-maker with at least G_{-i}. Its contribution function has to satisfy

$$C_i(\tau) \geq G_{-i} - \left[\sum_{j \neq i} C_j(\tau) + aW(\tau)\right] \tag{9}$$

in order to implement τ. This is the standard participation constraint in principal-agent problems. Naturally, the interest group has no desire to give the policy-maker more than necessary in order to induce a policy change. Therefore it choose a contribution function that satisfies (9) with equality at the equilibrium point. The policy vector that maximises the lobby's objective function $W_i(\tau) - C_i$ is then

$$\tau^i \in \arg\max_{\tau} W_i(\tau) + \left[\sum_{j \neq i} C_j(\tau) + aW(\tau)\right].$$

The contribution function is designed to *implement* this policy vector, and there typically exist many contribution functions that do it. Although lobby i is indifferent as to which contribution function it uses in order to implement this policy vector, its choice may affect the decision problems of other lobbies. Therefore there often exist many combinations of contribution functions that implement the equilibrium policy vector as well as equilibria with different policy vectors (see Bernheim and Whinston, 1986). An equilibrium consists of feasible contribution functions $\{C_j^o(.)\}_{j \in L}$ and a policy vector τ^o such that: (a) $\tau^o \in \arg\max_\tau W_i(\tau) + \left[\sum_{j \neq i} C_j^o(\tau) + aW(\tau)\right]$ for all $i \in L$; (b) $C_j^o(.)$ implements τ^o for all $j \in L$; and (c) $\sum_{j \in L} C_j^o(\tau) + aW(\tau) = G_{-i}$ for all $i \in L$.

To illustrate some of the relevant considerations, first suppose that there is only one organised interest group, say in sector i. Then the equilibrium policy vector maximises $W_i(\tau) + aW(\tau)$. Using (4) and (8) this implies

$$\tau_j - 1 = \frac{I_j - \alpha_i}{a + \alpha_i} \frac{X_j}{\left(-M_j'\right)},$$

where I_j equals one for $j = i$ and zero otherwise. First note that only sector i, which is represented by an organised interest group, is protected. All other sectors are afforded negative protection. The reason is that the special-interest group lobbies the policy-maker for high prices in sector i, in which it is a net seller, and for low prices in all other sectors, in which it is a net buyer. The rate of protection in sector i is higher the more concentrated is the ownership of the sector-specific factor in that sector (because the less the lobby cares then about excess burden), the less weight the policy-maker places on welfare relative to contributions (because the cheaper it is then to influence the policy-maker with contributions), the larger the output level of the sector (because it raises the benefit of the influence motive), and the flatter the import-demand function (because the lower is then the excess burden imposed on society, about which the policy-maker cares). Observe that the effects of output and slope of the import-demand function are the same as in the formulas that we derived from the direct democracy approach, the political support-function approach, and the tariff-formation function approach. In addition, the effect of the degree of concentration of ownership is similar to the tariff-formation function approach, while the role of the marginal rate of substitution between welfare and contributions plays a similar role to the marginal rate of substitution between welfare and profits in the political support- function approach. These analogies are not accidental. I have purposely constructed variants of the other approaches that enable us to draw these analogies with the influence-motive approach.

What happens when there is more than one organised interest group? Grossman and Helpman (1994) have shown that if we restrict the contribution functions to be differentiable around the equilibrium vector τ^o, then they have to be locally truthful – i.e. the gradient of $C_i^o(.)$ has to equal the gradient of $W_i(.)$ at τ^o. This leads to the tariff formula

$$\tau_j - 1 = \frac{I_j - \alpha_L}{a + \alpha_L} \frac{X_j}{\left(-M_j'\right)}, \tag{10}$$

where $\alpha_L = \sum_{j \in L} \alpha_j$ stands for the fraction of people that owns sector-specific inputs. The difference between this formula and the previous one, which was derived for the case in which only one sector had an organised lobby, is the replacement of α_i with α_L. Therefore the interpretation remains very much the same. Importantly, all sectors with organised pressure groups now enjoy protection while sectors without lobbies are afforded negative protection. In the extreme case, when all sectors have organised pressure groups and every individual has a stake in some sector, there is free trade. Under these circumstances, the lobbies battle for protection of their own interests and neutralise each other in the process. Despite the fact that none of them succeeds in securing higher prices for their clients, they typically spend resources in the process (as can be confirmed from the participation constraint). The role of the contributions in this case is to avoid being harmed by the other lobbies.

Equation (10) describes the resulting rates of protection when each lobby conditions its contributions on the entire tariff vector. In practice, this may not be the case. A lobby of the textile industry is obviously very much concerned with the protection of textiles, but its interest in subsidising imports of tea is much smaller. In the event it may choose to neglect the conditioning of its contributions on the policy towards tea, especially if it is costly to spread the lobbying effort across a large number of policy instruments. A complete model of the political process should include a specification of the lobbying technology, which will then determine the relative costs of lobbying. We would then expect pressure groups to focus on their core activity and get involved in the design of other policies only when the direct or indirect benefits from doing so would be large or when the marginal cost of doing so would be small. To see what difference a focused lobbying effort can make, suppose that the lobby of sector i conditions its contributions only on τ_i, for $i \in L$. In this event there will be free trade in each sector that does not have an organised interest group while in the sectors with pressure groups the rates of protection will be

$$\tau_j - 1 = \frac{1 - \alpha_j}{a + \alpha_j} \frac{X_j}{\left(-M_j'\right)} \, ; \, for \, j \in L.$$

We see that the effects of the sector's size and the slope of its import demand function are the same as in the other formulas. Compared to the case in which pressure groups lobby for all policies, however, there are two major differences. First, unorganised sectors are now not protected while in (10) they are accorded negative protection. Second, the rate of protection of an organised sector now depends on the fraction of voters who have a stake in the industry (i.e. α_i) while in (10) it depends on the fraction of voters who belong to any lobby, not necessarily the lobby of the industry under consideration (i.e. α_L). The implication is that now the degree of concentration of the ownership in a sector has a direct effect on its rate of protection; sectors with higher concentration of ownership attain higher protection. This is a desirable feature, as it finds support in reality.

My discussion has focused on trade taxes. It should be clear, however, that the same tools of analysis can be applied to other policy instruments as well.[22] There is a major question, however, concerning the choice of instruments of protection. Why use tariffs rather than output subsidies, for example, when the latter instrument is more desirable on efficiency grounds? Partial answers, based on political economy considerations, are provided by Rodrik (1986) and Grossman and Helpman (1994). But as Rodrik (1995) forcefully argues, the choice of instrument is a central question that has received only limited attention. Since good answers to this question are not yet available, I shall proceed to the next topic.

3   Double-edged diplomacy

We have so far examined situations in which trade policies are pursued by a single country facing constant world prices. This simplification helped us to focus on the internal politics – i.e. the interaction between lobbies and policy-makers. Much of trade policy is affected, however, by international constraints. As a result, even when a country sets its own trade-policy agenda it has to consider the international repercussions. This is particularly so for large countries. But countries also negotiate trade rules, tariff reductions, VERs, free trade areas (FTAs), and other items. Therefore an analysis of the formation of trade policies is incomplete without paying attention to the international interactions.

In view of these remarks it is only appropriate to consider the formation of trade policies in a framework that emphasises two levels of strategic interaction. On the one hand governments set trade policies facing each other in the international arena. On the other hand each government has to deal with its internal political system. This type of two-level interaction produces a simultaneous dependence between the internal and the external politics. A government that, say, negotiates an FTA, is aware in its dealings with the foreign government of the domestic consequences of such an agreement. At the same time, domestic pressure groups that wish to influence the policy outcome are aware of the negotiation process, and of the pros and cons of alternatives results. These dependencies are the source of the title of this section, which is taken from the title of a book by Evans, Jacobson and Putnam (1993). Their book describes a series of case studies, building on the conceptual framework that was developed by Putnam (1988) in order to study situations of this sort. In the rest of this section I describe three examples that build on two-level interactions: non-cooperative tariff setting, negotiated tariffs and negotiated FTAs.

3.1   Trade wars

Grossman and Helpman (1995a) have extended the influence-driven contributions approach to a setting with two countries that set trade policies non-cooperatively. In each country the economy is structured as in subsection 2.1, pressure groups lobby the domestic policy-maker in the manner described in subsection 2.5, and the policy-maker maximises a political objective function that is linear in contributions and aggregate welfare.[23] Both the lobbies and the policy-maker take as given the policy vector of the other country. But they do take into account the fact that domestic policies affect the terms of trade. In particular, denoting the countries by A and B and the international price by π_i, the world market-clearing condition for product i, $\sum_{K=A,B} M_i^K\left(\tau_i^K \pi_i\right) = 0$, defines implicitly the international price as a function of the trade policies in the two countries. Using this relationship, it is possible to derive a set of contribution schedules and a domestic policy vector that are the political response to the other country's trade policy. A similar political response can be defined for the other country. An equilibrium consists of contribution schedules and a policy vector for each country, such that the contribution schedules and the policy vector of each country represent a political response to the other country's trade policy. These equilibrium trade policies satisfy

$$\tau_j^K - 1 = \frac{I_j^K - \alpha_L^K}{a^K + \alpha_L^K} \frac{X_j^K}{\left(-\pi_j M_j^{K\prime}\right)} + \frac{1}{e_j^L} \; for \; K, L = A, B \; and \; L \neq K, \; (11)$$

where e_j^L is the export supply elasticity of country L in sector j (this elasticity is negative if the country imports the product). This formula has two parts: a political power index that is identical to (10) and a second part that captures terms of trade considerations. The latter, which is well known from Johnson (1953–4) and the now standard optimal tariff formula, states that a tariff should be higher the less elastic is the foreign export supply function.

The tax rate of country K in sector i, as given by (11), depends on the trade policy in the other country (i.e. it depends on it through the international price π_j). This interdependence has some interesting implications. In particular, for constant elasticity import demand and output supply functions, it implies that a lower weight on welfare relative to contributions in the political objective function of the importing country leads it to take a more aggressive policy stance. As a result, its terms of trade improve, its tariff is higher – and sufficiently so as to secure a higher domestic price for the protected industry – and the domestic price in the exporting country is lower. It follows that the same industry in the exporting country receives less protection, or that it is afforded more negative protection. This example demonstrates how a change in the political environment in one country affects the resulting degree of protection in each one of them. Evidently, this type of analysis helps us to see how trade policies of one country depend on the political environment in the other.

3.2 Trade talks

In subsection 3.1 trade taxes were set non-cooperatively. As a result, policy-makers inflicted deadweight loss not only on the residents of the two countries, but also on each other. To avoid some of this political damage they can set trade policies cooperatively, as governments often do.

When governments negotiate trade policies they are aware of the political repercussions at home, including those that are related to special-interest groups. These repercussions affect their strategy. At the same time, campaign contributions of special-interest groups are designed differently when they expect the policy-makers to negotiate than when they expect them to set policies non-cooperatively. In anticipation of negotiation a lobby designs its contribution schedule so as to tilt the agreement in its favour. The best schedule depends on the institutional framework in which the negotiations take place. As shown in Grossman and Helpman (1995a), however, as long as the negotiating procedure allows policy-makers to choose from the outcomes that are efficient from their own perspective, the resulting equilibrium policy vectors satisfy

$$\tau_j^A - \tau_j^B = \frac{I_j^A - \alpha_L^A}{a^A + \alpha_L^A} \frac{X_j^A}{\left(-\pi_j M_j^{A\prime} \right)} - \frac{I_j^B - \alpha_L^B}{a^B + \alpha_L^B} \frac{X_j^B}{\left(-\pi_j M_j^{B\prime} \right)}. \tag{12}$$

This formula determines only the relative values τ_j^A / τ_j^B, which are independent of the negotiation procedure. They ensure that the outcome is on the efficiency frontier of the governments. It is then possible to use the levels of these policy variables, or direct transfers between the governments (as in the CAP in Europe), to select a particular distribution of gains on the efficient frontier.[24] Which particular distribution the governments choose depends on the negotiation procedure, as well as on a variety of economic and political variables.[25]

Importantly, an industry is protected in country A but not in B if and only if the political power index of this industry is larger in A. Negotiations over trade taxes bring special interests of an industry from the two countries to take opposing sides of the issue; each one of them wants to be protected at the expense of the other. As a result they exert opposing pressures on the negotiating parties and the winner is the lobby with the larger political clout. Thus, for example, if the textile industry is organised in country A but not in B, textiles will obtain positive protection in A and negative protection in B, relative to free trade.

Equation (12) also shows that the governments will agree on free trade in textiles (or the same internal price in both countries) if and only if the political power indexes of the textile lobbies are the same in both countries.

Finally, observe that contrary to (11), no export supply elasticities appear in (12). This stems from the fact that in a trade war each government is using trade taxes to also better its nation's terms of trade. When the governments negotiate, however, the use of terms of trade as a means of income transfer is politically inefficient. Therefore they do not use them in the cooperative design of trade taxes.

3.3   Free trade agreements

Another important example of negotiated trade policies is provided by FTAs. Unlike negotiated trade taxes, however, FTAs involve discrete choices (although some continuity is available via the specified terms). The GATT Article XXIV allows countries to form an FTA in exception to the 'most favoured nation' (MFN) clause if the agreement eliminates duties and restrictions on 'substantially all trade' among the contracting parties. Grossman and Helpman (1995b) have studied the political economy of such agreements when interest groups that represent various industries express their concerns by means of campaign contributions. Each interest group can voice its support or opposition to an agreement by contributing money in case an FTA forms or in case an FTA is rejected.

First, suppose that a country contemplates joining an FTA with well specified terms that it cannot affect. Each sector is represented in the debate over the agreement, and the representatives of an industry seek to maximise the return to the sector-specific input. The government seeks to maximise $C + aW$, as in subsection 2.5. The economic model is the same as in subsection 2.1. In these circumstances the policy-maker has to choose one of two regimes: regime F (i.e. joining the free trade area), or regime N (i.e. not joining). Sector-specific income in regime $R = F, N$ equals Π_{iR} in sector i and welfare is given by W_R. Lobby i offers a pair of contributions (C_{iF}, C_{iN}), the first representing an offer in case regime F is adopted and the second representing an offer in case regime N is adopted. One of the offers equals zero.

The first question to ask is: what types of political equilibria arise in these circumstances? Grossman and Helpman show that two types may arise. If the regime that provides the higher aggregate welfare level generates a large enough welfare gain relative to the alternative, then there exists a political equilibrium in which the welfare-superior regime is chosen by the government and all lobbies contribute zero. The welfare gain is large enough for this purpose if the product of *a* with the welfare gain exceeds the largest loss that a single sector experiences when the welfare-superior regime is selected.[26] Clearly, with no contributions the government selects the welfare-superior regime. The point is, however, that under the specified circumstances no lobby stands to gain enough from inducing the government to choose the welfare-inferior regime in order to make it worthwhile for the lobby to contribute the required minimum that induces the policy-maker to switch regimes. Evidently, this equilibrium builds on a lack of coordination among the lobbying groups, and each one separately does not have a big enough stake to induce a switch of regimes on its own.

Minimal coordination by pressure groups, in the form of non-binding prior communication about preferable outcomes, leads to an equilibrium that is *coalition-proof*. In such equilibria the policy-maker chooses the regime that provides the highest joint welfare to the organised interest groups and the government.[27] Moreover, every equilibrium in which contributions by at least one lobby support the selected regime is of this nature. In these equilibria, contributions by opposing interest groups make the government just indifferent between the alternative regimes. The implication is that a delicate balance prevails in these equilibria, in the sense that about equal political strength supports each side of the issue.[28]

These results can be used to examine what pairs of countries are likely candidates for FTAs. An agreement requires both countries to select regime *F* in the political equilibrium. For this purpose, enough support in favour of the agreement has to be amassed in each country. Now, support for an agreement can come from one of two sources. Either *F* provides higher welfare, in which case the government will be happy to sign an agreement in order to please its voters. Or potential exporters to the FTA, who expect to sell at higher prices in the partner country, are willing to contribute enough money in order to open those markets. Sectors that expect to face fiercer import competition in the FTA oppose the agreement.

If the initial rates of protection reflect a political balance of power of the type described in subsection 2.5, then each country needs enough potential exporters that support the FTA in order to overcome the opposing political pressures. This means that the imbalance of trade between the countries has to be small enough, because one country's exports into the FTA are the other's imports. Unfortunately, potential exporters that support the agreement do so because they expect to be able to charge higher prices, and higher prices are bad for welfare. As a result, free trade agreements are most viable in situations in which the two countries are most likely to suffer joint welfare losses.[29]

Both countries are more likely to endorse an FTA if some politically sensitive sectors can be excluded from the agreement and allowed to maintain the original rates of protection. If given a choice, each country prefers to exclude sectors for whom the FTA produces the largest joint loss of welfare and lobby income per unit of the overall constraining factor, where the constraining factor represents the interpretation of the term 'substantially all trade' in Article XXIV. Examples of the constraining factor include the fraction of industries that can be excluded from the agreement or the fraction of trade that takes place in exempted products. All sectors can be ranked according to this criterion and the cutoff point then determined by the overall constraint.[30]

It is quite unlikely, however, that both countries will have the same ranking of sectors according to this criterion. Under these circumstances a conflict arises over the set of exemptions and the countries need to reach a compromise in order to enact an FTA. Grossman and Helpman (1995b) show that if the two governments engage in Nash bargaining over the exemptions, then they agree to exclude a set of sectors that is ranked according to a weighted average of the criterion that each country would like to use on its own.[31] The weights reflect the relative bargaining powers of the two governments. And a cutoff point is determined by the overall constraint imposed by the term 'substantially all trade'.

These examples show the power of an approach that emphasises two-way interactions between internal politics and international economic relations. They also show that – complications generated by such interactions notwithstanding – this approach yields interesting insights about important policy issues. Further enrichment of this framework is needed, however, in order to address problems of institutional design that are at the heart of the current debate about rules concerning trade, direct foreign investment (FDI), and intellectual property rights.

NOTES

I am grateful to the NSF for financial support and to Gene Grossman and Alan Winters for comments.
   1 When τ_i is larger than one and the good is imported, we have a proper tariff. Alternatively, when τ_i is smaller than one and the good is imported, we have a subsidy to imports. If the good is exported and τ_i is larger than one we have an export subsidy and if τ_i is smaller than one and the good is exported we have an export tax.
   2 Depending on context, it may be necessary to limit the choice of τ_i to some

feasible set. Obviously, it has to be non-negative. But some upper limit may also exist as a result of political constraints or international agreements.

3 The discussion in the text assumes that the distribution of the ownership of labour and sector-specific inputs is atomless – i.e. it is thinly dispersed in the population. As a result, γ_L^j is treated as the measure of labour owned by individual j, implying $\int_j \gamma_L^j dj = 1$.

4 I.e. $\int_j \gamma_i^{jdj} = 1$ for every $i = 1, 2, \ldots, n$.

5 When there are trade taxes only, the consumer price equals the producer price. As is well known, the utility function (1) has an associated standard indirect utility function $v(p, E) = E + \sum_{i=1}^n S_i(p_i)$, where E represents total spending and $S_i(p_i) = u_i[d_i(p_i)] - p_i d_i(p_i)$ is the consumer surplus from product i, where $d_i(p_i)$ is the demand function for product i. Imports of product i are given by $M_i(\tau_i) = -[S_i'(\tau_i) + \Pi_i'(\tau_i)]$.

6 The reduced-form indirect utility function (2) is given by $\hat{v}(\tau, \gamma^j) = \gamma_L^j + \sum_{i=1}^n \hat{v}_i(\tau_i, \gamma_i^j)$.

7 I use the term 'tariff' to mean $\tau_i > 1$ independently of whether the good is imported or exported. Also observe that under our normalisation of the population size (i.e. that the population equals one), the average ownership share of a sector-specific input equals one.

8 Output and the slope of the import demand function depend on the tariff rate, but these arguments have been suppressed in the following formula for convenience.

9 The assumption of linearity is inconsequential for our purpose. With a non-linear political support function the formula of the tariff rate has a marginal rate of substitution a_π that depends on the levels of income of sector-specific inputs and on aggregate welfare.

10 Observe that by substituting (4) into (5) we obtain an objective function in which every dollar of real income obtains a weight of 1, except for income from a sector-specific input that obtains a weight of $1 + 1/a_\pi$. These differential weights on different sources of real income drive the results. Long and Vousden (1991) have proposed a somewhat different approach to the formulation of political support functions, in which the weights vary across individuals rather than across sources of income.

11 Feenstra and Bhagwati (1982) take a similar approach, except that they view the government as the defender of the public interest. As a result, the lobbying costs of the pro-protectionist coalition rise with the price distortion. We will come back to this point at a later stage.

12 I exclude the constant term for labour income from this formula.

13 It is, of course, not realistic to assume that the anti-protectionist lobby consists of all other individuals in the economy. But it simplifies the exposition.

14 If only a fraction $\alpha_i^O < 1 - \alpha_i$ of individuals belong to the anti-protectionist lobby, then the first term on the right-hand side of (7) should be replaced with $[(1 - \alpha_i)(b_i - 1) + 1 - \alpha_i - \alpha_i^O]/(\alpha_i b_i + \alpha_i^O)$.

15 Electoral competition is implicit in both the political support function and the tariff-formation function approaches, while in the MBY approach it takes centre stage.

16 The influence motive generates benefits to the lobbies that are of the same order of magnitude as their contributions. This feature makes it desirable to exploit this motive for contributions even when there exists a large number of interest groups.

17 The political-support function approach can be interpreted as a reduced form of the influence-driven contributions approach. For some purposes the details of the influence-driven contributions approach are not needed. For other purposes, however, they are essential.

18 Each party seeks to maximise its expected number of seats. The probability of successfully promoting a policy depends on the number of seats in command. A party uses contributions from special interests to influence the voting pattern of uninformed or 'impressionable' voters. On the other hand, each informed voter casts her ballot on the basis of whichever party commits to a policy that she most prefers. Except that each voter may have preferences between the parties that are based on other considerations as well, such as their positions on non-economic issues. This leads to probabilistic voting. In this framework, a party can choose a policy that is desirable to the general public and thereby secure the support of informed voters. Instead it can tilt its policy position in favour of special interests in order to gain campaign contributions. In this event, it loses the support of some of the informed voters, but it can use the contributions to gain support from the impressionable voters. This trade-off between the support of the two groups of voters, and a party's objective to attain as many seats as possible in Parliament translate into a desire to maximise an objective function that is increasing in contributions and in the wellbeing of the general public. This function is linear when the distribution of preferences over non-economic issues is uniform. The parameters of the political objective function depend on the degree of dispersion of these preferences, on the non-economic bias in the preferences of voters, the number of informed relative to uninformed voters in the population, and the effectiveness of campaign spending in attracting impressionable votes.

19 As explained in n.18, in the Grossman and Helpman (1994b) model of electoral competition with special interests a depends on a variety of the underlying parameters.

20 Observe that unlike the example of the tariff-formation function here we include contributions to welfare by all goods, not only the product of sector i. The reason is that we shall allow each interest group to lobby for trade taxes in all sectors (i.e. not only in the sector in which they have a stake in the sector-specific factor). More on this point later.

21 In order to simplify notation, I use $\sum_{j \neq i} C_j(\tau)$ as a shorthand for the sum of contributions of all organised interest groups other than i.

22 See, for example, Dixit (1995) for an application to commodity taxation. Similar methods can be used to deal with quotas and other forms of quantitative restrictions.

23 It is also possible to allow pressure groups to lobby foreign governments, as shown in Grossman and Helpman (1995a).

24 See also Mayer (1981) on this issue.

25 See Grossman and Helpman (1995a) for an example.

26 Let R be the welfare-superior regime – i.e. $W_R > W_K, R \neq K$. Then there exists an equilibrium in which contributions are zero and the government chooses R whenever $a(W_R - W_K) \geq \max[0, \max_i(\Pi_{iK} - \Pi_{iR})]$.

27 Regime R is selected in this case if and only if $\sum_{j \in L} \Pi_{jR} + aW_R \geq \sum_{j \in L} \Pi_{jK} + aW_K$.

28 The fact that NAFTA has barely passed during the vote in US Congress can be interpreted as a reflection of this sort of equilibrium.

29 In this statement welfare is measure by W, and it does not include the wellbeing of the government.

30 Suppose there exists a continuum of sectors and that the overall constraint is given by $\int_{i \in E} T_i di \leq T$, where E represents the set of exempt sectors, T_i represents the contribution of sector i to the overall constraint, and T represents the overall constraint. If, for example, the overall constraint is on the number of sectors that can be granted an exemption, than $T_i = 1$ for every sector and T stands for the largest measure of sectors that are allowed to be excluded from the FTA under Article XXIV. On the other hand, if the constraint is on the trade volume, than T_i stands for the trade volume in sector i and T represents the maximum trade volume that can be excluded from the agreement. The ranking of industries builds on the index $g_i = (a\Delta W_i + \Delta\Pi_i)/T_i$, where ΔW_i represent the welfare gain in sector i from the FTA and $\Delta\Pi_i$ represents lobby i's income gain from the FTA. Indexing the sectors in an increasing order of g_i, the government wants to exclude the sectors for which g_i is negative, as well as sectors with positive values of g_i up to the constraint permitted by $\int_{i \in E} T_i di \leq T$.

31 Sectors are ranked according to $\omega^A g_i^A + \omega^B g_i^B$, where ω^K is the weight of country K. The overall constraint remains the same as in n.30.

REFERENCES

Bernheim, D. B. and Whinston, M.D., 1986. 'Menu Auctions, Resource Allocation, and Economic Influence', *Quarterly Journal of Economics*, **101**, 1–31

Coughlin, P. J., 1992. *Probabilistic Voting Theory* (Cambridge: Cambridge University Press)

Dixit, A., 1995. 'Special-interest Lobbying and Endogenous Commodity Taxation', Princeton University, mimeo

Evans, P., Jacobson, H. and Putnam, R. (eds.) , 1993. *Double-Edge Diplomacy* (Berkeley: University of California Press)

Feenstra, R. C. and Bhagwati, J.N., 1982. 'Tariff Seeking and the Efficient Tariff', in J.N. Bhagwati (ed.), *Import Competition and Response* (Chicago: University of Chicago Press)

Findlay, R. and Wellisz, S., 1982. 'Endogenous Tariffs, the Political Economy of Trade Restrictions, and Welfare', in J.N. Bhagwati (ed.), *Import Competition and Response* (Chicago: University of Chicago Press)

Flam, H., 1992. 'Product Markets and 1992: Full Integration, Large Gains?', *Journal of Economic Perspectives*, **6**, 7–30

Garber, P. M. (ed.), 1993. *The Mexico–US Free Trade Agreement* (Cambridge, MA: MIT Press)

Grossman, G. M. and Helpman, E., 1994. 'Protection for Sale', *American Economic Review*, **84**, 667–90

1995a. 'Trade Wars and Trade Talks', *Journal of Political Economy*, **103**, 675–708

1995b. 'The Politics of Free Trade Agreements', *American Economic Review*, **84**, 833–50

1996. 'Electoral Competition and Special Interest Politics, *Review of Economic Studies*, **63**, 265–86

Hillman, A. L., 1982. 'Declining Industries and Political-support Protectionist Motives', *American Economic Review*, **72**, 1180–7

1989. *The Political Economy of Protection* (London: Harwood)

Hillman, A. L. and Ursprung, H. 1988. 'Domestic Politics, Foreign Interests, and International Trade Policy', *American Economic Review*, **78**, 729–45

Johnson, H. G., 1953–4. 'Optimal Tariffs and Retaliation', *Review of Economic Studies*, **21**, 142–53

Jones, R. W., 1971. 'A Three-Factor Model in Theory, Trade and History', in J.N. Bhagwati *et al.* (eds.), *Trade, Growth and the Balance of Payments: Essays in Honor of C. B. Kindleberger* (Amsterdam: North-Holland)

Long, N. V. and Vousden, N. 1991. 'Protectionist Responses and Declining Industries', *Journal of International Economics*, **30**, 87–103

Magee, S. P., Brock, W.A. and Young, L. 1989. *Black Hole Tariffs and Endogenous Policy Formation* (Cambridge, MA: MIT Press)

Magelby, D. B. and Nelson, C.J. 1990. *The Money Chase: Congressional Campaign Finance Reform* (Washington, DC: Brookings)

Mayer, W., 1981. 'Theoretical Considerations on Negotiated Tariff Adjustments', *Oxford Economic Papers*, **33**, 135–53

1984. 'Endogenous Tariff Formation', *American Economic Review*, 74, 970–85

Mayer, W. and Li, J., 1994. 'Interest Groups, Electoral Competition, and Probabilistic Voting for Trade Policies', *Economics and Politics*, **6**, 59–77

Olsen, M., 1965. *The Logic of Collective Action* (Cambridge, MA: Harvard University Press)

Peltzman, S., 1976. 'Toward a More General Theory of Regulation', *Journal of Law and Economics*, **19**, 211–40

Putnam, R., 1988. 'Diplomacy and Domestic Politics: The Logic of Two-level Games', *International Organization*, **42**, 427–60

Rodrik, D., 1986. 'Tariffs, Subsidies, and Welfare with Endogenous Policy', *Journal of International Economics*, **21**, 285–96

1995. 'Political Economy of Trade Policy', in G.M. Grossman and K. Rogoff (eds.), *Handbook of International Economics, III* (Amsterdam: North-Holland)

Shepsle, K. A., 1990. *Models of Multiparty Electoral Competition* (London: Harwood)

Stigler, G., 1971. 'The Theory of Economic Regulation', *Bell Journal of Economics*, **2**, 3–21

Discussion

THIERRY VERDIER

It is always a pleasure to read a contribution by Elhanan Helpman, and chapter 4 is no exception. This survey presents in a clear-cut and compact way the recent formal literature on political economy of trade to which Helpman and his coauthor Gene Grossman have importantly contributed. Generations of scholars and students of international trade policy will have this chapter on their reading list and will be grateful to get to the frontier of the field in just about 30 pages!

The main strength of the chapter lies in grasping the various approaches of political economy of trade protection in a single simple framework and deriving elegant explicit tariff formulae that can be easily compared. In this way, the contributions of the different models are concisely explained and transparently related to each other.

The survey starts by reviewing the various political economy approaches to trade protection (direct democracy, political-support function, tariff-formation function, electoral competition). It follows Helpman and Grossman's recent work in the field (the so-called 'influence-driven contribution' approach), and discusses how their approach can fruitfully be applied to the political economy of international trade relationships (international trade negotiations and the formation of free trade areas (FTAs)). I will essentially organise my discussion in two sections. First, I point out a caveat to most models that Helpman presents. Second, I suggest some potential avenues for future research which were not mentioned in the chapter.

An important and nice feature of the literature that Helpman reviews is the fact that tariff formulae are derived from various political settings. From this, one gets a sense of clear empirical implications about the structure of protection across industries and one can distinguish which approach is most relevant when confronted with the data. However, it seems to me that all of them suffer from a particular caveat. They do not fit with the well known stylised fact that industries with high import-penetration ratios tend to be more protected, everything else being equal. To be more precise, one can see that all tariff formulae (except the electoral competition approach) look like :

$$\tau_i - 1 = c_i \frac{X_i}{-M_i'}$$

where c_i is a constant which takes various forms and depends on different political parameters according to the approach chosen. Using $T_i = M_i/(X_i + M_i)$ as the import penetration ratio and $\in_i^M$ the price elasticity of import demand, these formulae can be rewritten in the Ramsey-type optimal tariff form:

$$\tau_i - 1 = c_i' \left(\frac{1}{T_i} - 1 \right) \frac{1}{\in_i^M}$$

with c_i' another constant. As clearly appears in this form, these formulae predict that, controlling for import elasticity demands, more protection is granted to industry i the smaller its import-penetration ratio: exactly the opposite to what is observed empirically! Of course, one may still use the approach if a good case can be made that industries which have high import-penetration ratios are also industries with low price elasticities of import demand, but I do not see any reason why this should systematically be the case.

How to reconcile this perturbing stylised fact with political economy models of trade protection? Maybe, one should extend the political logic of of the models surveyed in chapter 4. A common feature of these models is the idea that egoistic individuals, knowing exactly their sectoral position, influence politics to get the level of protection which seems best to them. Starting from there, two natural extensions can be hypothesised. The first is the idea that individuals actually have a grain of social altruism, especially to those who are disadvantaged (here, by trade shocks or openness of the economy). Solidarity may after all play a role in societies! In that case, a high import-penetration ratio may simply reflect a signal on how badly hurt the disadvantaged are, triggering a social response for more protection to help them. The second route is to consider that people may decide to vote for an implicit social contract of trade protection before knowing exactly where they end up sectorally – social-insurance motivation against trade shocks. How such a social contract would be enforced and emerge as a political outcome remains, of course, to be investigated.[1]

Let me conclude this discussion by suggesting a couple of avenues for future research. A first interesting direction is to extend the models developed by Helpman to a dynamic context. Some issues have already been recently addressed in this perspective – domino effects (Baldwin, 1995), persistence of protection in declining sectors (Brainard and

Verdier, 1997), endogenous tariff cycles (Baldwin and Baldwin, 1992), but I think that still more needs to be done along this line.

A more ambitious line of research concerns going further into the micro foundations of the modelling of lobbying behaviour by interest groups. In this respect, a first aspect, not alluded to directly in the chapter, deals with the introduction of imperfect information in lobbying models of trade protection. Interest groups not only provide campaign contributions to politicians; they quite often influence the decision policy-making process in more indirect ways, providing good or bad information about the issues to politicians and the public. This may be quite important (sometimes even more important than providing contributions or bribes to elected officials). Incorporating asymmetry of information clearly paves the way for understanding better why politicians prefer the use of more distortionary but less 'transparent' redistribution instruments like trade restrictions rather than direct taxation to compensate people.

A second aspect concerns the implications of imperfect asset markets for lobbying behaviour. Typically in most models, there are no income effects nor cash constraints on the way lobbies can provide contributions. However when credit markets are imperfect, these effects occur naturally. In that case, the separability between policies and contributions (as obtained, for example, in Grossman and Helpman, 1994) no longer holds. In that setting, it will be then quite interesting to investigate the implications of liquidity constraints on lobbying behaviour and the level of protection. When insurance markets are imperfect, agents cannot perfectly insure themselves against bad trade shocks. This may affect their incentives to lobby to preserve their pre-shock income level, which in turn has implications for the resulting political equilibrium. Feeney and Hillman (1996) have started such an investigation with a black-box lobbying function; certainly, more remains to be done along these lines.

Finally one would want to have a theory of the internal organisation of lobbies. This is, I think, a necessary step towards a serious theory of endogenous lobby formation. How do lobbies get organised and coordinated, how do they deal with the free-riding problem of their members? What will be the consequences for the trade-policy outcome? What will be the impact of regional integration at the institutional level on the organisation of lobbies? All these questions are still unanswered in the literature and are definitely worth our attention to improve our understanding of the positive aspects between trade and politics.

Having such a number of potential lines of investigation may generate feelings of frustration or exasperation. My own feeling is rather that it will make the field of political economy of trade all the more lively and exciting for generations of scholars!

NOTES

1 Obviously in both cases the open question remains of why we should use trade-policy instruments when there are certainly less distortionary ways to help or insure people. Notice, however, that the models presented in the survey do not provide an answer to this question, which in some sense is fundamental for the political economy of trade protection.

REFERENCES

Baldwin, R., 1995. 'A Domino Theory of Regionalism', chapter 2 in R. Baldwin, P. Haaparantaa and J. Kiander (eds.), *Expanding Membership in the European Union* (Cambridge: Cambridge University Press for the CEPR)

Baldwin, R. and Baldwin, R., 1992. 'Endogenous Policy Cycles' (Geneva: GIIS), mimeo

Brainard, L. and Verdier, T., 1997. 'The Political Economy of Declining Industries: Senescent Industry Collapse Revisited', *Journal of International Economics*, **42**, 221–38

Feeney, J. and Hillman, A., 1996. 'Endogenous Trade Liberalization in the Presence of Domestic and International Asset Markets', paper presented at the CEPR European Research Workshop on International Trade, Glasgow

Grossman, G. M. and Helpman, H., 1994. 'Protection for Sale', *American Economic Review*, **85**, 667–90

5 Globalisation and labour, or: if globalisation is a bowl of cherries, why are there so many glum faces around the table?

DANI RODRIK

1   Introduction

The increasing pace of international economic integration, as a consequence of global convergence on liberal trade policies as well as advances in transportation and communication technologies, has opened an interesting chasm between economists and the common folk who often feel they bear the brunt of globalisation. Most economists tend to view expanding trade and foreign investment opportunities as inherently desirable, because they believe that these opportunities improve the efficiency with which market economies operate and enhance growth prospects. The troubled state of labour markets in advanced industrial economies, on the other hand, has led many influential groups in society – policy-makers, labour advocates, pundits in general – to link these ills directly to the process of globalisation. Intensified competition from low-wage countries, both as sources of imports and as hosts for foreign investors, is alleged by these groups to be largely responsible for the stagnation or decline of real wages of low-skilled workers in the Anglo-Saxon countries and for increasing unemployment in the continental European countries.

In absolving trade from any significant responsibility for these ills, many economists have taken a tack which sits uncomfortably with their faith in the benefits of free trade. The conclusion that trade with labour-abundant countries would reduce real wages in rich countries – or increase unemployment if wages are artificially fixed – is one that has been a cornerstone of traditional trade theory. Indeed, in the standard factor-endowments model, it is precisely through changing the effective relative abundance of different factors of production that trade creates gains for all nations. Hence, saying that the quantitative significance of this process in the real world is rather small and overshadowed by other phenomena (such as technological changes), which is what many trade

117

economists have found themselves arguing, is no different from saying that in practice the gains from trade amount to little more than peanuts. Put differently, if one believes that expanded trade has been a source of a lot of good things in the last couple of decades, one is also forced to believe that it has had many of the consequences that its opponents have alleged.

In this chapter, my purpose is not to take stand on the question of whether the (net) benefits of trade are large or small in practice. My objective is to emphasise some connections between international economic integration and labour markets in advanced industrial countries which have received insufficient attention in the economics literature. I discuss three issues in particular.[1]

First, globalisation has resulted in unskilled labour becoming more easily substitutable – through trade or investment flows – across national borders. While this is well recognised, its implications for the workings of the labour market has not received much attention. The economics literature has focused on identifying the magnitude of the *downward shift* in the demand curve for low-skilled labour, and not on the consequences of the *increase in the elasticity* of this demand. Focusing on the latter is important because it can account for many of the observed changes in the labour market without requiring large changes either in trade and investment flows or in relative goods prices (neither of which have by and large occurred). In particular, I will argue that the increased substitutability of low-skilled workers implies the following:

- The costs of increased benefits and improved working conditions can no longer be passed on (or shared with) employers. The larger the elasticity of demand for labour, the higher the share of any such costs that must be borne by the workers themselves. Hence globalisation makes it difficult to sustain the post-war bargain under which workers would receive continued improvements in pay and benefits in return for labour peace and loyalty.
- Shocks to labour demand – caused, say, by shocks in labour productivity – now result in much greater volatility in both earnings and hours worked (assuming that there is some positive elasticity to labour supply). This is important insofar as it can account directly for some of the widening wage inequality since the late 1970s, as well as for the increase in within-group inequality.
- Third, to the extent that wages are determined in bargaining between workers and employers, an increase in the substitutability of workers will result in a lower share of the enterprise surplus ending up with workers. The more substitutable are workers in Akron with those in

Monterrey or Bombay, the less bargaining power they have and the lower the wage they will receive.

From this perspective, the main story about globalisation is the change in the (actual or perceived) elasticity of demand for unskilled workers, and not the reduction in the demand *per se*.

The second issue I stress is labour standards. Expanding networks of trade and investment are bringing societies with very different standards for working conditions into increasing contact with each other. Much of these differences reflect income differentials and varying values across countries. At the same time, large discrepancies in labour standards – relating to working hours, collective bargaining, child labour practices, etc. – undermine the legitimacy of free trade and make it harder to sustain domestic consensus on trade policy in the industrial countries. They raise concerns about 'social dumping' and a 'race to the bottom'. I will provide some evidence here that labour standards do indeed affect labour costs across countries as well as trade and investment flows. Low-standard countries tend to have low labour costs, controlling for labour productivity, and a stronger revealed comparative advantage in labour-intensive manufactures. At the same time, contrary to the common presumption, low labour standards appear to deter, and not attract, inward investment by foreign firms.

The third issue I discuss has to do with the undermining of the role and effectiveness of national governments in the advanced industrial societies where international economic integration has moved beyond the boundaries of 'shallow integration' and into 'deep integration' territory.[2] A particular trade-off has gone unnoticed in this process. The post-war international economic system was founded on the principle that national governments would provide for domestic economic stability in an overall international environment characterised by multilateralism and open trade. Far from downplaying the role of government, post-war multilateralism gave it a central role: that of sheltering domestic society from excessive amounts of external risk. I will provide here some rather striking empirical evidence for this proposition. Contrary to what most economists would expect, economies that are more open and exposed to greater amounts of external risk have had *bigger* governments. In such economies, governments have consumed a larger share of society's resources and employed a larger proportion of the labour force.

The significance of this finding from the current perspective is that it identifies a serious dilemma in this new era of globalisation. Historically openness has been maintained thanks to strong governments, yet globalisation exerts forces that make national governments weak and ineffective. It is clear who stands to lose the most from the dilemma being resolved in favour of globalisation. Labour, and low-skilled labour in particular, is the least internationally mobile group in advanced industrial societies. Consequently, it is the group most exposed to external shocks and least able to protect itself in the absence of proactive government policies.

Once these considerations are taken into account, our perspective on the redistributive significance of globalisation may move closer to that of the average person on the street. In particular, we begin to see how the implicit post-war bargain between employers and workers is being undermined across a broad front, to the detriment of low-skilled workers.

2   Trade and wages

Since the mid-1970s, 'an economic disaster has befallen low skill Americans', as Freeman (1996) puts it. The real hourly wages of young males with 12 or fewer years of schooling has dropped by 20 per cent between 1979 and 1989, accompanied by an increase in inequality both within and across skill groups. In Europe, real wages at the bottom of the skill distribution rose, but unemployment increased significantly relative to the United States (Freeman, 1996). At the same time, international economic integration has continued apace and the world has become a much smaller place.

The link between internationalisation and labour market outcomes has been the subject of numerous empirical studies, including Borjas, Freeman and Katz (1992), Lawrence and Slaughter (1993), Wood (1995), Sachs and Shatz (1994) and Leamer (1995). There are also a number of useful surveys and evaluations of the literature, including Wood (1995), Richardson (1995), Freeman (1996), and Cline (1998).

These studies have focused on the factor-endowments model to answer the question: how much have trade and migration flows reduced the demand for unskilled labour in the developed countries? Since the relevant volumes of trade and migration are small relative to the domestic stocks of unskilled labour, the answer is almost a foregone conclusion: some but not a whole lot. In addition, in the canonical factor-endowments model the effect of trade on relative factor prices operates through relative commodity prices, and it has been difficult to find significant changes in these relative prices. Hence, the evidence neither on quantities nor on prices suggests that trade has been more than a minor factor in the rising skill premium in the United States and in the increasing unemployment in Europe.[3]

But suppose we ask a different question: how much has international economic integration affected the *elasticity of demand* for low-skilled labour? Since an elasticity concerns changes at the margin, this question cannot be simply answered by looking at volumes of trade and immigration. Nor would an increase in the elasticity of demand for labour necessarily be associated with changes in the relative price of labour-intensive goods.[4]

To see the point, consider what would happen if the rest of the world consisted of economies that were identical to the United States, in terms of their relative factor endowments and levels of wealth. Since there would be no comparative advantage, economic integration would result in little trade (save, of course, for trade based on scale economies) and no change in relative prices. But the services of US workers would now become more easily substitutable thanks to the possibilities of trade, migration and capital outflows. Hence, while US labour would not face a reduction in demand (since the rest of the world is assumed to be no more labour-abundant than the United States), it would certainly be confronted with a demand that is more elastic.

But could an increase in the elasticity of demand for low-skilled workers account for the labour market developments summarised above, in the absence of a downward shift in the demand as well? The answer is: quite possibly. For one thing, a more elastic demand implies that shocks to the demand curve will result in greater volatility both in wages and hours worked, and in greater dispersion in earnings within and across skill categories. Perhaps more fundamentally, a large increase in the substitut- ability of unskilled workers is likely to undermine the traditional implicit bargain between employers and workers to the detriment of the latter. I will now elaborate on these possibilities.

Consider the supply–demand framework in figure 5.1. Let the initial labour market equilibrium in an advanced industrial country be at *A*. Two labour demand curves are drawn for this equilibrium, one for a closed economy and one for an open economy. The open-economy labour demand curve is the more elastic. Consider now the consequences of an exogenous shock to labour demand, say because of a shock to labour productivity. As drawn, the shock is a positive one, and both labour demand curves shift up by an equal amount. For the closed economy the new equilibrium is at *B*, and for the open economy it is at *C*. There is a larger increase in wages and employment in the open economy than there is in the closed economy. Conversely, had the productivity shock been a negative one, wages and employment would have fallen by a greater amount in the open economy. In short, openness makes labour market outcomes more volatile.

This is important insofar as it can account for part of the widening

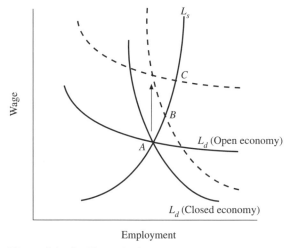

Employment

Figure 5.1   Incidence in the open economy

wage inequality since the late 1970s, as well as for the increase in within-group inequality. Table 5.1 reports the findings of a study by Gottschalk and Moffitt (1994) on the United States.

The table shows that between one-third and one-half of the widening wage distribution from the 1970s to the 1980s can be attributed to the increase in the *short-term variance* in earnings. Between the two periods (from 1970–8 to 1979–87), the permanent variance of real annual earnings rose by 41 per cent (from 0.20 to 0.28), reflecting the dispersion in permanent earnings. The transitory variance, which is roughly half as large as the permanent variance, rose by almost the same percentage amount (42 per cent). This indicates that fully one-third of the widening of the earnings distribution has resulted from an increase in the instability of earnings. Moreover, the increase in short-term volatility is greatest for the least-skilled groups – see the numbers for workers with less than 12 years of education – these being the ones for which demand has presumably become the most elastic. Hence the facts are consistent with a picture of labour markets in which greater openness to trade interacting with short-term fluctuations in labour demand (or labour productivity) has resulted in greater inequalities across and within skill groups.

Note that the focus on trade with (and immigration from) low-wage countries ignores the fact that unskilled workers in Germany or France are also in competition with similar workers in the United Kingdom or the United States, markets with which the former countries are considerably more tightly integrated than with India and China. And

Table 5.1. *Increasing instability in labour market outcomes, 1970–8 and 1979–87*

	Permanent variance				Transitory variance			
	1970–8	1979–87	Change	Percentage change	1970–8	1979–87	Change	Percentage change
Real annual earnings								
Whole sample	0.201	0.284	0.083	41	0.104	0.148	0.044	42
Workers with fewer than 12 years of education	0.175	0.272	0.097	55	0.106	0.208	0.102	96
Log weekly wage	0.171	0.230	0.059	35	0.075	0.101	0.026	35
Log of weeks worked	0.014	0.020	0.006	43	0.046	0.063	0.017	37

Source: Gottschalk and Moffitt (1994, Tables 1 and 2a).

while North–North trade may have little perceptible impact on the demand for unskilled labour, it certainly makes this demand more elastic in all countries involved.

But that is not all. As mentioned previously, the greater substitutability of labour also alters the nature of the bargaining between workers and employers. This part of the picture has received surprisingly little attention in the literature, primarily because the focus has typically been on perfectly competitive settings in which wages are determined in spot markets.[5] There is by now considerable evidence, however, of the presence of labour rents in manufacturing industries (see in particular Katz and Summers, 1989; Blanchflower, Oswald and Sanfey, 1996). This evidence indicates that part of labour remuneration in these industries comes in the form of rent-sharing with the employers. I will use a simple model to highlight the consequences of increased globalisation for the rent-sharing equilibrium.

3   The consequences of increased international mobility by firms for the rent-sharing bargain

We consider a small open economy with $K+1$ sectors and a total of L workers. All goods are tradable and their prices are fixed at unity. We assume that there exist rents in K of these sectors, with the remaining sector representing an aggregate of all competitive activities in the economy. Let these competitive activities use labour alone under constant costs, so that the competitive level of the wage can be fixed at w^* according to the marginal (and average) product of labour in the $K+1$st sector.

Let the level of wages and employment in the first K sectors be determined by Nash bargaining between workers and employers. We follow the framework in Blanchflower, Oswald and Sanfey (1996), and extend it slightly to consider the role of outside options for employers and the welfare and distributional implications in general equilibrium. A similar framework has also been considered in a paper by Borjas and Ramey (1994) devoted specifically to the trade and wages issue, but they focus on a reduction in demand in the goods market rather than on the impact of increasing mobility of firms. Hence let ϕ and $(1 - \phi)$ stand for the bargaining power of workers and employers, respectively, and π^* for the level of profits that employers could achieve by moving their operations offshore. I will capture the effects of globalisation by considering the consequences of an increase in π^*. This seems to be a natural way to parameterise the increasing mobility of firms: declining barriers to trade and investment and advances in communication reduce the employers' cost of moving abroad, and increase the value of their 'outside option'. The Nash bargaining outcome in the representative non-competitive sector is the solution to the following problem:

$$\max_{w,n} \ \phi \ \log[(u(w) - u(w^*))n] + (1 - \phi) \log(\pi - \pi^*)$$

where n is the number of employees in that sector, π and w are the profit and wage levels respectively, $u'(w) > 0$, and $u''(w) < 0$. Letting the production function be represented by the concave function $f(n)$, profits are written as $\pi = f(n) - wn$. The first-order conditions can then be expressed as:

$$w : \frac{\phi u'(w)}{u(w) - u(w^*)} - \frac{(1 - \phi)n}{\pi - \pi^*} = 0$$

$$n : \frac{\phi}{n} + (1 - \phi)\frac{f'(n) - w}{\pi - \pi^*} = 0$$

Note the implication from the first-order condition for n that $w > f'(n)$ in an interior equilibrium, that is labour will be paid above its value marginal product as long as it has some bargaining power ($\phi > 0$) and the industry has rents ($\pi > \pi^*$). This need not imply, however, that employment will be too high in these industries from a social standpoint. Since the social opportunity cost of labour is w^*, whether the industry employs too few or too many workers depends on the relationship between $f'(n)$ and w^*. I will return to this point below.

Following Blanchflower, Oswald and Sanfey (1996), we can take a first-order approximation to express $u(w^*)$ as follows:

$$u(w^*) \cong u(w) + (w^* - w)u'(w).$$

Substituting this into the first-order expression for w, we have

$$w \cong w^* + \frac{\phi}{1 - \phi}\left(\frac{\pi - \pi^*}{n}\right)$$

This expression states that in this bargaining equilibrium workers receive a premium above the competitive wage. The premium equals a per worker share of the firm's rents *above* the level of outside profits available to the firm (say, in Malaysia or the Dominican Republic). Workers can share only the part of the rents in excess of those that the firm can make by outsourcing. This can be checked by doing the comparative statics of the pair of first-order conditions above that

$$\frac{dw}{d\pi^*} < 0$$

i.e. wages must fall if it becomes less costly for the firm to set up shop abroad.[6] The level of employment in turn is given by

$$n = \frac{\phi}{1-\phi}\left(\frac{\pi - \pi^*}{w - f'(n)}\right)$$

It can also be checked that $dn/d\pi^* < 0$, so employment in rent-sharing sectors must fall as well as a consequence of globalisation. Profits, by contrast, increase for two reasons: one is the direct effect of reduced wages, the other is the effect of reduced employment in a context where the wage being paid out, due to bargaining and rent-sharing reasons, is above the value marginal product of labour:

$$\frac{d\pi}{d\pi^*} = -n\frac{dw}{d\pi^*} + [f'(n) - w]\frac{dn}{d\pi^*} > 0$$

Hence, what we have shown is that increased mobility by employers and an enhanced ability to outsource will redistribute income away from workers in rent-sharing sectors and in favour of profits. Note that these important changes can occur, as in the present model, with no change in relative prices and no increase in international trade (outsourcing) taking place.

Now consider the consequences for national welfare. Let m stand for the number of workers in the competitive sector. This sector acts as the absorbing sector for workers who lose their jobs in the rent-sharing sectors ($L = nK + m$). National income is $Y = wnK + w^*m + \pi K$. Differentiating this expression with respect to π^*, and noting that $dm = -Kdn$, we get after simplifying:

$$\frac{dY}{d\pi^*} = K[f'(n) - w^*]\frac{dn}{d\pi^*}$$

Since $dn/d\pi^* < 0$, national income falls if $f'(n) > w^*$, that is, if the value marginal product of labour in rent-sharing sectors exceeds the social opportunity cost of labour (which is the wage in the competitive sector). Note that the model predicts $w > f'(n)$, but is silent on the relationship between w^* and $f'(n)$. Hence increased globalisation will hurt national welfare if the following pattern of inequalities holds: $w > f'(n) > w^*$. In this case, globalisation will result in both a deterioration of income distribution and an aggregate income loss.

3.1   Downward-sloping demand for labour in competitive sectors

In the preceding exercise, we fixed the 'outside' wage (w^*) by assuming that labour is employed under constant costs in the competitive sectors of the economy. As the high-wage sectors release workers to the rest of the economy, however, it is natural to expect that this will exert a depressing effect on the 'outside' wage. This can be taken into account by assuming that there is diminishing marginal product to workers in the competitive sectors of the economy. More specifically, let $g(m)$ stand for the production function in these sectors, with $g'(m) > 0$ and $g''(m) < 0$. To abstract from demand-side considerations, continue to assume that the relative price of the competitive good is fixed at unity. Employers in this sector will hire labour up to the point where the (value) marginal product of labour equals the competitive wage, $g'(m) = w^*$. This additional equation is needed to determine the now endogenous value of w^*. Other than re-writing the expression for national income as $Y = wnK + \pi K + g(m)$, nothing else is affected in the specification of the model.

Since w^* is now endogenous, however, the expressions for $dw/d\pi^*$ and $dn/d\pi^*$ cannot be determined from the first-order conditions in the high-wage sectors alone, and need to be solved in full general equilibrium. This is easily done, and rather than repeat the algebra, I will simply state the results. Once again, employment and wages both fall as a consequence of a rise in π^*. The downward effect on wages is now exacerbated by the reduction in w^* (as displaced workers bid down the wage in the competitive sectors). For this same reason, however, fewer workers get laid off from the high-wage sectors. The loss for workers is magnified, but the efficiency loss to the economy as a whole (assuming $w > f'(n) > w^*$ in equilibrium) is reduced.

3.2   Unemployment

The model so far is perhaps more reminiscent of the United States than Europe, in that sufficient flexibility in competitive sector wages is assumed to prevent unemployment. To see how a 'European' version of the model would produce different outcomes, assume now that w^* is fixed by fiat (by minimum-wage laws, say), despite diminishing marginal product to labour in the competitive sectors. The fixed wage implies $dn/d\pi^* = 0$, so that the workers who are laid off from the high-wage sectors (in the amount $-K\, dn/d\pi^*$) now become unemployed. The impact on national income is:

$$\frac{dY}{d\pi^*} = K f'(n) \frac{dn}{d\pi^*}$$

which is unambiguously negative. The 'European' version of the model generates worse efficiency outcomes on two accounts: first, some unemployment is generated; and second, there is a higher loss of employment in the high-wage sectors due to the smaller reduction in w. (The latter assumes that w^* continues to be used as the reference wage in bargaining.) Workers who remain employed in the rent-sharing sectors are of course better off under the 'European' model.

4   Trade and labour standards

We now turn to the impact that low labour standards in developing countries can have on labour markets in rich countries through international trade.[7] Analytically, most cases of low labour standards can be thought of as an enlargement of the effective labour supply in the country concerned (see Brown, Deardorff and Stern, 1996).   For concreteness, think of the employment of under-age children in manufacturing industries in the South. This increases the labour supply in the South by (roughly) the number of children added to the labour force as a consequence. For countries that already have a comparative advantage in unskilled labour-intensive industries such as clothing and footwear, this results in a strengthening of their comparative advantage. Southern exports of such products increase and Northern imports must correspondingly increase as well. If collectively Southern exporters amount to a large enough share of total supply – which is likely – the increase in import penetration in the North is achieved via a *fall* in the relative price of labour-intensive manufactures in world markets. The real wages of unskilled workers in the North are likely to decline as well, to the extent that Southern exports compete head-on with Northern production and Northern production is also intensive in unskilled labour.

That much should be straightforward and uncontroversial. From this point on, the viewpoints diverge. To a trade economist, what has just transpired is the creation of gains from trade for the North. Essentially the North is now being offered goods at a cheaper price than before. The fall in the relative price of labour-intensive goods represents an *improvement* in the terms of trade of the North since the North is a net importer of such goods. While unskilled labour may lose, the North is richer as a whole, and if governments in the North wished to do so they could compensate the losers and still come out ahead.

To a labour advocate (and the average person on the street), however, things look very different. While the gains to other groups (and to all workers *qua* consumers) are undeniable, what has just happened is that unskilled workers in the North have been displaced from their jobs and their earnings reduced because of employment practices in the South that would be considered unconscionable in the North. While it would be nice if full compensation were to take place, it is extremely unlikely in practice. Consequently, it is unfair that unskilled workers in the North should have to compete with child workers in the South and have to bear the costs for others' gains.

What is clearly at issue here is the *legitimacy* of the process through which net gains are being created in the North. In thinking about this issue, it helps to de-mystify international trade by recognising that from the perspective of any individual country trade is *just like* an additional technology with which goods can be produced. In the domestic context, we think of a 'production function' as representing the technology through which a set of intermediate inputs and primary factors is transformed into final goods. International trade is entirely analogous to such a production function: the goods that we sell abroad allow us to purchase imports in return, and hence our exports can be thought of as the inputs which get transformed into imports (the outputs). Prevailing international prices indicate the 'input–output' coefficients used in this transformation. And, continuing the analogy, a terms of trade improvement (due, for example, to lower labour standards in a partner country) acts just like a technical advance in this technology, by reducing the input–output coefficients.

This is a helpful way of looking at trade, for a number of reasons. For one thing, this perspective clarifies that the opening up of new trade opportunities is no different from the kind of technological progress that governments routinely pursue and encourage, even when such progress has sharp distributional considerations. We would not dream of banning the electric bulb to please the candle makers!

At the same time, the analogy with technology clarifies a central issue: nations do have collective preferences over what kinds of production technologies are admissible ('fair' or 'legitimate'), and governments have always had restrictions on technologies that violate these boundaries, even on those that promise a large increase in a nation's productive potential. The ban on slave labour is, of course, the example that comes immediately to mind. But there are many, many more. Experimentation on human subjects, for example, is generally illegal, even when there is full consent and when the potential medical benefits from a discovery are large. Experiments on animals are heavily regulated, and there is much support for the idea of banning them altogether. And, of course, over the last two centuries rich countries have developed labour legislation and standards that heavily circumscribe the nature of the production process.

One big difference is that the trade technology involves foreigners, and as such can become subject to an 'us' versus 'them' distinction. The Bangladeshi children, Chinese prisoners or Indian women who labour under substandard conditions are not part of 'our' community, and we may not feel it appropriate or practical to extend to them the protection that we provide our own workers. But once it is granted that the process by which goods are 'produced' can be legitimately subject to regulation, the case for not interfering with trade because only foreigners are involved becomes one of degree and not of kind. Simple introspection will reveal that citizens of the rich countries are not utterly indifferent to the wellbeing of workers in other countries. As Freeman (1994) points out, most of us would be willing to pay a few additional cents (if not a dollar or two) to buy a shirt that we knew was manufactured by foreign workers under safe and adequate working conditions. Moreover, our willingness to pay for labour standards abroad is presumably even higher when standards in *our own* community as well would be otherwise affected negatively.

The previous discussion focused on the case where low labour standards in the South exerted downward pressure on Northern wages. A more common complaint is that low labour standards create downward pressure on importing countries' labour standards as well. This is the well known 'race-to-the-bottom' argument, according to which workers in the North will have to acquiesce in standards that are low enough to prevent footloose capital and employers from deserting them for the South.

The argument has surface appeal, but is correct only in a limited sense to be explained below. The case against it has been put well by Freeman (1994): any country that wants higher labour standards can purchase them for itself, regardless of the level of standards in other countries, in one of the following three ways. First, a currency devaluation can be used to reduce domestic costs in foreign currency terms, thereby offsetting the loss in competitiveness. Second, there could be a downward adjustment in wages directly. Third, the cost of higher labour standards can be paid for by the government, and financed through an increase in taxes. Provided one or a combination of these approaches is followed, the presence of demanding labour standards does not put competitiveness and jobs at risk in the rich countries. The race to the bottom need not take place.

There is a sense, however, in which the race to the bottom becomes more likely as integration with low-standard countries increases. That is because increased trade and investment opportunities make it almost certainly more costly *for labour* to maintain high standards.

The point is best seen by returning to our simple supply–demand framework (figure 5.2). Let the initial labour market equilibrium in the North be at *A*. Now consider the consequences of raising labour

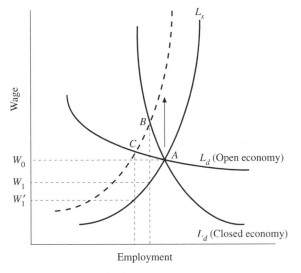

Figure 5.2   Volatility in the open economy

standards. From the perspective of employers, labour standards can be
viewed as a tax on employment. The result is a shift up in the effective
labour supply curve (as shown in figure 5.2), by an amount corresponding to the additional (per-worker) cost of maintaining the standard.
In the new equilibrium, as in the usual tax-incidence analysis, some of the
additional cost will be borne by employers and the rest by workers. What
determines the distribution of the cost between employers and workers is
the elasticity of demand for labour. Two cases are shown in figure 5.2.

As discussed earlier, in an economy that is more open to foreign trade
and investment the demand for labour will generally be more elastic.
And as figure 5.2 makes clear, the more elastic is labour demand, the
greater the part of the cost increase due to the labour standard that is
borne by workers: wages have to fall from w_0 to w_1', rather than from w_0
to w_1. The reduction in domestic employment is larger as well. Hence, in
an integrated world economy, higher labour standards cost workers
more, in terms of both wages and jobs.

Relating this result to the Freeman argument, it is still the case that
higher labour standards can be maintained if there is a willingness to pay
for them. What increased openness to trade and foreign investment does,
however, is render it more difficult for workers to make other groups in
society, and employers in particular, share in the costs. Consider the
three options mentioned earlier: devaluation, taxation and wage cuts. As
long as employers and capitalists have the option of moving (or

importing from) abroad, they cannot be induced to take a loss in terms of real after-tax earnings. Therefore, devaluation can work only insofar as it results in a disproportionate cut in take-home real wages. The same is true for taxation. One way or another, it is workers that must pay the lion's share of the cost.

5   Quantifying labour standards and their consequences

There is no universal, common definition of labour standards, but such standards are usually thought to cover areas like child labour, working conditions and collective bargaining. The International Labour Organization's (ILO) Conventions come perhaps closest to representing a universal set of labour standards. Since its first session in 1919, the ILO has approved no less than 174 Conventions, of which 171 are considered to be in force. (The remaining three, as of 1 June 1994, had not yet received the required number of ratifications to enter into force.) These range from the Hours of Work (Industry) Convention of 1919 to the Prevention of Major Industrial Accidents Convention of 1993. Once ratified by a member government, a Convention has the force of law in the country concerned. In addition to these Conventions, 181 Recommendations, which are purely advisory, have been adopted. The ILO does not have enforcement power, and it relies on persuasion and voluntary compliance with ratified Conventions. It does exercise a fair amount of monitoring and surveillance over the application of ratified Conventions.

There is a great amount of variation in the ratification coverage of Conventions by country. Oddly enough, the United States has ratified a very small number of Conventions – 11 in all, with the 1985 Labour Statistics Convention one of them! – and stands as one of the laggards in this respect. India, meanwhile, has ratified 36, Iraq 64, Haiti 23, Cuba 86 and the Central African Republic 35. Some recent Conventions that have not been ratified by the United States include: Night Work Convention (1990), Chemicals Convention (1990), Safety and Health in Construction Convention (1988), Asbestos Convention (1986), Occupational Health Services Convention (1985), Termination of Employment Convention (1982), and Occupational Safety and Health Convention (1981). Among other developed countries, the United Kingdom has ratified 80 Conventions, Japan 41, France 114 and Germany 73.[8]

There is of course plenty of anecdotal evidence about lax standards in many developing countries. In order to obtain some rough quantitative feel for the disparities among countries and in order to see how different countries stack up against each other, it is useful to take a look at some statistical indicators that relate to labour standards. I will describe a number of these indicators here. Some of these are based on adherence to ILO Conventions, while the rest are taken from other databases and deal with either specific legislation or actual practices.[9]

- *TOTCONV.* This indicator is simply the total number of ILO conventions ratified by a country. It ranges from 0 (the Gambia, Oman, Vanuatu) to 123 (Spain).
- *BWRCONV.* Not all of the ILO Conventions are regarded as equally central to labour standards. This indicator is the number of Conventions ratified by a country among six of the Conventions relating to 'basic worker rights': Conventions 29 (Forced Labour), 87 (Freedom of Association and Protection of the Right to Organise), 98 (Right to Organise and Collective Bargaining), 105 (Abolition of Forced Labour), 111 (Discrimination) and 138 (Minimum Age). It ranges from 0 to 6.
- *CIVLIB, PRIGHTS.* These are the Freedom House (1994) indicators of civil liberties and political rights, respectively. While these deal with human and political rights that go considerably beyond labour standards, one expects that they would also capture workers' rights of organisation and self-expression. Indeed, the Freedom House checklist for civil liberties includes questions on the presence of free trade unions, effectiveness of collective bargaining and freedom from exploitation by employers. Unlike the previous two indicators, these are based mostly on actual practice rather than formal obligations: as Freedom House (1994, p. 673) puts it, '[we do] not mistake constitutional guarantees of human rights for those rights in practice'. *CIVLIB* and *PRIGHTS* are each measured on a scale of 1 to 7, with larger values indicating *fewer* rights.
- *DEMOC.* Since *CIVLIB* and *PRIGHTS* are highly correlated, it is convenient to combine the two into a synthetic indicator I call *DEMOC*, using a transformation due to Helliwell (1994): *DEMOC* = $(14 - (CIVLIB + PRIGHTS))/12$. *DEMOC* ranges from 0 to 1, with 1 indicating a full set of civil and political rights.
- *CHILD.* This is an indicator meant to capture the extent to which child-labour practices are condoned. It is coded with the help of a US Department of Labor survey[10] based in turn on US embassy and ILO reports. For each country, the survey indicates whether there are inadequacies either in 'legislation' or 'enforcement' relating to standards on child labour. Problems with legislation refer to lack of child labour legislation or provisions in the legislation that do not meet ILO

criteria. Problems in enforcement usually relate to lack of a sufficient number of inspectors to implement the child-labour legislation. I use the following score: a country receives 0 if no problems are reported on either score, 1 if there is a problem with either legislation or enforcement, and 2 if problems are reported on both scores.

- *HOURS*. This is the statutory hours of work in a normal working week, in manufacturing or construction (when no data on manufacturing is reported). It ranges from 40 to 48.
- *LEAVE* . Days of annual leave with pay in manufacturing. It ranges from 5 (El Salvador, Sudan, and Tunisia) to 38 (Finland).
- *UNION*. Percentage of the labour force that is unionised. It ranges from 1 per cent to over 100 per cent.

While all of these indicators have their problems, I have deliberately cast a wide net in the hope that collectively they may provide an accurate and useful picture. The detailed information on each country is reported in the appendix to Rodrik (1995a). In table 5.2, I provide the matrix of correlations between the indicators, as well as their correlations with *per capita* income (*GDPSH589*). The correlations are mostly in the expected direction. Hence, *DEMOC*, *TOTCONV*, *LEAVE*, and *UNION* are strongly positively correlated with *per capita* income, while *CHILD* is strongly negatively correlated with it. High labour standards in one dimension tend to go with high standards in other dimensions, although the correlations are not always very strong, pointing to the need to use a diverse set of indicators. There are a few counter-intuitive findings: for example, democracies seem to have longer working hours.

We now use the indicators discussed above to look for evidence that labour standards – or lack thereof – have consequences for trade and foreign investment patterns. I will focus on three questions in particular: (1) Do labour standards affect labour costs? (2) Do labour standards affect comparative advantage, and thereby trade flows? (3) Do labour standards affect foreign direct investment (FDI)?

Labour costs are determined first and foremost by productivity. To see whether labour standards make a difference as well, I regress annualised labour costs in dollars (*LABCOST*) on *per capita* income, to control for productivity[11] and on the indicators of labour standards for which there are enough observations. Table 5.3 reports the results. Unfortunately, the labour cost variable is available for less than 40 countries. Nonetheless, the results are interesting. Not surprisingly, *per capita* income is strongly correlated with labour costs. But so are some of the labour indicators. The coefficients on *BWRCONV* and *TOTCONV* are both positive and statistically significant, as is the coefficient on *DEMOC*. The

Table 5.2. *Correlation matrix*

	DEMOC	BWRCONV	TOTCONV	CHILD	HOURS	LEAVE	UNION	GDPSH589
DEMOC	1.00							
BWRCONV	0.22	1.00						
TOTCONV	0.40	0.65	1.00					
CHILD	-0.21	-0.07	-0.14	1.00				
HOURS	0.14	-0.18	0.17	0.12	1.00			
LEAVE	0.43	0.50	0.65	-0.37	-0.41	1.00		
UNION	0.28	0.33	0.31	-0.37	-0.19	0.47	1.00	
GDPSH589	0.67	0.12	0.39	-0.44	0.21	0.57	0.42	1.00

Table 5.3. *Labour standards and labour costs, 1985–8*

Independent variables	Dependent variable: *LABCOST* (annual labour cost in US dollars, 1985–8)				
	(1)	(2)	(3)	(4)	(5)
Constant	−4685 (3690)	1596 (4037)	3205 (3553)	−2830 (4691)	−1755 (4865)
GNPCAP85	2.203* (0.265)	1.450* (0.331)	1.545* (0.308)	1.351* (0.327)	1.470* (0.335)
BWRCONV	1707** (751.0)	2524* (784.5)		1736*** (889.0)	
TOTCONV			143.9* (3.720)		
CHILD			−8710* (2508)	−6240* (2272)	−6965* (2533)	−4849*** (2391)
DEMOC				9968*** (5813)	15836* (5197)
N	36	35	35	35	35
R^2	0.71	0.78	0.79	0.80	0.77

Notes: See pp. 133–4 for variable definitions. Standard errors are reported in parentheses:
*   significant at 1 per cent level
**   significant at 5 per cent level
***   significant at 10 per cent level.

coefficient on *CHILD* is negative and often statistically significant at the 1 per cent level. The small sample size notwithstanding – 35 or 36 countries, depending on the regression – these are fairly strong results, indicating that labour costs tend to increase as standards become more stringent.

Moreover, the estimated coefficients are large, implying that the economic magnitude of the effects are significant as well. For example, an increase of one step in our measure of child labour (going, say, from no child labour legislation to having such legislation) is associated with an increase in annual labour costs of $4,849–$8,710. These are very large numbers. Note, however, that child labour practices are likely to be correlated with other shortcomings in labour standards. Consequently, what the parameter estimates are probably giving us is an indication of the aggregate effect of all of these.

Next we turn to comparative advantage. As discussed previously, the impact of labour standards is likely to be felt most strongly on labour-intensive goods. Consequently, I use as my dependent variable a measure of comparative advantage in labour-intensive goods: the ratio of textile and clothing exports to other exports, excluding fuels (*TXTNTXT*). I use the following two controls for the natural determinants of comparative advantage: population:land ratio (*POPAREA85*), which is a proxy for the labour endowment of a country relative to its land endowment; and average years of schooling in the population aged over 25 (*HUMAN85*), which is a proxy for human capital.[12] The results indicate that these two variables are associated with comparative advantage in labour-intensive goods in the expected manner. The benchmark regression with just these two explanatory variables is shown in column (1) of table 5.4. The population:land ratio is positively associated with comparative advantage in textiles and clothing, and human capital is negatively associated with it. While both parameter estimates are statistically significant, the overall fit of the equation is not as good as in the case of labour costs.

The other columns in table 5.4 experiment with adding different combinations of labour standard indicators in the benchmark regression. With one exception, there are no statistically significant results. The exception is the regression including *HOURS*, which indicates that longer statutory hours is associated with a stronger comparative advantage in textiles and clothing. The signs on *DEMOC* and *UNION* are negative, but the parameter estimates are not statistically significant. The parameter estimate for *CHILD* is consistently positive, and at times borderline significant (at the 10 per cent level). Hence, while the pattern of signs is supportive of the hypothesis that low labour standards can help create comparative advantage in labour-intensive goods, the results are not very strong.

The sample of countries used for the regression in table 5.4 includes both rich and poor nations. To see whether the presence of rich countries plays a confounding role, I have repeated the exercise after removing from the sample high-income countries, defined as countries with Summers–Heston (1985) *per capita* GDP larger than $6,000. The results are reported in table 5.5. We note first that the fit of the benchmark equation is now much improved, although still not extraordinary. In addition, we find that *CHILD* is statistically significant (with a positive sign) in a couple of the regressions, along with *HOURS* as before. The signs on *DEMOC* and *UNION* are in the expected direction, although these variables are still not statistically significant. The restricted sample, therefore, provides somewhat stronger support for the idea that labour standards can influence comparative advantage.

The final set of empirical estimates focus on direct FDI, and these are shown in table 5.6. The dependent variable in these regressions is the value of investment during 1982–9 by majority-owned US affiliates

Table 5.4. *Labour standards and comparative advantage*

Independent variables	Dependent variable: *TXTNTXT* (ratio of textile and clothing exports to other exports, excluding fuels)						
	(1)	(2)	(3)	(4)	(5)	(6)	(7)
Constant	0.42* (0.11)	0.45** (0.20)	0.44** (0.12)	0.22*** (0.12)	−1.60** (0.80)	0.24 (0.17)	0.32** (0.13)
POPAREA85	1.13E-07** (4.50E-08)	1.12E-07**** (5.74E-08)	1.55E-07 (2.42E-07)	1.57E-07 (2.40E-07)	1.92E-07 (2.54E-07)	4.29E-07*** (2.42E-07)	1.09E-07 (2.36E-07)
HUMAN85	−0.04* (0.01)	−0.04* (0.02)	−0.03 (0.03)	−0.02*** (0.01)	−0.08** (0.04)	−0.02 (0.02)	−0.03** (0.01)
BWRCONV		−0.01 (0.05)					
TOTCONV		0.00 (0.00)					
DEMOC			−0.11 (0.25)				
CHILD				0.14 (0.09)	0.15 (0.10)	0.15 (0.11)	0.06 (0.07)
HOURS					0.04** (0.02)		
UNION						−0.16 (0.17)	
LEAVE							0.00 (0.00)
N	84	84	83	83	54	46	36
R^2	0.10	0.11	0.09	0.13	0.20	0.15	0.38

Notes: See pp. 133–4, 137 for variable definitions. Heteroskedasticity-consistent standard errors are reported in parentheses: *significant at 1 per cent level **significant at 5 per cent level *** significant at 10 per cent level.

Table 5.5. *Labour standards and comparative advantage, excluding high-income countries*

Independent variables	Dependent variable: TXTNTXT (ratio of textile and clothing exports to other exports, excluding fuels)						
	(1)	(2)	(3)	(4)	(5)	(6)	(7)
Constant	0.42* (0.11)	0.44*** (0.24)	0.47* (0.12)	0.19 (0.15)	-1.81** (0.73)	0.28 (0.27)	0.38 (0.23)
POPAREA85	1.43E-06** (4.50E-08)	1.54E-06** (5.74E-08)	1.54E-06* (2.42E-07)	1.50E-06* (2.40E-07)	1.57E-06** (2.54E-07)	7.92E-07 (2.42E-07)	1.50E-06** (2.36E-07)
HUMAN85	-0.07** (0.03)	-0.09** (0.03)	-0.05 (0.04)	-0.06** (0.03)	-0.10* (0.03)	-0.04 (0.05)	-0.10* (0.03)
BWRCONV		-0.03 (0.07)					
TOTCONV		0.00 (0.00)					
DEMOC			-0.30 (0.30)				
CHILD				0.18*** (0.10)	0.14 (0.10)	0.18 (0.14)	0.15** (0.07)
HOURS					0.05* (0.02)		
UNION						-0.44 (0.47)	
LEAVE							0.00 (0.00)
N	56	56	56	56	49	30	17
R^2	0.22	0.25	0.24	0.28	0.36	0.10	0.62

Notes: See pp. 133–4, 137 for variable definitions. Heteroskedasticity-consistent standard errors are reported in parentheses: *significant at 1 per cent level **significant at 5 per cent level ***significant at 10 per cent level.

Table 5.6. *Labour standards and foreign investment, 1982–9*

Independent variables	Dependent variable: Manufacturing FDI by US majority-owned foreign affiliates, 1982–9 (divided by the stock of FDI at year-end 1982)			
	(1)	(2)	(3)	(4)
Constant	0.03 (0.32)	−0.26 (0.62)	−1.46** (0.69)	0.19 (0.29)
BMP6L	−0.93** (0.42)	−0.73 (0.45)	−0.16 (0.51)	−0.31 (0.49)
POP89	−3.00E-09* (5.58E-10)	−3.05E-09* (6.37E-10)	−3.08E-09* (5.76-10)	−2.88E-09* (5.23E-10)
GROWTH82–89	38.05* (10.43)	40.64* (11.51)	46.76* (11.35)	40.18* (10.53)
BWRCONV		−0.01 (0.14)		
TOTCONV		0.00 (0.01)		
DEMOC			1.44** (0.57)	
CHILD				−0.43** (0.20)
N	40	40	39	39
Adj. R^2	0.53	0.51	0.57	0.55

Notes: See pp. 133–4, 140 for variable definitions. Heteroskedasticity-consistent standard errors are reported in parentheses:
*   significant at 1 per cent level
**   significant at 5 per cent level
*** significant at 10 per cent level.

abroad, normalised by the stock of such investment in the relevant countries at year-end 1982. I have selected the period 1982–9 for analysis because the last two available benchmark surveys undertaken by the US Department of Commerce are those for 1982 and 1989. Since the theory of FDI is nowhere as complete as that for comparative advantage, we do not have a good empirical model to use as a reference. Therefore the benchmark regression, shown in column (1) of table 5.6, takes an eclectic approach and includes the following three explanatory variables: the black market premium for foreign currency (*BMP6L*) as a proxy for policy distortions, population (*POP89*), and income growth in host country (*GROWTH82–89*).[13] With the exception of population, there is a reasonable *a priori* prediction regarding the sign on these variables, and the expectations are borne out. Countries with low black-market premia and high growth receive more FDI.

As in the previous set of regressions, the other columns in table 5.6 report the results when the labour standard indicators are introduced. In this case, we find statistically significant relationships for *DEMOC* and *CHILD*. But these go in opposite directions from what one might have predicted. Countries with a lower democracy score and a higher *CHILD* score have received *less* foreign investment during 1982–9 than would have been predicted on the basis of other country characteristics. Taken at face value, these results indicate that low labour standards may be a hindrance, rather than an attraction, for foreign investors. One can speculate about the reasons for this finding. In particular, it is possible that *DEMOC* and *CHILD* are proxying for omitted country character-istics, leading to omitted-variable bias. Nonetheless, it is interesting that the conventional wisdom about low-standard countries being a haven for foreign investors is far from being borne out.

We conclude that labour standards do exert a statistically and economically significant effect on labour cost differentials across coun-tries. Low labour standards tend to increase the comparative advantage of *domestic* firms in labour-intensive manufactures. However, their effect on inward foreign investment is, if anything, negative. In view of the weakness of the data on labour standards and the difficulties involved in quantifying differences across countries on such a complex set of issues, I find the results overall suggestive. Indeed, I am rather surprised to have found any statistical regularities at all.[14]

6   Trade, external risk and the role of government

Openness to foreign trade exposes society, and labour in particular, to shocks of external origin. The post-war bargain on multilateralism was contingent on, and sustained by, a commitment on the part of national governments to shelter and insulate labour from the vicissitudes of global markets. Strong, stabilising governments at home were the domestic counterpart of the global expansion of free trade. However, globalisation and 'deep' integration are rendering this post-war bargain unsustainable. Governments are losing their ability to perform the sheltering function because globalisation undercuts the effectiveness of government policies. In addition, since internationally mobile groups can evade taxation, the revenue base of national governments has been collapsing. All this at a time when the legitimacy of government is at a low ebb in many advanced industrial countries. These trends expose groups that are not internationally mobile – low-skilled labour all the way through middle management – to risks that they have not had to face until recently.

The ideas expressed in the preceding paragraph are not meant to be self-evident to economists. In particular, the notion that governments have traditionally used their powers to insulate domestic groups from external risk requires some explaining and substantiation. I will offer here one very concrete piece of evidence in favour of this idea: contrary to what most economists would predict, *more open economies have had bigger governments*. This correlation turns out to be statistically very strong and quite robust. It is insensitive to the inclusion of a wide range of control variables; it holds for all available measures of government size; and it exists for low- as well as high-income countries. I have discussed the evidence relating to measures of government spending in two other papers (Rodrik, 1995b, 1996), to which the reader is referred for more details. Here I will provide a brief overview, as well as some new evidence on government *employment*.

In a paper published in 1978 and which is well known in political science (but not in economics), David Cameron (1978) showed that the best single predictor of the increase in an OECD government's size between 1960 and 1975 was the economy's openness in 1960, with a correlation coefficient of 0.78. Cameron proxied the size of the public sector by the share of government revenue in GDP and openness by the share of trade (exports *plus* imports) in GDP. In interpreting this finding, Cameron argued that more open economies have higher rates of industrial concentration, which tends to foster higher unionisation, greater scope for collective bargaining, and stronger labour confederations. These in turn result in larger demands for government transfers – social security, pensions, unemployment insurance, job training, etc. – which mitigate external risk.

Cameron's study was limited to 18 OECD countries, and the small sample raises doubts both about the generality of the finding and the interpretation. For example, it is impossible to distinguish Cameron's hypothesis from one that relates the scope of government to a third variable, country size. Small countries like the Netherlands, Norway and Belgium trade more and tend to have larger governments. It turns out, however, that the correlation exists also in a much larger sample of countries and that it survives the inclusion of control variables such as country size, level of income and other determinants of government size. Of course, Cameron's specific arguments are unlikely to be relevant to a 100-plus country sample. In particular, it is not plausible to attach such importance to the role of labour organisations in most developing countries. And in any case, it turns out that the empirical relationship between openness and government spending holds at the level of government *consumption* as well (and not just for transfers). But the evidence is consistent with the central idea that public expenditures and employment are a risk-reducing instrument on which there has been greater reliance in more open economies.

Table 5.7 summarises the evidence. Three different measures of government size are used as the dependent variable in these regressions: (1) government expenditures, net of interest payments (per centage of GDP); (2) government consumption (percentage of GDP); and (3) government employment (percentage of workforce). The sources for these variables are the World Bank's *World Data 1995*, Penn World Tables (5.6a), and the World Bank Labor Market Data Base, respectively. In addition to variables relating to openness and external risk, all regressions contain the following three independent variables, dated according to the dependent variable: (1) *per capita* GDP; (2) dependency ratio in the population; and (3) urbanisation rate. A set of country grouping and region dummies were also used in each regression, but only those that were significant at the 10 per cent level or better were selected for the final run. A large range of additional variables were tried on the right-hand side (including measures of country size), but they did not affect the results and are not shown here (see Rodrik 1995b, 1996).

For each regression, two versions are shown. The first version includes a measure of openness to trade averaged over the 1970–9 or 1975–84 decades (*OPENAVG7079* or *OPENAVG7584*). This measure is the sum of exports and imports (as a share of GDP). The second version includes in addition a measure of terms of trade volatility (*TOTDLOGSTD*), both on its own and interacted with openness. *TOTDLOGSTD* is calculated by taking the standard deviation of the first differences (in logs) of the terms of trade for each included country over the period 1971–90. Note that openness multiplied by this measure of terms of trade volatility gives us a theoretically appropriate measure of *external risk*.[13]

The results show that openness and external risk have been significant determinants of the size of government expenditure and employment. When openness is entered on its own, it always has a positive sign, and in all but one of the regressions its estimated coefficient is significant at the 1 per cent or 5 per cent level. That this relationship between openness and size of government is mediated through external risk is strongly suggested by the regressions in which openness is interacted with terms of trade volatility. When the interaction term is included, the coefficient on openness turns either insignificant or becomes *negative*. The interaction term itself enters always positively and is significant at the 1 per cent level in two out of the four regressions in which it is included. Figure 5.3

Table 5.7. Openness and size of government, 1985–92

Independent variables	Government spending excluding interest exp., 1990–2 (% of GDP)		Government consumption 1985–9 (% of GDP)		General government employment, c.1980 (% of labour force)			
Constant	−1.693*	−1.556*	2.626*	2.939*	−4.510*	−3.901*	−4.364*	−3.692*
GDP/cap.	1.48E-05	6.23E-06	−2.45E-05***	−1.55E-05	6.92E-05**	6.02E-05***	9.14E-05**	6.51E-05**
Dependency ratio	−0.243	−0.292	0.769*	0.835*	1.324***	0.932	1.416**	0.918
Urbanisation	0.001	0.004	−0.004***	−0.004***	0.011**	0.012**	0.007	0.010**
LAAM	−0.455*	−0.421*	−0.229**	−0.177***				
ASIAE	−0.336**	−0.285**	−0.347*	−0.332*				
SAFRICA			−0.168***	−0.147	−0.629*	−0.656*	−0.658*	−0.711*
OPENAVG7079	0.006*		0.002*		0.004**		0.002	
OPENAVG7584		0.004		−0.004***		−0.003		−0.007**
TOTDLOGSTD		−1.951		−3.234*		−2.958		−3.656**
OPENAVG7079 × TOTDLOGSTD		0.016		0.051*		0.070		0.097*
OPENAVG7584 × TOTDLOGSTD								0.097*
N	72	64	125	109	56	51	57	52
Adj/ R^2	0.56	0.57	0.43	0.46	0.72	0.74	0.70	0.75

Notes: See text for explanation   **significant at 5 per cent level   *** significant at 10 per cent level.
*significant at 1 per cent level

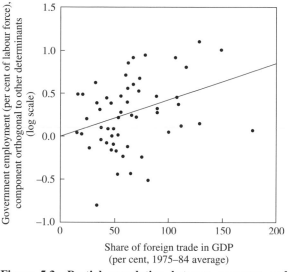

Figure 5.3   Partial correlation between openness and share of workforce in government employment

provides a graphical perspective on these results, also showing that these findings are not generated by the presence of outliers.

Among our three measures of government, the measure with which external risk is most strongly and robustly associated turns out to be government *consumption* (Rodrik, 1996). This may well be due to the superiority of the Penn World Tables as a data source: government consumption data are available for a larger sample of countries, and they are in principle free of problems having to do with purchasing-power differentials.

I interpret these results as follows. More open economies have greater exposure to the risks emanating from turbulence in world markets. We can view larger government spending in such economies as performing an insulation function, insofar as the government sector is the 'safe' sector (in terms of employment and purchases from the rest of the economy) relative to other activities and especially compared to tradables. Hence in countries significantly affected by external shocks the government can mitigate risk by taking command of a larger share of the economy's resources.[16]

In principle, external risk should be diversifiable for small countries through participation in international capital markets. In practice, this does not prove possible, either because full capital market openness conflicts with other objectives of government policy or because incentive and sovereign-risk problems restrict the range and extent of financial instruments available to countries. One might also object that the government's risk-reducing role could be best played through the establishment of a safety net, in which case it would show up only in government spending on social security and welfare, and not at all in government *consumption*. However, social security systems are difficult to set up even in the most advanced countries, and it stands to reason that the developing countries which predominate in our cross-section would rely on a broader set of instrumentalities to achieve risk reduction.

The idea that greater openness to foreign trade increases the risk to which residents are exposed also deserves comment. It is generally not the case that the world economy as a whole is more volatile than the economy of any single country. In fact, we would expect the world market to be less risky than any of its constituent parts. But note that openness to trade generally implies *specialisation* in production through the forces of comparative advantage. Hence, all else being equal, we would expect the production structure to be less diversified in more open economies. And in an economy that cannot purchase insurance from the rest of the world, what matters is not the stability of the world economy as a whole, but the stability of the stream of earnings from *domestic* production. Consequently, it is not implausible that greater openness translates into greater risk for domestic residents.

If, as argued here, societies have traditionally demanded a greater government role in exchange for accepting larger doses of external risk, globalisation now presents a dilemma. Either governments have to continue to be responsive to the need to provide some degree of shelter from uncertainties arising from global markets, or societies must learn to live unprotected from the risks of a global market. On current trends, the safe bet would have to be the latter of these options. The burden will be naturally greater for groups that have the least ability to diversify internationally and take advantage of cross-border opportunities. Labour, and low-skilled labour in particular, is likely to be a loser on both accounts.

7   Conclusions

I have discussed here a number of reasons why labour regards globalisation with a suspicious eye: a generalised increase in the elasticity of labour demand; a collapse of the implicit bargain between labour and employers; the downward pressure placed on labour standards in advanced industrial countries; and the abdication by governments of their traditional role of providing shelter against external risk. These go considerably beyond the question of whether recent trends in international trade have reduced the relative demand for low-skilled workers, this being the question on which the economics literature has overwhelmingly focused. Whatever the answer may be to the last question, the issues raised in this chapter are of a more permanent nature, and in the long run their cumulative effects are likely to be much more serious.

The standard reaction to these concerns is to stress the role of education and training. The more flexible, skilled, and differentiated workers in the advanced countries become, the more they too can take advantage of the opportunities that globalisation brings. This is true enough. On the other hand, who is to mobilise and deploy the resources needed for education and training if not governments themselves? And can these governments pull this off in an environment in which their resources are restricted by the unwillingness of internationally mobile groups to pay for the necessary programmes?[17] The answers are not self-evident.

NOTES

I thank Martin Rama for making data from the World Bank Labor Market Database available, and André Sapir and Alasdair Smith for helpful comments.

1 These issues are discussed at greater length in Rodrik (1998).
2 The terms are due to Robert Lawrence (see Lawrence, 1998).
3 Wood (1994) constitutes a significant exception. By making a number of adjustments to the data – increasing the unskilled labour content of displaced production, incorporating induced technological change, etc. – Wood concludes that a much larger share of the increased inequality can be attributed to trade.
4 Leamer (1995) has stressed the point that a key aspect of the open economy is that the demand for domestic labour becomes infinitely elastic (assuming the economy is small) over the range of labour demand for which the economy is in the diversification cone. However, his empirical analysis focuses on the implications of a shift in the location of the demand curve, rather than of an increase in the elasticity of demand.
5 Borjas and Ramey (1994, 1995) are two significant exceptions.
6 If workers are risk-neutral instead ($u'' = 0$), we would have $dw/d\pi^* = 0$.
7 This section and the next rely heavily on a previous paper (Rodrik, 1995a).
8 The information in this paragraph is obtained from International Labour Office, *Lists of Ratification by Convention and by Country*, Report III (part 5) (Geneva, 1994).
9 Unless otherwise specified, all labour market data come from the World Bank Labor Market Data base. I thank Martin Rama for making these data available. Other sources of data are Barro and Lee (1994); UNCTAD, *Handbook of International Trade and Development Statistics*; Penn World Tables (5.6a); and World Bank, *World Data 1995*.
10 United States Department of Labour, *Foreign Labour Trends: International*

Child Labor Problems (Washington, DC: Bureau of International Labor Affairs, 1992).

11 I also included an educational variable to control for the skill level of the workforce, but it turned out that this variable was insignificant when *per capita* GNP was included. Using GNP per worker instead of GNP *per capita* in these regressions made no difference to the results.

12 The use of these proxies for relative factor endowments is inspired by Berge and Wood (1994).

13 I thank James Hines for helpful discussions on the FDI data. The benchmark specification here is influenced by Hines (1995).

14 The only other empirical study on the trade consequences of labour standards that I am aware of is the study by the OECD (1996). This study focuses on violations of ILO Conventions 87 and 88 (relating to trade unions and collective bargaining). It finds no effects on trade flows.

15 To see this, let x, m, and y stand for volumes of exports, imports and GDP, respectively. Let p be the price of exports relative to imports (the terms of trade). Let the (log) of the terms of trade follow a random walk, possibly with drift (a hypothesis which cannot be rejected for most countries). The unanticipated component of the income effects of the terms of trade shock can then be expressed as a per centage of GDP as $\frac{1}{2}[(x+m)/y][d\log p - \alpha]$, where α is the trend growth rate of the terms of trade. The standard deviation of this is $\frac{1}{2}[(x+m)/y]$ st.dev.$(d\log p)$, which is one-half times our interaction variable.

16 In Rodrik (1996) I list alternative explanations for the empirical association between openness and government, and show that they can all be rejected.

17 See Rodrik (1997) for evidence that the tax burden in the OECD countries has shifted from capital towards labour as openness has increased.

REFERENCES

Barro, R. and Lee, J.W., 1994. 'Data Set for a Panel of 138 Countries', Harvard University, mimeo

Berge, K., and Wood, A., 1994. 'Exporting Manufactures: Trade Policy or Human Resources?', *IDS Working Paper*, **4**, Institute of Development Studies, University of Sussex

Blanchflower, D. G., Oswald, A.J. and Sanfey, P., 1996. 'Wages, Profits, and Rent-Sharing', *Quarterly Journal of Economics*, **111**, 227–52.

Borjas, G., and Ramey, V., 1994. 'The Relationship between Wage Inequality and International Trade', in J. Bergstrand *et al.* (eds.), *The Changing Distribution of Income in an Open US Economy* (Amsterdam: North-Holland)

     1995. 'Foreign Competition, Market Power, and Wage Inequality', *Quarterly Journal of Economics*, **110**, 1075–1110

Borjas, G., Freeman, R. and Katz, L., 1992. 'On the Labour Market Effects of Immigration and Trade', in G. Borjas and R. Freeman (eds.), *Immigration and the Work Force* (Chicago: University of Chicago Press)

Brown, D., Deardorff, A. and Stern,R., 1996. 'International Labour Standards and International Trade: A Theoretical Analysis', in J.N. Bhagwati and R.E.

Hudec (eds.), *Fair Trade and Harmonization: Prerequisites for Free Trade?* (Cambridge, MA: MIT Press)

Cameron, D., 1978. 'The Expansion of the Public Economy', *American Political Science Review*, **72**

Cline, W.R., 1998. 'Trade and Wage Inequality' (Washington, DC: Institute for International Economics)

Freedom House, 1994. *Freedom in the World: The Annual Survey of Political Rights and Civil Liberties 1993–1994* (New York: Freedom House)

Freeman, R., 1994. 'A Hard-Headed Look at Labour Standards', in W. Sengenberger and D. Campbell (eds.), *International Labour Standards and Economic Interdependence* (Geneva: International Institute for Labour Studies)

1996. 'Will Globalisation Dominate US Labour Market Outcomes?' paper prepared for the Brookings Conference on 'Imports, Exports, and the American Worker' (January)

Gottschalk, P. and Moffitt, R., 1994. 'The Growth of Earnings Instability in the US Labour Market', *Brookings Papers on Economic Activity*, **2**, 217–54

Helliwell, J., 1994. 'Empirical Linkages Between Democracy and Economic Growth', *British Journal of Political Science*, **24**, 225–48

Hines, J., 1995. 'Forbidden Payment: Foreign Bribery and American Business After 1977', Harvard University (September), mimeo

Katz, L.F. and Summers, L.H., 1989. 'Industry Rents: Evidence and Implications', *Brookings Papers on Economic Activity (Microeconomics)*, 209 75

Lawrence, R., 1998. *Regionalism, Multilateralism, and Deeper Integration* (Washington, DC: Brookings)

Lawrence, R. and Slaughter, M., 1993. 'Trade and US Wages in the 1980s: Giant Sucking Sound or Small Hiccup?', *Brookings Papers on Economic Activity (Microeconomics)*, 161–210

Leamer, E., 1995. 'In Search of Stolper–Samuelson Effects on US Wages', paper prepared for the Brookings Conference on 'Imports, Exports, and the American Worker' (January)

OECD, 1996. *Trade and Labour Standards* (Paris: OECD) (April)

Richardson, J.D., 1995. 'Income Inequality and Trade: How to Think and What to Conclude', *Journal of Economic Perspectives* (Summer)

Rodrik, D., 1995a. 'Labour Standards in International Trade: Do They Matter and What Do We Do About Them?', Columbia University (December), mimeo

1995b. 'International Trade and Big Government', Columbia University, mimeo

1996. 'Why Do More Open Economies Have Bigger Governments?', *NBER Discussion Paper*

1998. *Has International Economic Integration Gone Too Far?* (Washington, DC: Institute for International Economics)

Sachs, J. and Shatz, H., 1994. 'Trade and Jobs in US Manufacturing', *Brookings Papers on Economic Activity*, **1**

Wood, A., 1994. *North–South Trade, Employment and Inequality: Changing Fortunes in a Skill-Driven World* (Oxford: Clarendon Press); see also chapter 6 in this volume
   1995. 'How Trade Hurt Unskilled Workers', *Journal of Economic Perspectives*, **9/3**, 57–80

Discussion

ALASDAIR SMITH

In his wide-ranging and characteristically thought-provoking chapter 5, Dani Rodrik tackles several aspects of the controversial relationship between global integration and inequality.

Many trade economists argue that trade has a small effect on income distribution, and Dani Rodrik opens with the observation that this implies a belief that trade has a small effect on welfare. Now income distribution and welfare are not the same, but it is true that in the standard models in which comparative advantage derives from the factor endowments of countries and the factor intensities of products, large differences in factor endowments between countries and in factor intensities between products imply that trade will cause large changes both in welfare and in income distribution. More briefly, with given factor endowments, changes in real national income will be associated with changes in the distribution of that income.

However, the loaded phrase 'saying that in practice the gains from trade amount to little more than peanuts' implies that economists characteristically argue that the gains from trade are large. In fact, it is the long-standing conventional wisdom in the welfare economics of trade that in the standard trade model, the gains from trade are indeed small, whether represented by triangles in partial equilibrium models or the curvature of transformation surfaces in general equilibrium models. Most economists would look to the effects of trade on competition, on product variety, on rent-seeking and on innovation for the large gains from trade and a belief that such effects are large is not inconsistent with a belief that the conventional gains from trade and the effects of trade on income distribution are both small. The charge of inconsistency is not proved though, of course, it is possible to be consistent and wrong.

The first substantial part of the chapter looks at ways that trade might affect income distribution through its effect on the elasticity of demand for labour. The intuitive idea, which is appealing, is that the increased substitutability of foreign for domestic labour through trade, migration and capital mobility makes the demand curve for labour more elastic. (The simplest version of the proposition that the labour demand curve in an open economy is elastic is in the standard textbook small open unspecialised economy, where all factors of production have horizontal demand curves.)

Figure 5.1 shows that a comparable labour productivity shock has a larger effect on wages and employment in an open than a closed economy. This is perhaps a slightly artificial example: the exposure of an open economy to a different range of shocks than a closed economy is likely to be at least as relevant as the differential response to comparable shocks.

In any case, the formal argument is as applicable to labour as to any other factor, and needs elaboration if it is to support the proposition that globalisation has had more impact on income from labour than from capital, or income from unskilled labour than from skilled labour. As the chapter makes clear, what actually follows from figure 5.1 is the proposition that globalisation may make labour incomes more volatile, and volatility is not the same as inequality. Indeed it is not clear how one should think about the observation that 'fully one-third of the widening of the earnings distribution has resulted from an increase in the instability of earnings'. Is instability causing inequality; or only causing a mis-measurement of life-cycle inequality? Ultimately, the view one takes on this should depend on the extent to which workers have access to capital markets.

The model to which Dani Rodrik turns in section 3 gets away from the standard competitive model of the trade textbooks to a bargaining model which seems more successful as a way of modelling the intuitive idea that international competition weakens the position of workers.

The link with the debate about labour standards is made in section 4. The popular argument is that high labour standards damage 'competitiveness'; the economists' response is that high labour standards are just one element of the payment of labour and if workers demand a high non-cash element in their pay, they will have to accept a lower real value of their cash wage through wage cuts or currency depreciation if they are to maintain 'competitiveness' and employment. The model of section 4 shows that if we model labour standards as a tax on employment, then the incidence of the tax depends on the elasticity of demand for labour – globalisation increases the wage-depressing effect of labour standards. However, modelling labour standards as a wedge between the cost to employers and the benefit to employees is appropriate only if workers attach no value to higher labour standards. Such 'standards' are simply wasteful. If globalisation increases resistance to forms of labour market regulation that are of value neither to employers or employees, so much the better for globalisation!

Dani Rodrik says that there can be no absolute bar to legitimate interest in the labour standards of foreigners. That is indeed true, but there are two good reasons to minimise the internationalisation of labour standards (or, indeed, other kinds of social policy, and many aspects of environmental policy). The first is that there is a presumption that local communities are the best judges of their own interests. The other side of the world is not the best vantage point from which to decide whether excluding children from factories will send them to school or on to the streets. And to argue that we have a legitimate interest in the social policy of foreigners is to give them a legitimate interest in our policy. I would prefer the UK government to abstain from encouraging equality of opportunity in Saudi Arabia than to give the Saudi government any say in the employment prospects of my daughters. Secondly, we all know that many expressed concerns about foreign standards are in reality the cloaks of expressions of the self-interest of particular groups of workers in rich countries. Opening up new channels for such interventions in policy-making is not a good idea.

The empirical results on the international relationships between labour standards and trade are suggestive. High standards on child labour seem to raise labour costs even controlling for national income and to influence the pattern of comparative advantage even controlling for other likely influences on comparative advantage. But the results of this kind of exercise are so likely to be affected by measurement error and by excluded variables that the results can be no more than suggestive.

By contrast, the results of the final section 6, indicating that more open economies tend to have larger governments, are argued to be quite robust. They provide a useful counterpoint to the standard argument that globalisation limits the tax-raising power of governments and therefore tends to reduce the size of government.

In short, Dani Rodrik shows us here that, in spite of all that has been written in recent years about globalisation and policy, there is still much of interest to be said.

6 Openness and wage inequality in developing countries: the Latin American challenge to East Asian conventional wisdom

ADRIAN WOOD

Greater openness to trade in developing countries is conventionally argued to be doubly blessed. It not only increases efficiency, but also reduces inequality, by boosting the relative demand for unskilled workers and hence narrowing the gap in wages (and in unemployment rates) between them and skilled workers. However, this optimistic view has been challenged by the experience of Latin America since the mid-1980s, where greater openness to trade has been accompanied by rising rather than falling wage inequality.[1]

This chapter is a response to that challenge. Section 1 outlines the theory underlying the conventional wisdom; section 2 provides an overview of the empirical evidence, both in favour of and against it. Sections 3 and 4 attempt to resolve the conflict of evidence, the first in terms of differences between East Asia and Latin America, the second in terms of differences between the 1960s and the 1980s. Section 5 sums up.

1 Heckscher–Ohlin theory

The belief that increased openness reduces wage inequality in developing countries rests on an apparently unchallengeable fact – that the supply of unskilled labour, relative to skilled labour, is larger in developing than in developed countries (Wood, 1994, table 3.1) – and on an often challenged but widely used theory of trade, that of Heckscher and Ohlin (hereafter H–O).

1.1 The simplest model

H–O theory asserts that countries export goods which use intensively those factors of production with which they are relatively abundantly endowed, and import goods which use intensively factors which are

153

relatively scarce at home. Trade thus increases demand for abundant factors, because of the expansion of export sectors, and reduces demand for scarce factors, because of the contraction of import-competing sectors, with corresponding effects on factor prices. In developing countries, where unskilled labour is abundant and skilled labour is scarce, trade tends to raise unskilled wages and lower skilled wages, and hence to narrow the gap between them.

To explain the effect on relative wages more precisely, consider a simple model with two countries (developed and developing), two factors (skilled and unskilled labour), and two goods (skill-intensive machinery and labour-intensive clothing). The developing country has a relatively large supply of unskilled labour, giving it a comparative advantage in clothing, while the developed country's relatively large supply of skilled labour gives it a comparative advantage in machinery.

Barriers to trade (transport costs and tariffs, for example) drive wedges between the prices of goods in the two countries, and may even result in no trade – or 'autarky'. In particular, they keep the price of clothing lower in the developing country than in the developed country, and vice versa for machinery. A reduction in barriers, and the resulting expansion of trade, would thus raise the price of clothing in the developing country and lower the price of machinery.

Such a change in relative domestic producer prices would raise the wage of unskilled, relative to skilled, workers. This linkage, known as the Stolper–Samuelson theorem, exists because H–O theory assumes technology (i.e. the production function for each good) to be given. In other words, it assumes a fixed functional relationship between outputs of goods and inputs of factors, which (with no excess profits) implies a similarly fixed relationship between the prices of goods and the wages of factors.

The outcome can be illustrated in a type of supply and demand curve diagram adapted from Leamer (1995). In figure 6.1, the vertical axis measures the unskilled wage, relative to the skilled wage, while the horizontal axis measures the number of unskilled workers, relative to the number of skilled workers. The downward-sloping line, dd, is the demand curve for unskilled labour that would prevail in a state of autarky. In the absence of trade, wages would be determined by the intersection of this demand curve with a supply curve (assumed for simplicity to be completely inelastic), whose position depends on the country's endowments of skilled and unskilled labour. With supply S_2, say, as in a country with many unskilled workers, the relative wage of unskilled labour would be at the low level, w_0.

The demand curve in a country open to trade is the line DD. It crosses

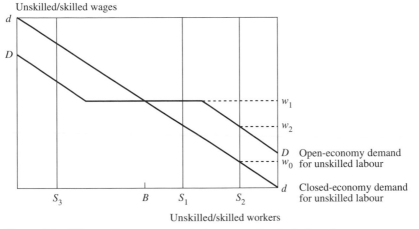

Unskilled/skilled wages

d

D

w_1

w_2

D Open-economy demand
w_0 for unskilled labour

d Closed-economy demand
for unskilled labour

S_3 B S_1 S_2

Unskilled/skilled workers

Figure 6.1   Effects of openness on relative wages: two traded goods

dd at point B on the horizontal axis: if it had this skill–supply ratio, even an open country would not trade. The developing country, with a relatively large supply of unskilled labour, and hence a net exporter of clothing, must lie to the right of B (and the developed country to the left of B). So for a developing country, opening to trade shifts the demand curve in favour of unskilled labour (DD lies above dd), and narrows the gap in wages. With skill–supply ratio S_2, the relative wage of unskilled labour would rise from w_0 to w_2.

The open-economy demand curve DD is an odd shape, with two downward-sloping segments separated by a flat segment in the middle: even to the right of B, in the developing-country range, there are two distinct segments. The flat segment covers the range of skill supplies in which a trading economy would be 'diversified', in the sense of continuing to produce both clothing and machinery (albeit in different proportions than under autarky), as for example in a developing country with skill supply S_1. But a country with a high proportion of unskilled workers, as at S_2, would produce no machinery, and specialise in clothing (a country with very few unskilled workers, as at S_3, would specialise in machinery). Such specialisation puts a country on a segment of the demand curve which slopes downwards because increases in the relative supply of unskilled labour have to be absorbed by relative wage-induced changes in the technique chosen to produce the single good.

Trade raises the relative wage of unskilled workers, whether the outcome is diversified or specialised. But the effects on wages of subsequent changes in domestic relative labour supplies differ. In a diversified country (as at S_1), relative wages are fixed by relative world prices, at the level w_1. Changes in domestic labour supply, unless they are big enough to affect world prices, do not change relative wages: they alter only the composition of output and trade. By contrast, in a specialised country, on a downward-sloping segment of *DD*, as at S_2, changes in domestic labour supply do affect relative wages. For instance, an increase in the relative number of skilled workers would raise the relative wage of unskilled labour.

1.2   More goods, countries and factors

This model can be extended to include many goods (differentiated by skill intensity), and many countries (differentiated by relative skill supplies), without fundamentally altering the conventional theoretical story about the beneficial effect of reduction of trade barriers on the relative wages of unskilled workers in developing countries. However, inclusion of non-traded goods and additional factors can in special cases yield contrary results.

Consider first a rise in the number of traded goods. Figure 6.2 is drawn on the same principles as figure 6.1, but with six rather than two goods (and at least six countries). The open-economy demand curve, *DD*, instead of having one flat segment, has five, which alternate with downward-sloping segments. Countries whose relative skill supplies put them on a flat segment produce two of the goods, adjacent in skill intensity, while those on a downward-sloping segment produce only one good.[2] All countries are specialised, since none produces all of the goods, but in those which produce two goods, as in a fully diversified country, relative wages are not altered by small changes in labour supplies. However, larger changes in labour supplies do alter relative wages, by moving the country to a different segment of *DD*.

The effects of trade on relative wages remain the same as in figure 6.1. In developing countries, to the right of *B*, reduction of trade barriers shifts demand in favour of unskilled labour, and narrows the skill differential in wages. The impact on wages is bigger, the larger the relative supply of unskilled labour in the country concerned (i.e. the further it lies to the right). For countries with middling skill supplies, in the vicinity of *B*, the effect of trade on wages is smaller – and could go either way. This is because trade causes contraction of both their most and their least skill-intensive sectors: such countries export goods of middling skill intensity, and import goods of high and low skill intensity from countries with higher and lower relative supplies of skilled labour.

In reality, there is a very large number of traded goods of differing skill

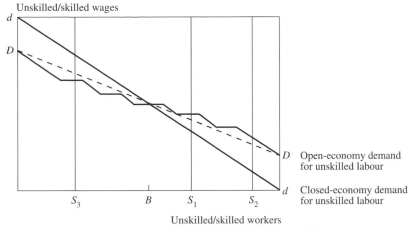

Figure 6.2   **Effects of openness on relative wages: many traded goods**

intensity. It is thus reasonable, as well as convenient, to approximate DD by a continuous line (shown with dashes in figure 6.2).[3] This formulation emphasises two important points: first, that in an open economy the demand curve is more elastic than in a closed economy, so that changes in factor supplies have *smaller* effects on relative wages; but second, and contrary to the impression given by the two-good model in figure 6.1, that even in an open economy, changes in factor supplies are in general likely to have *some* effect on relative wages.

Realism also requires inclusion of non-traded goods in the model (with the low ratios of trade to output in many 'open' economies as a reminder that transport costs are often more important barriers to trade than tariffs and quotas). Non-traded goods do not necessarily alter the conventional story about the effects of greater openness on relative wages, but they do create the possibility of 'perverse' outcomes, arising from particular patterns of substitution in consumption between traded and non-traded goods.[4] Consider, for example, an unskilled labour-abundant country in which labour-intensive non-traded goods are close substitutes for the more skill-intensive of two traded goods. Greater openness reduces the price of this traded good, inducing consumers to buy more of it, and less of the non-traded goods. The resulting drop in demand for unskilled labour in the non-traded sector might more than offset the rise in demand in the traded sector, leading to a fall rather than a rise in the relative wage of unskilled workers.

'Perverse' outcomes are also possible (though by no means inevitable) when the model is extended to include more factors than skilled and unskilled labour. Consider, for example, a third factor, infrastructure, which was a complement to skilled labour in production. There might in principle be a country with a low ratio of skilled to unskilled labour, but a large supply of infrastructure, and hence a comparative advantage in infrastructure-intensive traded goods. In such a country, greater openness to trade would increase the output of infrastructure-intensive goods, which also require a high ratio of skilled to unskilled labour, and could thus raise the demand for (and the wages of) skilled relative to unskilled workers.

2   Overview of empirical evidence

This section summarises the factor-content of trade and time-series studies which support the conventional wisdom about the effects of greater openness on relative wages in developing countries.[5] It also summarises the recent time-series studies which challenge this conventional wisdom. The conflict of evidence thereby exposed provides the focus for the rest of the chapter.

2.1   Factor-content of trade studies

Studies of this type calculate the amounts of skilled and unskilled labour used to produce a country's exports, and compare these with the amounts of skilled and unskilled labour that would be required to produce domestically the goods that it imports. If the ratio of skilled to unskilled labour is lower for exports than for imports, then increased openness to trade – more exports, more imports and less import-competing production – should raise the relative demand for (and so the relative wages of) unskilled workers.[6]

Table 6.1 encapsulates the relevant results from the classic study by Krueger et al. (1981), which calculated the factor content of trade in broadly defined manufactures in a range of developing countries in the early 1970s. Each number is the ratio of the average skill intensity of exporting sectors to that of import-competing sectors: column (1) is based on the relative numbers of skilled and unskilled workers (defined in most cases as white-collar and blue-collar), column (2) on the average wage in each sector (as a proxy for the skill composition of its labour force). In every case, the ratio is less than unity, implying that exporting sectors are less skill-intensive than import-competing sectors, usually by a wide margin.

Fischer and Spinanger (1986, retabulated in Wood, 1994, table 3.6) find the same for the trade in manufactures of 21 developing countries with

Table 6.1. *Skill intensity of trade in manufactures, 1966–73*
(exporting sectors as ratio of import-competing sectors)

| | | | Skilled/unskilled labour[a] | |
			Numbers measure (1)	Wages measure[b] (2)
Brazil	1971–2			0.92[+]
Chile	1966–8	H		0.26*
Colombia	1973		0.53[+]	
Hong Kong	1973	H	0.51[+]	
Indonesia	1971		0.55[+]	0.45*
Ivory Coast	1972	H	0.62[+]	
Tunisia	1972		< 1[+]	0.65[+]
Uruguay	1968		0.49	
Unweighted averages		0.54	0.58	

Notes:
* = trade with developed countries only.
+ = trade with all partners.
Absence of * or + indicates exports to developed countries only, imports from all partners.
H = includes home (non-traded) goods indirect labour use, otherwise direct use only.
Blank indicates data not available.
[a] 'Skilled' workers are white-collar, 'unskilled' blue-collar, except in Hong Kong (where skilled workers are defined as professional) and Ivory Coast and Tunisia (where some blue-collar workers are in the skilled category). For Tunisia, the precise number of skilled workers is not given in the source.
[b] 'Wages measure' of skill is based in some way on the average wage per worker: the precise nature of the calculation varies among the country studies
Sources: Krueger *et al.* (1981), Krueger (1983); for further details, see Wood (1994, table 3.2).

developed countries in 1965, 1973 and 1983: in 61 of the 63 cases, exports are less skill-intensive than imports. Similar results emerge for Taiwan around 1970 in Lee and Liang (1982, table 10.20), for India in the 1980s in Nambiar and Tadas (1994, table 10), and for several developing countries in Bourguignon and Morrisson (1989, p. 282). All these studies are limited to manufacturing, but Kim and Vorasopontaviporn (1989) show for Thailand that more trade would also increase the demand for low-wage agricultural labour.

Applying a somewhat different approach to three Latin American countries in the period 1970–85, Londero and Teitel (1996) compare the skill intensity of fast-growing manufactured exports with that of the manufacturing sector as a whole, using sectoral wage levels as their

Table 6.2. *Skill intensity of manufactured exports*
(percentage share of selected products)

	Number of products	Value of exports
Argentina		
High	25.0	18.0
Medium	52.1	53.6
Low	22.9	28.4
Total	100.0	100.0
Colombia		
High	13.5	38.4
Medium	32.7	27.2
Low	53.8	34.4
Total	100.0	100.0
Venezuela		
High	39.0	58.6
Medium	39.0	9.9
Low	22.0	31.5
Total	100.0	100.0

Source: Londero and Teitel (1996, tables 5, 6).

measure of skill intensity. As shown in table 6.2, all three countries export manufactures of low, medium and high skill intensity. In Argentina and Colombia, products of medium and low skill intensity account for three-quarters or more of the exports (discounting the value shares for Colombia, which are heavily influenced by two specific products). But in Venezuela, products of high skill intensity account for 40–60 per cent of the total.

That almost all factor-content calculations in developing countries show exports to be less skill-intensive than imports has generally been taken as strong support for the conventional view that greater openness particularly benefits unskilled workers. However, insufficient attention has been paid to variations among developing countries in the skill intensity of exports, which theory implies should be higher in better-educated (or middle-income) countries. Nor have the imports of middle-income countries usually been disaggregated between those from higher-skilled trading partners and those from lower-skilled partners, which, theory suggests, have different effects on the skill structure of domestic labour demand.[7]

An entirely different sort of evidence is provided by studies which attempt to relate movement of relative wages over time in particular countries to changes in trade barriers – sometimes casually, sometimes econometrically. Most such work has been done on countries in East Asia and Latin America: the results for the two regions are reviewed separately below, after a few remarks on methodology.[8]

2.2 Methodology

All time-series studies encounter serious problems of measurement of skill differentials in wages. The common division between white-collar (or non-production) and blue-collar (or production) workers is treacherous, because the skill composition of both groups changes over time (for example, fewer clerks and more engineers in the white-collar category). Data on wages by level of education are more satisfactory, but not always available. Nor is it easy to obtain accurate measures of changes in openness: information on trade barriers, particularly on the restrictiveness of non-tariff barriers, is often inadequate; and changes in the ratio of exports or imports to GDP are an unreliable proxy. To measure the impact of changes in openness, it is also necessary to control for changes in domestic influences on relative wages, of which two are particularly noteworthy.[9]

2.2.1 Changes in the relative supply of skilled and unskilled labour

As is clear from figures 6.1 and 6.2, the impact on relative wages of increased openness (a shift of demand from *dd* to *DD*) varies with the level of supply (the position of the vertical line *S*), and would not be accurately measured by the observed change in wages if it coincided with a shift of supply.[10]

The only developing-country studies to have attempted formally to isolate the effects of supply shifts are those of Robbins (e.g. 1995a), who uses two different methods. One is the 'inner-product' test, which asks whether relative wages and relative employment in the various skill categories have moved in *opposite* directions (implying that supply shifts dominated), or in the *same* direction (implying that demand shifts dominated). Also, to test whether, as H–O theory predicts, changes in openness are affecting relative wages by altering the composition of output, Robbins decomposes changes in the skill structure of employment into between-industry and within-industry (between-occupation) components. However, this decomposition is vulnerable to the high level of aggregation of industries in most of his data (since changes in product mix can occur *within* statistically defined industries).

Robbins' second method of controlling for changes in supply is to estimate time series of implied shifts in the relative demand for skilled and unskilled labour, using information on relative wages and an equation of the form:

$$(\hat{d}_1/\hat{d}_2) = \sigma(\hat{w}_1/\hat{w}_2) + (\hat{s}_1/\hat{s}_2) \tag{1}$$

where d and s are demand and supply, the subscripts 1 and 2 denote skilled and unskilled labour, σ is the elasticity of the relative demand curve, and $\wedge$ over a variable indicates a logarithm. (1) is fundamentally an accounting identity but, if an assumption is made about the value of σ, it can be used to deduce shifts in demand from observed changes in supply and wages. The use of this method is complicated by the fact that the absolute value of σ is likely to become larger (and perhaps infinite) as a result of increased openness. Robbins (1995b) thus experiments with different values of σ. He also shows that even in apparently open economies, relative wages are inversely related to relative supply (with the significant exception of Taiwan after 1978), which gives support to the view that DD is usually less than infinitely elastic.

2.2.2 Changes in labour market institutions

Another likely internal influence on relative wages is changes in labour market institutions which increase or reduce wage flexibility, such as changes in the real or relative level of legal minimum wages, changes in the rights and powers of unions, and changes in the extent of employment in the public sector (within which wage differentials tend to be narrower than in the private sector). Thus, for example, even if demand and supply were tending to narrow the wage gap between skilled and unskilled workers, the gap might widen because of a decline in the minimum wage. This affects the accuracy of calculations based on (1), and more generally makes it harder to measure the impact of changes in openness.[11]

2.3 East Asia

Most of the time-series evidence from this region refers to the four 'little tigers' (Hong Kong, Korea, Singapore and Taiwan), whose experience is always quoted as confirmation that greater openness raises the relative demand for unskilled workers. In fact, this evidence, reviewed in more detail in Wood (1994, pp. 228–43), is by no means so clear-cut as is commonly supposed. There are gaps and deficiencies in the data on relative wages, and few rigorous attempts to control for internal influences on their movement.

Nonetheless, most of this evidence does support the conventional view that adoption of more outward-oriented policies increases the demand for workers with only a basic general education, relative to those with more education and skills. It is also consistent with the theoretical prediction that a switch of trade regime causes a step (or once-and-for-all) change in the composition of demand, whose effects on skill differentials in wages appear to be spread over a period of about ten years. In three of the four cases, the gap in wages between skilled and unskilled workers narrowed during the decade in question (the 1960s in Korea and Taiwan, the 1970s in Singapore). In Hong Kong in the 1950s (where the change in trade regime was of a rather different nature), the wage gap widened, but this was probably caused by a simultaneous large increase in the relative supply of unskilled labour.

Expansion of post-basic education is an alternative possible explanation of narrowing skill differentials in wages. However, in all three of the cases in which differentials narrowed, the change in trade regime appears to have been at least partly responsible – either because the narrowing was faster than in adjacent decades, or because expansion of higher education was deliberately restrained during the period concerned. After their initial decades of export-oriented industrialisation, expansion of higher education did further compress wage differentials in all four economies (albeit with periods of widening in all of them, too, for a variety of reasons).[12]

There is less evidence for other countries in East Asia. Robbins (1994a) finds persistent compression of wage differentials by level of education in Malaysia from 1973 to 1989, particularly between university graduates and less-educated workers. This continued in the early 1990s, with skilled and semi-skilled blue-collar workers in manufacturing gaining relative to other groups. Robbins ascribes this compression mainly to the rising relative numbers of highly educated workers (the inner-product test shows that supply shifts dominated demand shifts), perhaps augmented by the policy of discrimination towards indigenous Malays, and argues that this was not a case of increased openness. However, his data show that there were demand shifts in favour of less-skilled workers within industries, for which a plausible reason is trade-related changes in product mix – expansion of export-oriented labour-intensive activities within the textiles and machinery sectors.[13]

Robbins (1994b) also analyses movements in wages by education level in the Philippines between 1978 and 1988, a period of modest trade liberalisation, but with a severe recession in 1982–6. Skill differentials in wages show no clear trend: they widened during the recession, but then narrowed again. The initially remarkably large relative supply of university graduates increased somewhat, but inner-product tests yield conflicting results about the relative importance of demand and supply pressures on relative wages.

2.4 Latin America

Other studies by Robbins cover Argentina, Chile, Colombia, Costa Rica and Uruguay. Table 6.3 summarises their results: it focuses on seven periods in which efforts were made to increase openness, by lowering tariffs, easing quantitative import restrictions (QRs), or devaluation (which, in the presence of QRs, reduces anti-export bias by lowering the 'quota premia' on – or tariff equivalents of – these restrictions). In Argentina in 1989-93, there was little if any net increase in openness, because the reduction of barriers was offset by exchange rate appreciation. It also seems unlikely that openness increased in Chile during 1984–92 because, although there was a large devaluation, there were by that time almost no QRs on imports.

In all the five remaining periods (one in each country), in which openness did increase, skill differentials in wages (by level of education) widened, contrary to the conventional wisdom. The widening occurred from the mid-1970s to the early 1980s in Argentina and Chile, and between the mid-1980s and the mid-1990s in Colombia, Costa Rica and Uruguay. In all five cases, the relative number of skilled workers was rising, and thus the dominant influence on the change in wages was a rise in demand (as indicated by the results of the inner-product tests, except for part of the period in Costa Rica). The time-series calculations (based on (1)) confirm that the relative demand for skilled labour rose in all five of these episodes.

Mexico is another Latin American country where skill differentials in wages widened after the mid-1980s in parallel with radical liberalisation of the trade regime. The wage gap between non-production and production workers in manufacturing widened from 1984 to 1990 (Feenstra and Hanson, 1995; Hanson and Harrison, 1995; Revenga and Montenegro, 1995). This finding is corroborated for wage differentials by level of education over the period 1987–93 by Robbins (1996b), who also shows, by controlling for changes in relative supply, that the driving force was a shift in relative demand.

In some of these countries, liberalisation of labour market institutions is a possible alternative explanation of the widening of skill differentials, but one which is rejected by the authors of these studies. Robbins (1996b) finds no correlation in Chile, Colombia or Costa Rica between movements in relative wages (or in his relative demand time-series) and changes in legal minimum wages.[14] He also argues that reduced union

Table 6.3. *Effects of increased openness in five Latin American countries, 1974–95*

	Argentina (Buenos Aires)	Chile (Santiago)	Colombia (seven cities)	Costa Rica	Uruguay (Montevideo)
Periods of increased openness	(a) 1976–82 (b) 1989–93	(a) 1974–9 (b) 1984–92	1985–94	1985–93	1990–5
Changes in trade regime	Barrier reduction, but appreciation, in both periods	Barrier reduction 1974–9, devaluation in both periods	Devaluation to 1989 barrier reduction 1990–2	Barrier reduction and devaluation	Barrier reduction
Skill differentials in wages	(a) Widened (b) Narrowed	(a) Widened (b) Fluctuated	Widened	Widened	Widened
Predominant influence (inner-product test)	(a) Demand (b) Supply	(a) Demand (b) Demand	Demand	Supply, except in 1988–90	Demand
Relative demand for skill (time series)	(a) Rising (b) Falling	(a) Rising (b) Rising	Rising	Rising	Rising

Sources: Robbins (1995a, 1995b, 1996a, 1996b); Robbins and Gindling (1997); Robbins, Gonzales and Menendez (1995).

power is unlikely to have been the cause, with the possible exception of Argentina. In Mexico, the widening of skill differentials during 1984–90 coincided with a steep decline in the real minimum wage, but Feenstra and Hanson (1995) and Hanson and Harrison (1995) reject this as an explanation, citing Bell (1995), who finds that even in 1984 the average production worker was paid more than the minimum in 97 per cent of the manufacturing plants in their data set.

These rejections are not entirely convincing. In particular, the widening of wage differentials in Chile in the late 1970s, following the military overthrow of the Allende government, did coincide with a severe curtailment of union activity (Edwards and Edwards, 1995), and moreover simply restored differentials to the levels which had prevailed in the late 1960s (Robbins, 1995a, figure 5). The widening of wage differentials in Argentina in the late 1970s also occurred after a military coup, and in parallel, as Robbins points out, with a decline in the union movement. The counter-evidence for Mexico also needs to be treated with caution: because wages vary among production workers, the legal minimum could affect the average even if it set only the lowest wage (well below the average). Moreover, Bell (1995) finds that it did affect the wages of many workers in the informal sector.

2.5   Assessment of time-series evidence

All the time-series studies – those which support the conventional wisdom that increased openness reduces wage inequality in developing countries, as well those which contradict it – are open to doubts of one sort or another. But it is hard to avoid the conclusion that there is a genuine conflict of evidence: in some countries and periods, increased openness does appear to have caused a narrowing of skill differentials, but in others the opposite seems to have happened (even allowing for possible non-trade influences).

The conflict is particularly sharp between, on the one hand, the evidence from East Asia in the 1960s (Korea and Taiwan) and 1970s (Singapore and probably Malaysia) and, on the other, the evidence from Latin America in the late 1980s and early 1990s. Increased openness was also associated with widening wage differentials in Chile and Argentina in the late 1970s, but in both these cases labour market liberalisation under military rule is a plausible alternative explanation. It is harder to explain away the rise in wage inequality in Colombia, Costa Rica, Mexico and Uruguay since the mid-1980s.

For the rest of this chapter, while acknowledging various residual doubts and the need for further research on the countries concerned, which might erase the apparent conflict of evidence, it will be taken as a working assumption that there was a genuine difference between the effects of greater openness on wage inequality in East Asia in the 1960s and 1970s, and its effects in Latin America in the late 1980s and early 1990s. This assumption not only allows the following pages to focus on possible reasons for the difference, but also suggests a convenient framework for the discussion. The conflict involves two regions in two periods: section 3 will thus ask whether it might be due to *differences between East Asia and Latin America*, and section 4 whether it might be due to *differences between the 1960s–1970s and the 1980s–1990s*.

3   Differences between East Asia and Latin America

Some important differences between the two regions have already been taken into account in the preceding review of evidence: the much faster growth of the supply of skilled labour in East Asia, and the more regulated nature of labour markets in most Latin American countries. This section examines two other possibly important differences: in natural resource availability, and in the choice of policy instruments for increasing openness.

3.1   Natural-resource endowments

Latin America is far better endowed with natural resources than East Asia, and consequently has a comparative advantage in primary products (including processed products, such as canned fish), whereas East Asia's comparative advantage lies in narrowly defined manufactures requiring few local natural resource inputs (such as clothing).[15] The difference is clear from data on land per worker in the two regions, and on the composition of their exports (Owens and Wood, 1997, figures 6 and 7). It emerges also from the sectoral pattern of the output response to increases in openness: in East Asia, the growth of exports was concentrated on manufacturing, while in Latin America the gains were mainly in primary and processed primary exports, with other (non-primary-processing) parts of manufacturing often shrinking – except in the parts of Mexico adjacent to the United States.

As explained in section 1, the introduction of a third factor such as land into the H–O model could in principle cause greater openness to widen wage differentials even in a country with a relatively low ratio of skilled–unskilled labour. The mechanism, for Latin America, would have to be that skill and natural resources were complementary inputs, so that expansion of primary output raised the relative demand for skilled labour. In practice, however, primary production is not generally skill-intensive, by comparison with import-competing manufacturing. Mining and oil refining do require a highly skilled labour force, but account for only a small share of total employment. Agriculture, a far larger employer, has a low ratio of skilled–unskilled workers.[16] Nor is most primary processing skill-intensive.[17]

It remains possible that some more complicated process, involving non-traded sectors as well as natural resources, could explain the difference in wage outcomes between the two regions.[18] For instance, if all manufactures were import substitutes in Latin America, but only skill-intensive manufactures in East Asia, non-traded sectors (of given absolute skill intensity) might be *more* skill-intensive than import-competing sectors in Latin America, and *less* skill-intensive than import-competing sectors in East Asia. Hence, if greater openness (through substitution in consumption) caused expansion of non-traded as well as export sectors (with contraction of import-competing sectors), the net effect might be a rise in the relative demand for skilled labour in Latin America, but a fall in East Asia.

This specific chain of causation may seem far-fetched, but the correlation between the regional differences in natural resources and in wage outcomes is so strong that one should hesitate before dismissing it without further empirical research. (It might also be worth checking whether the wage data for Latin America are hiding increased demand for unskilled workers because of gaps in their coverage of primary sectors and rural areas.[19])

3.2   Trade-policy instruments

East Asian opening to trade, particularly in Korea and Taiwan in the 1960s, was achieved mainly by increasing incentives for exporters, while keeping fairly high levels of protection against imports in most sectors. Most of the Latin American openings, by contrast, have involved large reductions in barriers to imports.

From a macroeconomic viewpoint, the two approaches are equivalent: it does not matter whether bias against exporting is reduced by giving subsidies to exports or by lowering barriers to imports. However, because neither the subsidies nor the barriers are uniform across sectors, their effects on the sectoral structure of output, and so on the skill composition of the demand for labour, may be different. For example, labour-intensive manufacturing subsectors such as clothing and footwear were initially highly protected in most Latin American countries (as in developed countries), so that making barriers against manufactured imports lower and more uniform tended to hurt unskilled workers more than skilled workers.[20]

This possibility may deserve further investigation (and comparison with the liberalisation of imports in Korea and Taiwan after the mid-1980s), but is not a promising explanation of the difference in wage outcomes between the two regions. For if Latin America had a comparative advantage in unskilled labour-intensive goods (manufactured or primary), then the effects of import liberalisation in sectors such as clothing and footwear should have been more than offset by growth of exports in (these or other) labour-intensive sectors. And if in fact the outcome was a rise in the relative demand for skilled workers because Latin America did *not* have a comparative advantage in labour-intensive sectors, the explanation must be sought somewhere other than in the details of its trade regime.

4   Differences between 1960s–1970s and 1980s–1990s

This section examines the possibility that the observed difference in wage outcomes occurred because the world had changed in some respect between the 1960s and 1970s, to which the East Asian time-series studies refer, and the late 1980s and 1990s, to which the most convincing Latin American evidence refers. One such change was the entry of the largest low-income countries into world markets in the 1980s. Another change may have been in the skill bias of technology.[21]

4.1   Entry of large low-income exporters

Half the world's population, and an even higher proportion of the world's unskilled workers, lives in five low-income Asian countries: China, India, Indonesia, Pakistan and Bangladesh. In the 1960s and 1970s, all of them were largely closed to trade, and thus their workers did not form part of the effective world labour supply. By the mid-1980s, they were all opening to trade, led by Indonesia and China, with the South Asian countries also making some progress. Their manufactured exports grew rapidly: in the six years 1987–93, OECD imports of manufactures from low-income countries rose nearly four times, from $28 billion to $110 billion (about one-third of all manufactured imports from developing countries), while imports from middle-income countries rose by less than 50 per cent.[22]

This opening of the low-income half of the world is likely to have altered the comparative advantage of middle-income countries, whose ratio of skilled–unskilled workers is above the global average, though below that of developed countries. Thus in the economic world of the 1960s and 1970s, which consisted effectively only of developed and middle-income countries, the latter had a comparative advantage in goods of low skill intensity, but in the 1980s, when low-income Asia started to realise its own comparative advantage in goods of low skill intensity, the comparative advantage of middle-income countries shifted to goods of intermediate skill intensity.[23]

The effect on relative wages in a middle-income country of opening to trade is thus likely to have changed over time. In the 1960s, increased openness would have raised the relative wage of unskilled workers, because it would have caused sectors of above-average skill intensity to shrink, and sectors of below-average skill intensity to expand. In the 1980s, however, greater openness had conflicting effects on relative wages, by causing contraction of sectors both of high skill intensity (replaced by imports from developed countries) and of low skill intensity (replaced by imports from low-income countries). The net effect might be in either direction, but could well be to widen the wage gap between skilled and unskilled workers, as happened in the middle-income countries of Latin America in this period.

This change can be interpreted in theoretical terms as a shift in the open-economy demand curve, caused by an increase in the effective world relative supply of unskilled labour, which lowers the relative world market price of unskilled labour-intensive goods. This is illustrated in the simplest case of a two-good model in figure 6.3, which is the same as figure 6.1, except that the lower relative world price of clothing is shown (with a dashed line) as a downward shift of the horizontal segment of DD.

A better way of depicting what has happened is figure 6.4 which, in the case of a many-good model (as in figure 6.2), approximates the open-economy demand curve by a continuous downward-sloping line. The world of the 1960s is the North-West quadrant (with diagonal dd_1), consisting of developed countries (with unskilled/skilled labour ratios in the range $0A$) and middle-income countries (in the range AB), but excluding the low-income Asian countries (with unskilled/skilled labour ratios beyond B). The open-economy demand curve in the 1960s is the line DD_1. The world of the 1980s is the whole of the figure: the closed-economy demand curve extends to d_2, and the open-economy demand curve pivots down to DD_2 (drawn for simplicity to cross dd_2 at B). For the middle-income countries, with skill supply ratios between A and B, DD_1 is above dd, but DD_2 is below it, so that opening to trade would have reduced wage inequality in the 1960s, but increased it in the 1980s.

The near-simultaneous expansion of exports from low-income Asian

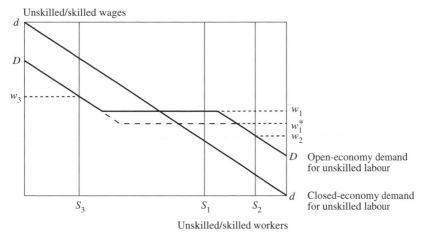

Figure 6.3   Entry of low-income Asia: two traded goods

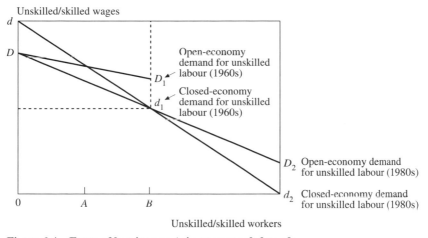

Figure 6.4   Entry of low-income Asia: many traded goods

countries is a plausible explanation for the widening of wage differentials in Latin American countries which opened to trade in the late 1980s. This expansion of supply does appear to have caused a downward shift in the open-economy demand curve: from the mid-1980s to the mid-1990s, as shown in figure 6.5, there was a drop in the world price of unskilled labour-intensive, relative to more skill-intensive, goods.[24] There is also anecdotal and case-study evidence (e.g. Kaplinsky, 1993) that labour-intensive Latin American manufacturing sectors have suffered

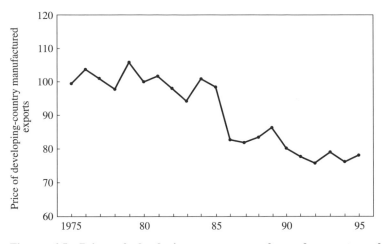

Figure 6.5   **Price of developing-country manufactured exports, relative to developed-country exports of machinery, transport equipment and services, 1975–95**

Note: Manufactured export prices are unit-value indexes from UN trade data; service-price index refers to the United Kingdom only and has a weight of 0.27 in the combined developed-country index.
Source: Update of Minford, Riley and Nowell (1995, figure 6).

from competition from Asian imports both domestically and in third markets such as the United States.

A downward shift of the open-economy demand curve should also have affected relative wages in other countries which were already open to trade (through the Stolper–Samuelson linkage between product and factor prices), but only in those which produce both labour-intensive and other goods. Figure 6.3, in the simple two-good case, thus shows that the downward shift of *DD* reduces (from w_1 to w_1^*) the relative wage of unskilled workers in the country with skill supply S_1, which produces clothing and machinery, but does not change relative wages in countries that are specialised in one of the goods (S_2 in clothing, S_3 in machinery).[25] This distinction is less clear in figure 6.4, but however the diagrams are drawn, it must be open *middle-income* economies – with intermediate unskilled–skilled labour ratios – which are most likely to produce both labour-intensive and more skill-intensive goods, and thus to have experienced external pressure for wider wage differentials.

An indirect test of this explanation of why wage differentials widened in opening Latin American countries is thus whether, when low-income Asia entered world markets, the same happened in other, already open, middle-income countries. The time-series studies reviewed earlier reveal a mixed picture regarding wage differentials: in Hong Kong, they widened throughout the 1980s; in Taiwan and Singapore, they widened in the early 1980s, but narrowed in the late 1980s; in Korea and Malaysia, they narrowed throughout the decade; and in Chile, they fluctuated (Robbins, 1995b, figure 3; Wood, 1994, pp. 228–43). The estimated relative demand for skilled labour also moved in different directions in the three countries for which data are available – Taiwan, Malaysia and Chile (Robbins, 1995b, figure 6). The test, on this small set of fairly open middle-income countries, is thus inconclusive.

The hypothesis that the difference between the experience of East Asia in the 1960s and Latin America in the 1980s was due to the entry of low-income Asian countries into world markets clearly requires further research. This should include a larger sample of open middle-income countries, and should also examine the opening low-income countries themselves (within which wage differentials should have narrowed). Even more vitally, further research would need to look more closely at the consistency of this hypothesis with the experience of the middle-income countries which have opened since the mid-1980s (again with a larger sample), and particularly to check by factor-content analysis whether reduction of trade barriers did cause sectors of intermediate skill intensity to expand and sectors of low skill intensity to contract.

4.2   Skill-biased technical progress

Another possible reason why opening to trade had different effects on wage inequality in the 1980s than in the 1960s is that world technology changed between these periods in a way which raised the relative demand for skilled labour. This explanation assumes that increased openness in a developing country affects the skill structure of labour demand in two different ways: by altering the sectoral composition of production (as in H–O theory), and by changing the production technology available – through increased imports of advanced capital goods, for example, or through exporters learning from foreign buyers and exposure to foreign markets. The net impact on relative wages depends on the sizes of these two effects, and on the exact nature of the difference between domestic and world technology, but could be contrary to the predictions of standard H–O theory, which assumes that all countries always have access to the same technology. (It could also result in the *real* wage of unskilled workers rising, even if their *relative* wage fell, whereas under strict H–O assumptions, including constant returns to scale, real and relative wages should move in the same direction.)

This explanation, put forward by Robbins (e.g. 1995a), who calls it

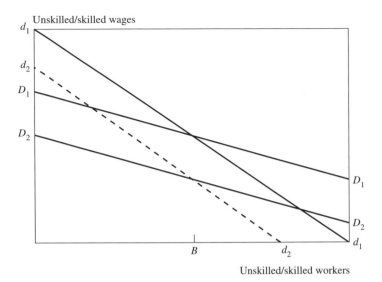

Figure 6.6   Effects of openness and technology transfer

Note: d_1d_1 and d_2d_2 are the closed-economy demand curves for unskilled labour based on 1960s' and 1980s' technology, respectively. D_1D_1 and D_2D_2 are the open-economy demand curves for unskilled labour based on 1960s' and 1980s' technology, respectively.

'skill-enhancing trade', is depicted in figure 6.6, in which there are two pairs of closed-economy and open-economy demand curves: dd_1 and DD_1 are based on the use of 1960s' technology, dd_2 and DD_2 on the use of 1980s' technology, which is assumed to have changed over time in a biased way, requiring a generally lower ratio of unskilled to skilled labour.[26] It is also assumed that the new technology is available only to open economies, so that a country which remained closed to trade over this period would have continued to use 1960s' technology. For most developing countries (to the right of B), opening to trade would thus have had different effects on wage inequality in the 1960s (decreasing it, by movement from dd_1 to DD_1) than in the 1980s (increasing it, by movement from dd_1 to DD_2). Even in the 1980s, the H–O tendency for openness to reduce inequality remains – reversion to a closed economy, with 1980s' technology and demand curve dd_2, would aggravate the increase in wage inequality – but it is dominated by the effect of the change in technology.

The skill-enhancing trade explanation has considerable plausibility. It is likely that increased openness does alter the availability of technology. It is also widely believed that technical progress over the past couple of decades has in fact been biased against unskilled workers, and that this is why wage inequality has increased in most *developed* countries. More-over, Robbins (1996b) provides econometric support for this explana-tion: pooling the time series for six of the developing countries in his sample, he finds the relative demand for skilled labour to be positively correlated with the rate of growth of GDP, and with the ratio of the imported capital stock to GDP, interpreting both variables as proxies for access to new technology.

However, there is also considerable room for doubt about this explanation. The opening countries had not been completely cut off from new technology. There is little hard evidence of an autonomous skill-using bias in recent technical progress, and there is another plausible explanation – increased openness to trade with developing countries – for the rise in inequality in developed countries (Wood, 1995). Nor, as mentioned earlier, is there consistent evidence of a rise in wage inequality, or in the relative demand for skilled labour, in open middle-income economies. And the econometric results of Robbins are open to alternative interpretations. Again, then, there is a need for further research, both to determine whether or not the open economy demand curve has shifted down over time – an assumption common to the technological bias and low-income Asia hypotheses – and to establish which hypothesis provides a better explanation of this shift (including examination of movements in the *real* wages of unskilled workers, concerning which the two hypotheses make different predictions).

5   Summary and conclusions

A substantial amount of empirical evidence supports the conventional wisdom that increased openness to trade in developing countries tends to raise the demand for unskilled, relative to skilled, labour and thus to reduce wage inequality. However, there is also some recent evidence to the contrary: in particular, there is a conflict in the time-series evidence between the experience of East Asia in the 1960s and 1970s, which is consistent with the conventional wisdom, and the experience of Latin America in the late 1980s and early 1990s, where increased openness appears to have widened rather than narrowed skill differentials in wages.

Possible explanations fall into two classes: differences between East Asia and Latin America; and differences between the 1960s–1970s and the 1980s–1990s. Preliminary assessment of more specific explanations within these classes suggests that the reason is more likely to be the difference between the two time periods than the difference between the two regions. East Asia and Latin America differ in several respects, not least their endowments of natural resources, but it is not easy to establish a convincing causal link between any of them and the difference in the impact of increased openness on wage inequality.

By contrast, there are two plausible reasons why the effects of increased openness on wage inequality might have differed between the earlier and the later periods. One is that the entry of China and other large low-income Asian countries into the world market for labour-intensive manufactures in the 1980s shifted the comparative advantage of middle-income countries into goods of medium skill intensity, with the result that increased openness in middle-income countries reduced the relative demand for unskilled workers by causing sectors of low skill intensity to contract. The other reason is technical progress between the 1960s and the 1980s which was biased against unskilled workers, and to which developing countries were exposed when they opened to trade.

The available evidence does not permit any strong conclusion as to which of these two period-difference explanations is the right one. More generally, the slender empirical basis of this whole exercise should be emphasised. The sample of developing countries in which there is recent evidence on trade and wage inequality is extremely limited – not only small, but also confined to East Asia and Latin America, with no low-income countries, and none from Africa or South Asia. Within each country, too, there are gaps and other problems with the data and analysis. More research is needed to confirm whether, and how, the impact of increased openness on wage inequality has changed in recent years, as well as on possible reasons for the change.

NOTES

Financial support for the preparation of this chapter was provided by the UK Overseas Development Administration through its support of research at IDS, and by the World Bank, but the views expressed are those of the author, not of either organisation. Special thanks are due to Don Robbins, whose work motivated this chapter and who provided many unpublished papers and comments. Valuable comments were provided also by Shahen Abrahamian, Riccardo Faini, Richard Freeman, Edward Leamer, Jörg Mayer, Patricio Meller, Jeffrey Sachs, Wolfgang Stolper, three anonymous referees, and participants in seminars at Harvard and MIT, at conferences at the Universities of Oxford, Reading and the Auvergne (CERDI), as well as at the CEPR conference on Regional Integration (La Coruña, 26–27 April 1996). The chapter was originally published, with some stylistic editing, in the *World Bank Economic Review* , **11(1)** (1997), whose permission to reprint it in this volume is gratefully acknowledged.

1 By contrast, the debate over trade and inequality in *developed* countries is now over the *magnitude* of the effects, with their *direction* – adverse to unskilled workers – being largely agreed (Wood, 1995).

2 Alternative diagrammatic presentations of the H–O model with two factors and many goods, including the usual Lerner–Pearce diagram, may be found in, for example, Leamer (1984, pp. 16–21). The potential overdeterminacy with more goods prices than factor prices is avoided because no country produces more than two goods.

3 Formal models which assume an infinity or continuum of traded goods are Dornbusch, Fischer and Samuelson (1980) and Feenstra and Hanson (1995).

4 This was pointed out to me by Edward Leamer. Robinson and Thierfelder (1996) also present a formal model in which the effect of changes in world prices on factor prices can be either 'normal' or 'perverse', depending on the elasticity of substitution in consumption.

5 Two other types of evidence are neglected here (but are covered in Wood, 1994, pp. 220–7): cross-country studies, of which there are few, owing to lack of data; and simulation studies, which for the purposes of this chapter seem too vulnerable to disagreements about model and experiment specification.

6 Moreover, most factor-content calculations under-estimate the impact of trade on the relative demand for skilled and unskilled labour, because they fail to allow for non-competing imports (Wood, 1994, pp. 72 4, 87–91, 121–6).

7 The Krueger *et al.* study is an honourable exception, but there have been large changes in the pattern of world trade since the period to which it refers.

8 The few studies of countries in other regions are severely limited by lack of relevant data – e.g. Bourguignon and Morrison (1989) on Malawi and Morocco, and Fontana (1994) on Ghana and Sri Lanka. There are also several studies of the impact of trade liberalisation on unemployment (reviewed and extended by Edwards and Edwards, 1995), but they rarely distinguish between skilled and unskilled workers, and are mainly concerned with transitional dislocation rather than enduring changes in the labour market.

9 Others include changes in supplies of factors complementary with skilled or unskilled labour, in the composition of demand and in cyclical forces.

10 This would be less of a problem if *DD* were infinitely elastic over the relevant range: the observed change in wages would be an accurate measure of the impact of increased openness at the *initial* level of supply (though not at the *final* level of supply, where the closed-economy wage would have been different). But if *DD* is less than infinitely elastic, as was argued to be usually the case, the change in wages does not accurately measure the impact of increased openness even at the initial level of supply.

11 In principle, this problem can be solved by using data on unemployment rates by skill level (since the *combination* of changes in relative wages and relative unemployment rates should indicate the direction of demand and supply shifts), but in practice such data are rarely available.

12 For more details on their experiences in the 1970s and 1980s, see also Fields (1994) and Robbins and Zveglich (1995).

13 These two sectors account for a big and rising share of all employment – up from 13 per cent in 1984 to 16 per cent in 1989 (Robbins 1994a, table 22). Moreover, between 1984 and 1989, the share of university-educated workers declined in textiles and was static in machinery, despite the rising relative supply of such workers (Robbins, 1994a, tables 1–3, 15). See also the information on Malaysia in Bourguignon and Morrison (1989, 116–17).

14 By contrast, Bell (1995) finds that minimum wages do have an effect in Colombia, but her study focuses on average rather than relative wages, and ends earlier (the panel data in 1987 and the time-series data in 1990).

15 In other respects, the two regions are similarly endowed: both are well educated by comparison with Africa and South Asia, with few illiterates in their labour forces; and both have fairly well developed infrastructure.

16 However, it was suggested to me by a referee that in Latin America the least skill-intensive agricultural subsector, staple food, may be an import substitute, so that increased openness may raise the relative demand for skilled labour *within* agriculture.

17 Except for Hong Kong, most of the 'manufactured' exports in the Krueger *et al.* factor-content study summarised in table 6.1 were processed primary products (as defined in Owens and Wood, 1997). Londero and Teitel (1996, table 5) show that, in Argentina and Colombia, only 13 per cent of manufactures intensive in natural resources are of high skill intensity, and in Venezuela, only 30 per cent. The cross-country regressions of Owens and Wood (1997) suggest that primary processing needs a literate labour force, but uses a smaller proportion of highly skilled workers than other sorts of manufacturing.

18 This was suggested to me by Jeffrey Sachs.

19 The data for Argentina, Chile, Colombia and Uruguay cover only cities, and most of the data for Mexico are limited to manufacturing. However, the Costa Rican data, which show much the same wage pattern, are nation-wide. Moreover, even in the other countries, the data include factory-based primary processing. And if labour markets work properly, changes in relative wages in sectors that are not covered by the surveys should be transmitted into the sectors that are covered.

20 E.g. in Chile in 1974, textiles and footwear were the second and third most protected manufacturing sectors, with effective rates of protection over 200 per cent (Edwards and Edwards, 1995, table 2). And in Mexico, Revenga and Montenegro (1995, table 2) show the nominal tariff on apparel and footwear in 1985 to have been among the highest in manufacturing, although it stands out less in the calculations of Hanson and Harrison (1995, table 2).

21 These two seem the most promising explanations in this category: others considered were the debt crisis, greater international mobility of capital, and migration. Feenstra and Hanson (1995) present a model in which capital flows could explain the widening of wage differentials in Mexico.

22 World Bank (1989, indicators table 17; 1995, indicators table 16, with Indonesia moved into the low-income group for consistency): the figure for the middle-income group is slightly inflated by the reclassification of countries in Eastern Europe and the former Soviet Union.

23 Rapid accumulation of skills in the East Asian economies which opened in the 1960s also helped to shift their comparative advantage towards goods of intermediate skill intensity. In the 1960s, these East Asian economies were closer in their skill endowments to today's low-income Asian countries than they are today, and than Latin America is today.

24 These data were kindly provided by Patrick Minford. For discussion of earlier movements of a similar terms of trade index, see Sarkar and Singer (1991) and the October 1993 issue of *World Development*.

25 This is because, with only one good produced, there can be no change in

domestic relative producer prices. But the world price (or terms of trade) change does alter relative *consumer* prices, and thus the *real* wages of all workers in the specialised countries (downward in S_2, and upward in S_3).

26 In this context, it is not necessary to make the otherwise important distinction between *sectoral* and *factoral* bias (Leamer, 1995; Wood, 1995). All that needs to be assumed is that technology changed in some way which raised the relative demand for skilled labour.

REFERENCES

Bell, L. A., 1995. 'The Impact of Minimum Wages in Mexico and Colombia', *Policy Research Working Paper*, **1514** (Washington, DC: World Bank)

Bourguignon, F. and Morrisson,C., 1989. *External Trade and Income Distribution* (Paris: OECD)

Dornbusch, R., Fischer, S. and Samuelson, P., 1980. 'Heckscher–Ohlin Trade Theory with a Continuum of Goods', *Quarterly Journal of Economics*, **95**, 203–24

Edwards, A. C. and Edwards, S., 1995. 'Trade Liberalisation and Unemployment: Evidence from Chile', California State University and UCLA, unpublished paper

Feenstra, R. and Hanson, G., 1995. 'Foreign Investment, Outsourcing and Relative Wages', in R. Feenstra, G. Grossman and D. Irwin (eds.), *Political Economy of Trade Policy: Essays in Honor of Jagdish Bhagwati* (Cambridge, MA: MIT Press)

Fields, G., 1994. 'Changing Labor Market Conditions and Economic Development in Hong Kong, the Republic of Korea, Singapore, and Taiwan, China', *World Bank Economic Review*, **8**, 395–414

Fischer, B. and Spinanger, D., 1986. 'Factor Market Distortions and Export Performance: An Eclectic Review of the Evidence', *Kiel Working Paper*, **259** (Kiel: Institut für Weltwirtschaft an der Universität Kiel)

Fontana, M., 1994. 'Trade Liberalisation and Income Distribution in Developing Countries', MPhil dissertation, Institute of Development Studies, University of Sussex

Hanson, G. H. and Harrison, A., 1995. 'Trade, Technology and Wage Inequality', *NBER Working Paper*, **5110**

Kaplinsky, R., 1993. 'Export Processing Zones in the Dominican Republic: Transforming Manufactures into Commodities', *World Development*, **21/11**, 1851–65

Kim, K. S. and Vorasopontaviporn, P., 1989. 'Foreign Trade and the Distribution of Income in Thailand', *Working Paper*, **124**, Helen Kellogg Institute for International Studies, University of Notre Dame

Krueger, A. O., 1983. *Trade and Employment in Developing Countries: 3. Synthesis and Conclusions* (Chicago: University of Chicago Press)

Krueger, A. O., Lary, H. B., Monson, T. and Akrasanee, N. (eds.), 1981. *Trade and Employment in Developing Countries: 1. Individual Studies* (Chicago: University of Chicago Press)

Leamer, E. E., 1984. *Sources of International Comparative Advantage: Theory and Evidence* (Cambridge, MA: MIT Press)

  1995. 'A Trade Economist's View of US Wages and "Globalisation"', in S. Collins (ed.), *Imports, Exports and the American Worker* (Washington, DC: Brookings)

Lee, T. H. and Liang, K. S., 1982. 'Taiwan', in B. Balassa (ed.), *Development Strategies in Semi-Industrial Economies* (Baltimore: Johns Hopkins Press for the World Bank)

Londero, E. and Teitel, S., 1996. 'Industrialisation and the Factor Content of Latin American Exports of Manufactures', *Journal of Development Studies*, **32/4**, 581–601

Minford, P., Riley, J. and Nowell, E., 1995. 'The Elixir of Growth: Trade, Non-Traded Goods and Development', *CEPR Discussion Paper*, **1165**

Nambiar, R. G. and Tadas, G., 1994. 'Is Trade Deindustrialising India?', *Economic and Political Weekly* (15 October), 2741–6

Owens, T. and Wood, A., 1997. 'Export-oriented Industrialisation Through Primary Processing?', *World Development*, **25/9**, 1453–70

Revenga, A. and Montenegro, C., 1995. 'North American Integration and Factor Price Equalisation: Is there Evidence of Wage Convergence between Mexico and the United States?', in S. Collins (ed.), *Imports, Exports and the American Worker* (Washington, DC: Brookings)

Robinson, S. and Thierfelder, K., 1996. 'The Trade–Wage Debate in a Model with Non-traded Goods: Making Room for Labor Economists in Trade Theory', *TMD Discussion Paper*, **9** (Washington, DC: Trade and Macro-economics Division, International Food Policy Research Institute)

Robbins, D., 1994a. 'Malaysian Wage Structure and its Causes', Harvard University, unpublished paper

  1994b. 'Philippine Wage and Employment Structure, 1978–93', Harvard University, unpublished paper

  1995a. 'Earnings Dispersion in Chile after Trade Liberalisation', Harvard University, unpublished paper

  1995b. 'Trade, Trade Liberalisation and Inequality in Latin America and East Asia: Synthesis of Seven Country Studies', Harvard University, unpublished paper

  1996a. 'Stolper–Samuelson (Lost) in the Tropics: Trade Liberalisation and Wages in Colombia 1976–94', Harvard University, unpublished paper

  1996b. 'HOS Hits Facts: Facts Win. Evidence on Trade and Wages in the Developing World', Harvard University, unpublished paper

Robbins, D. and Gindling. T., 1997. 'Educational Expansion, Trade Liberalisation and Distribution in Costa Rica', in A. Berry (ed.), *Poverty, Economic Reform and Income Distribution in Latin America* (Boulder: Lynne Reinner)

Robbins, D. and Zveglich, J., 1995. 'Skill-bias in Recent Taiwanese Growth', Harvard University, unpublished paper

Robbins, D., Gonzales, M. and Menendez, A., 1995. 'Wage Dispersion in

Argentina, 1976–93: Trade Liberalisation Amidst Inflation, Stabilisation and Overvaluation', Harvard University, unpublished paper

Sarkar, P. and Singer, H., 1991. 'Manufactured Exports of Developing Countries and their Terms of Trade since 1965', *World Development*, **19/4**, 333–40

Wood, A., 1994. *North–South Trade, Employment and Inequality: Changing Fortunes in a Skill-Driven World* (Oxford: Clarendon Press)

1995. 'How Trade Hurt Unskilled Workers', *Journal of Economic Perspectives*, **9/3**, 57–80

World Bank, various years. *World Development Report* (New York: Oxford University Press for the World Bank)

Discussion

RICCARDO FAINI

There is something paradoxical in the attitude of international trade economists in the 'trade and jobs' debate. Most international economists would argue that trade did not matter much in determining the economic (mis)fortunes of unskilled workers in industrial countries, thereby denying the empirical and policy relevance of the very same theory that is covered at length in most of the standard textbooks on trade. When, however, trade economists turn to the developing countries case, they typically conclude that openness is a major determinant of the wellbeing of unskilled workers, with protectionism being a source of substantial inequality. Adrian Wood's previous research on industrial countries has contributed significantly to redress this imbalance, by arguing on the basis of a modified net factor-content approach that trade with developing countries can have sizable distributional effects in industrial countries. This should solve the paradox and re-establish the symmetry in the effects of trade between industrial and developing countries. This is not the end of the story, however. In this new piece of research, Adrian Wood collects extensive empirical evidence to show that quite often trade liberalisation has a negative impact on unskilled workers even in developing countries. We have come full circle, with the paradox simply reversed.

That trade liberalisation may have the opposite effects to those predicted by the standard H–O–S theory does not certainly come as a surprise to theorists. It is not difficult to build models, fully rooted in factor-endowment theory, where trade can lead to an income fall for the supposedly abundant factor. The true challenge is to find an explanation which is both consistent theoretically and empirically relevant. Wood's chapter 6 in this respect is refreshing, well argued and, as usual, provocative. It consists of basically two parts. In the first section of the chapter, Wood assesses the existing empirical evidence on the link between openness and inequality in developing countries. He finds that while the distributional effects of trade liberalisation in developing countries during the 1960s were typically favourable, this is no longer case when we turn to the 1980s. Most of the evidence from the 1960s comes from South-East Asia, while in the 1980s it is Latin America that provides the main basket-case to assess the effects of liberalisation. The obvious question, then, is whether a time or a region effect is at work, namely whether the 1980s are different in some substantive way from the 1960s or Latin America has some characteristics that sets it apart from South East Asia. According to Wood, both time and regional effects are part of the explanation. With regard to the latter, differences in factor endowments and trade-policy orientation could explain why the distributional impact of trade liberalisation differed between Latin America and East Asia. With respect to time effects, it is plausible that the entry of China and other densely populated low-income countries into world trade during the 1980s must have played a role in determining the different impact of trade liberalisation during the two periods.

In what follows, I would like to discuss the role of three factors, which are mentioned, but not emphasised by Wood.

1   Greater international mobility of capital

The fact that the mobility of capital increased during the 1980s is undisputed. Could that account for the widening wage differentials between skilled and unskilled workers in both industrial and developing countries? Two sets of models have been developed to this effect. In the former (Feenstra and Hanson, 1995), there is a continuum of goods ordered by levels of skill intensity. Skilled-(unskilled-) intensive goods are produced in the North (South). If capital flows from the North to the South, it will shift the dividing line and more (fewer) goods will be produced in the South (North). However, the commodities at the margin that are shifted from the North to the South are unskilled-intensive from the point of the North but skilled-intensive from the point of view of the South. Greater capital mobility is therefore associated with a fall in the relative unskilled wage both in the North and in the South. Empirical evidence in support of this model is presented in Feenstra and Hanson (1997). Markusen and Venables (1997) distinguish between a competitive low-skilled-intensive sector and an imperfectly competitive sector where multinationals may also operate. Multinationals' headquarters are more skilled-intensive than plant operations. In the initial equilibrium, with high trade costs, the South is specialised in the unskilled-intensive sector; only national firms operate in the skilled-intensive sector in the North. When trade costs fall, multinationals will emerge with headquarters in the North and plants in the South. In both regions, therefore, the demand for skilled workers will increase.

2   Discriminatory trade liberalisation

One difference between East Asia and Latin America which is not mentioned in the chapter is that the former region tended to liberalise globally, whereas countries in the second region tended to favour regional integration agreements. Could that account for the differing impact of trade liberalisation? Probably not. The problem with this explanation is that it works in the wrong direction. Indeed, if countries in Latin America have liberalised mostly among themselves or with the United States they should have been less exposed to the impact of competition from labour-abundant densely populated countries in Asia.

3   Perverse trade-policy effects

It could well be that Latin American countries tended to protect some of their labour-intensive sectors, so that trade liberalisation would hurt unskilled workers. Wood tends to dismiss this explanation by noting that

> if Latin America had a comparative advantage in unskilled labour-intensive goods ..., then the effects of imports liberalisation ... such as clothing and footwear should have been more than offset by growth of exports in (these or other) labour-intensive sectors.

However, it is fully possible that, due to the presence of factor intensity reversal, unskilled-labour-intensive sectors are not the same in the North and the South (Bhagwati and Dehejia, 1994). Suppose for instance that agriculture is a labour-intensive activity in Mexico, but is capital-intensive in the United States. Let us introduce these assumptions in a simple general equilibrium models with two goods (agriculture and industry) and two factors (labour and capital). It could well be that the United States has a comparative advantage in agriculture while Mexico holds a comparative advantage in industry. Trade liberalisation between

Mexico and the United States would then imply that the price of the labour-intensive commodity falls in both countries with a negative impact on the relative wage in both Mexico and the United States. Is that merely a theoretical curiosum? Probably not, when we consider the case of maize. Maize is a very important crop in Mexico's agriculture (most farmers grow maize) and a highly protected one. There are no barriers in the United States against maize imports. Moreover, it is labour-intensive in Mexico, but capital-intensive in the United States. Lowering trade barriers on maize would then lower the relative wage in both countries.

These comments are meant only to indicate some further avenues of research in addition to those already outlined by Wood. The author himself is keen to admit that his chapter does not seek to provide conclusive answers to many of the questions that are raised there. Most of his analysis is indeed a plea for more research, on the role of resource endowment, differences in trade policy, the entry of low-income Asian countries and the bias of technical progress.

REFERENCES

Bhagwati J. and Dehejia. V., 1994. 'Free Trade and Wages of the Unskilled. Is Marx Striking Again?', in J. Bhagwati and M. Kosters (eds.), *Trade and Wages. Leveling Wages Down?* (Washington, DC: American Enterprise Institute)

Feenstra R. and Hanson, G., 1995. 'Foreign Investment, Outsourcing, and Relative Wages', in R. Feenstra, G. Grossman and D. Irwin (eds.), *Political Economy of Trade Policy: Essays in Honor of Jagdish Bhagwati* Cambridge, MA: MIT Press)

  1997. 'Foreign Direct Investment and Relative Wages: Evidence from Mexico's Maquilladoras', *Journal of International Economics*, **42**, 371–93

Markusen J. and Venables, A., 1997. 'The Role of Multinationals in the Wage-Gap Debate', *Review of International Economics*, **5**, 435–51

Part Two
Market integration and regionalism

7 Operationalising the theory of optimum currency areas

TAMIM BAYOUMI AND
BARRY EICHENGREEN

1 Introduction

In the literature on optimum currency areas (OCAs), theory has always run ahead of empirics. The classic contributions of Mundell (1961), McKinnon (1964) and Kenen (1969) were essentially theoretical. Beyond some casual observations – Mundell's to the effect that Western Canada and the Western United States were subject to many of the same disturbances, McKinnon's that Canada was more open and trade-dependent than its neighbour to the south, Kenen's that the US economy was more sectorally diversified and less susceptible to idiosyncratic national shocks – little was done to fill the analytical framework with empirical content. This is not a criticism of the founding fathers of the theory of OCAs; the real puzzle is that so little systematic empirical work seeking to operationalise this literature has been undertaken over the course of the succeeding quarter-century.

In this respect, the debate over European monetary unification provoked by the Delors Report and the Maastricht Treaty has served as a healthy corrective. Recent years have seen a wave of empirical studies attempting to operationalise the theory of OCAs as a way of marshalling evidence on EMU's costs and benefits. It is that empirical literature that we seek to survey in this chapter. The fact that recent empirical work is itself a product of the debate over EMU necessarily lends our discussion a European cast.

There exist a number of recent surveys of the theory of OCAs, including several which take into their compass both theoretical and empirical studies.[1] Our purpose here is different: we focus on empirical work, examining the success with which theory has been operationalised.[2] After providing a critical assessment of the empirical literature in section 2, we report some extensions and sensitivity analyses in section 3. Section 4, in concluding, offers an agenda for research.

187

2   A review of theory and empirics

Mundell suggested that two countries or regions will wish to adopt a common currency area when the saving in transactions costs dominates the rise in adjustment costs. The reduction in transactions costs is an increasing function of openness, since more open economies suffer more severe disruptions to trade and production from currency fluctuations. Adjustment costs are a function of the symmetry of disturbances and the inter-regional mobility of labour. Not surprisingly, most research on OCAs, as applied to the European Union, rests squarely in the Mundellian tradition.

2.1   Symmetry of shocks

We are not aware of studies which made a serious attempt to estimate the symmetry of disturbances across and within currency areas prior to the debate over European monetary unification. In that literature, early contributors examined the correlation across countries of output movements (sometimes detrended output movements) and argued that countries whose GDPs tended to move together experienced relatively symmetrical disturbances. Cohen and Wyplosz (1989), Weber (1990) and European Commission (1990) are illustrative of this approach, which continues to be utilised to the present day (see, for example, Garrett, 1995).

From the point of view of faithfulness to Mundell's model, the problem with this approach is that observed output movements reflect the influence of both disturbances and responses. Imagine that two economies experience identical temporary disturbances, but that one responds more rapidly. In the first economy, output returns quickly to its initial level, while the second remains away from its equilibrium for an extended period. Although the correlation of disturbances is high, the correlation of output movements is low, and the latter tell us little about Mundell's first criterion for an OCA.[3]

Initial attempts to distinguish disturbances from other components of observed output movements identified shocks as the residuals from an autoregression. Caporale (1993), for example, regressed nominal and real GDP for various European countries on three own lags and examined the correlation of the residuals across countries. It is not clear that his results for nominal GDP are particularly useful, however, and those for real GDP are somewhat peculiar: the correlation of 'shocks' to the Dutch and German economies are if anything negative; only in Denmark and Portugal do shocks follow those of Germany. There is no evidence here, in other words, of an EMU 'hard core' and 'periphery'.

The difficulty of interpreting Caporale's results may reflect the fact that his estimated residuals incorporate the effects of a number of disturbances: aggregate demand disturbances associated with policy, which have only temporary effects on output in the textbook aggregate supply–aggregate demand model, and aggregate supply disturbances associated with other factors, which should have permanent output effects. Distinguishing the two types of disturbances requires more information and more structure. In our own work (Bayoumi and Eichengreen 1993a, 1993b, 1994) we utilised a method of Blanchard and Quah (1989) to distinguish aggregate supply and aggregate demand disturbances. We estimated bivariate autoregressions using data from 1968 through 1988 for output and prices, restricting demand disturbances to affect only prices in the long run while allowing supply disturbances to have long-run effects on both prices and output.[4] This exercise yielded clear evidence of an EU core and an EU periphery. The core, whose disturbances are highly correlated with those of Germany, includes Austria, Switzerland, France, Denmark and the Benelux countries. Included in the periphery are Italy, Spain, Portugal, Ireland, Greece, the United Kingdom and Finland. Sweden occupies something of an intermediate position.[5] Funke (1995) has replicated this analysis using data through 1992, finding similar results but somewhat lower correlations with Germany, not surprisingly since his period includes the highly asymmetric German unification shock.[6]

Subsequent work estimated larger dimension VARs in the attempt to distinguish a larger number of different disturbances. Chamie *et al.* (1994) utilise the same data and approach but distinguish monetary and non-monetary shocks on the demand side. When three shocks are specified, the distinction between and EU core and EU periphery is less clear-cut. Only Germany and Switzerland have highly correlated disturbances; Austria, Belgium, France, the Netherlands, Spain and the United Kingdom occupy an intermediate position, while Greece, Italy, Norway, Portugal and Sweden form a European periphery subject to relatively idiosyncratic shocks. Erkel-Rousse and Melitz (1995) estimate six-equation VARs on quarterly data for six European countries, finding a positive covariance between supply shocks to the Netherlands and supply shocks to Germany, but a negative association with Germany in the cases of France, the United Kingdom, Italy and Spain.[7]

The fact that some studies find disturbances to the members of the EU 'hard core' to be more highly correlated than those to the EU 'periphery' does not tell us that the disturbances to the core are sufficiently well correlated to support the operation of a monetary union. Neither do comparisons with existing monetary unions, although the results are suggestive. In the previously mentioned studies, we found that the correlation of disturbances to the eight Bureau of Economic Analysis regions of the United States are high but far from perfect. Indeed, the correlation is little different than that evinced by the members of the EU core, though significantly higher than that of the EU periphery. Funke, on the other hand, contrasts disturbances to EU countries with disturbances to German *Länder*, finding a noticeably higher correlation among the supply disturbances to the German states.[8] In the end, then, the jury remains out on whether the observed correlation of disturbances within existing monetary unions provides encouragement for EMU.[9]

The methodology used in these studies is not uncontroversial. Lippi and Reichlin (1993) point out that the Blanchard–Quah procedure incorporates the assumption that the error terms in the model are fundamental; they show that non-fundamental representations can give different results. This is a general problem which permeates all dynamic econometric analyses, however, and is not specific to the procedure at hand. Faust and Leeper (1994) observe that the identifying restriction that demand disturbances have no long-run output effects may be difficult to implement accurately using finite-horizon data and that problems of time aggregation complicate the task of accurately identifying supply and demand shocks. While this provides more grounds for worry, neither is their critique specific to this methodology; it applies equally to other strategies for distinguishing shocks from responses and analysing the speed with which equilibria are restored.

In this context, it is worth noting the work of Decressin and Fatas (1993), who examine employment rather than output. They regress employment in individual European regions (US states) on employment in Europe (the United States) as a whole, and find that the R^2 from these regressions averages 0.6 for the United States but only 0.2 for Europe.[10] Controlling for country-specific shocks diminishes but does not eliminate this differential.

2.2   Regional specialisation

While Mundell and later contributors to the OCA literature focused on the symmetry of disturbances, Kenen (1969) noted that asymmetric disturbances may be of little consequence if they are small. Only if disturbances are both large and asymmetric do they create a case for national policy autonomy. Kenen's article pointed to regional specialisation as a determinant of the magnitude of shocks. When a region possesses a sectorally diversified 'portfolio' of jobs, sector-specific shocks will tend to cancel out, minimising the amplitude of aggregate disturbances, much in the manner that shocks to individual asset returns cancel out in a well diversified financial portfolio. Two countries whose 'employment portfolios' are diversified so as to overlap will also tend to experience relatively symmetric aggregate disturbances *if* most shocks are sector-specific.

That is a big 'if'. Stockman (1988) finds that country-specific shocks account for as large a share of the variance of output as do sector-specific shocks that are common to different nations. This is not surprising if one thinks that demand shocks are important (since demand management policy is made at the national level).[11] But none of this is to question that both national and industrial disturbances matter; it is possible for many shocks on the supply side to be sector-specific (due to changes in technology and productivity that affect particular industries regardless of the country in which they are located), while most demand shocks are country-specific.

Bayoumi and Eichengreen (1997) attempt to test for evidence of a connection between such factors and observed policy toward the exchange rate. Using data on the network of bilateral exchange rates among the industrial countries in the 1960s, 1970s and 1980s, they relate the variability of bilateral rates to a vector of variables which includes the dissimilarity of the commodity composition of two countries' exports (defined as the sum of the absolute values of the differences in the shares of manufactured goods, food and minerals in total merchandise trade for each country).[12] They find strong evidence in support of the existence of this linkage.

Assuming a significant incidence of sector-specific shocks, it then becomes important to know the diversification and overlap of regional employment portfolios. Bini-Smaghi and Vori (1993), Helg *et al.* (1994) and Masson and Taylor (1993) have examined this question using data for European countries and the United States. They find a greater degree of diversification and overlap among member states of the European Union than among the 50 US states. The problem with basing inferences on this finding, as Krugman (1993) notes, is that these differences may themselves be artefacts of the historical degree of integration of the US and European economies. Because the 50 US states constitute a highly integrated internal market, each can specialise along lines of comparative advantage and exploit economies of scale and scope. As European integration deepens it will become more likely that EU member states will do likewise, and the observed overlap and diversification of member state employment portfolios will decline.

Two objections can be raised to this reasoning. One concerns the identification of regions with nations. Even if economies of scale and scope increasingly dominate locational decisions as the process of European integration proceeds, there is no reason to think that industrial concentrations will respect national borders. What was true in the past of the iron and steel complex of the Ruhr, the Saar and Lorraine will also be true, to an extent, in the future. A second objection is to the notion that external economies necessarily dominate location decisions. The advantages of agglomeration have to be balanced against lower costs of labour, land and other factor services outside the industrial heartland. (The attractions of peripheral locations are evident in the tendency for US industry to relocate away from the traditional manufacturing belt in the 1980s.) If this tendency dominates the evolution of Europe's economic geography as well, Bini-Smaghi and Vori may be right in assuming the continued expansion of intra-industry trade and growing overlap of regional employment portfolios.[13]

Additional light is shed on this question by Bayoumi and Prasad (1995), who distinguish global-, regional- and industrial-specific shocks. Comparing US regions with eight European countries, they find that the share of the variance in output explained by region-specific shocks is slightly higher in Europe than in the United States (31 per cent of the variance explained as against 26 per cent). For employment, in contrast, region-specific shocks dominate in Europe, industry-specific shocks in the United States. The lesser importance of region-specific shocks in the United States points to the higher degree of integration of the US labour market, a topic to which we now turn.

2.3   Labour market adjustment

Blanchard and Katz (1992) is the most widely cited study of the contribution of labour mobility to regional adjustment. Using data for US states, they find that inter-state migration plays a major role in adjustment to shocks. The contribution of migration to the elimination of labour market disequilibria, according to their results, dominates those of wage flexibility and labour force participation.[14] Decressin and Fatas (1993) obtain different results for the regions of Europe. In the first three years following a disturbance, they find, the largest portion of a decline in regional labour demand is met by lower labour force participation; immigration is important only after four years. Together, these results support the presumption that Europe is less well suited for monetary union than the United States on the grounds of its lesser responsiveness of migration to region-specific shocks.[15]

These conclusions are supported by the analysis of Eichengreen (1993a), who finds that the elasticity of inter-regional migration with respect to unemployment and wage differentials is significantly smaller in the United Kingdom and, especially, in Italy than in the United States.[16] De Grauwe and Vanhaverbeke (1993) similarly find that the migratory response across regions is significantly less in Southern than Northern Europe.

It is worth recalling that Mundell emphasised the role of migration in the operation of currency areas because he presumed that the social costs of relocation were less than the social costs of unemployment. But in fact neither Blanchard and Katz nor Decressin and Fatas find that the alternative to migration is unemployment; the former find that real wage flexibility is the other adjustment mechanism in the United States, while the latter identify changes in labour force participation as the main alternative in Europe. Neither team of authors finds much evidence that regional shocks result in persistent unemployment differentials. Their combined results support the notion that Europe is less well suited to monetary unification only if the social costs of migration are less than the social costs of reduced labour force participation, which is less than clear *a priori*.

It is worth noting (as does Buiter, 1995) that the finding that real wage flexibility plays a larger role in labour market adjustment in the United States than Europe has ambiguous implications for EMU. If real wages are rigid, they are unaffected by changes in nominal variables; any sacrifice of monetary autonomy associated with EMU is irrelevant from this point of view. However, few observers would go so far as to assert that real wages are impervious to exchange rate changes in the short run; the question, rather, is how the response divides into wage and employment effects. But there is the further question of whether the response of wages is itself a function of the exchange rate regime. Alogoskoufis and Smith (1992) and Eichengreen (1993b) provide evidence that this has been the case historically. Blanchard and Muet (1993) detect little sign that French wage behaviour has changed as the government's commitment to its exchange rate peg has hardened. Anderton and Barrell (1993), on the other hand, report some evidence of increasing wage flexibility in Italy over the period of that country's ERM membership.

2.4   Fiscal federalism

The labour market is not the only channel of adjustment to region-specific shocks. Since Ingram (1959), economists have argued that fiscal transfers within monetary unions provide an important cushion against asymmetric shocks. Sala-i-Martin and Sachs (1992) estimate the extent of the stabilisation provided by fiscal transfers among states within the US economic and monetary union, concluding that approximately a third of the impact of region-specific shocks is offset by the federal tax and transfer system. Their results have been criticised for neglecting the distinction between equalisation and stabilisation – in other words, transfers undertaken in response to persistent income differentials between regions and those extended in response to cyclical fluctuations.[17] (For our purposes, the distinction is equivalent to that between income differentials arising from permanent and temporary shocks.) Subsequent work by Bayoumi and Masson (1995) distinguishing equalisation from stabilisation scaled back Sala-i-Martin and Sachs' estimate of the stabilisation offset from a third to a quarter or a fifth.[18]

Bayoumi and Masson (1995) and Jones (1995), among others, have confirmed that fiscal equalisation and stabilisation are also important in other monetary unions, including those operated by individual European countries. The question is not whether equalisation and stabilisation take place, however, but whether they are indispensable to monetary union. The early literature pointed out that fiscal transfers were likely to be more important the less responsive was migration to regional wage and unemployment differentials; by implication, the absence of a system of fiscal federalism in Europe could be devastating, given the region's relative low levels of labour mobility.

Italianer and Pisani-Ferry (1992) have shown that installing a system of intra-state transfers that mimicked the regional stabilisation role of the US and Canadian systems would require increasing the size of the EU budget by approximately 50 per cent, assuming that the increased resources were targeted at this function. The problem with such a scheme is that the tendency for differences in national unemployment rates to persist would lead to large-scale redistribution across member states, not merely coinsurance. Even activating the scheme only after unemployment differentials exceeded a threshold level would fail to significantly diminish this effect (Melitz and Vori, 1992). A more sophisticated system that made intra-EU transfers a function of a vector of economic variables (not just unemployment) could finesse this problem in principle (von Hagen and Hammond, 1995) but would be difficult to implement in practice.

None of this is to suggest that such a programme is likely to be adopted in the foreseeable future.[19] Responding to these doubts about the prospects for significant fiscal centralisation, Bean (1992), Diba (1992) and Kletzer (1995), among others, have suggested that fiscal stabilisation can be carried out by the national governments of the countries that constitute the monetary union, operating on their own. National governments can run deficits and finance them externally in recessions and repay during expansions. Insofar as the inter-regional transfers accomplished by the institutions of fiscal federalism can be replicated by the unilateral actions of governments, the need for fiscal centralisation and coordination is obviated.[20]

Unfortunately, local jurisdictions may be inhibited by credit constraints from borrowing on the requisite scale. The smaller the region and the more mobile its tax base, the less scope it has for raising taxes relative to those prevailing in neighbouring regions to service and repay debts incurred in recessionary periods. This constraint will be further tightened by monetary union insofar as the removal of capital controls and reduction of transactions costs increase capital mobility.[21] Goldstein and Woglom (1994) show that this constraint binds in the United States when ratios of state debt to state product hit 9 per cent. Thus, it may not be realistic to rely on state borrowing to provide automatic stabilisation. Von Hagen and Fratianni (1991) and Kletzer (1995) suggest that credit rationing can be overcome if states undertake bilateral transfers on an ad hoc basis (a booming France can extend transfers to a slump-ridden Germany, and the favour can be returned when cyclical conditions reverse), and that the repeated nature of the game can support the continued cooperation of the parties concerned. But such ad hoc transfers are much more visible and politically contentious than automatic transfers flowing through a federal fiscal system, making their feasibility an open question.[22]

Fiscal stabilisation by local jurisdictions may also be less effective than stabilisation at a federal level. If the local jurisdiction runs higher deficits in order to offset a negative disturbances, the increase in government debt will generate an expectation of higher future taxation which will lower the impact of fiscal transfers on aggregate demand. If the stabilisation occurs at a higher level of government, however, a fiscal deficit in one region generated by a negative disturbance will on average be offset by fiscal surpluses in other regions with positive disturbances. To the extent that these effects cancel out, and hence there is no net impact on federal debt, there will be no expectation of future tax increases and hence no diminution of the impact on aggregate demand. Using Canadian provincial data, Bayoumi and Masson (1996) provide evidence that fiscal deficits which generate debt, and hence an expectation of future tax increases, have only one-third to one-half the effect on consumption as those which do not create debt.

2.5 *Relative prices*

An alternative empirical approach to assessing the suitability of a region for a currency union has been to compare movements in relative prices (measured in a common currency) between countries with those observed between regions within a country. The main advantage of having an independent exchange rate is that it provides a flexible instrument capable of moving relative prices between currency areas in the short term. An exchange rate appreciation of (say) 5 per cent will raise all prices in the appreciating country by 5 per cent compared to those in the country with the weaker rate (*ceteris paribus*). Comparing relative price movements within and between countries allows some assessment of the degree to which countries have actually used this flexibility in practice. If countries have not needed the relative price flexibility that an exchange rate provides in the past, in that the volatility of relative prices across countries with independent currencies has been no larger than those within countries with a single currency, then this would be powerful evidence that a flexible exchange rate was not necessary for the smooth functioning of the economy.

Vaubel (1978) was the first to use such an approach to look at the issue of OCAs. As interest in a single European currency engendered by the Werner Report of 1970 waned in the late 1970s, his paper compared the volatility of relative prices across and within European countries. He found that relative variability of CPIs (measured in a common currency) across European countries was several times that of three separate measures of variability within countries, using CPIs for German *Länder*, Italian cities, and US cities. He concluded that Europe was not well designed for a single currency.

Interest in such an approach was reinvigorated by Polosz (1990), who compared relative price movements across Canadian provinces with those across EU countries using GDP deflators. He found that the relative price variability between the raw material-producing provinces of Alberta and Saskatchewan was higher than that observed between Germany, France, Italy and the United Kingdom. Similar studies using US data, however, have found the opposite result. Both Eichengreen (1992), using regional CPIs, and Bayoumi and Thomas (1995), using regional GDP deflators, find variances across US regions to be much lower than those across European countries. The Bayoumi and Thomas result is particularly notable as, like Polosz, they used GDP deflators as their measure of the price level. GDP deflators are a better measure of movements in underlying costs across regions, and hence of the disruption to production caused by movements in relative prices, than are CPIs, which are heavily affected by the level of goods market integration.

Bayoumi and Thomas were the only authors to relate these movements in relative prices to changes in output. They estimated underlying demand and supply curves for goods both for European countries and US regions. They found that within the United States the larger relative price movements observed in the raw material-producing regions largely reflect the larger supply shocks that are prevalent in these regions.[23] By contrast, the much higher relative price movements observed within Europe compared to the United States reflected lower levels of integration on the demand and (particularly) the supply side across these economies. In the absence of greater integration, they concluded that large relative price movements are an important adjustment mechanism for coping with country-specific shocks to product markets within Europe.

Finally, von Hagen and Neumann (1994) and De Grauwe and Heens (1993) use relative price variability to gauge which countries are most suited to enter EMU. Von Hagen and Neumann find Austria and the Benelux countries to be good candidates for EMU using CPI data (with several other countries becoming better candidates over time) while De Grauwe and Heens, using unit labour costs, add France and Denmark to the list of good candidates. Bayoumi and Eichengreen (1997), who relate bilateral exchange rate volatility across industrial countries to OCA considerations, also find the Benelux countries to be relatively well suited for monetary union with Germany. For the other European countries, however, they find that the observed exchange rate variability for the 1980s was below what might be expected from their model.

A basic concern with this entire line of research comparing relative price variability within and between countries is that it assumes that all observed movement in relative prices reflect beneficial responses to underlying real disturbances. However, there are many who believe that much of the actual variability of nominal exchange rates simply reflects market froth, and hence that the exchange rate can itself become a source of economic disruptions. To the extent that this is true, the observation that relative prices are more variable across countries with independent currencies than across regions within a currency union simply reflects the nature of the exchange rate regime and tells us little about the suitability of countries for a single currency. The truth presumably lies somewhere between these two extremes. While all movements in exchange rate may not be beneficial, it is difficult to believe that they are completely unrelated to fundamentals. The problem is that we have little information on the relative importance of these two factors, which makes it difficult to assess the information in comparisons of relative price adjustments across and within countries. While we have learned much about volatility of relative prices across different exchange rate regimes, the exact relationship to OCA considerations remains unclear.

3   New evidence: German unification and economic integration

With this discussion as background, we will provide some new evidence on two topics involving the dynamic aspects of OCAs. Much of the existing work with respect to Europe focuses on the issue of whether Europe currently constitutes an OCA. However, Europe is also in a process of change. Two of the more obvious dynamic aspects of the current situation are the collapse of communism, which has affected plans for EMU most directly through the unification of the two halves of Germany, and the increasing economic integration within Europe caused by the widening and deepening of the Union over time.

As discussed earlier, our own earlier work on underlying disturbances within Europe (Bayoumi and Eichengreen, 1993a, 1993b, 1994) indicated the existence of a 'hard core' of countries with relatively similar underlying macroeconomic disturbances, made up of Germany and her immediate neighbours – France, Belgium, the Netherlands, Denmark, Austria, Switzerland and (possibly) Sweden – and a periphery made up of countries with significantly more idiosyncratic shocks – Italy, Spain, Portugal, Greece, Ireland, the United Kingdom, Norway and Finland. We used 1988 data, and hence did not include the effects of the reunification of east and west Germany in 1991. German unification has been generally interpreted as a large asymmetric shock to the anchor country in Europe, which led to policy divergences within Europe which were significant contributory factors in the exchange rate crises of 1992 and 1993. An asymmetric shock of such a magnitude might be expected to significantly alter estimated correlations of underlying disturbances across European countries.

Funke (1995) provided some evidence that German unification did indeed have such an effect. Repeating the structural VAR decomposition using data including German unification, he found that the correlations between the aggregate supply and demand shocks of Germany and other members of the European Union were consistently lower than those reported in our original work, an effect which he interpreted as being due to German unification. His analysis, however, focused exclusively on the bilateral correlations of underlying disturbances between Germany and other European countries. Our own earlier work indicated that underlying disturbances are also highly correlated between other members of the core. A natural question to ask, therefore, is whether German unification disrupted correlations of underlying disturbances between third countries within Europe or not.

To answer this question, we re-ran our earlier estimation using data on 16 European countries.[24] The underlying data on real and nominal GDP used in the estimation, which come from the *OECD National Accounts*, cover the period up to 1994. The data for Germany require some explanation. Up to 1990 they refer to the former West Germany, while from 1991 onwards they represent the reunified Germany. As a result of this change in definition real output jumps significantly in 1991 while the price level (measured using the GDP deflator) stays relatively constant. This impact from unification is limited to 1991; afterwards the output (and price) series behave in a very similar manner to what is seen prior to unification.

We estimated the structural VARs for Germany with no adjustment for the change in definition between 1990 and 1991. The results from the estimation indicate that in 1991 Germany experienced a very large positive aggregate supply disturbance combined with a positive aggregate demand shock whose size is similar to those found in other years.[25] Such results appear to be a reasonable interpretation of the macroeconomic impact of German unification using the aggregate demand–aggregate supply framework. Unification added a large, and chronically under-capitalised, labour force to the existing West German economy. This can be seen as a large positive shock to aggregate supply, generating a rise in potential output and a fall in output prices. At the same time, this was accompanied by a significant expansion in aggregate demand through fiscal expansion and the chosen conversion rate of the East German currency, which negated the deflationary impact of the aggregate supply shock. Hence, the decomposition appears to provide a reasonable interpretation of the impact of unification on the German economy.

Table 7.1 reports correlations of the estimated aggregate supply disturbances between 1963 and 1994 across our sample of countries using these structural vector autoregressions. Correlations which are significantly different from zero at the 5 per cent level are shaded.[26] So as to better gauge the impact of German unification, the bottom panel shows correlations using the same aggregate supply disturbances, but using only the estimated supply shocks from 1963 to 1990, the period prior to German unification. We focus initially upon aggregate supply disturbances as they are less likely to be affected by macroeconomic policy decisions, and hence probably provide a better estimate of underlying behaviour.

The results for the full 1963–94 period clearly illustrate the impact of German unification on the correlation of underlying disturbances between Germany and other countries in Europe. Only two of the bilateral correlations between Germany and other European countries are significantly different from zero, and even these are only very

Table 7.1. *Correlation matrices of aggregate supply shocks, 1963–93*

1963–93

	GE	FR	NT	BE	AT	SZ	DE	SW	IT	UK	IR	FI	SP	PO	NO
GE															
FR	0.31														
NT	0.29	0.59													
BE	0.35	0.63	0.68												
AT	0.32	0.48	0.45	0.53											
SZ	0.20	0.53	0.64	0.61	0.54										
DE	0.36	0.53	0.39	0.32	0.22	0.23									
SW	0.15	0.49	0.50	0.24	0.15	0.49	0.29								
IT	0.22	0.50	0.57	0.29	0.22	0.24	0.23	0.55							
UK	0.18	0.49	0.24	0.29	-0.00	0.20	0.16	0.42	0.38						
IR	-0.03	-0.05	0.14	0.00	0.06	0.05	-0.08	0.13	0.19	-0.05					
FI	-0.03	0.48	0.23	0.30	0.31	0.39	0.44	0.48	0.22	0.27	0.06				
SP	0.20	0.09	0.19	0.26	0.27	0.19	0.06	0.30	0.02	0.03	-0.16	0.23			
PO	0.08	0.21	0.13	0.25	-0.01	0.12	0.02	0.30	0.12	0.41	0.01	0.07	0.49		
NO	0.26	0.17	0.43	0.32	0.19	0.20	0.27	-0.01	0.22	-0.31	-0.00	0.11	0.03	-0.31	
GR	-0.02	0.10	0.08	-0.05	0.14	0.04	-0.20	-0.02	0.26	-0.20	0.03	0.04	0.11	0.05	0.17

Table 7.1. (contd)

1963–90

	GE	FR	NT	BE	AT	SZ	DE	SW	IT	UK	IR	FI	SP	PO	NO
GE															
FR	0.31														
NT	0.29	0.59													
BE	0.52	0.57	0.65												
AT	0.46	0.47	0.41	0.49											
SZ	0.34	0.51	0.62	0.61	0.52										
DE	0.52	0.50	0.35	0.27	0.20	0.21									
SW	0.34	0.46	0.52	0.21	0.14	0.49	0.37								
IT	0.35	0.34	0.54	0.11	0.16	0.18	0.16	0.51							
UK	0.34	0.46	0.18	0.21	-0.09	0.16	0.13	0.43	0.34						
IR	0.05	-0.22	0.08	-0.07	0.04	0.01	-0.18	0.09	0.09	-0.09					
FI	0.37	0.36	0.08	0.20	0.26	0.35	0.44	0.46	0.02	0.17	-0.09				
SP	0.27	0.16	0.22	0.31	0.29	0.20	0.08	0.38	0.10	0.04	-0.14	0.30			
PO	0.18	0.29	0.14	0.30	-0.01	0.13	0.02	0.40	0.24	0.43	0.02	0.07	0.49		
NO	0.29	0.06	0.41	0.29	0.18	0.20	0.19	-0.01	0.12	-0.36	-0.10	0.08	0.07	-0.30	
GR	0.03	0.09	0.10	-0.02	0.19	0.04	-0.20	-0.12	0.29	-0.20	-0.01	0.01	0.13	0.07	0.19

marginally so. By contrast, when the data are truncated in 1990 Germany has large and highly significant correlations with all of her immediate neighbours except Switzerland. German unification does not, however, appear to have significantly disrupted the cohesion of the other countries in the European core. All of the correlations between France, the Netherlands, Belgium, Austria and Switzerland are significant in both time periods. Indeed, the addition of the 1991 to the 1994 data appears to have generally increased these correlations. Hence, while German unification clearly had an important impact on the estimated level of cohesion between Germany and her neighbours, it does not appear to have caused disruption within the later group. It was, in other words, an asymmetric shock which purely affected Germany.

The results in table 7.1 also broadly confirm our original analysis as to the existence of a European hard core and periphery. The correlations up until 1990 still point to an inner group of countries – Germany, France, the Netherlands, Belgium, Austria and Switzerland – whose underlying disturbances are almost all significantly correlated. Denmark, Sweden and (possibly) Italy also have reasonably high correlations with the larger members of the core, Germany, France and the Netherlands. The underlying aggregate supply disturbances for the remaining countries show relatively little systematic correlation either with the core or with each other. Hence, with the potentially important exception of Italy, whose connection with the core appears somewhat closer than our earlier results would have suggested, the distinction of the core and periphery appear consistent with our earlier analysis.[27]

Truncating the data in 1990 represents one method of eliminating the impact of German unification from the data. Two other methods for achieving the same goal were also investigated. The first involved using the estimated disturbances over the full 1963–94 sample but excluding the data for 1991 from the calculations of the underlying correlations. The second involved re-estimating the German structural vector auto-regression with dummy variables in the estimation for 1991, so as to exclude the effects of the 1991 structural break from the estimation. Both of these approaches gave very similar results to those reported in the lower panel of table 7.1.

The correlations using the estimated aggregate demand disturbances are shown in table 7.2. Confirming the results of our earlier work, the distinction between the core and the periphery is less clear, although there is still a tendency for correlations to become more prevalent in the upper-left corner of the matrix. Another interesting feature of the results is that, unlike the results for the aggregate supply shocks, excluding the period after German unification has little impact on the analysis. As

Table 7.2. Correlation matrices of aggregate demand shocks, 1963–93

1963–93

	GE	FR	NT	BE	AT	SZ	DE	SW	IT	UK	IR	FI	SP	PO	NO
GE															
FR	0.28														
NT	0.19	0.32													
BE	0.20	0.51	0.48												
AT	0.35	0.31	0.21	0.58											
SZ	0.23	0.34	0.38	0.25	0.41										
DE	0.24	0.21	0.02	0.19	0.23	0.09									
SW	0.25	0.25	0.23	0.31	0.02	0.06	0.08								
IT	0.37	0.56	0.26	0.43	0.51	0.37	0.02	0.17							
UK	0.12	-0.02	0.21	0.03	-0.25	-0.11	-0.18	0.43	-0.06						
IR	-0.03	-0.00	0.43	0.03	-0.18	0.18	0.16	0.19	-0.09	0.50					
FI	-0.05	0.29	0.20	0.40	0.24	0.25	0.14	0.03	0.44	0.10	-0.02				
SP	0.01	0.53	0.08	0.20	0.34	0.14	-0.03	0.10	0.37	0.06	-0.09	0.17			
PO	0.24	0.28	0.04	0.30	0.51	0.36	-0.04	0.20	0.58	0.08	0.01	0.25	0.42		
NO	0.32	-0.00	0.21	0.26	0.17	0.17	0.34	0.23	0.36	-0.00	0.17	0.05	-0.11	0.10	
GR	0.17	0.05	0.11	0.04	-0.03	0.08	-0.15	0.32	0.05	0.32	0.26	-0.32	0.16	0.46	-0.02

Table 7.2. (contd)
1963–90

	GE	FR	NT	BE	AT	SZ	DE	SW	IT	UK	IR	FI	SP	PO	NO
GE															
FR	0.29														
NT	0.18	0.28													
BE	0.25	0.48	0.47												
AT	0.36	0.27	0.18	0.57											
SZ	0.19	0.30	0.35	0.23	0.41										
DE	0.26	0.19	0.00	0.18	0.20	0.09									
SW	0.21	0.11	0.15	0.28	−0.10	−0.14	0.07								
IT	0.33	0.55	0.22	0.43	0.50	0.32	0.01	0.02							
UK	0.17	−0.13	0.16	−0.04	−0.32	−0.23	−0.21	0.33	−0.14						
IR	0.01	−0.03	0.44	0.00	−0.18	0.17	0.18	0.17	−0.10	0.48					
FI	0.03	0.29	0.20	0.39	0.29	0.25	0.17	−0.03	0.49	−0.01	−0.10				
SP	−0.09	0.48	−0.02	0.12	0.27	0.03	−0.09	−0.26	0.31	−0.07	−0.14	0.19			
PO	0.21	0.27	−0.01	0.28	0.56	0.35	−0.05	−0.01	0.62	0.08	−0.01	0.33	0.28		
NO	0.29	−0.04	0.19	0.26	0.19	0.10	0.38	0.12	0.33	−0.09	0.15	0.02	−0.23	0.05	
GR	0.06	0.03	0.12	0.03	−0.11	0.03	−0.17	0.32	−0.04	0.52	0.36	−0.32	0.01	0.25	−0.08

Table 7.3. *Coherence of aggregate supply disturbances, 1963–94*
(percentage of variance explained by the first principal component)

	1963–72	1973–83	1984–94
EU core[a]	44	66	53
Extended core[b]	37	52	45
Other EC[c]	40	41	35
Total EU[d]	26	38	32
Control group[e]	47	50	57

Notes:
[a] 'EU core' refers to Germany, France, the Netherlands, Belgium, Austria and Switzerland.
[b] The 'extended core' adds Denmark, Sweden and Italy.
[c] 'Other EU' refers to the United Kingdom, Ireland, Spain, Portugal, Greece and Finland.
[d] 'Total EU' refers to the 14 current members of the European Union in the data set (i.e. the EU-15 excluding Luxembourg).
[e] The control group is made up of the United States, Japan, Canada, Australia and New Zealand.

might be expected, unification is identified as an idiosyncratic aggregate supply shock.

The focus to date has been on analysing correlations across the full 1963–94 sample. However, it is evident that the level of integration of the European economy has changed greatly over the period. The EEC in 1963 contained only six members, compared to the current European Union's 15, and intra-regional trade has risen steadily over time. It is of some interest, therefore, to consider whether the coherence of the underlying disturbances has risen over time. As estimates of individual bilateral correlations become highly unstable over short sample periods, we elected to use the explanatory power of the first principal component of the estimated underlying disturbances across various groupings of countries to analyse trends in the cohesion of disturbances.[28] To control for the impact of external trends in coherence caused by world events – for example, the oil price shocks in the 1970s – which affect all countries, we also include in the analysis a group of five non-European OECD countries (the United States, Japan, Canada, Australia and New Zealand).

Table 7.3 shows the results from the analysis using the estimated aggregate supply disturbances.[29] It reports the percentage of the overall variance of the aggregate demand and aggregate supply disturbances explained by the first principal component for four country groupings over three approximately equal periods, 1963–73, 1973–83 and 1984–94.

The country groupings are: the EU 'core' (Germany, France, the Netherlands, Belgium, Austria and Switzerland); an 'extended core' which includes Denmark, Sweden and Italy; the other EU members in the data set (excluding Luxembourg); the 14 members of the European Union in the data set; and the five non-European countries discussed above. It should be noted at the outset that the explanatory power of the first principal component will generally fall as the number of countries increases, so the primary interest in the analysis is in changes in explanatory power within the same groups across time.

The four European groupings follow a fairly similar pattern. The percentage of the variance explained by the first principal component rises between 1963–72 and 1973–83 and then falls from 1973–83 to 1984–94, ending up in most cases higher in the 1980s and 1990s than it was in the 1960s. By contrast, in the control group the percentage of the variance explained by the first principal component rises throughout the sample. Compared to the control, therefore, there appears to be little evidence that increasing close economic ties within Europe has promoted convergence in underlying disturbances. Indeed, if anything, the evidence points to the reverse, although with such a small control group we would certainly not wish to push such a conclusion too far.

In addition to increasing trade between regions, economic integration will also increase the specialisation of production. This specialisation of production may well explain why there appears to have been no move towards greater correlation of underlying disturbances within Europe over time. To the extent that disturbances are industry-specific, greater specialisation of production will tend to make underlying disturbances across regions less similar (Krugman, 1993). Much of the discussion of this issue, reviewed earlier in this chapter, has focused on the degree to which specialisation across regions of the European Union compares with specialisation across US regions. Estimates of trends in the degree of industry specialisation over time, by contrast, has attracted less attention.

Table 7.4 shows some estimates of how the level of industrial specialisation in the EU has changed between the 1970s and the 1980s for eight industries. For each industry the level of specialisation is calculated as the coefficient of variation of the share of that industry in total output for each of across eight EU countries.[30] The more diverse the shares of output across countries, and hence the greater the amount of regional specialisation of production, the larger is the coefficient of variation (the coefficient of variation – i.e. the standard deviation divided by the mean of the observations – was used in the calculations as some industries were significantly larger than others). To control for general trends in geographic specialisation caused by factors such as technological innova-

Table 7.4. *Trends in regional specialisation of production for the European Union and the United States, 1972–87*
(coefficient of variation across eight countries/regions)

	1971–9	1980–7	Difference
European Union			
Primary goods	0.67	0.67	0.00
Construction	0.18	0.21	+0.03
Manufacturing	0.23	0.22	−0.01
Transportation	0.15	0.19	+0.04
Retail and wholesale trade	0.22	0.21	−0.01
Finance	0.33	0.36	+0.03
Other private services	0.64	0.73	+0.09
Government	0.17	0.23	+0.06
United States			
Primary goods	0.92	0.80	−0.12
Construction	0.14	0.20	+0.06
Manufacturing	0.32	0.26	−0.06
Transportation	0.09	0.12	+0.03
Retail and wholesale trade	0.08	0.04	−0.04
Finance	0.15	0.09	−0.06
Other private services	0.18	0.16	−0.02
Government	0.15	0.13	−0.02

Notes: The EU data consists of Austria, Belgium, Denmark, Germany, Greece, Italy, the Netherlands and the United Kingdom. The US data consists of the eight standard BEA regions. For details about the data see Bayoumi and Prasad (1995).

tion, the bottom half of table 7.4 reports the calculations for the same industries across eight US regions.[31]

The results from table 7.4 indicate some trend toward greater specialisation across EU countries (for further empirical evidence on increasing specialisation in Europe see Smith's discussion of chapter 9 by Venables in this volume). All five of the industries in the European Union which had a change in their coefficient of variation of more than 0.01 between 1971–9 and 1980–7 showed an increase in regional specialisation. By contrast, within the United States over the same period in six of the eight industries the coefficient of variation across regions fell (construction and transportation bucked this trend), which is consistent with the view that easier communications have increased the attractions of locating in more peripheral regions. Thus, over a period in which regional specialisation in the United States appears to have been declining, specialisation within the European Union appears to have increased.

While acknowledging the limitations of this exercise, in particular the very broad definitions of industries being used in the calculations, these results support the notion that increasing economic integration has been accompanied by a measurable in rise in economic specialisation. If anything, this process has generated some decrease in the correlation of underlying disturbances, a result which is in line with the analysis provided in Krugman (1993).

4   Conclusion

Empirical analyses building on the theory of OCAs have come a long way since the Delors Report and its background studies (European Commission, 1990). Relatively successful techniques have been developed for measuring the size and correlation of underlying disturbances across different regions, the role of labour mobility in restoring equilibrium within existing currency unions and the level of insurance provided by federal tax systems. More generally, the criteria identified in the theoretical literature – asymmetric shocks, labour mobility and fiscal transfers – do indeed appear to matter in actual currency unions. There may not be agreement on answers, but the questions have gained definition. There is, in short, a framework for debate.

Much of the dispute which remains revolves around the issue of the inferences that can be validly drawn from historical data. Monetary unification, in Europe as elsewhere, will be a structural break. It will alter market structures and policy processes. Correlations that held in a past of segmented national markets and independent policies may not hold in the integrated Europe of the future. Some authors have taken this point on board by searching for changes in economic relationships over the period when European integration has deepened and by comparing Europe with existing monetary unions such as the United States. Others, including ourselves in this chapter, have attempted to look at the impact of changes over time within Europe on OCA criteria. But whether either of these approaches provides the guidance needed to forecast the changes that will take place with EMU remains an open question, and one on which reasonable people can (and do) disagree.

Despite these concerns, the impact of economic change on OCA criteria is clearly becoming an increasingly important issue. The implication is that future empirical work is likely to be increasingly concerned with these dynamic aspects of OCAs, and in particular with the interaction between economic integration and the net benefits from adopting a currency union. In addition to being central to much of the debate about EMU, such issues have a much wider resonance in an world of increasing globalisation. If the next five years of empirical work on OCAs are as productive as the last five, the progress will be impressive indeed.

NOTES

This is a revised version of a paper prepared for the CEPR conference on 'Regional Integration' (La Coruña, 26–27 April 1996).

1 See for example Masson and Taylor (1993), Tavlas (1994).

2 Melitz (1996) covers some of the same ground.

3 One may argue that differences across economies in both the symmetry of disturbances and the speed of response are in fact relevant to the decision of whether to fix the exchange rate or adopt a common currency, and that insofar as the speed of response heavily reflects Mundell's second consideration, the mobility of labour between depressed and booming regions, the information contained in output movements is still highly relevant. But from an analytical point of view, it is still important to know whether a high correlation of output movements reflects symmetric shocks or rapid, symmetric responses. About this, observed output movements tell us little.

4 Blanchard and Quah's original study utilised data on output and unemployment, with the assumption that demand disturbances had no long-run output effects. The problem with this implementation is that it is not clear why demand disturbances should be permitted to affect unemployment in the long run cither, as permitted by Blanchard and Quah. In contrast, our implementation using output and prices can utilise the textbook prediction that a rightward shift in the aggregate demand curve should, in the presence of a vertical long-run supply curve, raise prices permanently. The prediction that prices should rise rather than fall in the long run is not imposed in estimation and may be utilised to check the consistency of the results.

5 Our 1994 paper also extended this type of approach to East Asia and the Americas.

6 A more surprising aspect of Funke's results is that, unlike the present authors, he finds supply shocks to the United Kingdom to be relatively highly correlated with supply shocks to Germany. This result may reflect the fact that the United Kingdom's post-1990 recession set in relatively early (as did Germany's), raising the correlation.

7 For completeness, we mention also Ghosh and Wolf (1994), who use a genetic approach to identify country groupings. While their method identifies several natural clusters of EU member states, they appear to find that Germany is not a natural member of any group.

8 De Grauwe and Vanhaverbeke (1993), on the other hand, can be read as showing that the shocks to regions within EU countries are relatively large, implying that the observed asymmetry of shocks to the various candidate nations for EMU are not a prohibitive barrier to its successful operation.

9 Inference suffers from the further problem, as we have noted in our own work, that the observed pattern of disturbances may shift with EMU. This Lucas Critique is less likely to apply to permanent, or supply, disturbances, insofar as those are associated with economic structure, than to temporary, or

demand, disturbances associated with policy. Hence, our discussion here, as elsewhere, focuses primarily on the correlation of supply disturbances. We return to this point below.

10 An earlier study which reported essentially the same finding is Eichengreen (1990).

11 Costello (1993) has undertaken a similar exercise using measures of productivity growth (Solow residuals): she finds that nation-specific factors are substantially more important than industry-specific components.

12 'Manufactured goods' were defined as the total of basic manufactures, chemicals, machines and transport equipment, miscellaneous manufactured goods and other goods. 'Food' is the sum of food and live animals, beverages and tobacco and animal, vegetable oils and fats. 'Minerals' amalgamate data on crude materials excluding fuel with mineral fuels, etc.

13 For similar arguments, see Gros and Thygesen (1991) and Spahn (1992).

14 Buiter (1995), while not denying that labour mobility is higher in the United States than in Europe, questions whether the degree of labour mobility in the United States is really sufficient to contribute importantly to adjustment to macroeconomic shocks.

15 Thomas (1994) also provides a VAR-based analysis of US and European data. While confirming Blanchard and Katz's findings for the United States, he suggests that in Europe the substitute for inter-regional migration is not changes in labour force participation rates but persistent unemployment. Part of the explanation for the discrepancy appears to be the unit of observation: Thomas analyses time series at the national level for various European countries rather than a panel of regional data like the other authors. One can imagine that a national shock to employment could give rise to persistent unemployment, while a shock specific to a region within that country did not. But this cannot be the entire difference, since Thomas also finds that region-specific shocks give rise to persistent unemployment differentials in a panel of British regions.

16 For other analyses that point in the same direction, see Muet (1991, 1995) and Mantel (1994).

17 See von Hagen (1993).

18 They also find a smaller stabilisation effect operating through taxes and transfers in Canada than in the United States, which is offset to a large extent by the greater freedom of Canadian provinces (compared to US states) to borrow and run deficits in recessions.

19 Von Hagen (1993) suggests that this resistance is rational, on the grounds that a system of federal fiscal transfers to depressed states, say through the operation of an EU-financed unemployment insurance programme, would give rise to serious moral hazard problems that are more easily contained within existing EU member states by national solidarity. Goodhart and Smith (1993), however, propose a mechanism with which potential moral hazard problems might be contained.

20 An obvious question at this point is why households need the intervention of government to carry out this function. Cannot households borrow externally in periods of recession to smooth their consumption, thereby stabilising the local economy? Atkesen and Bayoumi (1994) show that some private borrowing through capital markets in fact takes place in the US economic and monetary union but that its magnitude is small, presumably reflecting

liquidity constraints associated with the dominance of human capital in household wealth.

21 In addition, McKinnon (1995) suggests that the members of monetary unions can be rationed out of capital markets by rising default risk resulting from their lack of a central bank to backstop the market in public debt.

22 Recall how much more difficult it was in 1994 for Washington, DC to arrange Congressional support for an ad hoc transfer to Mexico than to continue to transfer resources automatically to a state of California with an unemployment rate in excess of that of the rest of the country. In addition, there is the fact that bilateral transfers, as in the Franco-German example cited in the text, place a heavy burden on the country that extends the transfer compared to a system of fiscal federalism involving a dozen EU member states or 50 US states, in which the burden of the transfer is shared among a number of separate jurisdictions, diversifying the risk. A Kletzer-like scheme of ad hoc transfers would clearly grow more difficult to arrange as the number of governments concerned continued to increase.

23 This may also help explain the very large relative price movements for Alberta and Saskatchewan within Canada.

24 The countries are 14 of the current 15 members of the European Union (Luxembourg is excluded as it is so small) plus two non-members (Switzerland and Norway). These represent all of the significant European economies which are actual or prospective members of the European Union over the estimation period.

25 The impulse response functions for the aggregate demand and aggregate supply shocks generated by the estimation also appear reasonable. In particular, the short-term impact of an aggregate supply shock is to lower the price level.

26 The statistic $1/2 \log((1+r)/(1-r))$, where r is the correlation coefficient, is distributed approximately normally with a variance of T-3, where T is the number of time periods in the data (Kendall and Stuart, 1967, pp. 292–3).

27 In particular, the more positive assessment of the place of the United Kingdom within Europe found by Funke (1995) using data up to 1992 does not appear to hold over our somewhat longer sample period.

28 The same approach was used in Bayoumi and Eichengreen (1993b).

29 We focus on aggregate supply disturbances as the results for the aggregate demand disturbances appear less satisfactory, presumably because they include the effect of macroeconomic policies.

30 The data come from the *OECD National Accounts*. The eight industries are agriculture, construction, manufacturing, transportation, wholesale and retail trade, finance, other private services and government. The eight EU countries are Austria, Belgium, Denmark, Germany, Greece, Italy, Netherlands and the United Kingdom (constraints on data availability led us to exclude other important European countries such as France). See Bayoumi and Prasad (1995) for more details about the data.

31 The US data come from the *Gross State Product Accounts* of the Bureau of Economic Analysis (BEA). The industry groupings for the European Union and United States are as closely lined up as is possible given the fact that the US gross state product data use slightly different industrial definitions from the OECD. The eight US regions are the standard BEA classifications: New England, Mid-East, Great Lakes, Plains, South-East, South-West, Rocky Mountains and Far-West.

REFERENCES

Alogoskoufis, G. and Smith, R., 1992. 'The Phillips Curve, the Persistence of Inflation, and the Lucas Critique: Evidence from Exchange Rate Regimes', *American Economic Review*, **81**, 1254–75

Anderton, R. and Barrell, R., 1993. 'The ERM and Structural Change in European Labour Markets: A Study of 10 Countries', *NIESR Discussion Paper*, **40**

Atkesen, A. and Bayoumi, T., 1994. 'Do Private Capital Markets Insure Against Risk in a Common Currency Area?', University of Chicago and International Monetary Fund, unpublished manuscript

Bayoumi, T. and Eichengreen, B., 1993a. 'Shocking Aspects of European Monetary Unification', in F. Torres and F. Giavazzi (eds.), *Adjustment and Growth in the European Monetary Union* (Cambridge: Cambridge University Press for the CEPR), 193–230

1993b. 'Is There a Conflict Between EC Enlargement and European Monetary Unification?', *Greek Economic Review*, **15**, 131–54

1994. 'One Money or Many? On Analyzing the Prospects for Monetary Unification in Various Parts of the World', *Princeton Essays in International Finance*, **76** (Princeton: International Finance Section, Princeton University)

1997. 'Optimum Currency Areas and Exchange Rate Volatility: Theory and Evidence Compared', in B. Cohen (ed.), *Frontiers of International Economics* (Cambridge: Cambridge University Press)

Bayoumi, T. and Masson, P.R., 1995. 'Fiscal Flows in the United States and Canada: Lessons for Monetary Union in Europe', *European Economic Review*, **39**, 253–74

1996. 'Debt-creating versus Non-debt-creating Policies: Ricardian Equivalence, Fiscal Stabilisation, and EMU', International Monetary Fund, unpublished manuscript

Bayoumi, T. and Prasad, E., 1995. 'Currency Union, Economic Fluctuations and Adjustment: Some Empirical Evidence', *CEPR Discussion Paper*, **1172**

Bayoumi, T. and Thomas, A., 1995. 'Relative Prices and Economic Adjustments in the US and EU: A Real Story about Monetary Union', *IMF Staff Papers*, **41**, 108–33

Bean, C., 1992. 'Economic and Monetary Union in Europe', *Journal of Economic Perspectives*, **6**, 31–52

Bini-Smaghi, L. and Vori, S., 1993. 'Rating the EC as an Optimal Currency Area', *Bank of Italy Discussion Paper*, **187**

Blanchard, O. and Katz, L., 1992. 'Regional Evolutions', *Brookings Papers on Economic Activity*, **1**, 1–75

Blanchard, O. and Muet, P.A., 1993. 'Competitiveness Through Disinflation: An Assessment of the French Macroeconomic Strategy', *Economic Policy*, **16**, 11–56

Blanchard, O. and Quah, D., 1989. 'The Dynamic Effects of Aggregate Demand and Supply Disturbances', *American Economic Review*, **79**, 655–73

Buiter, W., 1995. 'Macroeconomic Policy During the Transition to Monetary Union', *CEPR Discussion Paper*, **1222**

Carporale, G.M., 1993. 'Is Europe an Optimum Currency Area? Symmetric versus Asymmetric Shocks in the EC', *National Institute Economic Review*, **144**, 93–105

Chamie, N., Deserres, A. and Lalonde, R., 1994. 'Optimum Currency Areas and Shock Asymmetry: A Comparison of Europe and the United States', *Bank of Canada Working Paper*, **94/1**

Cohen, D. and Wyplosz, C., 1989. 'The European Monetary Union: An Agnostic Evaluation', *CEPR Discussion Paper*, **306**

Costello, D. M., 1993. 'A Cross-country, Cross-industry Comparison of Productivity Growth', *Journal of Political Economy*, **101**, 207–22

Decressin, J. and Fatas, A., 1993. 'Regional Labour Market Dynamics in Europe and Implications for EMU', International Monetary Fund and INSEAD, unpublished manuscript

De Grauwe, P. and Heens, H., 1993. 'Real Exchange Rate Variability in Monetary Unions', *Recherches Economiques de Louvain*, **59**, 105–17

De Grauwe, P. and Vanhaverbeke, W., 1993. 'Is Europe an Optimimum Currency Area? Evidence from Regional Data', in P. R. Masson and M. P. Taylor (eds.), *Policy Issues in the Operation of Currency Unions* (Cambridge: Cambridge University Press), 111–30

Diba, B. T., 1992. 'Discussion of Sala-i-Martin and Sachs', in M. Canzoneri, V. Grilli and P. R. Masson (eds.), *Establishing a Central Bank: Issues in Europe and Lessons from the US* (Cambridge: Cambridge University Press), 220–2

Eichengreen, B., 1990. 'One Money for Europe? Lessons from the US Currency and Customs Union', *Economic Policy*, **10**, 117–87

1992. 'Is Europe an Optimum Currency Area?', in S. Borner and H. Grubel (eds.), *The European Community After 1992: The View from Outside* (London: Macmillan)

1993a. 'Labour Markets and European Monetary Unification', in P.R. Masson and M.P. Taylor (eds.), *Policy Issues in the Operation of Currency Unions* (Cambridge: Cambridge University Press)

1993b. 'Epilogue: Three Perspectives on the Bretton Woods System', in M. D. Bordo and B. Eichengreen (eds.), *A Retrospective on the Bretton Woods System* (Chicago: University of Chicago Press), 621–58

1996. *Mediating Markets: A Short History of the International Monetary System* (Princeton: Princeton University Press)

Erkel-Rousse, H. and Melitz, J., 1995. 'New Empirical Evidence on the Costs of European Monetary Union', *INSEE Working Paper*, **9516**

European Commission, 1990. 'One Market, One Money', Special Issue of *European Economy*, **44** (October) (Brussels: European Commission)

Faust, J. and Leeper, E., 1994. 'When Do Long-run Identifying Restrictions Give Reliable Results?', Board of Governors of the Federal Reserve System, *International Finance Discussion Paper*, **462**

Funke, M., 1995. 'Europe's Monetary Future: One Market, One Money?', Humbolt University, unpublished manuscript

Garrett, G., 1995. 'The Political Economy of Economic and Monetary Union', in B. Eichengreen and J. Frieden (eds.), *The Future of European Integration* (Cambridge: Cambridge University Press)

Ghosh, A. R. and Wolf, H.C., 1994. 'How Many Monies? A Genetic Approach to Finding Optimum Currency Areas', *NBER Working Paper*, **4805**

Goldstein, M. and Woglom, G., 1994. 'Market-based Fiscal Discipline in Monetary Unions: Evidence from the US Municipal Bond Market', in M. Canzoneri, V. Grilli and P. R. Masson (eds.), *Establishing a Central Bank: Issues in Europe and Lessons from the US* (Cambridge: Cambridge University Press), 228–60

Goodhart, C., 1995. 'The Political Economy of Monetary Union', in P. B. Kenen (ed.), *Understanding Interdependence: The Macroeconomics of the Open Economy* (Princeton: Princeton University Press), 450–505

Goodhart, C. and Smith, S., 1993. 'Stabilisation', *European Economy*, **5**, 417–55

Gros, D. and Thygesen, N., 1991. *European Monetary Integration: From the European Monetary System to European Monetary Union* (London: Longman)

Helg, R., Manasse, P., Monacelli, T. and Rovelli, R., 1994. 'How Much (A)symmetry in Europe? Evidence from Industrial Sectors', *IGIER Working Paper*, **70**

Ingram, J., 1959. 'State and Regional Payments Mechanisms', *Quarterly Journal of Economics*, **73**, 619–32

Italianer, A. and Pisani-Ferry, J., 1992. 'Regional Stabilisation Properties of Fiscal Arrangements: What Lessons for the Community?', European Commission and CEPII, unpublished manuscript

Jones, E., 1995. 'The European Monetary Trade-off: Economic Adjustment in Small Countries', CEPS, unpublished manuscript

Kendall, M. and Stuart, A., 1967. *The Advanced Theory of Statistics*, vol. 2 (New York: Hafner Publishing Company)

Kenen, P., 1969. 'The Theory of Optimum Currency Areas: An Eclectic View', in R. A. Mundell and A. K. Swoboda (eds.), *Monetary Problems of the International Economy* (Chicago: University of Chicago Press), 41–60

Kletzer, K., 1995. 'The Implications of Monetary Union for Fiscal Policy in Europe', in B. Eichengreen and J. Frieden (eds.), *The Future of European Integration* (Cambridge: Cambridge University Press)

Krugman, P., 1993. 'Lessons of Massachusetts for EMU', in F. Torres and F. Giavazzi (eds.), *Adjustment and Growth in the European Monetary Union* (Cambridge: Cambridge University Press for the CEPR), 241–60

Lippi, M. and Reichlin, L., 1993. 'The Dynamic Effects of Aggregate Demand and Supply Disturbances', *American Economic Review*, **83**, 644–52

Mantel, S., 1994. 'The Prospects for Labour Mobility Under EMU', *Economie et Statistique*, Special Issue, 137–47

Masson, P.R. and M. P. Taylor, 1993, 'Currency Unions: A Survey of the Issues', in P. R. Masson and M. P. Taylor (eds.), Policy Issues in the Operation of Currency Unions (Cambridge: Cambridge University Press), 3–51

McKinnon, R., 1964. 'Optimum Currency Areas', *American Economic Review*, **53**, 717–25

    1995. 'Comment: A Fiscally Consistent Proposal for Reforming the European Monetary System', in P. B. Kenen (ed.), *Understanding Interdependence: The Macroeconomics of the Open Economy* (Princeton: Princeton University Press), 88–97

Mélitz, J., 1996. 'The Evidence About Costs and Benefits of EMU', INSEE, unpublished manuscript

Mélitz, J. and Vori, S., 1992. 'National Insurance Against Unevenly Distributed Shocks in a European Monetary Union', INSEE, unpublished manuscript

Muet, P.-A., 1991. 'Croissance, emploi et chomage dans les années quatre-vingt', *Revue de l'OFCE*, **35**, 21–55

    1995. 'Ajustements Macroéconomiques et Coordination en Union Monetaire', OFCE, unpublished manuscript

Mundell, R.A. ,1961. 'A Theory of Optimum Currency Areas', *American Economic Review*, **51**, 657–65

Polosz, S. 1990. 'Real Exchange Rate Adjustment between Regions in a Common Currency Area', Bank of Canada, unpublished manuscript

Sala-i-Martin, X. and Sachs, J., 1992. 'Fiscal Federalism and Optimum Currency Areas: Evidence for Europe from the United States', in M. Canzoneri, V. Grilli and P. R. Masson (eds.), *Establishing a Central Bank: Issues in Europe and Lessons from the US* (Cambridge: Cambridge University Press), 195–220

Spahn, P.B., 1992, 'The Case for EMU: A European View', *Working Paper*, **29**, Faculty of Economics, Johann Wolfgang Goethe University

Stockman, A. C., 1988. 'Sectoral and National Aggregate Disturbances to Industrial Output in Seven European Countries', *Journal of Monetary Economics*, **21**, 387–410

Tavlas, G., 1994. 'The Theory of Monetary Integration', *Open Economies Review*, **5**, 211–30

Thomas, A. H., 1994. 'The Response of Wages and Labour Supply Movements to Employment Shocks Across Europe and the United States', *IMF Working Paper*, **WP/94/158**

Vaubel, R., 1978. 'Real Exchange Rate Changes in the European Community: A New Approach to the Determination of Optimum Currency Areas', *Journal of International Economics*, **8**, 319–39

Venables, A. J. (1996), 'Geography and Specialisation: Industrial Belts on a Circular Plain', chapter 9 in this volume

von Hagen, J., 1991. 'Fiscal Arrangements in a Monetary Union: Evidence from the US', in D. Fair and C. de Boissieu (eds.), *Fiscal Policy, Taxation and the Financial System in an Increasingly Integrated Europe* (Dordrecht: Kluwer Academic Publishers), 337–60

    1993. 'Monetary Union and Fiscal Union: A Perspective from Fiscal Federalism', in P. R. Masson and M. P. Taylor (eds.), *Policy Issues in the Operation of Currency Unions* (Cambridge: Cambridge University Press), 264–96 von Hagen, J. and Fratianni, M., 1991. 'Monetary and Fiscal Policy in a European Monetary Union: Some Public Choice Considerations', in P. J. Welfens (ed.), *The European Monetary System: From German Dominance to European Monetary Union* (Berlin: Springer), 275–302

von Hagen, J. and Hammond, G.W., 1995. 'Regional Insurance Against Asymmetric Shocks: An Empirical Study for the European Community', *CEPR Discussion Paper*, **1170**

von Hagen, J. and Neumann, M., 1994. 'Real Exchange Rates Within and Between Currency Areas: How Far Away is EMU?', *Review of Economics and Statistics*, **76**, 236–44

Weber, A., 1990. 'EMU and Asymmetries and Adjustment Problems in the EMS: Some Empirical Evidence', *CEPR Discussion Paper*, **448**

Werner, P. *et al.*, 1970. *Report to the Council and the Commission on the Realisation by Stages of Economic and Monetary Union in the Community*, Supplement to Bulletin II-1970 of the European Communities (Brussels: European Communities)

Discussion

JEAN PISANI-FERRY

1   Introduction

In 1990, when European economists started discussing the economics of monetary union with policy-makers, they were at pains to explain to them what an asymmetric shock could look like; I had recently an occasion to listen to a French foreign affairs official who was almost routinely referring to the asymmetric shock problem. This is an indication of the progress in the policy debate on Economic and Monetary Union (EMU) we have been witnessing over the last few years, and an illustration of Tam Bayoumi and Barry Eichengreen's (hereafter BE) view that research has come up with an adequate 'framework for debate' on the economics of European monetary union. As a large part of this progress can be attributed to their (joint or separate) research effort since 1990, it is a great pleasure to comment on a new chapter by them which aims to take stock of what has been achieved, to provide new empirical evidence, and to suggest new horizons for research. I will first discuss the survey section of the chapter, before turning to a discussion of the empirical section.

2   Some shortcomings in the operationalisation of OCA theory

Section 2 of chapter 7 provides a clearly structured, well balanced and very comprehensive survey of recent empirical research on the costs and benefits of forming a monetary union in Europe. The authors' main conclusions are (1) that research has basically followed a strategy that consisted in building upon the Mundellian approach of currency unions and in finding ways to 'operationalise' it – i.e. to measure the size and degree of asymmetry of shocks, to investigate the origin of asymmetries and to assess the effectiveness of alternative adjustment channels; (2) that this strategy has by and large been highly successful, because it has both provided an overall quantitative assessment of the potential costs of monetary union and consistent evidence on the variation of costs among potential EMU members; and (3) that the major issue on the agenda for the next few years is now to progress in the understanding of the dynamic interaction between economic integration and monetary integration.

I essentially agree with these conclusions. By taking the US inter-regional monetary union as a benchmark and by implementing statistical techniques *à la* Blanchard and Quah, research has succeeded in transforming the rather abstract OCA approach into a effective instrument for evaluating the potential costs of forming a monetary union in the absence of significant labour mobility between participating countries, and for assessing the potential role of alternative adjustment instruments such as labour mobility, relative prices and fiscal stabilisation. However, I would like to point out three shortcomings that might deserve more attention in future research: an excessive disdain for the potential benefits of monetary union, the dependence of measured shocks on the exchange rate regime and some loose links in the derivation of policy conclusions.

2.1   Benefits versus costs

The Mundellian approach to monetary unification rests on a balance between costs and benefits. In his own seminal OCA paper, Mundell (1961) stresses that there are microeconomic benefits in adopting a single currency. But, by concentrating on the measurement of costs and of the effectiveness of adjustment mechanisms, recent research has essentially turned a blind eye on the benefits side. The only potential benefits for which measurement is available are the transaction cost savings which were evaluated by the EC Commission (1990). However, according to the Commission study these (debatable) benefits amounted to 0.1 per cent of GDP for both France and Germany.[1] No government would seriously consider that such ridiculous savings are worth the efforts undertaken in the name of EMU. At best, transaction costs savings are just a metaphor for wider micro benefits.

The main reason for this imbalance between costs and benefits is easy to find: as costs arise from the combination of nominal rigidities and structural or behavioural asymmetries, investigating the costs side requires implementing only the apparatus of macroeconomic analysis; investigating the benefits side requires linking two separate fields of economic research, namely micro and monetary theory. As pointed out early on by Paul Krugman (1989), this is a much more demanding research agenda. However, as the choice between monetary union and exchange rate flexibility depends on the net balance between costs and benefits, it would be pointless to refine on the measurement of costs if benefits remain unexplored.

Moreover, it is well known that monetary union may involve purely macroeconomic benefits related to (1) the elimination of financial shocks arising from the existence of separate currencies and (2) the automatic coordination of monetary policies in the presence of symmetric shocks. Although they are both frequently mentioned by policy-makers and well documented in theory, these potential benefits have not received much attention in recent research.

Finally, economists may consider that the potential benefits of forming a monetary union are political rather than economic. In this case, more attention should be devoted to the political economy of EMU: research should take more seriously the rationale for monetary union that policy-makers and industrialists put forward when they claim that misalignments are severely detrimental in a highly integrated economic union and that the disciplines associated with the Single Market, especially competition policy, would not survive floating exchange rates.

2.2   *The measurement of shocks and the exchange rate regime*

In the successive papers that they survey here, BE discuss the choice of an exchange rate regime as a function of the correlation of shocks between European countries and Germany. The implicit assumption behind their methodology is that measured shocks can be considered structural – i.e. independent from the exchange rate regime(s) in place over the observation period. However, Artis and Zhang (1996) examine how the correlation of industrial production among industrialised countries has been affected by changes in the exchange rate regime, and conclude that in Europe participation in a fixed exchange rate regime has in fact increased the correlation of output cycles between participating countries and Germany. This leads us to examine more carefully the dependence of measured shocks on the exchange rate regime.

In the Blanchard–Quah (1989) framework implemented by BE, supply shocks are those which have lasting effects on both output and prices whereas shocks that affect only prices in the long run are classified as demand shocks. As illustrated by standard simulations with macroeconometric models (see e.g. EC Commission, 1990, annex E), being in a fixed or a flexible exchange rate regime clearly affects an economy's pattern of response to shocks. More importantly, it also affects the impact multiplier effect and the international transmission effect of shocks to aggregate demand – i.e. both their magnitude and their correlation as measured by BE, at least when shocks are measured using yearly data. Whether being in a fixed exchange rate system increases or reduces the correlation of these shocks is an empirical issue and depends on the relative magnitude of spillover effects through the goods market and the capital market, which can differ from one country to another, but it cannot be disputed that measured demand shocks are regime-dependent.

The problem is in principle less severe for supply shocks, because although the slopes of the aggregate demand curve and the short-run aggregate supply curve depend on the exchange rate regime, shocks as measured by BE should not depend on it if the long-run aggregate supply curve is vertical. However, as observed by Mélitz (1997), the distinction between demand and supply shocks can be blurred if recovery from a demand shock is delayed: *de facto*, BE's distinction is between temporary and permanent shocks to output, and demand shocks can have persistent effects on output in the presence of rigidities. It is therefore likely that supply shocks measured by the VAR methodology are also regime-dependent.

If measured shocks are regime-dependent, their observed correlation across countries does not provide an adequate optimum currency area criterion. Assume, for example, that the degree of correlation of shocks with the anchor country is a decreasing function of the degree of exchange rate flexibility as represented in figure D7.1. Assume this relationship is represented by the AA curve for country A and by the BB curve for country B, and that country A has been for years in a fixed exchange rate regime while country B remained in a floating regime. Corresponding equilibria are represented by E_A and E_B, and the correlation of shocks as measured by BE by ρ_A and ρ_B. Clearly, comparing ρ_A and ρ_B leads to the wrong conclusion that the costs of

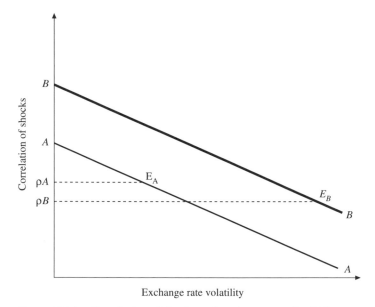

Figure D7.1   Correlation of shocks and exchange rate flexibility

participating in a monetary union with the anchor country are lower for country *A* than for country *B*.

How severe can this problem be in practice? Figure D7.2 plots the actual degree of real exchange rate volatility *vis-à-vis* the mark over the 1970–90 period (measured by the standard deviation of first differences in the logarithm of the real exchange rate)[2] against the correlation of supply shocks with Germany over the 1963–90 period (from BE's table 7.1). For the 15 countries in the sample (the same as in BE's chapter, i.e. EU15 *less* Luxembourg and Germany, *plus* Switzerland and Norway), figure D7.2 indicates a strong negative correlation between these two indicators (the correlation coefficient is −0.8). Clearly, there are two ways of interpreting the data. One view is that there is a tautological element in BE's measurement of the potential costs of monetary union. The alternative view is that shocks are exogenous and exchange rate policies endogenous, and that figure D7.2 indicates that the latter have actually been optimal, as countries subject to asymmetric shocks have tended to rely more on exchange rate flexibility. Even if one adopts this more optimistic reading, it should be noted that supply-shock correlations may provide only an indirect indicator of the cost of monetary union, as its true cost should in principle be measured by the welfare cost of moving from the (presumably optimal) regime *E* to full monetary union.

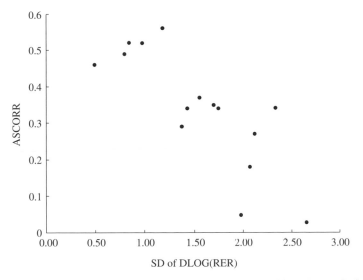

Figure D7.2   Real exchange rate volatility, 1970–90 and correlation of supply shocks

2.3   From measured shocks to policy conclusions

My last point relates to the policy conclusions one may draw from statistics on the distribution of shocks. Though useful as a framework for interpretation, the aggregate supply–aggregate demand setting has limitations that need to be kept in mind when jumping from the measurement of shocks to policy conclusions.

As mentioned above, a first limitation is that it is not clear to what extent the VAR methodology actually separates shocks from responses. Whether a disturbance is considered of the supply or the demand type depends on the economy's response as well as on the intrinsic nature of the shock: genuine demand disturbances will be classified as 'supply shocks' if the economy is characterised by strong unemployment persistence, while a genuine supply disturbance (e.g. a shock to the NAIRU) may fail to be classified as such if the economy's response to it involves long lags. As the economy's response clearly depends on the exchange rate regime, this is a significant limit to the approach.

Second, there is only scant evidence on the origin of the shocks. The framework for interpretation that is frequently used (and alluded to in the chapter) suggests that supply shocks originate in industry-specific disturbances, while demand shocks arise from country-specific behavioural disturbances or policy moves. There is indeed evidence that

Europe-wide, country-specific and industry-specific shocks all account for output fluctuations in Europe (Bayoumi and Prasad, 1995). However, there is no clear correspondance between this decomposition and the supply–demand classification: supply shocks can also arise from policies (e.g. tax policy changes, labour market deregulations, etc.) or from country-specific labour market disturbances; demand shocks can originate in industry-specific disturbances as well as in asymmetries in the transmission mechanism of monetary policy (Barran *et al.*, 1997) that lead to different reactions to a common policy action. This reduces the ability to draw conclusions from the observation of the statistical properties of shocks. It is therefore difficult to draw firm normative conclusions from the sole measurement of shocks.

Third, the link between the nature of the shocks and the implications one can draw for determining the optimum exchange rate regime needs to be refined. As BE mention, taking the US economy as a benchmark for evaluating how EMU would adjust to shocks should not be read as implying that the adjustment through migrations is optimal. Absent the Walrasian response through changes in relative prices, the optimal response to exogenous perturbations depends both on the origin of the shock and on its (temporary vs. permanent) nature. Borrowing can, for example, be a superior alternative to migration (and to devaluing) when facing temporary demand shocks.

3   Dynamic interactions between economic integration and monetary integration: are they already perverse?

Paul Krugman's (1993) conjecture on the dynamic interactions between economic integration and monetary integration was a blow to the perviously dominant view that whatever the costs of monetary union, they were bound to decrease over time as economic integration proceeded and removed structural asymmetries within Europe. In the second part of their chapter, BE attempt to measure changes in the asymmetry of shocks over time and to provide evidence of the existence of specialisation effects of economic integration that could account for an increase in the degree of asymmetry. Their conclusion is that the asymmetry of shocks has increased and that this could be attributed to specialisation effects *à la* Krugman.

As BE rightly point out in their conclusion, this is without doubt a major topic for research in the years to come. However, the preliminary evidence they present is not convincing.

Table D7.1. *Average standard deviation of GDP growth rates, 1964–94*

	1964–72	1973–83	1984–94	1984–94, excl. 1991	1984–94, excl. 1990, 1991
Core	0.99	1.37	0.71	0.68	0.67
Extended core	1.29	1.52	1.02	0.99	0.99
EU14	1.90	1.98	1.56	1.46	1.40

Source: Calculations based on OECD data.

3.1 Has the asymmetry of shocks increased?

The VAR methodology used by BE requires large sample periods and does not allow one to test easily for structural breaks in individual bilateral correlations of shocks between European countries. They therefore rely instead on an aggregate measure of the coherence of disturbances over three subsample periods: the explanatory power of the first principal component of the estimated underlying supply disturbances across various country groupings.

The result they obtain is that controlling for the 1991 effects of German unification, the coherence of disturbances was lower in 1984–94 than in 1973–83. This was true for members of the European 'core', for the 'extended core', and for the European Union as a whole. Therefore, BE's result suggests that the European Union has already entered a process of divergence.

This result is rather counter-intuitive, because raw statistics suggest the opposite. As an example, table D7.1 reports the standard deviation of yearly GDP growth rates accross the same country groupings and for the same subperiods as in BE's table 7.3. In spite of German unification, there was a decline during the last period in the discrepancy of growth rates across all three groupings, which is even more pronounced if one excludes 1991, or 1990 and 1991, to remove the effects of German unification. Of course, observed growth rates can *in principle* converge in spite of an increase in the asymmetry of shocks, but this requires at least some additional explanations. Results presented in BE's table 7.1 also point in the opposite direction. Excluding Germany, which was affected by the unification shocks, bilateral correlations of supply shocks have increased from 1963–90 to 1963–94 for eight out of ten bilateral pairs of core countries. This increase may be due to the German unification shock, but at least there is no evidence of increased divergence. (Incidentally, this suggests an alternative methodology for measuring changes in the degree of asymmetry of shocks.)

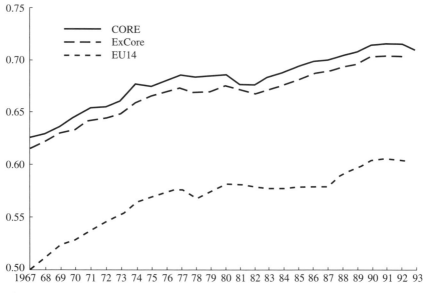

Figure D7.3   Finger index of export structure similarity (*vis-à-vis* Germany), 1967–93

Summing up, stronger evidence of increasing divergence over time would be needed in order to win out on the issue.

3.2   Has specialisation increased?

BE relate the increase in the asymmetry of shocks to a trend towards regional specialisation, for which they provide evidence in their table 7.4. Using an eight-sector classification, they compute coefficients of variation across eight EU countries and across US regions of the share of each sector in total output. They claim that the increase in most of the intra-EU coefficients of variation between 1971 and 1979 and 1980 and 1987 is an indication of a trend towards regional specialisation among EU countries.

This conclusion is debatable. First, data limitation prevented the authors from extending the comparison to all EU countries. Second, sectors for which the coefficient of variation increased the most are 'other private services', 'government', 'transportation', 'construction' and 'finance', the largest part of which are not traded. Most of the increase in 'specialisation' seems therefore to have taken place within the non-traded goods sector.

For measuring trends in specialisation, trade data provide a better

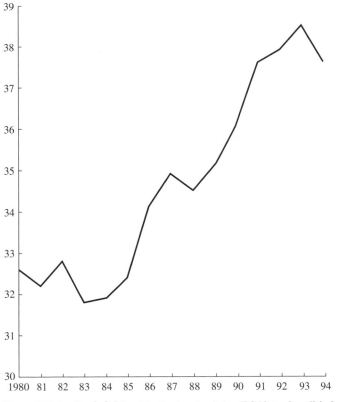

Figure D7.4   Grubel–Lloyd indicator for intra-EC12 trade, all industries, 1980–94 (per cent)

Source: Fontagné *et al.* (1997).

alternative to production data, first because they are available and comparable for all EU countries, and second because they provide more direct evidence of changes arising from specialisation effects. Their main limitation is that they ignore services, but if agglomeration effects are under way, they should show up in the goods sector.

Figure D7.3, which displays export similarity indexes with Germany for the three country groupings used by BE,[3] carries the opposite message : export similarity has been increasing over time for all three country groupings, indicating a decrease in inter-industry specialisation. Furthermore, export similarity is stronger for the core and the extended core than for the European Union as a whole, indicating a negative relationship between economic integration and specialisation. This evolution away from specialisation is confirmed by figure D7.4, which is taken from a study by Fontagné *et al.* (1997) and displays the Grubel–Lloyd index of intra-EU trade computed at a six-digit level.

Trade data therefore do not confirm that specialisation among EU countries has already increased. Obviously, this is no demonstration that agglomeration effects could not arise in the future as a consequence of economic integration: the extent to which specialisation is likely to increase in the coming decades is a matter for discussion. But, at least, the available empirical evidence should lead to more caution in the analysis of the joint dynamics of economic and monetary integration.

NOTES

1 EC Commission (1990, annex A, 264).
2 I was not able to assemble monthly real exchange rate data for 1960–70, but as all countries in the sample participated in the Bretton Woods system until 1973, this should not affect the conclusion.
3 For each country *i*, the Finger index of export structure similarity *vis-à-vis* Germany was computed, using a 70-good decomposition of exports. The Finger indexes are then averaged over the country goupings.

REFERENCES

Artis, M. and Zhang, W., 1996. 'International Business Cycles and the ERM: Is There a European Business Cycle?', paper presented at the CEPR conference on 'Regional Integration' (La Coruña, 26–27 April 1996)

Barran, F., Coudert, V. and Mojon, B., 1997. 'The Transmission of Monetary Policy in the European Countries', in S. Collignon (ed.), *European Monetary Policy* (London: Pinter)

Bayoumi, T. and Prasad, E., 1995. 'Currency Unions, Economic Fluctuations and Adjustment: Some Empirical Evidence', *CEPR Discussion Paper* , **1172**, May

Blanchard, O. J. and Muet. P.-A., 1993. 'Competitiveness Through Disinflation: An Assessment of the French Macroeconomic Strategy', *Economic Policy*, **16**

Blanchard, O. J. and Quah, D., 1989. 'The Dynamic Effect of Aggregate Demand and Supply Disturbances', *American Economic Review*, September

EC Commission, 1990. 'One Market, One Money', *European Economy*, **44**

Fontagné, L. *et al.*, 1997. 'Trade Patterns Inside the Single Market', *The Single Market Review*, Subseries IV, vol. 2 (Brussels: European Commission/Kogan Page Earthscan)

Krugman, P. R., 1989. 'Policy Problems of a Monetary Union', in *Currencies and Crises* (Cambridge, MA: MIT Press)

1993. 'Lessons of Massachussets for EMU', in F. Giavazzi and F. Torres (eds.), *Adjustment and Growth in the European Monetary Union* (Cambridge: Cambridge University Press for the CEPR)

Mélitz, J., 1997. 'Evidence about the Costs and Benefits of EMU', forthcoming in *Swedish Economic Policy Review*

Mundell, R. A., 1961. 'A Theory of Optimum Currency Areas', *American Economic Review*, **51**, 657–65

8 European migrants: an endangered species?

RICCARDO FAINI

1 Introduction

Economists and policy-makers alike typically complain about insufficient labour mobility within Europe. Yet, large internal migrations have been an enduring phenomenon in European economic history. Even in the nineteenth century, when Europeans went in great numbers to overseas destinations in an attempt to escape from deprivation and persecutions at home, intra-European migrations were quite large. During the 1890–1913 period, 6.596 million Italians migrated to the United States or to Latin America and 4.874 million went to European destinations (Ferenczi and Willcox, 1934). Similarly, a substantial share of Spanish migrants chose to migrate toward Europe, despite their cultural and political links with Latin America (Hatton and Williamson, 1994). The peak of intra-European migration came somewhat later, during the 1950s and 1960s, when overseas emigration fell abruptly and approximately 10.5 million migrants crossed European borders, mainly from Southern to Northern Europe (Razin and Sadka, 1995).

From an historical point of view, therefore, the lack of labour mobility within Europe is somewhat surprising. The evidence is however undisputed: intra-European labour mobility has indeed reached an historical low and compares quite unfavourably with similar findings for the United States. In turn, low labour mobility is a matter of great concern for European policy-makers. The reasons for this concern are well known. In the face of an idiosyncratic shock, regions can adjust by letting their exchange rate depreciate, by a drop in the real wage or by migration. The first option is unpalatable, as it may clash with the commitments of the European exchange rate system and the desire to fight off inflation. More crucially, devaluation will no longer be a policy option once European monetary unification has been completed. The second option, a drop in the real wage, is virtually ruled out, particularly

228

in the short to medium run, given the downward rigidity of European real wages. If the third option, labour migration, is also unavailable, regions will be unable to adjust to an idiosyncratic shock and will have to go through a period of protracted unemployment before the induced fall in real wages leads to the desired real depreciation. Empirical evidence (Blanchard and Katz, 1992) shows that even in the United States adjustment to regional shocks occurs mainly through labour outmigration rather than through wage flexibility. In Europe, where both labour mobility and wage flexibility are limited, regional adjustment is found to occur mainly through higher unemployment in the short run and lower participation rates in the long run (Decressin and Fatas, 1995; Bentolila and Jimeno, 1995).

Lack of labour mobility in Europe is typically attributed to the several barriers still hindering migrations among European countries. For instance, unskilled workers are not allowed to freely compete across national borders either by legal or by union regulations. The mobility of skilled workers is also hindered by insufficient recognition of national diplomas and other bureaucratic obstacles. There is a lot of truth in this approach. Yet, existing evidence shows that intra-European mobility is quite limited even within national borders. Despite the persistence of large unemployment differentials, workers in Southern Spain or in the Italian Mezzogiorno are not trying their way in the more prosperous Northern regions of their own countries. The search for an explanation of the low labour mobility in Europe must therefore look beyond the barriers of national borders.

The purpose of this chapter is to cast some light on the reasons underlying the fall in labour mobility within Europe. We rely on both theoretical analysis and empirical evidence, drawing mainly from the Italian and the Spanish cases. We also investigate whether the furthering of the integration process within Europe could provide a boost to labour mobility. The chapter is organised in the following way. In section 2, we review some explanations for the decline in intra-European labour mobility. In section 3, we turn to some evidence on the attitude toward mobility in Italy and Spain. We investigate in section 4 the effects of individual, family and regional factors in affecting the intention to migrate. We also take a closer look at the apparent paradox where regional unemployment is often found to discourage outmigration. In section 5, we focus on the impact of European integration on labour mobility. After arguing that theory alone cannot provide an unambiguous answer to this question, we provide some evidence suggesting that integration may spur migration to the extent that it will induce greater regional specialisation. Section 6 offers some brief policy conclusions.

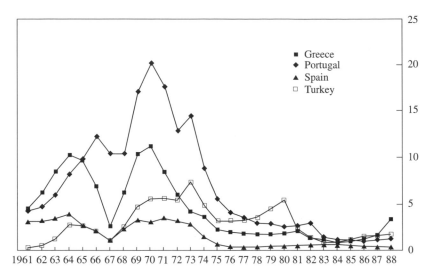

Figure 8.1   Migration rates from Southern Europe, 1961–88

2   The fall in intra-European mobility

2.1   International migrations

The fall in intra-European mobility can hardly be disputed. Both international and internal migrations have experienced a steady decline since the beginning of the 1970s. Figure 8.1 shows the evolution of international migrations from four Southern European countries, Greece, Portugal, Spain and Turkey. After reaching a peak around 1971, migrations rates show a sudden decline after 1973, in the wake of the first oil crisis and the adoption of restrictive migration policies in Northern Europe. Interestingly enough, however, migration from Southern Europe does not resume even when, during the 1980s, the economic recovery in the traditional receiving countries was well under way. Typically, one would attribute the fall in migration to a combination of demand and supply factors, in particular the decline in (expected) earnings differentials between receiving and sending regions and the continuation of restrictive immigration policies in Northern Europe (Salt, 1991). But the evidence is somewhat less than fully compelling. First, migration policies in receiving countries, while instrumental in accounting for the fall in immigration after 1973, cannot account for the virtual stagnation of migratory flows during the 1980s given that this decade coincided with a major liberalisation of labour flows from many of the sending countries. Second, the

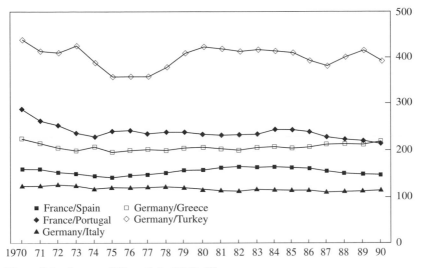

Figure 8.2   Income differentials, 1970–90

behaviour of economic incentives provides at best mixed signals as to the incentives for further migration. On the one hand, real income *per capita* differentials at international prices show no clear trend after 1971 (figure 8.2), suggesting that the economic incentive for mobility has been there throughout the period of declining mobility. If we focus on wage rather than income differentials, we find that the incentives to migrate declined somewhat (figure 8.3). However, existing estimates of the responsiveness of migrations to wage differentials indicate that the actual decline in the relative wage between receiving and sending countries can explain only a very small fraction of the observed drop in the rate of migration. Only Spanish migrations to France are likely to have been strongly affected by the evolution of the wage differential. That the incentive to migrate did not decline much is further corroborated by the consideration of unemployment differentials (figure 8.4). Except for France and Portugal, unemployment differentials have indeed increased sometimes conspicuously between origin and destination countries since the beginning of the 1970s, particularly between Spain and France. Searching for alternative explanations for the fall in migrations, social scientists would tend to emphasise the role of demographic factors, in particular of changes in the sending countries demographic structure. A plausible hypothesis would be that the falling weight of the young people cohorts – i.e. those more ready to migrate – could indeed explain the decline in the aggregate propensity to emigrate in the sending countries. Yet, we find little evidence in support of this claim. Table 8.1 shows that the population

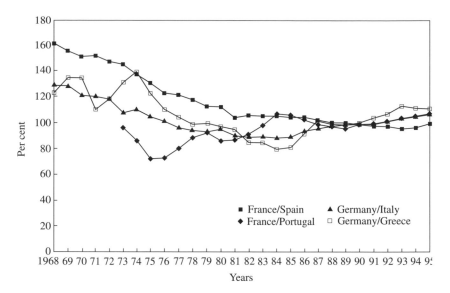

Figure 8.3　Real wage differentials, 1968–95 (receiving country–sending country: 1990 = 100)

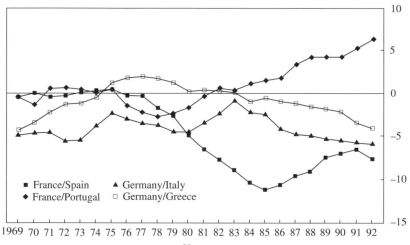

Figure 8.4　Unemployment differentials, 1969–92 (receiving country–sending country)

Table 8.1. *Demographic evolution in Southern Europe, 1960–90*

Year	Age structure (14–29 population)			
	Greece	Portugal	Spain	Turkey
1960	25.08	23.58	23.15	25.05
1965	23.40	22.92	22.34	25.26
1970	20.44	20.63	21.82	24.85
1975	21.63	23.84	22.80	27.02
1980	21.48	25.30	23.02	27.59
1985	22.07	25.29	24.12	28.19
1990	21.73	26.15	24.96	28.36

Source: ILO.

share of people aged 14–29 has been increasing rather than decreasing in Southern Europe. The results would be virtually unchanged if we considered the share of people aged 19–29.

Overall, neither the evolution of income and unemployment differentials nor demographic factors nor the changing stance of migration policies seem to provide a satisfactory explanation for the fall in intra-European migrations. One is therefore led to attribute the decline in labour mobility to a fall in the propensity to migrate. According to this view, the higher economic wellbeing in sending countries may have dissuaded many potential migrants from looking for better alternatives abroad. One way to rationalise this approach is to assume that potential migrants care both about wage goods and their home country's amenities. When wages grow at home, this will have a positive income effect that will prompt potential migrants to consume more of their home country's amenities; therefore the propensity to migrate will decline, even if wage differentials with the receiving countries are unchanged. Consider figure 8.5, where the two points N and S indicate the wage and the amenities associated with two alternative locations (North and South) for a potential migrant from region S. As drawn in the figure, utility is higher in N, prompting the individual to migrate. Suppose now that the wages in both regions increase by the same (relative) amount, leaving the wage differential unchanged. The level of amenities in the two regions is also unchanged at a_N and a_S, respectively. Clearly, it could well be that the new equilibrium at N' and S' will be such that utility is higher in the South and no migration will take place, despite the fact that the wage differential is unchanged. The (easily testable) empirical implication of this approach is that migration should be negatively affected by income growth at home, even after controlling for the wage differential. A

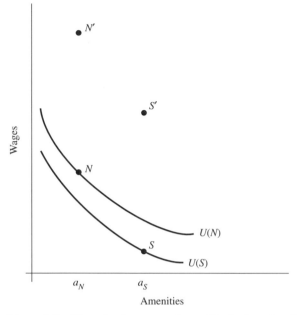

Figure 8.5   The role of wages and amenities in the migration choice

formal model and supporting econometric evidence are presented in Faini and Venturini (1994).

2.2   Internal migrations

The pattern of internal migrations shows many similarities with that of international migrations. There is indeed conspicuous evidence that mobility within most European countries has experienced a downward trend since the mid-1960s. International comparisons on internal labour mobility are somewhat problematic. Sources differ: some studies rely on Census data while others use information from population registers. Furthermore, the geographical definitions of the areas over which mobility is measured are often not comparable among different countries. Nonetheless, at the cost of some arbitrariness, we rely on the NUTS2 classification of geographical areas to measure the rate of inter-regional mobility of labour. We find that in Germany gross migrations between *Länder* declined from 18.4 per thousand population in 1970 to around 13 in 1975–80 and 10.5 in 1984–8 (Livi Bacci *et al.*, 1996). The more recent data are not fully comparable as they reflect the flows from Eastern to Western Germany. French data are based on census information and come at seven-year intervals. They show again a declining trend after the mid-1960s, with inter-regional labour mobility increasing from 13 in 1954–62 to 18 in 1968-75 and declining afterward to 17 in 1975–82 and 16 in 1983–90 (Courgeau and Pumain, 1993). Comparable Census data for Italy are available only for 1981 and 1991. We find that mobility declined somewhat from 20 in 1981 to 17 in 1991. Population-register data also show a steady fall in inter-regional mobility (Goria and Ichino, 1994). The picture changes somewhat when we focus on Great Britain and Spain. In both cases, the degree of labour mobility fluctuates markedly, apparently in response to changes in aggregate economic conditions.[1] In Great Britain, in particular, inter-regional labour mobility declined from 21 in 1975 to 17 in 1981 but then steadily increased to reach 26 in 1987 (Boden, Rees and Stillwell, 1992). Even in Spain, economic recessions appear to take a toll on internal labour mobility. If we focus on inter-town mobility, we find that it was equal to 9 per thousand in 1981–85 at the trough of the recession but then recovered to 14 per thousand in 1986–90 following the fall in aggregate unemployment. Similarly, inter-regional migration rates seemed to recover after 1984 (Bentolila and Dolado, 1991).

Comparisons of mobility levels across countries are somewhat trickier. Yet, the analysis of residence changes can provide a comparable benchmark. Census data indicate that 17–19 per cent of households have moved to a new residence in the year prior to the Census in Australia, New Zealand and the United States. The figure falls to 9.5–9.6 per cent for French and British households and to 6–8 per cent in other European countries (Livi Bacci et al., 1996). The evidence presented so far seems to suggest that Great Britain together with France stand as outliers among European countries with a relatively high mobility rate. Germany follows somewhat behind. Mobility appears to be lowest in Spain and Italy despite the persistence of very high inter-regional differentials of income and unemployment. In section 3, we take a closer look at the Italian and Spanish cases.

3 Migration and migration intentions in Italy and Spain

3.1 The main trends

The fall in labour mobility was most pronounced in the Italian and the Spanish cases. Spanish migrations have been extensively analysed in the recent literature. Bentolila and Dolado (1991) show that gross international migrations fell as a percentage of the domestic population from an yearly average of 0.3 per cent in 1960–74 to 0.06 per cent in 1975–86.

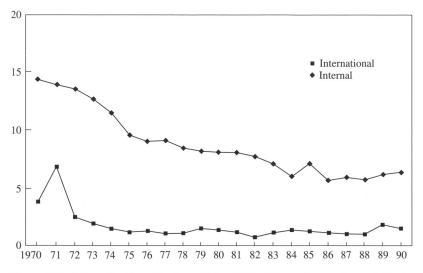

Figure 8.6   Migration from Southern Italy, 1970–90 (per thousand population)

Migration to France experienced the largest fall, from 0.18 in the 1960s to 0.03 per cent in the 1970s and 0.002 per cent in the 1980s (Antolin, 1994). As in other countries, the fall in international migration was not offset by rising internal mobility. Inter-regional migration dropped from 0.65 per cent in 1960–74 to 0.50 per cent in 1970–5 and to 0.36 per cent in 1975–86 (Bentolila and Dolado, 1991). The striking fact about inter-regional migration in Spain is the reversal in their geographical pattern, with migrations in the 1980s flowing from high-wage low-unemployment regions like Catalona and Madrid to low-wage high-unemployment regions in the South.

Turning to the Italian case, here too we find a steady decline in both internal migration and internal mobility. In what follows, we focus on the relatively backward regions of the Mezzogiorno. Figure 8.6 shows that the fall in the rate of inter-regional migrations from Southern Italian regions was quite marked. This pattern is, at first sight, somewhat puzzling. Wage convergence between Northern and Southern Italy had been basically achieved by the end of the 1960s. Moreover, starting in the 1980s, unemployment rates rise at much faster rate in the South than in the North (table 8.2). As a matter of fact, the unemployment rate in the Mezzogiorno increases from 4.89 in 1970 to 11.50 in 1979 to 21.13 in 1989. Yet, migration does not resume; quite the opposite, it keeps declining. In Italy as well, therefore, it would seem that regional unemployment rates have a perverse effect on the migratory choice.

Table 8.2. *Unemployment rates in Italian regions, 1963–94*

	Regional unemployment rates		
	North	South	Differential
1963	2.19	3.19	1.00
1970	2.35	4.89	2.54
1977	5.80	10.20	4.40
1980	5.80	11.50	5.70
1983	8.10	13.80	5.70
1986	8.50	16.50	8.00
1989	7.39	21.13	13.74
1992	7.07	20.45	13.37
1994	7.61	19.20	11.60

Source: Own elaborations on ISTAT data.

3.2 The impact of regional unemployment

In principle, migrations should reduce regional inequalities by flowing from high-unemployment to low-unemployment areas. As a result of immigration, wages should fall and unemployment rise in the receiving region. The opposite evolution should take place in the sending region. This equilibrating mechanism will not work, however, unless migration is responsive to unemployment differentials. Unsurprisingly, there have been many attempts in the literature to assess the impact of (regional) unemployment on migration. Most of the evidence relates to the case of Italy, Spain, the United Kingdom and the United States. One recurring finding is that, even after controlling for other determining factors, regional unemployment seems to discourage outmigration. Theory would suggest the opposite. It would seem therefore that the pattern of migration may be such that it aggravates the regional differentials in unemployment. A very careful analysis of the link between migration and unemployment is presented by Pissarides and Wadsworth (1989). They rely on household data for Great Britain. In their analysis, unemployment can affect mobility at three different levels: (1) the individual level, where unemployed workers should be more ready to migrate than employed workers (although financing mobility costs may be harder for an unemployed person); (2) the regional level, where higher regional unemployment should be associated with a lower probability of finding a job and a positive (negative) effect on outmigration (immigration); (3) the national level, where high aggregate unemployment should discourage mobility, mainly by reducing the expected gain from migration and hardening the financial constraint on would-be migrants. As in much of the US literature (DaVanzo, 1978), Pissarides and Wadsworth's results indicate that the effects of individual and national unemployment go in the expected direction. However, they cannot find a correctly signed effect for regional unemployment. Hughes and McCormick (1994) come to similar conclusions in their analysis of the mobility pattern of unskilled workers in the United Kingdom. These econometric findings support the notion that migration has not contributed to a reduction in the pattern of inter-regional differentials of unemployment.

One way to solve this puzzle, at least in the case of the United States, is to interact the level of regional unemployment with an unemployed person dummy. The positive coefficient on this newly defined variable (DaVanzo, 1978) indicates that regional unemployment will boost mobility of unemployed workers, in line with theoretical expectations. This simple trick does not work in the UK case, as shown both by Hughes and McCormick (1994) and by Pissarides and Wadsworth (1989). The puzzle continues when we turn to the case of Spain. Antolin and Bover (1997) pool five years of Labour Force Surveys data to investigate the impact of unemployment on migrations. They find again that regional unemployment has the 'wrong-signed' impact on the probability of migration, even when interacted with an unemployed individual dummy variable. The Spanish findings seem therefore to replicate those of the United Kingdom. Moreover, in the case of Spain, even individual unemployment does not have the correct sign. As the authors show, this is due to the 'perverse' behaviour of 'registered' unemployed who are more unwilling to migrate than employed workers. The authors speculate that this may be due to the fact that 'registered' unemployed may either be less active in the job search process or afraid of losing their priority in the regional job list if they migrate. Reassuringly, non-registered unemployed are found to be relatively more mobile than employed workers.

It is somewhat unfortunate that no comparable analysis on the link between regional unemployment and mobility based on individual or household data can be found for the Italian case. One cause of this state of affairs may lie in the fact that Italy's Labour Force Survey data have only recently become available for research. Furthermore, at least in the Italian case, the survey appears to be ill-suited for the analysis of migration.[2] We are therefore left with mainly aggregate analyses of regional migrations. Faini (1989) finds a correctly signed impact of regional unemployment on gross outmigrations from Southern Italy. However, the coefficient on regional unemployment may reflect both the (individual) effect, where unemployed workers are more likely to migrate, and the regional effect. Moreover, both studies refer to migration in the 1960s. When we focus on the most recent periods, the evidence is somewhat mixed. Attanasio and Padoa Schioppa (1991) can hardly find a significant impact of regional unemployment rates on outmigration, even though they work with aggregate data. In the next subsection, we take a different route to assess the link between regional unemployment and mobility. We rely on individual data but, short of information on actual migratory moves, we use migration intention data as provided by the Labour Force Survey.

3.3   Migration intentions among Italian unemployed: some econometric evidence [3]

There is an obvious drawback in concentrating on migration intentions rather than on actual migratory moves: a positive attitude toward migration may not translate in an actual move and may not be a good predictor of mobility. Yet, both the Spanish (Ahn, de la Rica and Ugidos, 1995) and the British literature (Hughes and McCormick, 1981, 1985) have used this kind of information extensively. Furthermore, Hughes and McCormick (1985) show that migration intentions are worth a careful economic analysis for their own sake: in particular, they share the same determining factors as actual migrations. As noticed earlier, Italy's Labour Force Survey provides little information on actual migration. However, all respondents are asked whether they would be willing to take a job: (1) only in their own city of residence, (2) in a neighbouring city at a commuting distance, (3) anywhere in Italy and abroad.

I concentrate on unemployed individuals, given that their behaviour is typically found to be different from that of employed workers. The striking fact is that 39.8 per cent of unemployed workers are willing to take a job only in their own city.[4] To put it differently, almost 40 per cent of unemployed in Italy are not even willing to commute to a nearby location. In part, this unwillingness to move may be predicated on particular family circumstances: spouses, for instance, may not be able to take a job in a close location because of their child-caring obligations. I distinguish therefore several categories depending on sex, location (Northern and Southern Italy), professional and family conditions. Table 8.3 provides a broad overview of the pattern of responses. Some interesting patterns stand out. First, as expected, mobility increases with education. For instance, only 16 per cent of Northern males with a basic education are willing to take a job everywhere against 51.7 per cent of those with a university degree. Second, women are less willing to migrate.

Table 8.3. *Mobility attitudes and job search*

All unemployed				
(a) Basic education	Males		Females	
	North	South	North	South
Own town	39.8	32.9	53.6	61.0
Nearby town	44.2	36.1	41.0	28.5
Everywhere	16.0	31.0	5.4	10.5
Total	100	100	100	100
(b) High school	Males		Females	
	North	South	North	South
Own town	27.7	23.8	36.3	44.8
Nearby town	46.5	33.5	52.0	31.1
Everywhere	25.8	42.7	11.7	24.1
Total	100	100	100	100
(c) University	Males		Females	
	North	South	North	South
Own town	20.7	26.9	27.9	31.8
Nearby town	27.6	30.8	44.3	38.6
Everywhere	51.7	42.3	27.8	29.4
Total	100	100	100	100
Son/Daughter (first time job-seeker)				
(a) Basic education	Males		Females	
	North	South	North	South
Own town	47.1	29.4	53.2	56.7
Nearby town	40.0	35.1	38.7	27.8
Everywhere	12.9	35.5	8.1	15.5
(b) High school	Males		Females	
	North	South	North	South
Own town	27.8	24.3	39.8	36.6
Nearby town	44.3	32.4	47.6	32.1
Everywhere	27.9	43.3	12.6	31.3
(c) University	Males		Females	
	North	South	North	South
Own town	13.6	25.0	27.3	35.7
Nearby town	31.8	30.0	39.4	25.0
Everywhere	54.6	45.0	33.3	39.3

Source: Faini, Galli and Rossi (1996).

Interestingly enough, the gender difference is more pronounced in Northern than in Southern Italy. Third, the propensity to migrate to distant destinations is systematically higher among unemployed workers in Southern Italy than in Northern Italy (with one significant exception: first-time job-seeker university graduates). Mezzogiorno workers, however, show a lower a propensity to take a job in a neighbouring location. This is a noteworthy result. It suggests that high regional unemployment, while providing an incentive to migrate to relatively distant locations, may deter short-haul mobility. One way to rationalise this finding is to assume that the rate of unemployment is highly correlated across space: high unemployment in one area would then be associated with high unemployment in neighbouring areas, thereby discouraging mobility among nearby locations.[5]

Table 8.3 provides only some simple cross-tabulations. To assess the effects of individual and regional characteristics on migration intentions and test the conjecture that regional unemployment may encourage mobility only to far-away destinations, I proceed as follows. I first run a simple logit model of the intention to migrate on a set of individual characteristics (age, education), family characteristics (household head, spouse, son, household's employment and unemployment rates) and regional characteristics (summarised by a set of regional dummies). Initially, I rely on an ordered logit specification (the results are not reported). This model assumes that mobility increases monotonically from response 1 (those who are willing to take a job only in their own town) to response 3 (those willing to take a job everywhere). In a second-stage regression, I then regress the regional dummy variables on regional unemployment rates. The latter is found to have any no statistically significant effect. As for Spain and the United Kingdom, therefore, regional unemployment does not seem to play a role in affecting mobility in Italy.[6]

An alternative strategy is to rely on a multinomial logit specification with three alternative (unordered) choices. Without loss of generality, I measure all coefficients with respect either to response 2 (willingness to commute) or to response 3 (full mobility). I get three set of coefficients measuring how the various characteristics affect the choice between responses 1 and 2, the choice between responses 3 and 2 and the choice between responses 1 and 3, respectively. I then run the second-stage regression of the three vectors of regional dummies on regional unemployment. The results are reported in table 8.4. Individual and family characteristics have the anticipated effect. More education is associated with higher mobility. Also, tied movers (i.e. spouses) are less mobile. Even after controlling for marital status, females are less mobile.

Table 8.4. *Econometric determinants of mobility attitudes* (multinomial logit)

	Mobility choice		
	Everywhere vs. nearby town (1)	Own vs. nearby town (2)	Own town vs. everywhere (3)
Spouse	− *	+ *	+ *
Son/daughter	+ *	+ *	+
Female	− *	+ *	+ *
University	+ *	− *	− *
Diploma	+	− *	− *
Age	+	−	−
(Age)²	−	+	+
Family's employment rate	+	− *	− *
Regional unemployment	+ *	+ *	− *

Note: * Statistically significant at a 5 per cent confidence level.
Source: Faini, Galli and Rossi (1996).

Turning to the effect of regional unemployment, this variable has a significant positive impact on the propensity to move to far-away destinations compared to both alternatives, namely moving to a nearby town (column (1)) or not moving at all (column (3)). At the same time, regional unemployment is associated with a greater preference for choice 1 (not moving at all) relative to moving to a nearby destination. This a fairly reasonable result if, as mentioned earlier, we are willing to believe that regional unemployment rates are highly correlated across space. High unemployment in one region would then mean also high unemployment in nearby regions, discouraging short-haul migrations but boosting mobility to far-away destinations. Whether aggregate outmigration falls in response to higher regional unemployment would then depend on whether the various destinations are good substitutes. If mobility costs are significantly higher for more distant destinations, then regional outmigration could definitely fall even in the face of rising regional unemployment.

From an econometric point of view, an ordered model cannot capture the non-linear effect of regional unemployment on mobility, given that it assumes that the positive attitude toward mobility increases monotonically from response 1 to response 3. We need to use a more appropriate specification that recognises that the impact of regional unemployment on the willingness to move may change sign depending on the geographical scope of migration. Doing so helps clarify why we could not find a significant effect of unemployment on the degree of mobility in the ordered logit model. The more general implication is that we need to control also for the behaviour of unemployment in neighbouring regions to assess the impact of regional unemployment on mobility. By doing so, the paradox of a negative regional unemployment effect may well disappear, as indeed it did in the Italian case.

4   Job-search and job-mobility attitudes

The question still remains of why inter-regional migration fell so much in Italy as well as in other European countries despite the large rise in unemployment differentials. I have argued in section 2 that one plausible explanation of this fact may lie on the supply side of migration – i.e. on the fact that higher economic welfare at home means that potential migrants are no longer willing to afford the disutility costs of migration. In this section, I investigate a complementary explanation, based, as in Gil and Jimeno (1993), on the inefficiencies of the job-matching process among regions. Consider the case where the probability of being hired in region i is significantly higher for a person located in that region. Formally, let h^i_j be the probability of being hired in region i while residing in region j. If $h^D_O < h^D_D$, i.e. if the probability of being hired in the destination region (D) is higher after migrating from the origin region (O), the inter-regional matching process is deemed to be quite inefficient. Suppose furthermore that mobility costs are very high. Given that h^D_O is low, migrants should move *before* they have found a job in the destination region. However, high mobility costs (and low hiring rates and/or high firing rate) mean that agents are willing to move only *after* having found a job. In the end, therefore, migration is unlikely to take place. If however h^D_O is close to h^D_D, then the matching process is quite efficient and migrants can migrate after having found a job: the probability of finding a job at a destination does not depend on where the migrant resides. Migrations could then take place even if migration costs were substantial. Unfortunately, we do not observe whether migrants moved before having found a job. Gil and Jimeno must therefore rely on indirect evidence, which in turn suggests that migration with employment is likely to be important. If we combine this finding with the fact that migration is low, we should then conclude that we are mainly in the first regime and that, for given migration costs, the quality of the matching process between unemployed and vacancies in different regions is likely to play a crucial role in affecting mobility. There is however a third interesting possibility, namely that $h^O_O > h^D_O \simeq h^D_D$. This will happen, for instance, if job search is more effective in the origin

Table 8.5. *Mobility attitudes and job search (first-time job-seekers)*[a]

Mobility attitudes	Job search	
	Family and friends	Other channels
Northern Italy:		
Own town only	36.60	34.71
Everywhere	30.57	32.75
Southern Italy:		
Own town only	42.19	37.18
Everywhere	16.41	20.22

Note: [a] Percentage of those willing to move to the stated location.
Source: Own elaborations on the 1995 Labour Force Survey.

than in the destination area, possibly because workers are better informed about job prospects in their own region and can count on family and friends' information networks to find a job. Migration would then be deterred both by informational problems and, possibly, by high migration costs.

Do we have any evidence that this may be the case? In table 8.5, I report the attitude toward mobility as a function of the type of job search actions. We see that those who are less willing to move are also those who rely to a greater extent on local information networks, i.e. on family and friends. Most likely, they are not willing to move because this would jeopardise their informational support to find a job. The policy implications of these findings are twofold. First, they stress the need to improve information flows about vacancies and job prospects in other regions (in Italy, private job agencies are prohibited). At the same time, the public sector agency is a blatantly inefficient monopolist: it does not provide information on labour market conditions in other regions, neither does it perform any training functions. The urgent policy message is that the public sector monopoly in Italy on job placement services should be rapidly abolished. There is, however, a further implication. One reason why information about job market conditions in other regions is so scarce is the lack of previous migrants. In the past, migrant chains proved instrumental in spreading information about job availabilities and attracting a steadily growing flow of migrants to low-unemployment and high-growth destinations. This network is no longer in place today, because of the long-standing stagnation in migration. Suppose, however, that less punitive housing policies and a thriving job placement private sector succeeds in fostering an initial increase in migration. Then, it is plausible that this may in turn overcome informational asymmetries, thereby generating a further increase in migrations. The economy could then move from a low-migration–high-unemployment differentials equilibrium to a new situation featuring higher mobility and greatly reduced unemployment differentials.

5   Economic integration and labour mobility

One explicit purpose of the Single Market programme is to foster labour mobility within Europe. The Cecchini Report (1988) acknowledged the existence of several hurdles to unimpeded labour mobility. For skilled workers, insufficient recognition of diplomas and professional qualifications still hinder the possibility of free movement across national European borders. For unskilled workers, labour and union regulations, particularly in non-tradable labour-intensive sectors such as services and construction, are still a powerful obstacle to the working of competitive forces. The inability of the European Commission to fully enforce regulations in the field of government procurement also reflects the attempt by some national governments to avoid opening construction activities to pan-European competition.

The completion of the internal labour market may also have other more indirect effects on labour mobility. In particular, European integration may favour the process of regional convergence in both income and unemployment, thereby further reducing the incentives for factor mobility. Economic theory, however, is deeply divided on this issue. Standard neoclassical models would predict that the reduction in trade barriers attendant on greater economic integration should favour the process of income convergence among countries and diminish the incentives for factor mobility. The 'new' geography models, however, come to different conclusions. In the increasing returns model of Krugman (1991a, 1991b), the reduction of trade barriers could improve the attractiveness of central locations and prompt workers to move there. Regional integration in this context will boost both factor mobility and regional divergence. The robustness of Krugman's conclusion is investigated in a number of studies by Krugman and Venables (1992; see also Venables, chapter 9 in this volume). They show, for instance, that if the basic model is extended to allow for intermediate inputs, regional polarisation is even more likely. On the one hand, final goods producers will tend to concentrate where the supply of intermediate goods is more abundant and their prices cheaper; on the other, intermediate goods producers will tend to move to those locations where the demand for their output is stronger.[7] The two effects will mutually reinforce each other, favouring the predominance of existing central locations. The role of increasing returns in affecting the interaction between factor mobility and economic convergence has also been investigated in a number of growth models by Bertola (1992), Rauch (1994) and Reichlin and Rustichini (1993). All rely on endogenous growth models, where the return to capital (or, more generally, to the reproducible factors) does not decline with an increasing capital stock. Introducing factor mobility invariably leads to a cumulative process of regional divergence (Reichlin and Rustichini, 1993; Rauch, 1994; Bertola, 1992). Factors will indeed move where their return is higher but, given the invariancy of the marginal productivity of capital, the incentives for further factor movements will not decrease. However, the hypothesis of constant returns to scale (CRS) for the reproducible factors is not necessary to generate a process of regional divergence. Faini (1996) develops a simple model of regional growth with mobile factors, increasing returns to scale and diminishing returns to capital to show that, even in the context of an exogenous growth model, convergence is not warranted. On the one hand, growth in the rich region is limited by the existence of diminishing returns to capital: with a fixed supply of labour, fast output growth would increase relative wages and depress the return to capital. Migration, however, can relax the labour supply constraint in the North: if mobility is sufficiently responsive to wage differentials, migration can even reverse the fall in the return to capital there. As in Lewis' (1954) classical analysis, growth in the North can proceed unimpeded provided that the rich regions can rely on a fairly elastic supply of labour from the South. Higher labour mobility is therefore found to strengthen the likelihood of regional divergence. Somewhat paradoxically, the lifting of barriers to labour mobility may then undermine the process of regional cohesion within Europe. Admittedly, the empirical evidence in support of this model is somewhat thin.

There are other ways for regional integration to affect the pattern of labour migration, in addition to its impact on factor returns and barriers to both trade and factor mobility. As the 'new' migration theory (Stark, 1991) has emphasised, migration does not occur only in response to wage and unemployment differentials. The desire to reduce risk exposure, the willingness to escape from relative deprivation or the attempt to exploit informational asymmetries are some of the factors which may prompt agent to migrate. These factors have been investigated in the more recent migration literature. There has not been, however, an attempt to integrate the insights of the new migration literature in trade models with factor mobility. A preliminary attempt to fill this gap is presented in Faini (1996a), whereas some supporting evidence is reported in Daveri and Faini (1999). The basic idea is quite simple. Suppose that migration is driven also by the desire to reduce risk (Levhari and Stark, 1982): a household may decide to have some of its members migrate if the returns in the receiving regions are negatively, or even only imperfectly, correlated with factor returns at home. One interesting implication of this approach is that households living in countries, or regions, which have a well diversified economy will have little incentive to migrate as a way to diversify risk. Conversely, if the regional economy is poorly diversified, migration may become a palatable strategy to reduce excessive risk exposure. We can see therefore a further channel through which economic integration may affect the incentive to migrate. European economies are still quite diversified, compared for instance to the states in the United States (Krugman, 1991a). To some extent, the lack of sectoral specialisation can be attributed to the effect of existing barriers to trade. By removing such barriers, the Internal Market programme would then foster economic specialisation (Krugman, 1991; Krugman and Venables, 1992). Regions would then be more subject to idiosyncratic shocks, prompting households to have some of their members migrate to reduce overall risk exposure. Clearly, this channel would work only to the extent that migration is a family rather than an individual decision. Empirical evidence on this issue is somewhat scant. Yet, there is growing evidence that migration flows are quite responsive to risk factors. Lambert (1994) studies the migration behaviour of households in Ivory Coast. Daveri and Faini (1996) consider regional migrations from Southern Italy and find that risk considerations play a substantial role in affecting both the decision to migrate and the choice of the migration destination. In their setup, potential migrants from relatively poor regions have three alternatives: they can stay home, migrate to a domestic destination or migrate abroad. They find that if the correlation between factor returns at home and in the domestic destination increases, then migrations to foreign destinations will rise. Again, this suggests that migration among European countries may increase if the completion of the Single Market programme leads to greater specialisation at the country's and the regional level. Therefore, even in a traditional trade model, trade integration may lead to more migrations.

6   Conclusions

The prospects for a resumption of a high level of labour mobility within Europe are not particularly bright. Higher economic welfare at home together with an extensive unemployment benefit system mean that migration is no longer the unavoidable choice for unemployed workers in poor regions. Moreover, family support can help defer the migratory decision and finance relatively long spells of unemployment. Cultural and linguistic barriers within Europe mean that the disutility costs of migrations (the 'loss of amenities') can be significant. Employed workers have therefore few incentives to move in search of better pay conditions, whereas unemployed workers can survive through long spells of unemployment thanks to family and public support.

Yet, the fact that mobility is also low within countries suggests that the difference in the degree of mobility between Europe and the United States cannot be entirely attributed to cultural and linguistic factors. Barriers to labour mobility are still quite high, as documented, for instance, by the European Commission. In addition to formal and informal barriers, there also economic obstacles to mobility. Punitive taxation of housing sales together with an a restricted rental market take a heavy toll on the willingness of European households to move. Similarly, the inefficiencies of the job placement system mean that job-seekers are often forced to rely on local job-search networks and are therefore unwilling to move to far-away locations. Policy intervention in these fields is imperative and may provide a substantial boost to labour mobility.

Finally, the completion of the Internal Market may contribute to higher labour mobility in a somewhat indirect way. If, as predicted both by factor endowment and geography models, production specialisation at a regional level increases following the reduction in trade costs, then it could well happen that risk-averse households may want to have some of their members migrate in an effort to reduce their exposure to risk. How realistic such a perspective is will depend on whether migration is a family rather than a individual decision (demography and smaller family size may work against the former) and on the strength of this effect. Further research on this issue is certainly warranted.

NOTES

I am very grateful to Dick Baldwin and Tony Venables for their comments on an earlier draft and to Elena Belli for outstanding research assistance.
1 For an econometric attempt to determine the impact of aggregate economic fluctuations (as measured by the national unemployment rate) on inter-regional mobility see Pissarides and Wadsworth (1989) for Great Britain and Bentolila and Dolado (1991) for Spain.
2 Surprisingly enough, we know only where the household currently resides. The fact that the same household is interviewed four times over a two-year interval does not help in identifying migrants either. If a household migrates, it will change residence and will almost certainly drop out from the next survey,

resulting in a severe attrition bias. Moreover, even households with a recent migration experience are unlikely to be part of the Labour Force Survey given the long delays in residence registration. Some of these considerations could apply also to the Labour Force Survey in other countries.

3 This section draws on Faini *et al.* (1996).

4 Results for Spain are not fully comparable. Ahn *et al.* (1995) show that 66.8 per cent of Spanish unemployed would not accept a job offer from a different region. They also find that mobility increases with education and is highest for a son/daughter.

5 For this interpretation to be valid, we need to assume that the attitude toward short-distance mobility reflects also a similar attitude toward job-search in nearby regions.

6 Notice also that we consider only unemployed workers. We cannot therefore exploit Da Vanzo's (1978) approach and interact regional unemployment with an unemployed worker dummy variable.

7 A similar result was derived by Faini (1984).

REFERENCES

Ahn, N., de la Rica, S. and Ugidos, S., 1995. 'Job-acceptance Attitudes and Unemployment Duration in Spain', Universidad del Pais Vasco, Bilbao, mimeo

Antolin, P., 1994. 'International Migration Flows: The Case of Spain (1960–1988)', Instituto Valenciano de Investigationes Economicas, **WP-EC 94-01**

Antolin, P. and Bover, O., 1997. 'Regional Migration in Spain', *Oxford Bulletin of Economics and Statistics*, **59**, 215–36

Attanasio, O. and Padoa Schioppa, F., 1991 'Regional Inequalities, Migration and Mismatch in Italy, 1960–86', in F. Padoa Schioppa (ed.), *Mismatch and Labour Mobility* (Cambridge: Cambridge University Press for the CEPR), 237–324

Bentolila, S. and Dolado, J., 1991. 'Mismatch and Internal Migration in Spain, 1962–86', in F. Padoa Schioppa (ed.), *Mismatch and Labour Mobility* (Cambridge: Cambridge University Press for the CEPR)

Bentolila, S. and Jimeno, J., 1995. 'Regional Unemployment Persistence (Spain, 1976–1994)', *CEPR Discussion Paper,* **1259**

Bertola, G., 1992. 'Models of Economic Integration and Localised Growth', *CEPR Discussion Paper*, **651**

Blanchard, O. and Katz, L., 1992. 'Regional Evolutions', *Brookings Papers on Economic Activity*, **1**, 1–75

Boden, P., Rees, P. and Stillwell. J., 1992. *Migration Processes and Patterns* (London: Belhaven Press)

Cecchini, P., 1988. *The European Challenge* (Aldershot: Gower)

Courgeau, D. and Pumain, D., 1993. 'Mobilité par temps de crise', *Population et Sociétés*, **279**

DaVanzo, J., 1978. 'Does Unemployment Affect Migration ? Evidence from Micro Data', *Review of Economics and Statistics*, **60**, 504–14

Daveri, F. and Faini, R., 1996. 'Where Do Migrants Go?', University of Brescia, mimeo; *Oxford Economic Papers*, forthcoming

Decressin, J. and Fatas, A., 1995. 'Regional Labor Market Dynamics in Europe and Implications for EMU', *European Economic Review*, **39**, 1627–55

Faini, R., 1984. 'Increasing Returns, Non-traded Inputs and Regional Development', *Economic Journal*, **94**, 308–23

1989. 'Regional Development and Economic Integration', in J. da Silva Lopes and L. Beleza (eds.), *Portugal and the Internal Market of the EEC* (Lisbon: Banco de Portugal)

1996a. 'Trade, Migration and Risk', paper delivered at AEA Annual meetings, San Francisco.

1996b. 'Increasing Returns, Migration and Convergence', *Journal of Development Economics*, **49**, 121–36

Faini, R. and Venturini, A., 1993. 'Trade, Aid and Migrations: Some Basic Policy Issues', *European Economic Review*, **37**, 435–42

1994. 'Migration and Growth. The Experience of Southern Europe', *CEPR Discussion Paper*, **964**

Faini R., Galli, G. and Rossi, F., 1996. 'Mobilità e disoccupazione in Italia', in G. Galli (ed.) *La mobilità nella società Italiana* (Rome: SIPI)

Ferenczi, I. and Willcox, W., 1934. *International Migrations* (Geneva: United Nations)

Gil, L. and Jimeno, J., 1993. 'The Determinants of Labour Mobility in Spain: Who are the Migrants ?', FEDEA, *Documento de Trabajo*, **93-05**

Goria, A. and Ichino, A., 1994. 'Migration and Convergence among Italian Regions', Fondazione ENI Enrico Mattei, *Nota di Lavoro*, **51.94**

Hatton, T. and Williamson, J., 1994. 'Latecomers to Mass Migration: The Latin Experience', in T. Hatton and J. Williamson (eds.), *Migration and the International Labor Market* (London: Routledge)

Hughes, G. and McCormick, B., 1981. 'Do Council Housing Policies Reduce Migration between Regions ?', *Economic Journal*, **91**, 319–37

1985. 'Migration Intentions in the UK: Which Households want to Migrate and which Succeed ?', *Economic Journal*, **95**, 76–95

1994. 'Did Migration in the 1980s Narrow the North–South Divide?, *Economica*, **61**, 509–27

Krugman, P., 1991a. *Geography and Trade* (Cambridge, MA: MIT Press)

1991b. 'History versus Expectations', *Quarterly Journal of Economics*, **106**, 651–67

Krugman, P. and Venables, A., 1992. 'Integration and the Competitiveness of Peripheral Industry', *CEPR Discussion Paper*, **363**

Lambert, S., 1994. 'La migration comme instrument de diversification des risques dans la famille ivoirienne', *Revue d'Economie du Développement*, **2**, 3–38

Levhari, D. and Stark, O., 1982. 'On Migration and Risk in Less-developed Countries', *Economic Development and Cultural Change*, **31**

Lewis, A., 1954. 'Economic Development with Unlimited Supplies of Labour', *Manchester School of Economic and Social Studies*, <at proof>, 139–91

Livi Bacci, M., Abbate, M., De Santis, G., Giovannelli, C. and Ricci, R., 1996. 'Mobilità e territorio', in G. Galli (ed.), *La mobilità nella società Italiana* (Rome: Sipi)

Meldolesi, L., 1996. 'L'elevata mobilità del lavoro nel Mezzogiorno della speranza', in G. Galli (ed.), *La mobilità nella società Italiana* (Rome: SIPI)

Pissarides, C. and Wadsworth, J., 1989. 'Unemployment and the Inter-regional Mobility of Labour', *Economic Journal*, **99**, 739–55

Rauch, J., 1994. 'Balanced and Unbalanced Growth', *NBER Working Paper*, **4659**

Razin, A. and Sadka, E., 1995. *Population Economics* (Cambridge, MA: MIT Press)

Reichlin, P. and Rustichini, A., 1993. 'Diverging Patterns in a Two Country Model with Endogenous Labor Migration', *CORE Discussion Paper*, **9332**

Salt, J., 1991. 'Current and Future International Migration Trends Affecting Europe', 4th Conference of European Ministers responsible for migration affairs (Luxembourg)

Stark, O., 1991. *The Migration of Labor* (Oxford: Basil Blackwell)

Discussion

RICHARD BALDWIN

Riccardo Faini has given us a very nice survey/synthesis piece on European migration in his chapter 8. If I may be so bold as to summarise it, Faini's chapter essentially tells us that European labour does not move – not between nations, not within nations and certainly not in response to wage differentials – as many economists would expect. Why does it not move? Faini evaluates and dismisses four popular explanations. The immobility is not due to a narrowing of the wage gap, it is not due to international regulation or subtle international regulatory barriers, it is not due to demographics and it is not due to changes in the gaps between unemployment rates. The real answer lies in four assertions. First, as the level of incomes has risen, European workers wish to consume more 'home amenities' – i.e. the ability to enjoy one's consumption near one's friends and family. Second, employment agencies have done a poor job of advertising job openings beyond the boundaries of their regional and national boundaries. Third, obstructionist housing market policies have greatly increased the cost of moving. Lastly, unemployment support has made it feasible for workers to survive without jobs.

I am not a migration specialist, so I cannot make clever points about his arguments, data and/or empirics. What I will do instead is attempt to draw some conclusions from Faini's findings. The first is to question the desirability of boosting European labour mobility. As a migrant myself, and citizen of a highly mobile society (the United States), I find the lack of European mobility a social plus. It is quite common for Europeans to have 'roots' – i.e. for them to grow up and work in the same community. Moreover, if they do move, they often stay in the same place for decades before moving again (if ever). This sort of stability must have implications for the types of socioeconomic relationships that develop. In terms of pure economics, it would seem that this would help avoid many of the prisoner's dilemma problems that plague US society. Moreover, it encourages positive consumption externalities. Everyone knows that a disproportionate amount of consumption goes on during weekends and the winter holiday season, despite convex of preferences. The answer may simply be that people get more utility out of a dollar's worth of expenditure when they can consume it in the company of friends and families. In any case, I think European society would be very different – and probably worse – if Europeans were as mobile as Americans. Factor immobility has clear economic costs, but I would argue that it also has hard-to-define economic benefits.

Second, I think Faini's chapter sheds some light on the types of economic geography models that are relevant to Europe. I view the recent economic geography as having two main types of model – the Krugman model (see Krugman, 1991, for instance) and the Venables model (see Venables, 1993). Both focus on agglomeration forces driven by supply and demand linkages, and both emphasise the possibility of extreme outcomes (such as one region emptying out all firms, or at least all firms in a given industry). The Krugman model, however, assumes that agglomeration forces act by moving workers to locations, and here one can get core–periphery outcomes like Wyoming and Los Angeles. The Venables model assumes that firms move to workers, agglomerating along industry lines. Here we get increased specialisation of the industrial make-up of regions, rather than empty and full regions as in the Krugman model.

Third, Faini's chapter has a simple policy implication for regional unemployment policies. If workers will not move to jobs, then policy-makers must accept pockets of unemployment, or they must encourage jobs to go to the workers. In other words, solving regional unemployment problems may necessitate policies that are similar in spirit to those of the European Union's Structural and Cohesion Funds.

REFERENCES

Krugman, P., 1991. *Trade and Economic Geography* (Cambridge, MA: MIT Press)
Venables, A., 1993. 'Equilibrium Locations of Vertically Linked Industries,' *CEPR Discussion Paper*, **802**

9 Geography and specialisation: industrial belts on a circular plain

ANTHONY J. VENABLES

1 Introduction

What forces determine the spatial pattern of industrial specialisation? Near the top of an economist's list of answers to this question would probably come differences in technology or endowments. A good deal further down we might find geography – the spatial position of locations – and agglomeration – the desire of firms or other economic agents to locate close to each other. This ranking comes in part from the intellectual tradition of economics. We naturally look to preferences, technology and endowments to determine everything. It also comes from the traditional focus of international economics on trade between countries with dissimilar endowments.

The 'new economic geography' literature of the last five years has started to redress the balance. Within deeply integrated regions such as the European Union it seems hard to argue that differences in technologies or in endowments of immobile factors are key determinants of patterns of specialisation and trade. And perhaps this also becoming true at the world level as more activities become tradable, and firms and factors of production become increasingly internationally mobile. We need a theory of the location of activity which is not dependent on assumed differences in locations' factor endowments or technologies, but which can address the pattern of location of economic activity in a world in which (almost) everything is mobile. Geography and agglomeration then come to the fore as possible determinants of the location of activity and the pattern of trade.

The 'new economic geography' literature focuses on agglomeration and provides analytical foundations for forces which induce agglomeration. It has given us a much better understanding of the sorts of interactions between agents that create these forces, in particular the role of technological and pecuniary externalities. It also establishes circum-

254

stances under which they are powerful enough to cause agglomeration to occur. This literature is surveyed in a recent paper by Fujita and Thisse (1996).

Much of the focus of the literature has been on the location of economic activity as a whole. If factors are mobile, then where does economic activity take place? Will activity agglomerate in a few locations? What structure of cities may form? In this chapter we focus on a different question. Suppose that factors of production are immobile and that there are several industries. What determines *which* industries locate where? This question was addressed in Krugman and Venables (1996), but for the very simple case in which there are only two industries (assumed to be identical) and two locations (also assumed to be identical). They showed that economic integration may lead to a spontaneous pattern of industrial specialisation. Above some critical level of trade barriers both locations have both industries, and below this level agglomeration takes over, causing each location to be specialised in a single industry. However, because of the very simple structure of the model they used, nothing could be said about what sort of industry locates in what sort of location.

The objective of the present chapter is to make a first attempt at answering this question. To do so we need to work with both a more heterogeneous geographical space, and a more heterogeneous mix of industries. For the former, we take as our geographical space a set of locations lying on a disc. The disc has two important characteristics. First, it is two-dimensional. And second, it has a well defined geography, in the sense that there is a centre and an edge. All points may have the same endowments and technologies, yet they are different by virtue of their location. Having this geographical structure is important, as the label 'new economic geography' has been something of a misnomer for much of the recent literature. Authors have typically stayed in the international trade tradition of working with countries as isolated points, or gone to the one-dimensional space used by much location theory. Hopefully, by working with a simple two-dimensional space this chapter will put some geography into the new economic geography.

The industrial heterogeneity we work with will be very simple. There is a background perfectly competitive sector, and attention is focused on two imperfectly competitive increasing returns industries. The structure of these industries will be exactly as in previous work (e.g. Krugman and Venables, 1996), except that we shall now allow for differences between industries. We focus on differences in the trade costs in the two industries (section 4) and on the input–output relationship between them (sections 5 and 6).

The cost of working with a richer geographical space and heterogeneous industrial sectors is that the chapter is entirely based on numerical simulation. However, we think these simulations are of interest in their own right, and possibly also as pointers to future analytical results. It has proved possible to obtain quite strong analytical results in the simpler models referred to above, and may yet turn out to be possible to obtain analogous results in this more general set up.

Many of the themes in the chapter are familiar from previous work, but their interaction, as so often in this literature, yields a rich set of quite surprising results. We shall see how zones of industrial activity form and how economic integration may modify these, in some cases completely reversing the pattern of industrial specialisation. In a concluding section we have a brief discussion of the implications of our findings, and of their relationship to empirical work on the evolution of specialisation.

2   Overview of the model

The mathematical structure of the model is given in the appendix, and in this section we give an informal overview of the model, together with some of the numerical detail required to understand the simulations.

2.1   Geographical space

Our locations lie on a disc of unit radius, and we approximate continuous space by taking a set of evenly spaced points on the disc. The points are formed by a square grid, and the number of points is set such that along the horizontal diameter of the disc there are 11 points.[1] In figures that follow these will be labelled from 1 (on one edge) through to 6 (the central point) and 11 (on the opposite edge). If our space were the unit square this would generate 121 locations. For a circle, we delete points which lie outside the unit radius of the disc, leaving 81 points. Distances, and hence trade costs, between a pair of points are measured by the Euclidean metric (there are no boundaries, road systems or other geographical or political features).

Ideally we would have worked with a very large number of points on the disc in order to approximate continuous space. This is infeasible as computational demands increase rapidly with the number of locations. For example, the number of elements in the matrix of distances between locations increases with the number of locations on the diameter to the power 4. However, working with our rather coarse square grid may bias results, and also has the disadvantage that the set of points has radial symmetry only of order 4.

Each of the locations is endowed with the same quantity of labour and land, both assumed to be immobile. They also have the same technologies, so there is no basis for traditional comparative advantage.

2.2   The perfectly competitive sector

There is a perfectly competitive sector which, in keeping with other papers, we shall refer to as 'agriculture'. It is the only sector to use land and produces a freely traded good which we shall use as numeraire. The sector plays two roles in the model. First, trade in this sector's output secures balance of payments balance for each location – some locations will be net exporters of manufacturing, and others net importers, with the surplus/deficit matched by agricultural imports/exports. Second, the sector employs labour, for which it has a downward sloping demand curve. This means that a location with more manufacturing will have a higher wage than one with less – it has less labour employed in agriculture, hence a higher land:labour ratio and higher wage rate. We set the share of labour in agriculture quite high (0.81), so that the elasticity of the wage rate with respect to manufacturing employment is low (this elasticity is not constant, but is of order 0.1).

2.3   Manufacturing industry

There are two manufacturing industries, each of them having the structure used in Krugman and Venables (1995, 1996). That is, both industries incorporate Dixit–Stiglitz (1977) monopolistic competition and 'iceberg' transport costs in shipping between locations. We shall look at some cases in which firms' only input is labour and all output is sold as a final good to consumers (sections 3 and 4). We shall then extend the model to allow firms to both use and produce intermediate goods (sections 5 and 6). Details of this are set out in the appendix, and here we just note the essential features of industry.

First, there is intra-industry trade – each firm sells some of its output in every location, although transport costs mean that less is sold to distant locations than to close ones. Transport costs in manufacturing are central to the model, as without them all points on the disc would be economically identical and there would be no economic geography. We model these costs as 'iceberg' trade costs – i.e. the resource used up in transport is the good itself, although this assumption is not necessary for results. The transport costs should be thought of as all the costs that are incurred in doing business with more distant locations and which give rise to the 'home market bias' we observe in firms' sales. We shall refer henceforth to this package of costs and trade barriers as 'trade costs'.

Second, firms have increasing returns to scale and the number of firms in each location is endogenously determined, with profits attracting entry and losses causing exit. It is this free entry and exit of firms which determines the equilibrium location of industries. At equilibrium no profits are earned, and there are no opportunities for profitable entry (or exit) by a single firm in any location.

Third, each firm is associated with a variety of product and entry of firms, by bringing in new varieties, brings a welfare gain. This can be measured as a reduction in an industry and location-specific price index. Changes in these price indices arise not only from changes in the total number of varieties on offer, but also from relocation of firms. Moving a firm into a location reduces the price index in the location, the mechanism being simply that this firm's sales no longer incur trade costs in supplying its new location.

When we add intermediate goods we do so in a very simple way, assuming that product varieties can be used both as final and as intermediate goods, and that firms enjoy the benefits of variety of intermediate goods in the same way as consumers enjoy variety in their consumption. The combination of imperfect competition, trade costs, and an input–output structure creates pecuniary externalities between firms and consequent forces for agglomeration. To see this, consider a location whose neighbourhood (in some sense) is somewhat more oriented toward manufacturing than the average. Such a location may well then turn out to be a place in which manufacturing is especially profitable, for two reasons. First, the availability of the inputs provided by nearby manufacturers will also encourage local industrial production – an effect which corresponds to the idea of 'forward linkage' or 'cost linkage'. This happens because proximity of firms reduces the price index of intermediate goods in each location. And, second, because manufactured goods are an input into manufactures production, a location that is surrounded by manufacturing-oriented locations will have access to a bigger market than one that is not; this 'backward linkage' or 'demand linkage' will tend to make industrial production there profitable.

These forward and backward linkages are centripetal forces, pulling in the direction of agglomeration. Pulling in the opposite direction are the usual centrifugal forces of factor and product market and competition. A location with many firms will have high labour demand and a high wage (factor market competition) and will have to divide local demand between many firms (product market competition). It is the interaction between the two forces for agglomeration – backward and forward linkages – and the two forces for dispersion of industry – factor market and product market competition – that drive the results of sections 5 and 6 of this chapter.

3   Centre vs. periphery

We commence our study by looking at the case where there are no intermediate goods and the two manufacturing industries are identical.[2] Where on the disc do manufacturing firms locate? The answer is the familiar one of market access benefits pulling firms into central locations at the expense of peripheral ones.

Rather than illustrate the location of industry directly, we illustrate the consequent distribution of real wages. Figure 9.1 plots real wages at locations on the diameter of the disc for three values of transport costs, lower transport costs giving rise to higher-placed curves.

If trade costs were infinitely high (autarky for each point on the disc) then real wages would be the same at all locations, so their representation on figure 9.1 would be a horizontal (and low) line. The lowest line illustrated on the figure is for a transport cost of 3, this meaning that if 4 units are shipped from the centre of the disc to the edge, only 1 unit will arrive (the other 3 'melting' according to the 'iceberg' trade costs). At this very high level of transport costs we see real wages at the edge of the disc significantly below their more or less flat value in central regions of the disc.[3] This pattern of real wages emerges as locations at the very edge of the disc are unattractive locations for firms – they have a market on only one side – so have low labour demand and low wages. Consumers also have to import a high proportion of their manufactures from far away, thus raising their price and reinforcing the real wage profile.

Moving to lower trade costs (the middle line is for transport costs of 1) we see, in addition to the poor performance of peripheral regions, the central area doing well relative to intermediate regions. This is driven by the fact that consumers in the immediate proximity of the firm are now less important in firms' location decisions. There is an incentive for firms to go to locations with good access to as many consumers as possible, this drawing firms to the centre of the disc.

At still lower trade costs, the wage schedule becomes less steeply humped. The top line in figure 9.1 is the real wage profile with transport costs of 0.12, i.e. just over 12 per cent of the product lost in shipping the whole way from the centre to the edge. Firms still want to locate in regions with good access to as many consumers as possible, but are now more sensitive to cost difference between locations. Industry starts relocating away from high-wage areas (the centre), giving the flattening

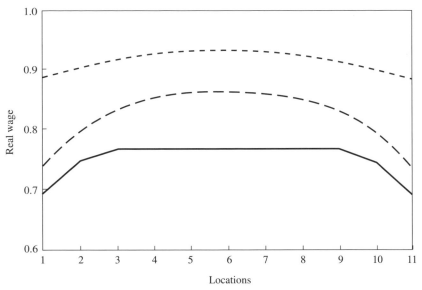

Figure 9.1   Centre and periphery

in the wage profile that is illustrated. At perfectly free trade the wage profile becomes flat because, as we have already noted, without trade costs all regions are economically identical.

The pattern of equilibria illustrated on figure 9.1 confirms what we know from simpler models (e.g. Krugman and Venables, 1990). If an imperfectly competitive manufacturing sector is subject to trade costs then market access considerations have a centripetal effect, drawing firms to central locations. Wage differences tend to act as centrifugal forces, and the relative strength of centripetal forces is strongest at intermediate values of trade costs. There is therefore a U-shaped relationship between levels of trade costs and regional wage inequalities.

4   Industries differing in trade costs

We now turn to cases in which the two industries have different demand or technological parameters. Which locations specialise in which industries?

The first set of results is unsurprising in view of section 3. Suppose that the industries differ only in the extent to which they mark up price over marginal cost. In our model this is measured by a single parameter, the elasticity of demand for each variety of differentiated product. An industry in which firms face lower elasticities can be regarded as more imperfectly competitive, in the sense that it has higher mark-ups, and is

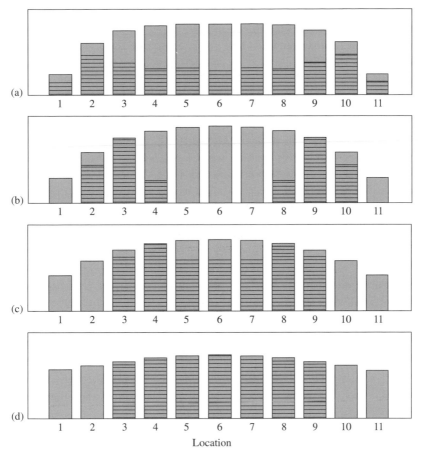

Figure 9.2   Differing trade costs

able to cover a larger fixed cost at a given scale of operation. We find that the more imperfectly competitive industry is relatively concentrated in central regions, while the less imperfectly competitive industry is (like agriculture) concentrated in peripheral regions.

What if the industries differ not in their demand elasticity, but instead in the level of trade costs they incur in shipping their output? Figure 9.2 reports results when industry 1 has trade costs twice as high as industry 2. Panels (a)–(d) of figure 9.2 correspond to four different values of trade costs which are, from (a) to (d), industry 1 trade costs of 2, 1, 0.5 and 0.12 and industry 2 costs of 1, 0.5, 0.25 and 0.06. In each panel the horizontal axis represents locations on the diameter, and the height of the bar is total manufacturing employment. The horizontally striped component of each bar is employment in industry 2 (the lower trade-cost industry) and the lower section of each bar employment in industry 1.[4]

The configurations reported are quite complex. At high trade costs (panel (a)) all locations have both industries, with edge locations biased towards industry 1 and the centre towards industry 2.

Moving to lower trade costs causes central *and* edge locations to specialise in industry 2. Between these regions a belt of intermediate locations specialise in 1. And between these three specialised belts are two non-specialised belts of activity (locations 2 and 4, and correspondingly 8 and 10, which have both industry 1 and industry 2 operating).

Reducing trade costs again (panel (c)) draws industry 1 into central regions. At the lowest trade costs (panel (d)) central regions specialise in industry 1 and peripheral regions specialise in industry 2 – an inversion of the pattern of location observed at high trade costs.

How are these patterns of specialisation to be explained? First the inversion in the pattern of specialisation. We saw in section 3 that the centripetal forces associated with market access considerations are strongest at intermediate levels of trade costs. In panels (a) and (b) of figure 9.2 industry 2 (the lower trade-cost industry) has 'intermediate' trade costs, so tends to concentrate in the centre while the higher trade-cost industry (industry 1) occupies a wider range of locations. As trade costs fall so industry 1 becomes the industry with 'intermediate' value trade costs, and gets drawn to the central region. The U-shape of the relationship between trade costs and the balance between centripetal and centrifugal forces now shows up, causing the inversion in the pattern of specialisation as trade costs are reduced.

Second, there are multiple rings of specialisation, particularly in panel (b). The reason for these is that, all other things being equal, firms do not want to locate close to competitor firms in the same industry. Looking at panel (b), central locations are attractive to firms in industry 2, and most of industry 2 is concentrated in these locations. However, some industry 2 firms are able to survive on the edge. The advantage of being on the edge is precisely that of being a long way away from most of their competitors, located in the centre. This creates a phenomenon of ripples of activity – industrial belts with industries occupying alternating concentric circles.

5   Industrial linkages

Suppose now that manufacturing output is used both as a final good and as an intermediate. As discussed in section 2, this creates forward and backward linkages between firms and hence an incentive for firms to cluster together. Firms want to be close to their intermediate suppliers and their customers, and the pattern of location to which this gives rise depends on the input–output structure. We start with the simple case in which firms only use the output of other firms in the *same* industry as an intermediate; the inter-industry transaction part of the input–output matrix therefore has zero off-diagonal elements, and positive diagonal elements. We set these so that costs in each industry are 70 per cent labour, and 30 per cent intermediates.

The presence of linkages means that the model exhibits multiple equilibria. Firms choose a particular location because other firms are located there, and this is consistent with many different equilibria. Given this multiplicity, what can we say? We proceed as follows. Because the industries have identical characteristics there is always an equilibrium in which both industries have identical location patterns, meaning that each industry accounts for half of manufacturing employment at every location. We shall call this the symmetric equilibrium, but note that it may be unstable. Starting from the symmetric equilibrium, consider a small perturbation away from it – i.e. a reallocation of some firms between locations. We allow a simple dynamic process to operate, in which firms enter at a location with positive profit levels, and exit from a location with negative profits. If the symmetric equilibrium is stable, then the model will return to this equilibrium. But if linkages are strong enough then the symmetric equilibrium is unstable; a location which has been assigned more than its share of a particular industry becomes a more attractive location for other firms in the industry, so our dynamic process will lead to divergence away from symmetry – a process of 'cumulative causation'. We simply let our dynamic entry–exit process run until the model converges to a new equilibrium.

Beginning from a situation with high transport costs, a random perturbation to the symmetric equilibrium typically leads to an outcome with what we shall term 'high-frequency agglomeration' 'Agglomeration' since each location comes to specialise in a single industry, and 'high-frequency' since industry 1 and industry 2 locations are interspersed over the space, rather than grouped into large regional concentrations.

Is there any pattern to these locations? Krugman and Venables (1995) show that, in a one-dimensional geographical space with one industry, random perturbations from an unstable equilibrium generate a completely regular pattern of agglomeration. No such regularity is apparent from the simulations undertaken in this model, probably because there are not sufficiently many locations to allow it to develop. Our procedure is therefore to start not with random perturbations from the symmetric equilibrium, but instead with small perturbations following a chequer-

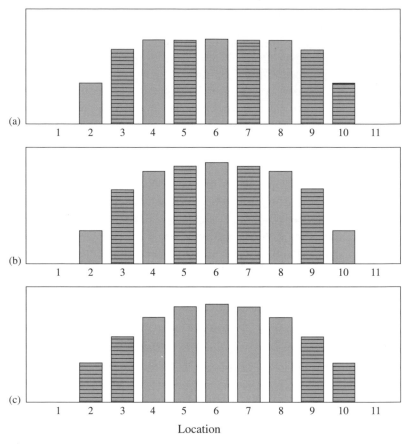

Figure 9.3   Industrial linkages

board pattern. Allowing firms to enter and exit in response to profits and losses, this pattern of perturbations evolves from the unstable equilibrium into an equilibrium with a chequerboard pattern of industry, as illustrated in panel (a) of figure 9.3. The two features of this panel are, first, high-frequency agglomeration – a general property which occurs whether we start with random or with chequerboard deviations. And, second, industries 1 and 2 occupy alternating locations. This tidy pattern is not general, but develops exactly because of the initial perturbations.

  Panel (a) of figure 9.3 has trade costs of 2. To see what happens at lower trade costs we reduce costs in a series of steps, each time using the previous equilibrium as starting values from which the numbers of firms evolve to a new equilibrium. As trade costs are reduced to 1 (panel (b)) so the chequerboard pattern remains an equilibrium, although central locations become more favoured. However, further reductions in trade costs (to 0.5, panel (c)) bring a switch to 'low-frequency agglomeration', destroying the previous high-frequency structure. This occurs as agglomeration forces induce firms in each industry to group together, and as distance from final consumers is now less costly. It is interesting to note that only one of the industries is able to reap the full benefits of agglomeration. One industry can occupy the central locations, but the other – despite the fact that it is identical in all respects – is forced out to occupy a peripheral belt.

Although the pattern traced out in figure 9.3 is not unique, it illustrates several general points. First, as trade costs are pulled down there is a transition from high-frequency agglomeration to low-frequency agglomeration. It occurs as the need to locate close to final consumers is reduced, so agglomeration forces become a relatively more important element in firms' location decisions. Krugman and Venables (1995) offer analytical foundations for this phenomenon.

Second, the equilibrium exhibits path-dependence. Following a change in parameters the new equilibrium established depends on the starting point. This applies both to the fine detail of the equilibrium – which location has which industry – and to the broader features, such as whether there is high or low frequency agglomeration. Thus, as transport costs are reduced the high-frequency structure remains for a wide range of costs, until below some level it reorganises into low-frequency agglomeration. This is the phenomenon of 'punctuated equilibrium' – stability of structure for a wide range of parameter values, followed by abrupt change.

6   Alternative input–output structures

In the analysis of section 5, firms used only their own industry's output as an intermediate. What if the input output structure takes a different form? The diametrically opposed possibility is that firms in one industry use only the output of the other industry. Since the pecuniary externality is now between, rather than within, industries, firms want to locate near firms in the other industry and symmetry (each location having half of its manufacturing employment in each industry) is a stable equilibrium. This gives a structure qualitatively similar to the one we saw in section 3, although quantitatively the presence of linkages greatly amplifies the centre–periphery wage differentials.

A further possible input–output structure is that one industry is upstream, and the other downstream, and the implications of this are illustrated on figure 9.4. Industry 1 (horizontally striped) is upstream,

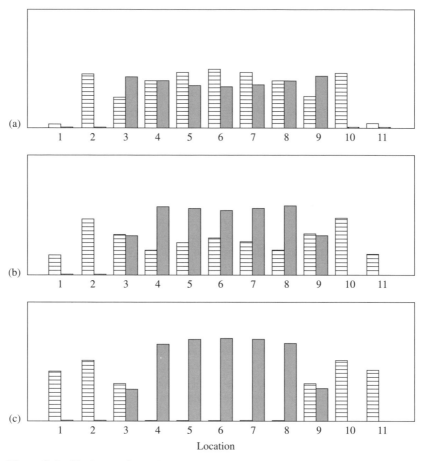

Figure 9.4   Upstream–downstream

using labour as its only input, and selling its output both as an intermediate and as a final consumer good. Industry 2 (shaded) is downstream, using labour and intermediate goods produced by industry 1 as inputs, and selling its output only to final consumers. To emphasise the *relative* scales of operation of each industry in each location we now illustrate employment in each industry by the adjacent columns (total manufacturing employment in each location being their sum).

Panels (a)–(c) of figure 9.4 give outcomes for trade costs of 2, 1 and 0.25. What do we learn from the figure? First, because linkages are between not within the industries, there is a tendency for all locations to have both industries (as compared to the total locational specialisation seen in figure 9.3). This force is stronger the higher are trade costs, because at lower trade costs the cost of shipping intermediates is reduced.

Second, peripheral regions specialise in the upstream industry. The reason for this is that wages are lower in the periphery than at the centre, and upstream industries are more labour-intensive. Some care is needed in interpreting this statement. Labour is the only primary factor used in manufacturing, but whereas upstream firms use labour only from their own location, downstream firms also use labour from other locations embodied in imported intermediates. The upstream industry is therefore more *local labour-intensive* than the downstream, and consequently more sensitive to inter-locational wage differentials. As trade costs fall so these factor price considerations become the main force in determining location (panel (c)).

Third, we see the production structure of central regions changing dramatically as trade costs fall. Whereas central regions specialise in downstream activities at low trade costs (panel (c)), at high trade costs they have more employment in upstream industries (panel (a)). Why should it be the case that at high trade costs upstream activities occupy the periphery *and* have a significant presence in the centre? The answer comes from two forces. First, at high trade costs upstream firms want to locate close to downstream firms. But second, upstream firms want to locate far away from other upstream firms (because of product market competition). The presence of upstream firms in the periphery creates an intermediate zone with few upstream firms, while in the central zone more upstream firms are present, benefiting from the advantage of distance from competitors. Just as we saw in section 4 (panels (b) and (c) of figure 9.2), this creates a force for alternating belts of industry.

Pulling together the information in figure 9.4, we see that there is a clear prediction that reducing trade costs will create a pattern of industrial specialisation in which upstream industries locate in low-wage peripheral regions, and downstream industries locate in higher-wage central regions.

7 Implications and conclusions

The model explored in this chapter contains none of the usual ingredients of comparative advantage – there are no differences in technology, endowments, or preferences – yet locations come to specialise in different industries. Two forces drive this specialisation. The first is the geography of the disc. Central locations are more profitable for manufacturing firms, by an amount which varies according to industry characteristics. Industries which are highly imperfectly competitive (in the sense of having high price–cost mark-ups) and which have intermediate levels of trade costs will tend to locate in more central locations. The second force driving the pattern of specialisation is agglomeration. Linkages between firms, captured here by supplier–customer relationships, induce clustering of the firms.

The main findings from the study can be grouped into three types. First is the discovery that, from a model with a quite simple structure, a remarkably rich set of patterns of industrial location can emerge. Industrial belts – concentric circles of industrial specialisation – arise as a consequence of the trade-off between the desire of firms to occupy locations with geographical advantages and the desire of firms to locate a long way away other firms in the same industry which are exploiting these advantages. Input–output linkages between firms can produce patterns of agglomeration which may be high frequency – neighbouring locations having different specialisations – or lower frequency, with large areas of specialisation forming.

Second, the patterns of specialisation we observed are very sensitive to levels of trade costs. A process of integration may lead to a complete inversion of the pattern of specialisation (as in the case of industries differing in transport costs) or lead to a change from high-frequency to low-frequency agglomeration (when there are intra-industry linkages). This raises some worrying policy concerns. It suggests that a process of integration may lead to substantial changes in industrial location, with all the adjustment costs that this will create. Countries and regions will lose a presence in traditional industries, and workers in these regionally declining industries will be hurt. The relocation of industry brings aggregate welfare gains, and resisting it would retard realisation of these gains. But it is easy to imagine how European countries, while enthusiastic about the gains from integration in the abstract, may be less enthusiastic if it turns out that the price of these aggregate gains is losses for many industrial sectors.

Third, the chapter suggests a number of testable hypotheses about the pattern of industrial specialisation. The model predicts increasing regional specialisation as trade costs are reduced (even if there are no sources of traditional comparative advantage). And it predicts that central regions are more likely to attract imperfectly competitive industries, and downstream industries. How do these predictions relate to actual European experience?

A number of authors have found evidence of growing industrial specialisation of European countries and regions. Brulhart and Torstensson (1996) compute locational Gini coefficients for each of 18 industries among 11 EU countries. These measure inequality in the distribution of each industry across countries, and they increase over the period 1980–90. They also find that these measures of specialisation are higher for industries with greater returns to scale, and that industries with greater returns to scale tend to be concentrated in central locations of the European Union.

Amiti (1997) works with a greater number of industries, and also finds increasing concentration of industries, the increase being positively associated with plant size, capital intensity and intermediate goods intensity of the industry. She also looks across countries, and measures the change in the specialisation (within manufacturing) of countries during the period 1968–90. Specialisation increases in Belgium, France, Germany, the Netherlands, Italy and Greece, and declines in Ireland, Portugal, Spain and the United Kingdom.[5]

Clearly, these results do not serve to discriminate between the sorts of specialisation forces described in this chapter and other forces – most trade theories predict increasing specialisation during a period of trade liberalisation. Nevertheless, they do suggest some empirical support for models which predict growing specialisation, especially of central areas in imperfectly competitive industries.

Results in this chapter are then suggestive of the possible effects of regional integration on industrial location, and point the way to formulating new hypotheses on these effects. Much further work remains to be done, both in theory and empirically.

APPENDIX: THE MODEL

There are N locations, each endowed with quantities L and K of labour and land. Each country can produce both manufacturing and agricultural output.

Agriculture

Agriculture is perfectly competitive. It produces under constant returns to scale a homogeneous output, which we choose as numeraire, and assume costlessly tradable. The agricultural production function is Cobb–Douglas in land and labour, with labour share θ. If manufacturing employment in location i is denoted m_i and the labour market clears, agricultural output is $(L_i - m_i)^\theta K_i^{(1-\theta)}$, and the wage in the economy is

$$w_i = \theta(L_i - m_i)^{(\theta-1)} K_i^{1-\theta}, \quad i = 1, \ldots, N. \tag{1}$$

Manufacturing

Manufacturing is composed of two different sectors or industries, each of which is assumed to be monopolistically competitive. The number of industry s (s = 1, 2) firms operating in location i is denoted n_i^s and endogenously determined. Each firm produces its own variety of differentiated product, and firms enter and exit in response to positive and negative profits, so at equilibrium profits are exhausted. The producer price set by an industry s firm at location i is denoted p_i^s. Shipments of industrial goods are subject to 'iceberg' transportation costs – that is, a fraction of any shipment melts away in transit. The number of units of industry s output that must be shipped from location i in order that one unit arrives at j is denoted τ_{ij}^s.

Each industry's products can be aggregated via a CES function to yield a composite that is used both as a consumption good and as an intermediate input. These CES functions may be represented indirectly by CES price indices, q_i^s. In each location each industry's price index is defined over products supplied from all sources, so takes the form:

$$q_i^s = \left[\sum_{j=1}^{N} n_j^s \, (p_j^s \, \tau_{j,i}^s)^{(1-\sigma)} \right]^{1/(1-\sigma)}, \tag{2}$$

where σ (> 1) is a measure of product differentiation.

The cost function of a single industry s firm in location i is:

$$C_i^s = (\alpha + \beta x_i^s) w_i^{(1-\sum_{r=1}^{2} \mu^{r,s})} \prod_{r=1}^{2} (q_i^r)^{\mu^{r,s}}. \tag{3}$$

We assume a fixed input requirement of α and a constant marginal input requirement β. The input is a Cobb–Douglas aggregate of labour, and manufactured products. The share of industry r in the s industry is $\mu^{r,s}$, and q_i^r is the price index of industry r in country i, where all industry r varieties enter the composite intermediate and are appropriately aggregated by the CES form of (2). Shares sum to unity, so the labour coefficient is as given, and its price is the local wage, w_i.

Preferences

Each consumer has Cobb–Douglas preferences over agriculture (the numeraire) and the two CES aggregates of industrial goods. The indirect utility of the representative consumer in country i is

$$V_i = 1^{-(1-\sum_{s=1}^{2} \gamma^s)} \prod_{s=1}^{2} (q_i^s)^{-\gamma^s} y_i, \tag{4}$$

where y_i is income.

Equilibrium

Expenditure on each manufacturing industry in each country can be derived from (3) and (4) as

$$e_i^s = \gamma^s \left[w_i m_i + (L_i - m_i)^\theta K_i^{(1-\theta)} \right] + \sum_{r=1}^{2} \mu^{s,r} n_i^r p_i^r x_i^r. \tag{5}$$

The first term is the value of consumer expenditure, and the second the value of intermediate demand. Consumers devote proportion γ^s of their income to expenditure on industry s products. In the square brackets, the first term is wage income in manufacturing, and the second is income generated in agriculture – agricultural rent is distributed across the population to equalise *per capita* incomes. The final term is intermediate demand, generated as industry r firms spend fraction $\mu^{s,r}$ of their costs (and, with zero profits, of their revenue) on the output of industry s.

The division of consumers' and producers' expenditure on each industry between individual varieties of industrial goods can be found by differentiation of the price index with respect to the price of the variety. Demand in j for a single s industry variety produced in i, x_{ij}, is

$$x_{i,j}^s = (p_i^s)^{-\sigma} \left(\frac{\tau_{i,j}^s}{q_j^s} \right)^{(1-\sigma)} e_j^s, \tag{6}$$

and each firm's total output is $x_i^s = \sum_{j=1}^{w} x_{ij}$.

Since the producer of an individual good faces an elasticity of demand σ, firms mark up price over marginal cost by the factor $\sigma/(\sigma - 1)$. We choose units of measurement such that $\beta\sigma = \sigma - 1$, so that the price is

$$p_i^s = w_i^{(1-\sum_{r=1}^{2} \mu^{r,s})} \prod_{r=1}^{2} (q_i^r)^{\mu^{r,s}}. \tag{7}$$

Firms are scaled such that they earn zero profits at size 1, achieved by choosing units such that $\alpha = 1/\sigma$. In equilibrium the number of firms has adjusted to give zero profits, so

$$x_i^s \leq 1, \ n_i^s \leq 0, \text{ complementary slack,}$$
$$\text{for all } i = 1, \ldots, N, \ s = 1, 2 \ldots \tag{8}$$

The manufacturing wage bill in location i, $m_i w_i$, is:

$$m_i w_i = \sum_{s=1}^{2} \left(1 - \sum_{r=1}^{2} \mu^{r,s} \right) n_i^s p_i^s x_i^s. \tag{9}$$

(1)–(9) characterise equilibrium.

Parameter values

In simulations the following parameter values are used: $\theta = 0.81, \sigma = 5, \gamma^1 + \gamma^2 = 0.3.$ $\gamma^1 = \gamma^2$ except in the upstream–downstream case, where these values are set such that employment levels in the two industries are equal.

$\mu^{s,r} = 0$ in sections 3 and 4. In section 5 $\mu^{11} = \mu^{22} = 0.3, \ \mu^{12} = \mu^{21} = 0.$ In section 6 $\mu^{12} = 0.3, \ \mu^{11} = \mu^{22} = \mu^{21} = 0.$

NOTES

This chapter was produced as part of the Programme on International Economic Performance at the UK Economic and Social Research Council funded Centre for Economic Performance, London School of Economics. Financial support from the Taiwan Cultural Institute is gratefully acknowledged.
1 The grid lines lie horizontally/ vertically.
2 This is equivalent to there being a single manufacturing industry.
3 There is in fact a slight dip in the centre. The fact that there are few firms on the very edge means that the locations with the most firms are somewhat in from the edge (around locations 3 and 9), since these are able to benefit from the absence of competition outside them.
4 The two industries are the same size in terms of both accounting for the same share of consumers' expenditure. Employment levels in the two industries are not necessarily equal, as, depending on their location, they face different factor prices.
5 Studies looking at trade data rather than at production give less clear-cut results. For example Sapir (1996) finds little change in specialisation indices for European countries' exports over the period 1977–92.

REFERENCES

Amiti, M., 1997. 'Specialization Patterns in Europe', Centre for Economic Performance, LSE, *Discussion Paper*, **363**
Brulhart, M. and Torstensson, J., 1996. 'Regional Integration, Scale Economies and Industry Location', *CEPR Discussion Paper*, **1435**

Dixit, A. K. and Stiglitz, J.E., 1977. 'Monopolistic Competition and Optimum Product Diversity', *American Economic Review*, **67**, 297–308

Fujita, M. and Thisse, J., 1996. 'The Economics of Agglomeration', *Journal of Japanese and International Economics*, **10**, 339–78

Krugman, P. R. and Venables, A.J., 1990. 'Integration and the Competitiveness of Peripheral Industry', in C. Bliss and J. de Macedo (eds.), *Unity with Diversity in the European Economy* (Cambridge: Cambridge University Press for the CEPR)

  1995. 'The Seamless World: A Spatial Model of International Specialization', NBER Discussion Paper, **5220**, July

  1996. 'Integration, Specialization and Adjustment', *European Economic Review, Papers and Proceedings* **40**, 959–67

Sapir, A., 1996. 'The Effects of Europe's Internal Market Programme on Production and Trade: A First Assessment', *Weltwirtschaftliches Archiv*, **132**, 457–75

Discussion

ALASDAIR SMITH

Chapter 9 addresses what many would see as the key question of economic geography: when there is agglomeration of economic activities because of locational externalities, will that agglomeration take place in locations which are recognisably central in a spatial sense? It is a curious feature of some of the recent literature on 'centre–periphery' development that it lacks the structure to make sense of its own terminology and to answer that key question.

The model presented here assumes that there is no mobility of factors between locations. Factor mobility is a powerful force in spatial agglomeration (Ottaviano and Puga, 1997), and by abstracting from this force, Venables aims to show us how the externalities associated with backward and forward linkages between imperfectly competitive industries are sufficient to give rise to rich and systematic spatial patterns of economic activity.

The results are derived by numerical simulation and are intuitively appealing. In the kind of model used in the chapter, agglomeration is associated with scale economies and imperfect competition, so with more than one industry it is natural for the less competitive industry to tend to be the one which occupies the central region. There is also a well established phenomenon of centripetal forces being strongest at intermediate levels of trade costs. Here, as trade costs change, the changing balance of centrifugal and centripetal forces as trade costs change produces switches in the spatial pattern of production. When there are inter-industry externalities, there is a natural tendency for firms from both industries to be found in all locations, though the effects of the other forces can still be seen in the complex patterns of industrial location that can emerge.

The analysis produces a rich set of results from a simple set of assumptions and it may seem churlish to suggest exploration of alternative assumptions, but there are two considerations that suggest it would be worthwhile investigating changes in the modelling of transport costs. One is the casual observation that as telecommunications costs have fallen and become distance-independent, telecommunications-based industries have moved in the UK to peripheral locations. This makes the rather obvious point that non-linearities in relative trade costs could have important effects on the location of different activities. It might be natural to model telecommunications costs as being the same between any pair of locations, independently of the distance between them. Centrifugal forces would surely be stronger in industries where a significant part of trade costs had this form.

The fact that computational complexity has limited the experiments described in the chapter suggests another kind of non-linearity in trade costs. Suppose that trade costs are prohibitive except between adjacent locations. From a point in the grid in the interior of the disc there are eight locations with which trade is possible. From a point near the edge of the disc there may be as few as three other locations within trading distance. Here the disadvantage of peripherality is simply the disadvantage of having fewer trading partners. I speculate that such a trading technology would produce as rich a range of outcomes as the iceberg costs modelled here, but the reduction in computing complexity would allow the use of much finer grids in the simulations.

REFERENCE

Ottaviano, G.I.P. and Puga, D., 1997. 'Agglomeration in the Global Economy: A Survey of the "New Economic Geography"', *CEPR Discussion Paper*, **1699** (October)

10 Convergence ... an overview

GIUSEPPE BERTOLA

1 Introduction

Does economic growth lead to convergence of *per capita* incomes across countries and/or smaller administrative units? This chapter does not provide a proper survey of the many ways in which recent theoretical and empirical work has motivated and posed this question and of the equally varied range of answers given to it.[1] Rather, it focuses on a few basic issues. It reads in the empirical evidence a qualified 'no' as the answer to question posed above, and moves on to examine the implications of this potentially disturbing finding for models of accumulation and growth and for the role and desirability of policy interventions in that context. As is the case in studies of personal income inequality, the extent and character of *laissez-faire* market imperfections bear importantly on the answers to such theoretical (and somewhat ideological) questions.

Section 2 briefly reviews recent and less recent empirical findings on growth behaviour across aggregate economies, and the following two sections outline theoretical motivations for interest in the convergence question. If each country is treated as an independent observation, then cross-sectional growth evidence can be used to test competing growth theories. Section 3 outlines the theoretical argument underlying this line of research: along the transition path towards neoclassical growth models' steady state of exogenous growth, capital intensity increases and further accumulation encounters decreasing returns; hence, capital-poor countries should 'catch up' with richer ones. In models where accumulation can sustain unceasing endogenous growth, conversely, returns to further accumulation are constant and there is no presumption that heterogeneous countries' incomes should converge in levels or rates of growth. Discriminating between exogenous and endogenous growth models is particularly important because the two approaches imply very

275

different views of *laissez-faire* markets, and assign very different roles to economic policy. While exogenous growth dynamic equilibria can be straightforwardly decentralised to complete competitive markets, most models of endogenous growth rely on market imperfections and/or incompleteness to ensure that accumulation avoids decreasing returns and sustain unceasing growth.

Section 4 points out that empirical answers to the convergence question are relevant to growth endogeneity at the individual countries' level only if income data across countries or regions are viewed as realisations of independent experiments. In reality, countries and regions do interact with each other, and are jointly affected by events at higher levels of aggregation. From this alternative standpoint, income-distribution dynamics may provide useful information on the intensity and character of economic interactions. Recent work on income distribution within a single macroeconomy has identified a variety of inequality-reducing and inequality-preserving mechanisms (see Bénabou, 1996, and his references). Section 5 reviews theoretical predictions as to income- and production-distribution dynamics in a partially or fully integrated economic system; reviews available evidence on empirical relationship between openness, growth and convergence; and briefly discusses, from a theoretical standpoint, the role of random shocks in rationalising empirical evidence on convergence in a variety of datasets. Section 6 concludes, recognising that many important issues remain open in the literature, and suggesting that more complex and realistic theoretical models are needed to interpret the accumulated body of empirical evidence.

2   What the data say

Kaldor (1961) identified a number of empirical regularities in national economies' long-run growth behaviour. Romer (1989) offers an updated exposition and revaluation of the most striking and robust stylised facts motivating theoretical work by both Kaldor's and Romer's contemporaries:

(1) growth rates and capital–output ratios are roughly constant *over time* for individual countries and the world as a whole;
(2) accumulated factors of production (or 'capital') earn a roughly constant share of aggregate production;
(3) growth and accumulation do display substantially heterogeneity *across* countries.[2]

Kaldor's fact (1) denies any systematic relationship between a country's

income level and its rate of growth: poor countries should not systematically grow faster (or slower) than richer ones. After some confusion
engendered by sample-selection biases, empirical research on newly
available international income data sets confirms this basic implication
of Kaldor's earlier observations. In samples which are free of selection
bias, regressing subsequent growth on initial income levels is more likely
to yield *positive* coefficients (indicating divergence) than the negative
ones that would be expected if poor countries did catch up with richer
ones.

Consistently with Kaldor's fact (3), however, growth rates do differ
systematically in other respects: population growth rates, saving rates,
educational levels and policy variables are relevant to subsequent growth
rates in economically – if not always statistically – significant ways
(Barro, 1991; Levine and Renelt, 1992). When estimated jointly with
those of other such empirically relevant variables, the effect of initial
income levels on subsequent growth *is* significantly negative in cross-
sectional regressions. Controlling for other growth-relevant characteristics, poorer countries do experience (slightly) faster growth of *per capita*
income levels: estimates of such 'conditional convergence' rates are
remarkably similar in a variety of cross-country and cross-region
regressions, which predict that about 2 per cent *ceteris paribus* of income
differentials vanish every year (Barro and Sala-i-Martin, 1992; Mankiw
et al., 1992; Sala-i-Martin 1995, 1996).

While statistically significant, conditional convergence is a relatively
minor force in the dynamics of income distribution. Other empirical
work takes a relatively unstructured prior to the data, and lets them
speak to the issue of whether relative income dispersion across countries
is accounted for by transitional dynamics or by permanent differences.
Using various (parametric and non-parametric, time-series and cross-
sectional) methods, Durlauf and Johnson (1994), Miller (1995), Ben-
David (1994), Canova and Marcet (1995), Quah (1996a, 1996b), and
others find that permanent income differentials are vastly more important than temporary, self-correcting ones. This is of course consistent
with Kaldor's fact (1) and – considering that country characteristics are
persistent and correlated with both income levels and growth rates – with
findings of 'conditional' convergence, too: persistently different growth-
relevant characteristics, combined with mild conditional convergence and
uncontrolled (random) factors driving individual countries' growth
experiences (Quah, 1993), result in stable or mildly increasing cross-
sectional dispersions for the initial and subsequent relative *per capita*
incomes. Income levels do not tend towards *un*conditional equality and,
when empirical techniques allow for them, the data also give evidence of

an important role for sources of persistent income differentials which appear to depend on initial income levels themselves rather than on individual countries' observable characteristics (the 'convergence club' or 'twin-peaks' phenomenon, whereby income levels within group of relatively rich or relatively poor countries gravitate towards each other even as divergence predominates across such groups).

3   Endogenous vs. exogenous growth theories

Interest in the strength and character of cross-country income convergence is largely motivated by the question of whether it might be technologically feasible for individual economic units to sustain their own growth indefinitely and independently of other other similar units' growth behaviour – i.e. of whether an individual economy's long-run growth experience is *endogenous* to its own saving and investment rates and to their determinants. In theoretical models, endogeneity of long-run growth depends on the character of technology and market interactions. From this point of view, lack of convergence is unfavourable evidence for Solow's (1956) neoclassical growth model, where complete competitive markets under a constant returns (CRS) technology offer decreasing returns to investment and, for realistic specifications, yield slowing and eventually ceasing growth.

To review such well known theoretical considerations, let country i's output $Y_i(t)$ be produced with (accumulated) capital K and (non-accumulated) other factors L according to

$$Y(t) = F_i(K_i(t), L_i(t)),$$ (1)

and let $Y_i(t)$ be allocated to consumption and capital accumulation according to

$$Y_i(t) = C_i(t) + I_i(t), \quad \dot{K}_i(t) = I_i(t) - \delta K_i(t).$$ (2)

If technology is the same for all i and offers constant returns to K and L together, $F(\lambda K, \lambda L) = \lambda F(K, L)$ for all λ and for $\lambda > 1$,

$$F(\lambda K, L) < F(\lambda K, \lambda L)$$ (3)

as long as the non-accumulated factors indexed by L have positive productivity: an increase in the accumulated factor K encounters *decreasing returns* if it is not accompanied by an proportional increase in L. This implies that the production function in intensive form is convex:

$$f(k) \equiv \frac{F(K,L)}{L} = F\left(\frac{K}{L}, 1\right) \Rightarrow f''(k) < 0, \tag{4}$$

and that accumulation should find it very hard (if not impossible) to sustain long-run growth. To see this, write the proportional growth rate of output as

$$\frac{\dot{Y}}{Y} = f'\left(\frac{K}{L}\right) + \frac{\dot{K}}{Y} + \frac{\dot{L}}{L}\left(1 - f'\left(\frac{K}{L}\right)\frac{K}{Y}\right): \tag{5}$$

in a closed economy, where $\dot{K} = Y - C - \delta K$ as in (2), the net saving rate $\dot{K}/Y$ is bounded above by unity; with $f''(\cdot) < 0$, its weight as the driving force of growth declines as capital intensity increases. If

$$\lim_{k \to \infty} f'(k) = 0, \tag{6}$$

unbounded capital intensity would tend to annihilate the first term on the right-hand side of (5), and before that happens the economy must settle in a steady state where K/L, K/Y, and $f'(\cdot)$ are constant.[3] In the long run, income growth is exogenous and determined by the rate of increase $\dot{L}/L$ of non-accumulated factors, in the second term on the right-hand side of (5).

A further crucial step brings neoclassical transitional dynamics to bear on cross-sectional findings of *per capita* income (non-)convergence: the non-accumulated factor L is identified with labour, and proportional to population; further, if $L_i = N_i A_i$ for N_i country i's population and A_i an index of its productive efficiency, A_i is given a technological interpretation and, like $F(\cdot, \cdot)$, is taken to be the same for all i.[4] Then, *per capita* income

$$y_i(t) = \frac{Y_i(t)}{N_i(t)} - f(k_i(t)).A(t)$$

may differ differ across countries only to the extent that k_i does – and poor countries should grow faster than richer ones.

Figure 10.1 summarises the argument just given and highlights its three key assumptions. The first (**A1**) states that identical technologies use accumulated (K) and non-accumulated (L) factors in all countries, and that population is identically proportional to the non-accumulated factor L. Thus, low *per capita* income levels are associated with low capital–labour ratios, which in turn are associated with high investment returns by the assumption (**A2**) of constant overall returns to scale (hence, decreasing returns to accumulation). Finally, accumulation of capital in

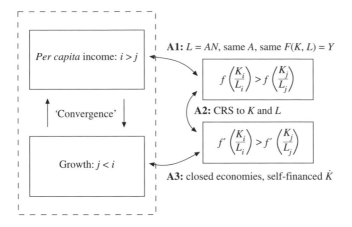

Figure 10.1 'Classical' approach to convergence

each closed economy is financed by its own savings (**A3**): accumulation-driven growth should move poor countries faster along a transition path towards an eventual steady state where growth is no longer driven, but only accompanied by accumulation.

How does the empirical lack of convergence bear on this theoretical argument? Persistent inequality of income levels and growth rates may lead to a relaxation of assumption (**A2**): if $f'(k)$ is *not* decreasing with k, individual countries' growth rates can be endogenous to their own saving rate and underlying economic circumstances. The largely undisputed Kaldorian fact (1) of rough constancy of growth rates and capital–output ratios did spur theoretical efforts by Romer (e.g. 1989) and other endogenous growth theorists to devise plausible technological and market mechanisms by which accumulation of capital and/or knowledge would not encounter decreasing returns in a closed economy.

Different rates of long-run growth across countries with access to similar technologies could then be explained by heterogeneous policies and institutions.

Whether long-run growth is endogenous to economically motivated accumulation choices, or determined by exogenous technological progress, is not an abstract ideological question. Rather, it has much practical and policy relevance in two inter-related respects. First, unlimited accumulation requires constant returns to capital: in the light of (5), this is incompatible with the constant-returns production technology needed to support complete competitive markets (at least if non-accumulated resources earn a non-vanishing share of aggregate output); accordingly, evidence of growth endogeneity means that the role of externalities and imperfectly competitive market interactions is important in general equilibrium. Second, the effects of economic policy are more dramatic in models where it can permanently affect the *growth rate* of resources rather than just their *level*: and policy interventions are quite naturally called for by externalities and market imperfections, which prevent the ultimate consequences of individual agents' choices from being fully internalised in *laissez-faire*.

Endogenous growth theorists were also comforted by the fact that, as already noted, cross-country growth heterogeneity is empirically related to a variety of theoretically sensible economic characteristics. When the neoclassical model is extended to allow for cross-country heterogeneity, however, it can provide an interpretation for the same empirical findings without relaxing assumptions **A1–3** of figure 10.1. The neoclassical model predicts eventual equality of production levels per unit of L, hence *per capita*, only if preferences (saving rates, population growth) are the same across countries; but if countries do not tend to identical $K–L$ ratios in the steady state, income levels can remain forever different. Under the assumptions highlighted in figure 10.1, countries should still be converging to their own, possibly very different, long-run income levels. Findings of conditional convergence, accordingly, are interpreted by Mankiw *et al.* (1992) and others as evidence of a particular variant of the neoclassical growth model, where exogenous and heterogeneous saving rates reconcile empirical evidence with decreasing returns to accumulation, and persistent inequality is unrelated to the growth process *per se*.

4   Relaxing neoclassical assumptions

If lack of convergence was evidence in favour of endogenous growth models with imperfect markets, significant rates of (conditional) income convergence indicate that returns to investment are lowered by higher capital–output ratios, technology is convex and perfect competitive markets can be supported by it. This line of thought (Sala-i-Martin's, 1996, 'classical approach' to convergence issues) offers an appealing and self-consistent rationalisation for findings of conditional convergence, while denying that lack of convergence is (by itself) evidence of increasing returns to scale and imperfect or incomplete markets.

The brief summary above, however, makes it clear that not only the constant-returns nature of technology (assumption (**A2**), but also its world-wide uniformity (assumption (**A3**) is crucial to the classical convergence argument. Quite as clearly, such uniformity need not be realistic: technology flows may *tend* to make the most advanced technology available in all locations, but this is far from implying that production methods are *always* the same throughout the world. Various countries and regions produce baskets of goods with different capital intensity (as may be captured by different $F(\cdot, \cdot)$ functional forms in the basic model above), different levels of technological efficiency or natural resources (as captured by A) and, perhaps most importantly, different rates of technological development – which should themselves be explained by theories of endogenous research and development expenditure and/or technological diffusion across countries (see Grossman and Helpman, 1994, and references therein). A more carefully disaggregated theoretical framework provides a related line of attack on the simplicity of the neoclassical growth model's technological assumptions. On the one hand, the accumulated factor K may be interpreted in terms of not only physical, but also 'human' durable factors of production (such as education and knowledge) in the context of the single-sector model of production outlined above – and A, the factor of proportionality between population and labour input, may well be endogenous to (human) capital accumulation choices.[5] On the other hand, the same factor of proportionality (and the *per capita endowment of the non-accumulated factor L*) might similarly correspond to a variety of real-life economic features such as land, natural resources and other country characteristics unrelated to population and accumulation, but heterogeneous across locations.

The main reason why the standard interpretation of empirical findings cannot provide definitive insights into the substantive aspects of the growth–endogeneity debate, however, is its maintained assumption (**A3**) that cross-country observations may be interpreted as independent of each other. In fact, whether growth at higher levels of aggregation is exogenous or endogenous is in principle irrelevant to the question of whether their incomes converge towards each other: if countries do share a similar technology, and take as given the dynamics of technological progress, it can still be the case that the latter are really endogenous at the world level. On the other side of the same coin, any convergence evidence can only be silent on the issue of whether technology is exogenous or (as it must be, at some level) endogenous to economic and non-economic interactions; hence, as suggested by Quah (1996b), growth mechanisms might best be treated separately from convergence mechanisms. As to the possibility or impossibility for individual countries to pull themselves out of relative poverty by intense accumulation, different countries' economies are jointly affected by world-wide developments, and interact with each other via technological transfers, trade and capital flows. Econometric work on non-experimental data can of course ascertain only whether countries do in actual fact diverge or 'catch up' – not whether it would be technologically feasible for them to do otherwise.

Section 5 discusses possible roles of international linkages and global developments in convergence processes.

5   Economic integration and income distribution

In a sample of Solow-style economies, *per capita* income levels should converge towards each other if tastes and technologies are common across countries, or when heterogeneity in either respect is properly controlled for. Empirical work of this type and the interpretation given to its results, however, are based on closed-economy dynamic relationships, where investment is identically equal to savings at all times, and neglect international flows of financial capital and trade imbalances. The neoclassical approach would tend to equalise *per capita* production if savings were allowed to differ from investment, or if assumption (**A3**) were lifted (maintaining the other two) in figure 10.1: as long as low capital intensity increases returns to investment by (**A2**), and determines *per capita* incomes by (**A1**), capital should flow towards poor countries and increase their GDP (if not their GNP). In the model proposed by Barro *et al.* (1995), returns to physical capital are equalised at all times (with no convergence dynamics) by financial capital mobility, while *per capita* production levels only slowly gradually converge towards possibly heterogeneous steady-state levels because investment in human capital must be self-financed by each country's (or location) residents.

Capital flows, if not overwhelmingly important, are far from irrelevant in the data, and certainly not uniformly small: their intensity, of course, depends crucially on the structure of markets and institutions and, like issues of growth endogeneity, issues of economic 'openness' are thick with policy implications. Obstfeld (1995) and others find that capital markets appear increasingly integrated in recent periods, and more closely inter-connected among groups of developed countries than in the global economy. 'Convergence' or lack thereof (with income levels remaining permanently different across all or some countries after shorter-run dynamics unwind) may accordingly be interpreted as evidence on the degree of economic openness rather than on the extent to which growth is endogenous.

To see whether this interpretation is warranted and evaluate its implications for convergence issues, consider convergence of incomes within a (potentially) integrated economy. Whereas in the basic closed economy model above Y_i denoted both income and production of country (or region) i, for discussing distribution within an integrated economy it will be useful to let $\hat{y}_j$ denote *income* of family j, and $\bar{y}_f$ denote *production* of firm f.

At time t, let family j own $l_j(t)$ units of the non-accumulated factor L and $k_j(t)$ units of accumulated capital. In a completely general specification, the unit compensation rate of the former (denoted w) and that of the latter (denoted r) may be allowed to depend not only on time, but also on the family's index j: period t's income is then

$$\hat{y}_j(t) = w_j(t)l_j(t) + r_j(t)k_j(t), \tag{7}$$

and the family may consume or save it according to the accumulation constraint

$$k_j(t+1) = k_j(t) + \hat{y}_j(t) - c_j(t) = w_j(t)l_j(t) + \big(1 + r_j(t)\big)k_j(t) - c_j(t). \tag{8}$$

Each firm indexed by f rents factors of production from families, and uses them in possibly heterogeneous production functions to produce $\tilde{y}_f = F_f(k_f, l_f)$ units of homogeneous (by choice of units) output. Again allowing for factor units to receive different compensation, firm f's profit-maximization problem is

$$\max_{K_f, L_f} \big(F_f(K_f, L_f) - rK_f - wL_f\big).$$

In (7), families' sources of income are fully determined by factor ownership, if only loosely linked to it by possibly heterogeneous factor compensation; hence, 'factors' should be interpreted widely to include pure profits accruing to owners of monopolistic firms (which may, of course, result from past innovation) and any rents accruing to fixed, non-accumulated factors of production. Under this convention, viewing each $F_f(\cdot, \cdot)$ as a first-degree homogeneous function entails no loss of generality: writing

$$k_f \equiv K_f/L_f, \quad f_f(k_f) \equiv F_f\left(\frac{K_f}{L_f}, 1\right),$$

the first-order conditions for profit maximization

$$f_f'(k_f(t)) = r_f(t), \quad f_f(k_f(t)) - k_f(t)f_f'(k_f(t)) = w_f(t) \tag{9}$$

determine firm f's capital intensity k_f in terms of its factors' prices w_f and r_f and of its production function's functional form $f_f(\cdot)$.

5.1   A fully integrated economy

Let all 'families' and 'firms' interact in fully integrated factor and product markets, and let no wedges be introduced between producers' and families' factor prices: then, $r_f = r_j = r$ and $w_f = w_j = w$ for all j and all f. Further, if all firms have access to the same set of technologies then the best one will be chosen, and $f_f(\cdot) = f(\cdot)$ for all f implies that capital intensity $K_f/L_f \equiv k$ is the same for all f: to fully employ a given stock $L = \sum_{ff}$ of non-accumulated factors, capital is allocated so that the integrated economy produces according to the same constant-returns function as each firm. The sum of all families' income of course coincides with the sum of all firms' production levels, and is given by

$$Y \equiv \sum_f F(K_f, L_f) = \sum_f L_f f(K_f/L_f) = LF(k) = F(K, L).$$

The dynamics of the integrated economy obey the accumulation constraint obtained by aggregation of (8), in the same form as (2), and the endogeneity or exogeneity of long-run growth rates depends on the same considerations outlined in section 4 above.

In an inter-linked world economy, the concepts of 'family' and/or 'firm' within a fully integrated economy may be associated with administrative or geographical subunits' national or domestic income flows.[6] Is there any reason to expect incomes to be equalised, or at least a tendency to 'converge,' across such subunits?

Consider first the dynamics of relative incomes and production in a steady-state situation where aggregate output, capital, and consumption all grow (exogenously or endogenously) at the same rate,

$$\frac{K(t+1)}{K_t} = \frac{Y(t+1)}{Y_t} = \frac{C(t+1)}{C_t} \equiv \theta \quad \forall t, \tag{10}$$

and output's capital intensity $A \equiv Y(t)/K(t)$ is constant. If the growth rate θ is exogenous, then the economy's capital intensity $A = F(1, L/K)$ is endogenously determined in the neoclassical steady state; endogenous growth models, conversely, take A to be a structural constant (explained by technology and/or market structure), and determine theta endogenously. The distinction is irrelevant to relative income dynamic issues.

If individual families maximise standard time-separable utility functions, and can transfer resources over time at the non-contingent (gross) rate r, their consumption levels should satisfy the Euler relationship

$$U'(c_j(t)) = \beta(1 + r)U'(c_j(t + 1)) \tag{11}$$

across consecutive time periods, for β the rate of utility discount across periods and $U(\cdot)$ the period utility function. Sufficient conditions for a stable income distribution are that the return r to savings be constant, and that the elasticity of marginal utility $U''(\cdot)/U'(\cdot) \equiv \sigma$ be the same across families:[7] then, the growth rate of each family's consumption is constant both over time and in cross-section,

$$\frac{c_j(t+1)}{c_j(t)} = (\beta(1+r))^{1/\sigma}, \tag{12}$$

and it coincides with the integrated economy's growth rate since

$$\theta \equiv \frac{\sum_j c_j(t+1)}{\sum_j c_j(t)} = \frac{\sum_j (\beta(1+r))^{1/\sigma} c_j(t)}{\sum_j c_j(t)}.$$

Thus, in a steady state of balanced (exogenous or endogenous) growth all families' consumption levels grow in parallel to each other, and so do their incomes as savings behaviour perpetuates any initial difference in the relative size of income flows as well as in their accumulated and non-accumulated components (Bertola, 1993a). Accordingly, permanent income differences are perfectly compatible with full market integration across families, and arguably across nations as well if endowments of non-accumulated factors (such as natural resources) differ across residents of different nations.

The size of individual firms' production flows (which may be related to domestic, rather than national income measures in international data) can similarly be and remain heterogeneous in a fully integrated economy with homogeneous technology. Under constant returns, in fact, capital intensity must be homogeneous across firms, but each firm's scale of operation may be fixed by *specific factors*: firm f's production flow is given by

$$\tilde{y}_f(t) = F\left(1, \frac{1}{k}\right) K_f = F\left(1, \frac{1}{k}\right) k L_f$$

for k the aggregate (exogenous or endogenous) K–L ratio, and the scale of its operations is well determined only if some component of the non-accumulated factor services flow L_f must be used by firm f (or, in an international interpretation, by any of the firms located in a specific geographical region). Any such source of heterogeneity across firms' (or regions') production flows will in general perpetuate itself in a steady state.

Consider next how capital-deepening transitional dynamics at the aggregate level may affect the distribution of measured income and production across families and firms inhabiting an integrated (world) economy. Chatterjee (1994) studies such issues under the assumption of quasi-homothetic preferences (so that aggregate savings are independent of wealth distribution), and neatly shows that theory has no sharp implications on such issues: as an aggregate economy becomes richer on its way to a neoclassical steady state, the relative standing of different individuals in terms of total (accumulated and non-accumulated) remains or evolves towards greater or smaller inequality depending on whether saving propensities are positively or negatively related to wealth, and remains unchanged under the standard homothetic-preferences assumption. Ventura (1995) models the world economy as a collection of fully integrated small open economies which, by trading intermediate inputs, can essentially 'rent' each other's baskets of accumulated and non-accumulated factors even in the absence of financial capital flows. Trade can equalise factor prices across fully open economies but, of course, their income will differ inasmuch as they are endowed by different baskets of (immobile) factors; from this point of view, small open economies are isomorphic to the standard disaggregation's families. Ventura shows that conditioning upon differences in productive efficiency (or 'non-accumulated income') will yield empirically plausible convergence rates if the rate of return to aggregate accumulation is (mildly) decreasing along the transition to a steady state of endogenous or exogenous growth.

In summary, standard aggregate models do not unambiguously predict that income and production levels of such subunits as 'families' or 'firms' should absolutely converge within an integrated economy: if non-accumulated endowments 1 differ across families or firms, or *initial* accumulated wealth differs across families, then production, income and consumption may or may not converge towards each other along a transitional dynamic path, and can very well remain different (barring random shocks, considered in the next subsection) once a steady state is reached.

5.2   Incomplete economic integration

Real-life nations and regions, of course, are not quite so immediately identified with families or firms interacting in a single factor and product market: to the extent that the factor reward rates r and w can differ across countries (and across the families and firms located in different countries), the intensity and character of international economic integration does arguably matter for the size and dynamics *of per capita* income differentials.

Consider first the obviously realistic possibility of different returns to saving and investment. Within an aggregate economy, financial market imperfections may require accumulation to be self-financed at the individual level – especially when what is being accumulated is *human* capital, which is purchased (by education) and bears fruit (in the form of labour income) under conditions of heavily imperfect and asymmetric information. As noted by Chatterjee (1994), self-financing constraints imply that each family invests in a specific 'firm': in an international context, the resulting model is one of complete (or partial, as in Barro, Mankiw and Sala-i-Martin, 1995) closure to international financial flows. Somewhat unintuitively, such imperfect integration *reduces* the inequality of wealth and consumption distributions if the conditions for GDP convergence are met – i.e. if further accumulation by relatively rich families (or relatively capital-intensive countries) encounters decreasing returns as in (4). Just as an asymptotically positive return to aggregate accumulation would make it possible for an economy to determine its own rate of long-run growth, so ultimately non-decreasing returns to family-level investment would allow a dynasty's income to diverge endlessly from others'. Galor and Zeira (1993) in a closed economy, and Quah (1996a) in an international context, consider the possibility of multiple steady-state equilibria for interacting individuals or countries when technology displays 'threshold' non-convexities – i.e. when microeconomic non-convexities and indivisibilities imply low returns to investment for very poor economies/families as well as for very rich ones (and very high for intermediate income levels).

If lack of interaction in accumulated factor markets somewhat ironically tends to equalise the long-run distribution of income, integration of non-accumulated factor markets may or may not have equalising effects across national or geographical units. If $\epsilon_i(t) = l_i(t)w_i(t)$ is the non-accumulated component of i's income, and accumulated wealth k_i yields the same return r for all i in an integrated capital market, then the level and dynamics of unit i's income,

$$\tilde{y}_i(t) \equiv rk_i(t) + \epsilon_i(t), \qquad (13)$$

depend on accumulation as well as on the amount and unit compensation of non-accumulated factor endowments. Bertola (1996) shows that interactions between non-accumulated income flows and accumulation rates can result in convergence across such units since, in the steady state of a growing economy, non-accumulated income flows grow at the same mean rate across economies, while savings are needed to ensure growth of capital income.

As to the level and dynamics of the non-accumulated income component $\epsilon_j = w_j l_j$, factor mobility (or simply trade if the conditions for factor-price equalisation are met) should tend to bring unit factor rewards towards equality ($w_j = w$ for all j). This, however, need not reduce inequality of total non-accumulated income, depending on whether higher l_j endowments are associated with larger or smaller autarkic compensation rates. In turn, this depends on whether factor returns are increasing or decreasing, and also on the extent to which the initial distribution may be altered by factor mobility. Integrated markets need not be perfect, and indeed cannot be perfect under increasing returns: in the presence of agglomeration economies, production and accumulation should concentrate in relatively better developed regions, increasing production level disparities as well as consumption level differentials across owners of mobile and immobile factors (see e.g. Bertola, 1993b).

5.3 Empirical evidence on economic integration

In theory, then, economic integration may or may not imply a tendency towards *per capita* income equalisation. But does it in practice? Designers of EU institutions were certainly aware of potential inequality-enhancing effects of free goods and factors mobility of goods and factors, and accompanied the '1992' liberalisation measures with 'structural funds' support programmes for peripheral regions. Sachs and Warner (1995b) provide a wealth of quantitative and institutional information on the growth behaviour of many countries over a long time span, and argue that poor countries grow fast (hence 'converge') when they implement economies policies which *open* them to international markets, while their measures of economic 'closeness' (in particular, restrictive trade policies) are actually associated to income level divergence instead. Openness, of course, has a variety of dimensions (trade, capital, technology) and is not uncorrelated to economic features which may be expected to speed up (endogenous) growth. Most importantly, policies which protect private property are likely to be implemented by the same countries which choose a liberal trade policy; both types of policies are arguably conducive to faster growth, hence to convergence as far as relatively poor countries are concerned (Sachs and Warner, 1995a). Such identification issues notwithstanding, factor mobility does appear to be associated empirically with equalisation of *per capita* income. Taylor and Williamson (1994) and their references find that income per worker displayed strong convergence in 1870–1913, when unrestrained and intense migration tended to arbitrage away wage differentials (and to equalise GDP *per capita*: the distinction between GDP and GNP, of course, becomes quite blurred when individuals' residence can and does change).

5.4   *Randomness*

Random variability is essential to real-world data-generating processes, to empirical regression equations and to inferences drawn from the latter on the former. When evaluating and interpreting cross-sectional evidence, one should keep in mind that *per capita* income data may be better represented by a stationary steady-state distribution than by steady convergence towards steady-state uniformity (or permanent difformity). Stationarity, of course, is not literally apparent in the data, as the cross-sectional distribution of relative income levels is far from stable in the time span for which data are available. Still, extrapolation of its dynamics to the indefinite future is problematic from the statistical point of view; as stressed by Quah (1993), a (quasi-)stationarity view of distributional developments almost by definition ensures that empirical estimation will give evidence of 'convergence'. On average, in fact, relatively poor countries must become richer and relatively rich ones must become poorer if the proportion (but not the identity) of countries in different relative income positions remains (almost) unchanged.

Leaving a review of formal econometric issues Quah (1998, chapter 11 in this volume), we can simply note that cross-sectional analysis provides meaningful information only if random shocks are 'idiosyncratic' (i.e. at least partly specific to individual observations), and consider briefly possible theoretical interpretations of idiosyncratic randomness in the context of the models reviewed above. Relative incomes within an integrated economy are affected by many kinds of uninsurable random shocks (including birth and death of individuals, if not of their families); at the level of countries (or regions), two broad classes of random shocks are presumably most relevant to aggregate and *per capita* income fluctuations: governmental policies, and natural resource prices. Chari, Kehoe and McGrattan's (1996) model suggests that stationary policy-regime switches may make an important contribution towards explaining empirical regularities, and Sachs and Warner (1995c) find that natural resource abundance was an important determinant of cross-country growth performances in 1970–90, a period when the world economy experienced sharp and far from predictable natural resource price fluctuations.[8] In this context, it may be interesting to note that convergence regressions in the form

$$\log(Y_T^i / Y_0^i) = \alpha + \beta \log(Y_0^i) + \epsilon^i \tag{14}$$

(or in the substantially similar non-linear form estimated by Sala-i-Martin, 1995, and his references) may fail to approximate satisfactorily the functional forms implied by models which explicitly distinguish accumulated and non-accumulated (e.g. natural resource-related) income flows. As suggested by the simple analysis above, in an integrated economy there are many economic reasons for permanent *per capita* income and production level differentials. The 'fixed-effect bias' discussed by Canova and Marcet (1995) will affect empirical estimates when permanent income level differences are subsumed into the error term by a specification which, like (14), imposes a single constant term rather than a collection $\{\alpha_i\}$ of observation-specific constants. Further, the log-linear specification of (14) is far from warranted in a world where data are sums of accumulated and non-accumulated factor income flows, as in (13) above. More generally data are based on *additive* aggregation of sectoral and regional income processes which the literature takes to themselves follow log-linear (hence *multiplicative*) dynamics. By Jensen's inequality, the sum of log-linear processes is different from the logarithm of their sum in levels: the discrepancy is typically neglected in macroeconomics, but it could easily be of the same small order of magnitude as common estimates of conditional convergence rates.

6   Conclusions

This chapter has analysed possible theoretical motivations and implications of the question posed on p. 275, from two inter-related and complementary points of view. If cross-country growth experiences are viewed as unrelated realisations of independent experiments, then empirical work can try and draw implications for the exogenous or endogenous nature of long-run growth; when theory emphasises international linkages instead, then relative income dynamics can give evidence on the extent and nature of economic integration across countries or regions. Unfortunately, strong maintained assumptions are needed to draw precise implications in either setting: theory does not offer a precise view on whether relative incomes should or should not converge under realistic conditions and, consequently, firm theory-based conclusions can hardly be drawn from the accumulated body of evidence.

Economic theory, of course, is to some extent irrelevant if what is wanted is simple measurement of *per capita* incomes' tendency to converge – whether in the cross-sectional sense of 'sigma' convergence, whereby the dispersion of log incomes becomes smaller, or in the ongoing sense of 'beta' convergence, whereby poorer countries tend to catch up with richer ones (and vice versa) even as random shocks continuously reshuffle income distribution. Whatever its theoretical source, both notions of convergence are relevant to long-run inequality issues; sigma-convergence would indicate that individual incomes become more equal to each other, and beta-convergence would lead us to be less concerned by current and future income disparities which, to the extent that they are quickly reversed, have a smaller impact on long-term welfare. On their own empirical terms, unfortunately, the data tend to give rather gloomy answers to convergence questions. Income differentials are not quickly reversed over the available span of data and, given that unconditional growth rates are roughly unrelated to initial income levels, appear just as likely to increase as to decrease in the foreseeable future. More complex and sophisticated theoretical approaches, paying more attention to international interactions, will hopefully ascertain the structural causes of persisting inequality and indicate whether policy interventions are desirable.

NOTES

I am grateful to the discussant Daniel Cohen, to other participants at the CEPR conference on 'Regional Integration' (La Coruña, 26–27 April 1996), and to seminar participants at the Università di Ancona for their comments on a previous draft.

1 De La Fuente (1995) and Temple (1995) offer comprehensive surveys of empirical results and theoretical interpretations; see also Sala-i-Martin (1995) and Galor (1996) for more succinct accounts of the subject matter.
2 From a longer-run perspective, growth rates clearly differ across historical periods as well as across countries: the world certainly did not grow as fast in the Middle Ages as in the post-Industrial Revolution era, and there is plentiful evidence of synchronised growth accelerations and slowdowns in the world economy since the Second World War.
3 Even under constant returns, as recognised by Solow (1956), growth can be indefinitely fuelled by accumulation iff $f''(k)$ declined to a positive asymptote rather than to zero. The limit behaviour of such an economy, studied by Jones and Manuelli (1990), is similar to that of Rebelo's (1991) AK economy and implies a vanishing (marginal productivity-determined) income share for non-accumulated factors of production. If L is identified with labour, this is inconsistent with Kaldor's fact (2).
4 The labour-augmenting specification of the technological parameter A is equivalent to other formalisations if, as is roughly realistic, the production function $F(\cdot, \cdot)$ is written in Cobb–Douglas form.
5 Benhabib and Spiegel (1994), Cohen (1995), and others explore theoretically and empirically the implications of separately accounting for physical and human capital accumulation. Young (1994) offers an informative account of the qualitative character of disaggregated factor accumulation in specific fast-growing countries.
6 The distinction between 'domestic' and 'national' income measures, like that between production and income flows, has no place in a constant-returns closed economy inhabited by homogeneous consumer–investors, but is potentially very important in more realistic circumstances. Either interpreta-

tion may be more or less appropriate to real-life statistical measures of production and income.

7 More generally, homogeneous intertemporal preferences are needed to obtain a well defined limit distribution of income: if the willingness to substitute future and current consumption were heterogeneous, in fact, the more patient families would eventually tend to own all of the economy's resources.

8 Oil-producing countries are typically excluded from cross-country growth regressions, presumably because the underlying theory does not satisfactorily model the role of natural resources in income determination.

REFERENCES

Barro, R.J., 1991. 'Economic Growth in a Cross-section of Countries', *Quarterly Journal of Economics*, **106**, 407–43

Barro, R.J. and Sala-i-Martin, X., 1992. 'Convergence', *Journal of Political Economy*, **100**, 223–51

Barro, R., Mankiw, N.G. and Sala-i-Martin, X., 1995. 'Capital Mobility in Neoclassical Models of Growth', *American Economic Review*, **85**, 103–15

Bénabou, R., 1996. 'Inequality and Growth', in B. Bernanke and J. Rotemberg (eds.), *NBER Macroeconomics Annual 1996* (Cambridge, MA: MIT Press), 11–90

Ben-David, D., 1994. 'Convergence Clubs and Diverging Economies', *CEPR Discussion Paper*, **922**

Benhabib, J. and Spiegel, M., 1994. 'The Role of Human Capital in Economic Development: Evidence from Aggregate Cross-country Data', *Journal of Monetary Economics*, **34**, 143–73

Bertola, G., 1993a. 'Factor Shares and Savings in Endogenous Growth', *American Economic Review*, **83**, 1184–98

1993b. 'Models of Economic Integration and Localized Growth', in F. Giavazzi and F. Torres (eds.), *The Transition to Economic and Monetary Union in Europe* (Cambridge: Cambridge University Press)

1996. 'Uninsurable Shocks and International Income Conversion', *American Economic Review, Papers and Proceedings*, **85**, 301–6

Canova, F. and Marcet, A., 1995. 'The Poor Stay Poor: Non-convergence across Countries and Regions', *CEPR Discussion Paper*, **1265**

Chari, V.V., Kehoe, P.J. and McGrattan, E.R.M., 1996. 'The Poverty of Nations: A Quantitative Exploration', *NBER Working Paper*, **5414**

Chatterjee, S., 1994. 'Transitional Dynamics and the Distribution of Wealth in a Neoclassical Growth Model', *Journal of Public Economics*, **54**, 97–119

Cohen, D., 1995. 'Tests of the "Convergence Hypothesis": Some Further Results', *CEPR Discussion Paper*, **1163**

De La Fuente, A., 1995. 'The Empirics of Growth and Convergence: A Selective Review', *CEPR Discussion Paper*, **1275**

Durlauf, S. and Johnson, P., 1994. 'Multiple Regimes and Cross-country Growth Behavior', *Journal of Applied Economcs*, **10**, 365–84

Feldstein, M. and Horioka, C., 1980. 'Domestic Savings and International Capital Flows', *Economic Journal*, **90**, 314–29

Galor, O., 1996. 'Convergence? Inferences from Theoretical Models', *CEPR Discussion Paper*, **1350**; *Economic Journal*, **106**, 1056–9

Galor, O. and Zeira, J., 1993, 'Income Distribution and Macroeconomics', *Review of Economic Studies*, **60**, 35–52

Grossman, G. and Helpman, E., 1994. 'Endogenous Innovation in the Theory of Growth', *Journal of Economic Perspectives,* **8**, 23–44

Jones, L.E. and Manuelli, R., 1990. 'A Model of Optimal Equilibrium Growth', *Journal of Political Economy*, **98**, 1008–38

Kaldor, N., 1961. 'Capital Accumulation and Economic Growth', in F.A. Lutz and D.C. Hague (eds.), *The Theory of Capital* (New York: St Martin's Press)

Levine, R. and Renelt, D., 1992. 'A Sensitivity Analysis of Cross-country Growth Regressions', *American Economic Review*, **82**, 942–63

Mankiw, N.G., Romer, D. and Weil, D.N., 1992. 'A Contribution to the Empirics of Economic Growth', *Quarterly Journal of Economcs*, **107**, 407–37

Miller. R., 1995. 'Time-series Estimation of Convergence Rates', Columbia University, mimeo

Obstfeld, M., 1995. 'International Capital Mobility in the 1990s', in P.B. Kenen (ed.), *Understanding Interdependence: The Macroeconomics of the Open Economy* (Princeton: Princeton University Press), 201–60

Quah, D.T., 1993. 'Galton's Fallacy and Tests of the Convergence Hypothesis', *Scandinavian Journal of Economics*, **95**, 427–43

    1996a. 'Empirics for Economic Growth and Convergence', *European Economic Review*, **40**, 1353–75

    1996b. Twin Peaks: Growth and Convergence in Models of Distribution Dynamics', *CEPR Discussion Paper*, **1355**

    1998. 'Convergence as Distribution Dynamics (With or Without Growth)', chapter 11 in this volume

Rebelo, S., 1991. 'Long-run Policy analysis and Long-run Growth', *Journal of Political Economy*, **99**, 500–21

Romer, P.M., 1989. 'Capital Accumulation in the Theory of Long Run Growth', in R.J. Barro (ed.), *Modern Business Cycle Theory* (Cambridge, MA: Harvard University Press and Oxford: Basil Blackwell)

Sachs, J.D. and Warner, A., 1995a. 'Economic Convergence and Economic Policies', *NBER Working Paper*, **5039**

    1995b. 'Economic Reform and the Process of Global Integration', *Brookings Papers on Economic Activity,* **1**, 1–118

    1995c. 'Natural Resource Abundance and Economic Growth', *NBER Working Paper*, **5398**

Sala-i-Martin, X., 1995. 'The Classical Approach to Convergence Analysis', *CEPR Working Paper*, **1254**

    1996. 'Regional Cohesion: Evidence and Theories of Regional Growth and Convergence', *European Economic Review*, **40**, 1325–52

Solow, R.M., 1956. 'A Contribution to the Theory of Economic Growth', *Journal of Economics*, **70**, 65–94

Taylor, A.M. and Williamson, J.G., 1994. 'Convergence in an Age of Mass Migration', *NBER Working Paper*, **4711**

Temple, Jonathan, 1995. 'New Growth Theory and New Growth Evidence', chapter in PhD dissertation, Oxford University

Ventura, J., 1995. 'Growth and Interdependence', *Working Paper*, MIT

Young, A., 1994. 'The Tyranny of Numbers: Confronting the Statistical Realities of the East Asian Growth Experience', *NBER Working Paper*, **4680**

Discussion

DANIEL COHEN

Chapter 10 offers a useful entry into the recent literature on growth and convergence. Although selective, the chapter provides a rich perspective on the issues at hand.

It starts with the standard neoclassical model whose prediction regarding growth and convergence lies at the heart of the 'conditional convergence' analysis of Barro (1991) and Sala-i-Martin (1995) and to which Mankiw, Romer and Weil (1992) have given a compact formulation. The critical assumption behind the empirical tests of conditional convergence offered by these authors is that countries are viewed as realisations of independent experiments of independent countries. The weakness is that countries do interact. If they were so well integrated as to be subject to the same intertemporal prices then one might equalise instantaneously the capital labour ratio of all economies at a level that would perpetuate indefinitely any initial diversity of *per capita* income. *Per capita* output, on the other hand, would be instantaneously equalised, and the empirical implication (that we would want to see, but which is likely to be falsified) would be that the pattern of convergence of income *per capita* is slower than the patterns of convergence of *per capita* output (and all the more so when the economies are financially integrated). The irony, of course, is indeed that integration is bad for convergence of welfare.

If we trust the work by Sachs and Warner (1997), it seems, however, the opposite is true: openness (at least trade liberalisation) appears to be good for convergence. How can we reconcile these findings? If one follows the line pursued in the chapter, one is left with a sense of an incomplete agenda regarding the analysis of convergence patterns and openness.

To start with, one would like to have more precise information on the difference between *per capita* income and output. Countries such as Singapore have relied extensively on FDI. Where do they stand in terms of *per capita* consumption?

Second, the work that has been performed by Barro and Sala-i-Martin on regions reaches the conclusion that the patterns of conditional convergence are quite similar to that of nations. Barro, Mankiw and Sala-i-Martin (1995) offer a potential explanation for this result by showing that the lack of tradability of human capital might be enough to reach this conclusion. Yet, in the experiment in which one country suddenly 'opens up' to financial integration or trade, one should observe a discontinuity of *per capita* output, although – again – not necessarily of *per capita* consumption. The example of East Germany is one case one might have in mind. Barro once extrapolated for the *Wall Street Journal* the patterns of β convergence observed for nations or regions to the case of German reunification. In theory, he should be wrong, but one would want to know if, in practice, enough time has elapsed to see where we stand in that matter.

Another difficulty with the Sachs and Warner results is that we cannot quite disentangle what arises from trade liberalisation *per se* and other policy variables which are often taken simultaneously with the decision to liberalise trade. One puzzle that this literature should address is the fact that openness itself (conventionally measured by imports *plus* exports over GDP) does not appear to be a significant determinant of growth. It might of course be that this is due to the fact that conventional measures of openness are a bad proxy for what they are meant to capture: the free ability to import and sell goods from or to the rest of the world. To put the question in other terms, it is not quite clear where we should stand when comparing the results found by Young on the domestic determinants of growth and those of Quah and others who do make a convincing case that contagion across borders is a powerful argument for growth.

I do then subscribe to the conclusion of the chapter: 'More complex and sophisticated theoretical approaches, paying more attention to international interactions, will hopefully ascertain the structural causes of persisting inequality and indicate whether policy interventions are desirable.'

REFERENCES

Barro, R. J., 1991. 'Economic Growth in a Cross-section of Countries', *Quarterly Journal of Economics*, **106**, 407–43

Barro, R., Mankiw, N. G. and Sala-i-Martin, X., 1995. 'Capital Mobility in Neoclassical Models of Growth', *American Economic Review*, **185**, 103–15.

Mankiw, N. G., Romer, D. and Weil, D. N. (1992) 'A Contribution to the Empirics of Economic Growth', *Quarterly Journal of Economics*, **107**, 407–37.

Sachs, J. D. and Warner, A., 1997. 'Economic Convergence and Economic Policies', *NBER Working Paper*, **5039**

Sala-i-Martin, X. 1995. 'The Classical Approach to Convergence Analysis', *CEPR Working Paper*, **1254**

Young, A. 1994. 'The Tyranny of Numbers: Confronting the Statistical Realities of the East Asian Growth Experience', *NBER Working Paper*, **4680**

11　Convergence as distribution dynamics (with or without growth)

DANNY T. QUAH

1　Introduction

Convergence is a catchy idea, but one that organises serious thinking in areas as diverse as economic growth, theoretical econometrics, finance, European politics and monetary union, regional planning and geography, up through but not ending at entertainment and multi-media technology and the software industry.

Some growth economists define 'convergence' as a single economy approaching its theoretically-derived steady-state growth path. Others translate this to whether poor economies are catching up with rich ones. Yet others think of these two – conceptually quite different – statements as being identical, and thus of either indicating convergence.

At one extreme, econometricians and probabilists have found it useful to work with different notions of convergence of sequences of random variables. At a different extreme, economists and policy-makers in Europe have been obsessed with the Maastricht convergence criteria. Finally, when high-tech, fast-growth market participants – people who actually create value in modern economies – get together, they too excitedly discuss convergence, but now between biological and machined products, or between communications, computers and content (e.g. Kelly, 1994; Tapscott, 1996). In every instance, the term 'convergence' is used with a different meaning – and rightly so.

That 'convergence' suffers from this meaning overload should not disguise its importance. This chapter concerns 'convergence' in the sense of poor economies catching up with the rich. If by economies, one means countries, then magnitudes of the numbers alone should already show why convergence is important. Some countries have been doubling *per capita* incomes every decade; yet others have been stagnant, with levels of *per capita* income a hundred times lower than those of the leading economies.

298

Such back-of-the-envelope facts are obvious and easy to obtain. But are there empirical regularities beyond them that could be useful for advancing economists' understanding of convergence? If the current situation continues, how will cross-country income distributions look in the future? Will rich economies always remain in a 'club' of rich countries, and similarly the poor? What possibilities are there for switches across relatively poor and relatively rich?

Consider the same question, but now with the economies being regions within countries: are poorer regions languishing, currently and forever behind richer ones, or do they face any possibility of catching up? As before, one seeks an empirical characterisation on such dynamic possibilities sufficiently precise and apposite that one can understand the implications of alternative scenarios.

Such questions concern the behaviour over time of cross-section distributions of income (or output or welfare): the issues are, writ large to the scale of macroeconomies or regions, the same as those that have traditionally been the concerns of research on the dynamics of inequality and personal income distributions. Are the distributions collapsing, so that everyone shows a tendency to become equally well off? Instead, are the distributions increasing in dispersion, so that those relatively better off are getting more so? Or are the distributions tending towards shapes that show clusters and subgroups, so that the population is polarising and then stratifying into distinct classes? Questions like these are useful for appreciating patterns of cross-country growth, just as they are for understanding patterns of dynamics and mobility in individuals' incomes within societies.

Such questions also show that economic growth – while unquestionably important for welfare – need not be the only mechanism permitting understanding of convergence. In the framework adopted below, convergence might occur because of growth. Or convergence might occur without growth. Pinning down a theory of growth is not essential to understanding whether poor economies will become rich, or whether they will remain poor.[1] The more central question is: what determines the dynamics of cross-economy income distributions? Mechanisms of growth might be an important part of the answer; then again, they might not.

This chapter provides an overview of recent research that takes this distribution-dynamics approach to analysing convergence. It clarifies how this work differs from more traditional analysis, and it points to where subsequent work is needed and suggests alternative theoretical ideas to explore.

To clarify how such an approach to studying convergence differs from more traditional ones, section 2 develops a series of theoretical models. It begins with models that underpin conventional understanding on growth and convergence, and progresses to models that focus on convergence as distribution dynamics and where growth occurs almost mechanically. In this last set of models, despite the near-trivial specification of economic growth, intricate patterns of convergence and divergence nevertheless emerge.

Section 3 provides the empirical counterpart to the analyses in section 2: once again, we study how configurations of convergence and divergence – or, alternatively, of stratification and polarisation – appear in the cross-section of economies. While section 2 does this theoretically, section 3 studies this empirically. Section 4 briefly concludes.

2   Theoretical models

This section develops a series of models to make precise the notion of convergence across economies. I begin with a deterministic, classical growth model, and consider its convergence implications. These predictions are the ones traditionally taken to be useful for understanding the dynamics of rich and poor economies. In one interpretation, they are also the implications that have importantly influenced thinking on exogenous and endogenous growth. It is this framework that has traditionally tied together so closely discussions of growth on the one hand and convergence on the other.

Next, I provide a stochastic version of essentially the same growth model: this permits clarifying where the original interpretation of convergence is useful, and where it is not. Finally, I develop a model where convergence – catch-up between rich and poor across a rich cross-section of economies – becomes the central concern. In this last model, growth in each of the economies is fairly mechanical: nevertheless, what emerges are intricate patterns of convergence and divergence, and of stratification and polarisation.

2.1   Neoclassical deterministic growth and convergence

The development given here of deterministic, neoclassical growth theory's convergence predictions is well known (e.g. Romer, 1994). Nonetheless, it will be useful as a starting point for the analyses that follow.

Assume that, in the representative economy, aggregate output is produced by a multiplicative-technology, constant returns to scale (CRS) production function in capital and labour. Normalising by labour, per worker output can be written as the product of technology A and a function f of per worker capital k (lower-case symbols denoting per worker quantities):

$$y = A f(k), f \text{ differentiable and invertible.} \tag{1}$$

It is traditional to refer to y as productivity (in the sense of average per worker output), and to A as the Solow or productivity residual. Taking growth rates on both sides of (1) gives

$$\dot{y} = \dot{A} + \left[\frac{f'(k)k}{f(k)}\right]\dot{k}. \tag{2}$$

Two points are immediate, both relating to the factor $f'(k)\, k/\, f(k)$ that multiplies $\dot{k}/k$ on the right-hand side. First, if the economy is one that compensates factor inputs according to marginal product, then this multiplicative term has an economic interpretation: it is physical capital's factor share in national income. Second, it follows that – regardless of how compensation actually occurs – that multiplicative term is bounded between 0 and 1. This therefore restricts how much capital deepening $\dot{k}/k$ can hope to contribute to productivity growth $\dot{y}/y$.

Such a bound applies regardless of how $\dot{k}/k$ is itself determined. That determination, however, is useful to develop explicitly. Call N the total quantity of labour. In our convention of lower- and upper-case symbols, the aggregate quantity of capital is $K = k\,N$ and aggregate output is $Y = y\,N$. Then,

$$\dot{k}/k = \dot{K}/K - \dot{N}/N.$$

Suppose that the (technology-adjusted) rate of aggregate capital accumulation is constant:

$$\sigma = \frac{\dot{K}}{Y/A} \in (0, 1).$$

Substituting this into the previous equation,

$$\begin{aligned}
\hat{k} &= ((Y/A)/K)\sigma - \hat{N} \\
&= ((y/A)/k)\sigma - \hat{N} \\
&= \frac{(y/A)}{f^{-1}(y/A)}\sigma - \hat{N},
\end{aligned}$$

where (1) has been inverted to solve for k. Using this expression for $\dot{k}/k$ in (2) gives y's proportional growth rate as a function of, among other things, its level:

$$y = \left(A - \left[\frac{f'(k)k}{f(k)}\right]N\right) + \left[\frac{f'(k)k}{f(k)}\right]\sigma \times \frac{(y/A)}{f^{-1}(y/A)}. \tag{3}$$

For analysing convergence, what matters is the last levels term on the right-hand side. If the production technology in (1) has the power form

$$f(k) = k^\gamma, 0 < \gamma \le 1, \tag{4}$$

then that last term in levels becomes

$$\frac{(y/A)}{f^{-1}(y/A)} = (y/A)^{1-\gamma^{-1}},$$

where, by construction, $1 - \gamma^{-1} \le 0$. This technology specification (4) also gives that the restricting factor $[f'(k)k/f(k)]$ is not just bounded (possibly varying) between 0 and 1 but actually constant at γ. Using these in (3) we have

$$y = (A - \gamma N) + \gamma\sigma A^{-(1-\gamma^{-1})} \times y^{1-\gamma^{-1}} \tag{5}$$

$$= \xi_0 + \xi_1 \times y^{1-\gamma^{-1}} \tag{6}$$

(with ξ_0 and ξ_1 defined in the obvious way).

From a convergence perspective, abstracting away inessentials, (6) gives the theory's predicted relation between income growth $\dot{y}/y$, income levels y, and physical capital's productivity coefficient γ. Since $1 - \gamma^{-1} \le 0$ and increases in γ, tending to 0 as γ goes to 1, one might read (6) to say that rich economies grow slower, while poor ones grow faster. Convergence is faster, the smaller is γ. Abstracting away from differences and scale effects in ξ_0 and ξ_1, the convergence situation is as in figure 11.1, where the different time paths illustrate different economies.

To see the algebra through completely, one might proceed as follows. Rearrange (5) to get

$$y - A = \gamma\left[\sigma(y/A)^{1-\gamma^{-1}} - N\right]. \tag{7}$$

A steady state in y/A thus exists when $\dot{N}/N$ is positive and (eventually) constant. That steady-state level for y/A is given by the unique zero of (7) at

$$(y/A)_* = \left(\sigma^{-1}N\right)^{(1-\gamma^{-1})^{-1}}.$$

Moreover, since $1 - \gamma^{-1}$ is negative, the ratio y/A is globally stable around its steady state. (At that steady state, y of course grows at the same rate as A.)

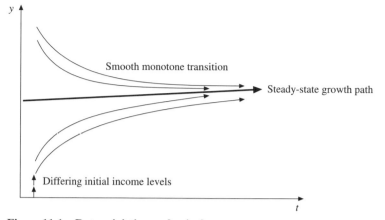

Figure 11.1   Deterministic neoclassical convergence

How rapidly does convergence occur? Define $z \overset{\text{def}}{=} y/A$, and log-linearise (7) around steady state $z_* = y_A$ to get

$$\dot{z} = -(1 - \gamma)(N) \times (\log z - \log z_*). \tag{8}$$

This is simply a first-order differential equation in $\log z - \log z_*$. The larger is γ, the slower is the rate of convergence of $\log z$ to $\log z_*$.

Such a depiction of convergence gives rise to a research programme with a number of features (see, e.g. Barro and Sala-i-Martin, 1992). First, the researcher might consider ξ_0 and ξ_1 in (6) or N/N and z_* in (8) to vary, plausibly, with differing structural characteristics of different economies. Examples of such characteristics might include democracy, political stability, tax regime, religious ethos, colonial heritage and so on. The researcher then seeks 'conditional convergence' where figure 11.1 obtains only after conditioning on those other characteristics. Such conditioning, however, leaves unchanged the basic message: those auxiliary variables, after all, entered the discussion only *after* the derivation of convergence in (1)–(6) and figure 11.1 Conditioning can affect neither the intuition nor the interpretation surrounding the convergence of figure 11.1.

Second, to investigate empirically (6) or (8) or figure 11.1, the researcher seeks a convergence regression: there, one is interested if growth (on the left-hand side) depends negatively on levels (on the right). That regression would formalise the intuition where as one looks across the different economies in figure 11.1, one expects to see richer ones growing relatively slower, and poorer economies, relatively faster. On the left-hand side of such a regression, one might proxy growth rates by an average of log first-differences. On the right-hand side, one might have a range of auxiliary conditioning variables, and then income levels. When negative, the coefficient on income levels denotes convergence (in the sense of figure 11.1); its magnitude measures the speed of convergence and varies negatively with physical capital's productivity coefficient. In this model, a zero coefficient on income levels would imply physical capital's productivity coefficient γ equal to 1.

If one were to interpret (6) and (8) as applying only over the long run, then the averaged log first differences appearing on the left-hand side of the regression should be averages taken over an appropriately long time horizon. Consequently, the regression would be estimated effectively only over the cross-section (and not time-series) dimension. As usual in such work, the researcher investigates the convergence regression equations (6) and (8), tacking on a stochastic residual at the end.

When one carries out this research programme – either using explicit regression analysis (e.g. Barro and Sala-i-Martin, 1992) or informal comparison (e.g. Romer, 1994), one concludes that in the data the growth–levels relation implies that γ should be close to 1. More significantly, however, one concludes that γ is much larger than would be implied by capital's factor share in national income accounts. This, by itself, has been an important spur to the development of growth models that feature externalities, increasing returns, endogenous technical progress or other possibilities breaking the link between γ and capital's measured factor share. Researchers like Barro and Sala-i-Martin (1992), moreover, claim to find conditional convergence, and thus conclude that figure 11.1 is operative, and that the poor do catch up with the rich, if slowly.[2]

Throughout this discussion, we have considered only a single, representative economy. Thus, in this research programme, one implicitly identifies convergence of that representative economy's z to its z_* also as cross-sectional convergence of different economies towards each other (as in figure 11.1).

2.2 Stochastic growth

Above, I described the empirical implementation of (6) and (8) in terms of tacking on a stochastic residual at the end. Since the equations cannot be expected to fit perfectly, something like this is obviously necessary. Two issues, however, then arise. First, there might be interesting economics omitted when one simply adds on a stochastic residual as an afterthought. And, second, the interpretation of figure 11.1 in terms of the poor catching up with the rich might no longer be appropriate. We consider these in turn.

Stochastic disturbances induce uncertainty: a rich cross-section of economies might then not behave just as a collection of individualistic, autarkic elements, as implicitly assumed in the previous development. In this case, one fruitful approach might be to explore insurance arrangements across the distribution of aggregate economies (using ideas from, e.g. Bertola, 1995; Lucas, 1992; Thomas and Worrall, 1990). Groupings of selected economies might endogenously emerge – depending on patterns of insurable and uninsurable disturbances across economies – with growth patterns then varying across different groupings. Because identification becomes important – which economies go in which groupings – such an outcome would depart from the 'representative economy' analysis above. To keep within space restrictions, however, I will not analyse this further here: the model developed in the next subsection will carry similar predictions (although it will not be stochastic, and thus groupings will occur for other than insurance reasons).

A different, more direct possibility is that stochastic disturbances might, properly considered, break the link between convergence, capital's productivity coefficient γ and factor income shares. This idea has been explored in den Haan (1995), Kelly (1992) and Leung and Quah (1996). I follow the last of these in developing this possibility, but keep as close as I can to the deterministic model previously studied. Some properties of the stochastic model will translate directly from the deterministic case; however, to be clear where the new subtleties are, it helps to be more explicit about economic behaviour than I have been thus far.

In the cross-section distribution, index economies by j; it will be convenient now to suppose that time is discrete. Variables specific to economy j at time t will have subscript j and be parenthesised t.

Assume that each economy behaves autarkically and that, in equilibrium, can be described by the following social planning problem: at time t_0, solve

$$\sup_{\{(c_j(t),k_j(t+1)):t\geq t_0\}} E_{t_0} \sum_{t=t_0}^{\infty} (1+\rho)^{-t} \log c_j(t), \ \rho > 0 \tag{9}$$

$$\text{s.t. } y_j(t) = A(t)k_j(t)^{\gamma(t)} \tag{10}$$

$$c_j(t) \leq y_j(t) - k_j(t+1), \ \tilde{} \, t \geq t_0,$$

$$k_j(t_0) > 0 \text{ given.}$$

In (9), ρ describes the discount factor. The last two relations state, respectively, the capital accumulation constraint and that the time t_0-extant capital stock is fixed.

The stochastic elements introduced are encapsulated in the technology and productivity terms A and γ: these can now vary randomly through time. Assume that $\{(A(t),\gamma(t)) :$ integer t$\}$ is a jointly stationary vector process with all entries (almost surely) positive.[3] When this process is degenerate, (10) collapses to the production technology of the previous section. By contrast, with A and γ non-degenerate stochastic processes, we will see that they give rise to the stochastic disturbances that, in the previous subsection, had been simply tacked on at the end. Keeping to our earlier interpretation, A and γ are taken to be common across economies: thus, while they might vary over time, they are constant over the cross-section.

Assume that at time t every economy observes the same history,

$$\mathcal{F}(t) = \{ A(s), \gamma(s), y_j(s), k_j(s) : s < t,\ \text{all } j \}.$$

Expectations conditioned on this history will be denoted $E_t = E(\cdot | \mathcal{F}(t))$, a notation already used in (9). By this timing assumption, in general, $E_t A(t) \neq A(t)$ and $E_t \gamma(t) \neq \gamma(t)$. Not allowing economies, at time t, to know time-t productivity disturbances is not crucial for the discussion but simplifies notation.

In equilibrium, in each time period t, economies behave as if a social planner chooses consumption and investment functions based on what is observable at time t. Under regularity conditions, those optimal decision rules lead to

$$k_j(t+1) = \left((E_t\gamma(t))(1+\rho)^{-1} \right) y_j(t), \tag{11}$$

so that from (10) output behaves as

$$y_j(t+1) = A(t+1) \left[\left((E_t\gamma(t))(1+\rho)^{-1} \right) y_j(t) \right]^{\gamma(t+1)}.$$

Taking logs and defining $\tilde{y} \overset{\text{def}}{=} \log y$ and $\log k$ gives the first-order stochastic difference equation:

$$\forall t \geq t_0 : \quad \tilde{y}_j(t+1) = \log A(t+1) + \gamma(t+1)\log(E_t\gamma(t))$$
$$- \gamma(t+1)\log(1+\rho) + \gamma(t+1)\tilde{y}_j(t)$$
$$= \eta(t+1) + \gamma(t+1)\tilde{y}_j(t) \tag{12}$$

with initial condition

$$\tilde{y}_j(t_0) = \log A(t_0) + \gamma(t_0)\tilde{k}_j(t_0), \tag{13}$$

and where η in (12) is defined as:

$$\eta(t) = \log A(t) + \gamma(t) \log(E_{t-1}\gamma(t-1)) - \gamma(t) \log(1+\rho). \quad (14)$$

Immediate from the assumptions on $\{(A(t), \gamma(t)) : \text{integer t}\}$ we have that the stochastic process $\{\eta(t) : \text{integer t}\}$ is stationary and common across economies.[4]

All the model's dynamics – and hence all its convergence implications – are embedded in (12)–(14). To make those implications explicit, first take the case where $\gamma(t) = \gamma \in (0, 1]$: this has capital's productivity coefficient constant as in the previous section, but the Solow productivity residual A is stochastic. Then, (14) becomes

$$\eta(t) = \log A(t) + \gamma \log((1+\rho)^{-1}\gamma);$$

up to a shift in mean, η simply inherits all the stochastic properties of log A. From (12) and (13), the distribution of output across economies evolves as

$$\tilde{y}_j(t+1) = \gamma \tilde{y}_j(t)\eta(t+1) \quad \text{for } t \geq t_0, \quad (15)$$

$$\tilde{y}_j(t_0) = \log A(t_0) + \gamma \tilde{k}_j(t_0). \quad (16)$$

Iterating (15) forwards from the initial condition (16), we get

$$\tilde{y}_j(t) = \gamma^{t-t_0}\tilde{y}_j(t_0) + \sum_{s=0}^{t-1-t_0} \gamma^s \eta(t-s). \quad (17)$$

Since η is stationary, if γ is 1, then $\tilde{y}_j$ for each j is an integrated (order 1) process.[5] If, further, A is iid through time, then (15) says that $\tilde{y}_j$ (for each j) is a random walk with drift

$$E\eta = E \log A + \gamma \log((1+\rho)^{-1}\gamma)$$

which could be positive, negative, or zero. Should the discount rate ρ be large (relative to the technology terms γ and E log A), then $\tilde{y}_j = \log y_j$ diverges to $-\infty$ (when $\gamma = 1$), implying then that y_j converges to 0, independent of initial conditions.

This case is, however, relatively uninteresting: it is when economic agents discount the future so heavily that accumulation does not occur and the economy thus collapses on itself. More relevant is when the drift $E\eta$ is non-negative. Then there are two possibilities: when γ is strictly less than 1, and when γ is exactly 1.

Take first the case with $\gamma < 1$. From (17), as t grows large, $\tilde{y}_j$ (for each j) converges to a random variable having a unique stationary or invariant distribution given by the distribution of

$$\zeta(t) \overset{\text{def}}{=} \sum_{s=0}^{\infty} \gamma^s \eta(t-s)$$

for any integer t. (If, for example, η is distributed iid normal with mean $E\eta$ and variance var(η), then that invariant distribution is normal with mean $E\eta$ (1- gamma) and variance var(η)/$(1-\gamma^2)$ identically across $\zeta(t)$s).

That unique invariant distribution, by definition, must be attained independent of initial conditions. It is, moreover, typically non-degenerate. What happens, however, to the cross-section distribution of $\tilde{y}_j$s across j? Since the limiting $\zeta(t)$s are the *same* for all j, the cross-section distribution turns out to collapse to a single point: it behaves not at all like the time-series distribution of $\tilde{y}_j$ for a fixed (but arbitrary) j.

This difference between cross-section and time-series dimensions arises for a quite trivial and easily identified reason: the model has taken A and γ, and thus η, to be common across economies.

The same insight applies to when γ is 1: once again, simply study (17). Although for each j, the sequence $\tilde{y}_j(t)$ does not converge in t to any invariant distribution, the cross-section distribution across js is completely stable, and does not diverge. That cross-section distribution just moves up and down, perturbed by a single common factor: no intra-distribution relative movements occur.

Again, this happens because A and γ have been assumed to be common across economies. It thus seems fairly trivial. The conceptual difficulty arises, however, when one asks: what assumption should replace this commonality property? *Any* assumption – especially an iid one – is going to be equally arbitrary, and more to the point, will give predictions for the cross-section distribution as mechanically and simply as those just obtained. In this kind of 'representative economy' analysis, economic theory plays almost no role in helping us understand the behaviour of the cross-section distribution. Depending only on arbitrary assumptions on unobservable disturbances, the cross-section distribution across economies on the one hand and the time-series distribution of any single economy in the cross-section on the other can behave completely differently.

The point is emphasised if we return to the general case in (12)–(14). Then, iterating (12), we obtain the counterpart of (15):

$$\tilde{y}_j(t) = \left[\prod_{s=1}^{t-t_0} \gamma(t_0+s)\right]\tilde{y}_j(t_0) + \sum_{s=0}^{t-1-t_0}\left[\prod_{r=0}^{s-1}\gamma(t-r)\right]\eta(t-s). \quad (18)$$

Kelly (1992) and Leung and Quah (1996) prove that (18) converges to a

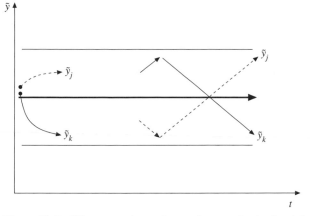

Figure 11.2   Divergence towards non-degenerate steady-state invariant distribution

degenerate cross-section distribution across economies, even when $\gamma(t)$ has expectation 1 and exceeds 1 with positive probability. Put another way, (12) could show a coefficient on lagged $\tilde{y}_j$ that is large – the technology (10) could show, on average, physical capital having productivity coefficient 1 – yet convergence of the cross-section distribution to a degenerate point could still occur.

The stochastic model thus far has been used to argue that a convergence regression coefficient indicating no convergence – in the sense of subsection 2.1 – can be consistent with the cross-section distribution collapsing to a point. The opposite can also occur: a convergence regression coefficient indicating convergence is also consistent with the cross-section distribution expanding. An easy way to understand this is to use (17) with $\gamma < 1$, and allow η to be iid across economies. Then, by the Glivenko–Cantelli Theorem, the cross-section and time-series distributions coincide. Since the (time-series) invariant distribution is unique, the cross-section distribution tends to it from wherever that cross-section distribution might happen to be. In particular, this must happen even when the cross-section distribution is already more tightly concentrated than the invariant distribution (see figure 11.2). Under such circumstances, the cross-section distribution will be seen to diverge, even when $\gamma < 1$, and convergence regressions indicate convergence.

What I have just described is an instance of the general message from Galton's fallacy reasoning (see, e.g. Friedman, 1992; Quah, 1993b). Here, one can usefully regard its lesson as the following: the dynamics of a representative or average economy in the cross-section say little about the behaviour of the entire cross-section distribution.

To conclude, the message from this subsection can be stated in two different ways, First, in the kind of 'representative-economy' model studied thus far, it is the assumptions on exogenous stochastic disturbances that are dominant for the behaviour of the cross-section distribution: economic theory gives no useful guide to those dynamics. Second, even a complete characterisation of the dynamic behaviour of a representative economy tells little about the dynamics of the entire cross-section distribution.

These statements suggest how misleading is the apparently obvious message of figure 11.1 – of poor catching up with rich provided only that technology coefficients take particular values or that certain regression coefficients take particular signs. To make progress on analysing convergence, one needs an economic model that theorises explicitly in terms of the cross-section distribution.

2.3 Cross-section dynamics and convergence

Quah (1996d) develops a model of convergence for a rich cross-section distribution of economies.[6] In the model, a balance between a force for consolidation and a force for fragmentation results in coalitions forming across different parts of the distribution of economies. Those coalitions then turn out to behave like convergence clubs (e.g. Baumol, 1986). The model explains the dynamics of the entire cross-section distribution, and directly gives predictions on convergence.

The model is most naturally viewed as one where growth and convergence arise from human capital or the generation of ideas.[7] We therefore switch from the earlier models where accumulating physical capital k is important to one where it is accumulating human capital h that matters. Let $\mathcal{J}$ be the index set of economies, taken as fixed throughout the discussion. A *coalition* of economies is a subset C of $\mathcal{J}$. Each economy l in $\mathcal{J}$ is characterised by an economy-specific stock of human capital h_l. That stock is used in two non-rival ways: first, it represents the potential for generating ideas, and second, it produces non-storable output for consumption. Ideas that are further developed then increment the stock of human capital, thereby driving economic growth.

Production occurs from coalitions of economies forming to jointly produce a single non-durable consumption good. Denote the total output of coalition C by Y_C. Assume that Y_C depends on the distribution of h_l across l in C, and is increasing in each h_l. Assume also that out of the total coalition output, economy l in C gets $\psi(Y_C, h_l)$, with ψ increasing in both arguments, and satisfying exact product exhaustion:

$$\sum_{l \,in\, C} \psi(Y_C, h_l) = Y_C.$$

(Primitive assumptions sufficient for these properties would be first, compensation according to marginal product and second, the CES technology

$$Y_C = \left[\sum_{l \,in\, C} h_l^{\theta} \right]^{1/\theta}, 0 < \theta < 1$$

(with θ, describing the elasticity of substitution in the CES production function, giving isoquants between linear and Cobb–Douglas technologies). Quah (1996d) gives the natural interpretation of these properties as economies of scale deriving from specialisation.

By the assumptions above, enlarging the coalition always increases total output Y. Then the compensation scheme ψ ensures that all economies unanimously agree to be in the single grand coalition comprising the entire cross-section. This, therefore, is a force for consolidation.

Consider next how the distribution of hs evolves. In every instant of time, economy l generates ideas of average quality h_l. Assume that it first gets to use those ideas and then shares them with others in its coalition. Ideas propagate freely within coalitions, but do not transmit across them.[8] Call H_C the *average* quality of ideas generated in coalition C, and suppose that human capital in economy l evolves as:

$$\dot{h}_l = \tilde{\phi}(h_l, H_C) \text{ for } l \text{ in } C,$$

with $\tilde{\phi}$ increasing in both arguments and homogeneous degree 1. Dividing throughout by h_l we get:

$$\dot{h}_l / h_l = \tilde{\phi}(1, H_C/h_l) \stackrel{\text{def}}{=} \phi(H/h_l).$$

By construction ϕ is increasing in the ratio H_C / h_l.

It is now easy to understand the force for fragmentation. Economies in higher average h coalitions have faster proportional growth rates. The problem with allowing a coalition to get too large – expanding below – is that the coalition thereby lowers its average H_C: this would slow growth for all economies already in the coalition. Economies already in good coalitions would, *ceteris paribus*, refuse to admit economies that lower the coalition average H_C.

The force for consolidation (the compensation ψ (Y_C, h_l)) is a *level* effect – it affects current consumption. The force for fragmentation (the growth

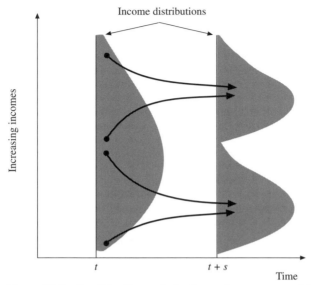

Figure 11.3   Stratification, polarisation and convergence clubs

ϕ (H_C / h_l)) is a *slope* effect – it affects future consumption. Parameterising economies' discount rates for intertemporal consumption allows calibrating the trade-off across level and slope effects, and thus provides a theory of coalition formation. Quah (1996d) describes an equilibrium where non-trivial consecutive subsets of the cross-section distribution of economies form coalitions. The distribution of income across economies within the same coalition converges towards equality; those across different coalitions separate and then diverge (figure 11.3).

In equilibrium, rich economies converge towards each other, but remain rich; similarly the poor remain poor. The middle class eventually vanishes, and the income distribution stratifies. Those in the middle part of the income distribution might begin close to each other, but over time diverge apart: small differences here become magnified eventually into large disparities. By contrast, within extreme parts of the distributions, economies, over time, have their differences diminish. Because only two convergence clubs form in figure 11.3, it is natural to consider the dynamics here as showing an *emerging twin-peaks* character. In general, multiple clubs may form, the number of which will then be the number of emerging modes in the long-run cross-section distribution of incomes.

In this model, conditional convergence occurs. This is a conditional convergence, however, that depends critically on the coalition structure in equilibrium. Different rules for how coalitions form would lead, in general, to different distribution dynamics. Appreciating those rules provides an understanding on the stratification and polarisation that emerges across the cross-section.

More generally, the model in this subsection draws attention to two features in figure 11.3 relevant for convergence. First is the abeyant emergence of peaks in the cross-economy income distribution. Second is the intra-distribution dynamics, where different economies in the cross-section, over time, transit to different parts of the distribution.

3   Empirics

Conventional wisdom on cross-section regression analyses of convergence is that cross-economy convergence occurs, once appropriate conditioning is applied (Barro and Sala-i-Martin, 1992; Sala-i-Martin, 1996). In this conventional wisdom, such convergence is stable and uniform at 2 per cent per year.

Quah (1996c) has argued that such empirical stability might be simply a statistical artifact. He provides Monte Carlo evidence that heterogeneous unit root data – that, by construction, contradict stable uniform convergence in the sense described above – could nevertheless generate a stable 2 per cent convergence rate, given the sample sizes of observations typically used. In those Monte Carlo experiments, the cross-section income distributions diverge over time; yet, the 2 per cent convergence regression finding is reproduced, on average.

But the theoretical analysis in section 2 provides yet other reasons for doubting the usefulness of such results for analysing convergence. Whether or not the 2 per cent estimate is statistically reliable, it can provide *no* guide for convergence behaviour across the cross-section. The interesting features in figure 11.3 can certainly never be captured by cross-section (conditional or unconditional) convergence regression analysis.[9] However, it is exactly such dynamics that will shed light on convergence patterns across economies.

The most apposite empirical approach parallels the theoretical analysis of subsection 2.3 in modelling directly the dynamics of the entire cross-section distribution. Note that such a motivation differs from the technical ones traditionally given of either exploiting simultaneously cross-section and time-series dimensions of the data for great precision in estimation and inference or permitting 'flexibility' in estimating time-varying and non-linear regression or distribution functions.[10] Instead, the goal is to provide a picture of how the entire cross-section distribution evolves over time, and to understand the long-run or limiting behaviour of that cross-economy income distribution.

Figure 11.4 gives a first preliminary look at cross-economy distribution dynamics. The different panels in figure 11.4 show point-in-time snapshots of the density of normalised productivity across countries.[11] Thus, figure 11.4 cannot show intra-distribution or churning dynamics in the evolving distributions. It can, however, and evidently does show an emerging twin-peakedness.

The econometric task in studying convergence, therefore, is to formulate a model that (1) is capable of capturing the different possibilities in figure 11.3 (including, significantly, the intra-distribution dynamics as well as the shapes of the point-in-time distributions); (2) accepts data in the form of distributions as in figure 11.4 and (3) allows analysis of long-run or out-of-sample behaviour in the distributions. Call a structure allowing (1)–(3) a *model of explicit distribution dynamics* (or *medd*). Desdoigts (1994), Lamo (1996), Paap and van Dijk (1994) and Quah (1993a, 1993b, 1996b, 1997) have studied convergence in terms of *medd* structures.[12] The underlying framework common to all this research is the following.

Let F_t denote the time t cross-economy income distribution. Associated with each F_t is a probability measure λ_t, where

$$\forall y \in \mathbb{R}: \quad \lambda_t((-\infty, y]) = F_t(y).$$

A stochastic difference equation describing distribution dynamics is then

$$\lambda_t = T^*(\lambda_{t-1}, u_t), \text{ integer } t, \tag{19}$$

where $\{u_t : \text{integer } t\}$ is a sequence of disturbances, and T^* is an operator mapping the Cartesian product of probability measures with disturbances to probability measures. (Needless to say, the first-order specification in (19) is just a convenience for the discussion. Nothing substantive hinges on it, and the model easily generalises to higher-order dynamics.)

For *medd* analysis, one is also interested in intra-distribution dynamics. Equation (19) therefore has to record more than just means and standard deviations or, more generally, a finite set of moments of the distribution sequence $\{F_0, F_1, \ldots\}$. Equation (19) takes values that are measures, rather than just scalars or finite-dimensioned vectors, and thus differs from the typical time-series model.

The structure of T^* reveals if dynamics like those in figure 11.3 occur. Estimated from observed data, T^* allows empirical quantification of those dynamics. Economic hypotheses restrict T^* in particular ways: they therefore provide predictions on how λ_t, and thus the distributions F_t, evolve over time.

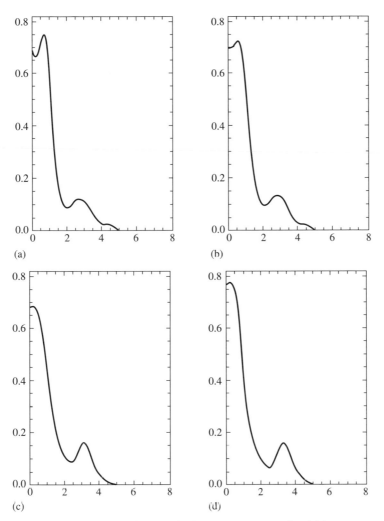

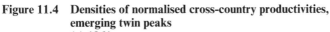

**Figure 11.4   Densities of normalised cross-country productivities,
emerging twin peaks
(a) 1961
(b) 1970
(c) 1980
(d) 1988**

Just as in time-series analysis, the researcher might seek to understand T^* by its 'impulse response function': set the disturbances u to $\mathbf{0}$ (whatever $\mathbf{0}$ means here) and run out the difference equation:

$$T^*(\lambda_{t+s-1}, \mathbf{0}) = T^*(T^*(\lambda_{t+s-2}, \mathbf{0}), \mathbf{0})$$

$$\vdots$$

$$= T^*(T^*(T^*(T^*(\lambda_t, \mathbf{0}), \mathbf{0},)\ldots\mathbf{0}), \mathbf{0}), \tag{20}$$

with the result being a proxy for λ_{t+s}. Then, convergence in country incomes to equality might be represented by (20) tending, as $s \to \infty$, towards a degenerate point mass. Alternatively, the world polarising into rich and poor might be represented by (20) tending towards a two-point measure: the implied limit distribution F_{t+s}, $s \to \infty$, would then be bimodal or twin-peaked. More generally, stratification into different convergence clubs might manifest in (20) tending towards a multi-point, discrete measure, or equivalently, a multi-modal distribution. How quickly a given initial distribution, F_0, evolves into the limiting distribution, F_{t+s}, $s \to \infty$, can be read off T^*'s (spectral) structure.

Finally, T^* also contains information on intra-distribution dynamics. Exploiting that structure, one can quantify the likelihood of the poor catching up with the rich, and characterise the (random) occurrence times for such events.

While this framework borrows ideas from standard time-series analysis, certain conceptual differences are critical. To appreciate those differences, first consider when the researcher discretises the underlying income state space so that distribution λ is given by just a probability vector. The researcher might be tempted to write (19) as

$$\lambda_t = M\lambda_{t-1} + u_t \tag{21}$$

(with M a square matrix representing the operator T^*), and then call (21) simply a vector autoregression (VAR) taking values on the unit simplex. This, however, would be incorrect. If (19) could be written as the VAR in (21), matrix M would be identified from (i.e. uniquely determined by) the sequence $\{\lambda_t : \text{integer } t\}$. However, for describing distribution dynamics, multiple Ms in (21) can be associated with any given distribution sequence: as just one example, the distribution sequence $\lambda_t = (1/2, 1/2)$ for all t is fit perfectly in (21) by any of

$$M_1 = \begin{pmatrix} 1 & 0 \\ 0 & 1 \end{pmatrix}$$

$$M_2 = \begin{pmatrix} 1/2 & 1/2 \\ 1/2 & 1/2 \end{pmatrix}$$

$$\text{or } M_3 = \begin{pmatrix} 0 & 1 \\ 1 & 0 \end{pmatrix}$$

Thus, the difference equation (19) must contain strictly more information than the VAR formulation (21).

Next, a time-series researcher might ask: since (19) describes the joint dynamics of a collection of individual time-series processes, why not just characterise the behaviour of the underlying variables directly? One might do this by estimating univariate or small multivariate time-series representations for subsets of those underlying income series. Suppose the researcher estimated univariate representations for each of the underlying variables. What can the researcher learn about 'emerging twin-peaks' tendencies from those? The answer is nothing. Knowing univariate representations for each of the underlying income series can give no information on *comovements* across the cross-section: establishing, say, that the first income series is a first-order autoregression with coefficient 0.8, while the second is a mixed moving average autoregression and so on can provide no understanding of how the different incomes covary. Thus, there might be a tendency towards twin peaks in the cross-section distribution; or there might not: one cannot tell from the collection of all univariate representations. Moreover, this negative conclusion extends from when the researcher is studying only univariate representations to when studying multivariate time-series models for subsets of the cross-section: there too one learns nothing about 'emerging twin-peaks' possibilities for the entire cross-section distribution.[13]

The time-series researcher might then consider building a model for the joint dynamics of a rich cross-section of individual time series (e.g. Canova and Marcet, 1995; Forni and Reichlin, 1995; or Quah and Sargent,1993). It is tautological that a rich enough model must be able to capture all the features of interest in the original data set. The question then becomes what is the most direct and transparent way to capture characteristics of interest. In my view, when one is concerned with an 'emerging twin-peaks' property, then a model of explicit distribution dynamics of the form (19) is best: the distribution λ_t becomes the fundamental object of study.

Following the notation above, the estimated T^*s in Desdoigts (1994),

Lamo (1996), Paap and van Dijk (1994) and Quah (1993a, 1993b, 1996b, 1997) all show an emerging twin-peaks character in the cross-country income distributions.[14] Because estimated T^*s qualify as *medds*, they can shed light on that seductive intuition – the poor growing faster and thereby catching up with the rich – that growth-on-levels regressions wish to exploit. Quah (1996b) calculates, from an estimated T^*, the probability density of passage times from poor parts of the income distribution to rich parts. He finds that although growth miracles – the Hong Kongs, the South Koreas and the Singapores – can happen with reasonable positive probability, the passage time from the bottom 5 per cent percentile to the top, given the magnitude of the gap extant, averages in the hundreds of years. Thus, persistence and immobility characterise the world cross-section of country incomes.[15]

The evidence therefore suggests, in the large, keeping figure 11.3, but modifying it so that the arrows showing intra-distribution dynamics are allowed to cross. Why this crossing comes about is not yet well captured in explicit distribution-dynamics models like those in Quah (1996b, 1996d). However, these calculations can be viewed as the econometric formalization of the 'miracles' (e.g. Lucas, 1993) that theory should continue to seek to explain.

The natural next step then is to ask: what explains the observed emerging twin-peaks patterns in cross-country income distributions? Of course, in a sense, models like those in Quah (1996b, 1996d) already explain those patterns; what such a question must intend instead is: what *measured* variables empirically account for patterns like emerging twin peaks? When the fundamental object of study is an entire distribution, empirically accounting for the patterns of interest in it has a subtle interpretation. For one, it cannot mean just getting a high R^2 or significant *t*-statistics in a regression: a regression, at best, helps us understand conditional means; it does not account for the entire distribution.

The approach I take here – described in detail in Quah (1997) – is analogous to constructing a conditional distribution from the unconditional distribution, in classical probability theory. In this framework, explaining features like emerging twin peaks means obtaining conditional distributions so that such features *no longer appear*.

Figures 11.5 and 11.6 show cross-country income distributions conditioning *on trade* and *on space*; Figures 11.7 and 11.8 show stochastic kernels transforming the original income distributions in figure 11.4 into the corresponding distributions in figures 11.5 and 11.6.

What I mean by 'conditioning' is the following: instead of taking incomes relative to the world average – and then finding their cross-

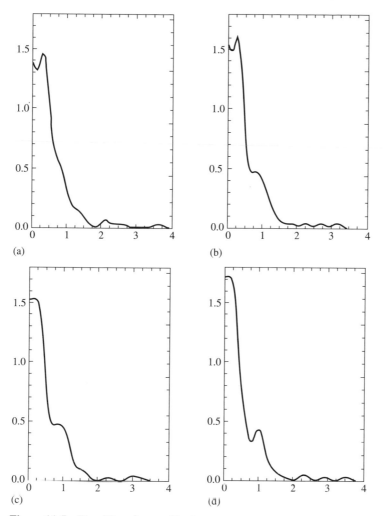

Figure 11.5   **Densities of normalised cross-country productivities,
trade conditioning**
(a) 1961
(b) 1970
(c) 1980
(d) 1988

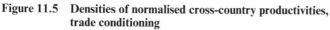

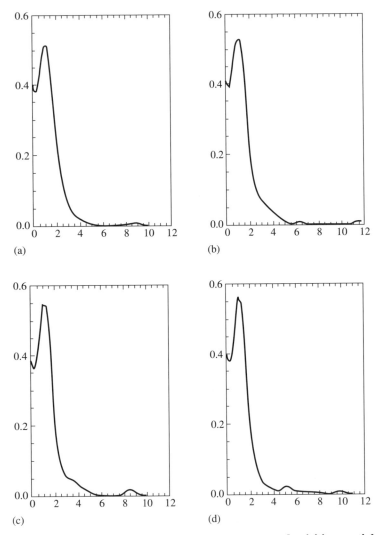

Figure 11.6   Densities of normalised cross-country productivities, spatial
              conditioning
              (a) 1961
              (b) 1970
              (c) 1980
              (d) 1988

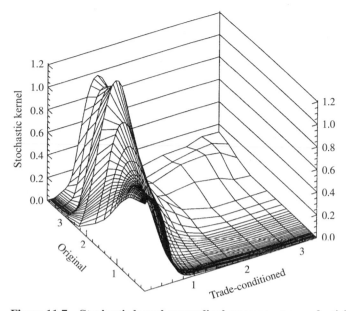

Figure 11.7   Stochastic kernel, normalised cross-country productivities, trade conditioning

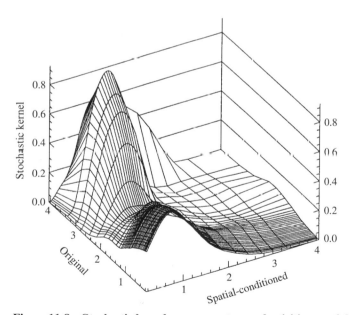

Figure 11.8   Stochastic kernel, cross-country productivities, spatial conditioning

section distribution – take instead incomes relative to those of the economy's principal trading partners (conditioning on trade), or relative to those of the economy's physical neighbours (conditioning on space). By 'trade', I mean the sum of exports and imports; by 'principal trading partners', I mean those economies such that their total trade with a given economy exceeds 50 per cent of that economy's total trade. Obvious variations on this are easy: one might look only at exports or at imports rather than their sum; one might look at the 3 (or n) largest trading partners, rather than a variable number of them; one might use 80 per cent as the threshold rather than 50 per cent for defining the group of trading partners; and so on.[16] Within a reasonable range of variation, however, perturbations along these lines do not dramatically alter the conclusions below.

To appreciate better what is involved here, take, for instance, Algeria: its trade-conditioned income is defined to be its income relative to the average of incomes in France, the United States, Italy and Morocco, with that average weighted by these economies' trade shares in Algeria. By contrast, Algeria's spatial-conditioned income is its income relative to the average of incomes in Mali, Mauritania, Morocco, Niger and Tunisia, weighted by the number of workers in those economies. For Singapore, its trade-conditioned income is relative to Guinea-Bissau, Oman, the United States, Japan, Malaysia, Mauritius and Qatar, while its spatial-conditioned income is relative to Malaysia and Indonesia.

As for spatial conditioning, if economies across the world formed a seamless web in physical geography, then one might expect the resulting (conditioned) distribution to be tightly concentrated about 1. After taking into account spatial factors, all economies would be just about average: all the poor economies in sub-Saharan Africa might be poor relative to the rest of the world, but not relative to each other. Similarly, the relatively rich economies – rich relative to the world – would again be just about average, relative to their also-rich neighbours.

The stochastic kernel shows how the unconditional distribution is transformed into a conditional one. If the mass of the kernel piled up on the 45-degree diagonal, then the transformation is one that leaves unchanged the original distribution's features. If, on the other hand, the kernel swings counter-clockwise – with most of its mass then lying in swathes parallel to the *Conditioned* axis – then that conditioning operation has successfully explained the original distribution's characteristic.

Figures 11.5 and 11.6 display exactly that counter-clockwise pivot. They thus show the importance of space and trade in explaining the 'emerging twin peaks' of figure 11.4. Quah (1997) explores these issues further.

4   Conclusions

This chapter has argued that convergence – because it concerns poor economies catching up with rich ones – forces the researcher to study what happens to the entire cross-sectional distribution of economies. What matters for convergence is *not* whether a single economy is tending towards its own, individual steady state. Instead, what matters is the behaviour of the entire distribution.

Moreover, while understanding economic growth is undoubtedly important, convergence can be insightfully studied by itself. This chapter shows that taking such an approach leads to theoretical and empirical analyses that, in turn, raise further interesting questions.

In section 2, a series of growth models progressively emphasised the importance of understanding the dynamics of the cross-sectional distribution. Section 2 argued that 'representative-economy' reasoning would be unlikely to shed much light on whether the poor can catch up with the rich. A model that departs usefully from such reasoning might then involve ideas about coalition and group formation, as analysed above, but would help explain the dynamics of cross-economy income distributions.

Section 3 described empirical analyses that adopt this distribution-dynamics perspective. Cross-country empirical findings thus far have confirmed the importance of studying convergence in this way: they have revealed a range of behaviour in the cross-section that is hidden from 'representative-economy', convergence regression analysis.

Statistical analysis of *medd*s is, in economics, in its early stages. (Extensions to what I have described above are in, among others, Desdoigts, 1996; Magrini, 1995; Quah, 1995a, 1995b; and Trede, 1995.)

Viewing convergence as distribution dynamics diverts focus away from economic growth as just boosting the arguments of a production function and towards understanding interaction across economies. Such interaction could take the form of ordinary merchandise trade. Or, as in subsection 2.3 above, it could take the form of coalition formation. Theoretical models of individual cross-section interaction and group formation have also begun to be explored elsewhere (already mentioned above, for instance, are Bénabou, 1996 and Durlauf, 1993). Much, however, remains to be done.

Finally, in this chapter I have emphasised convergence only in the context of cross-economy behaviour. Many of the same ideas and techniques, of course, apply directly to other types of distribution dynamics: a leading example would be the behaviour of personal and family income distributions (e.g. Johnson and Reed, 1996). 'Convergence' there – in the sense of dynamic inequality – is as important as convergence across economies. While, through Kuznets-based reasoning, dynamic inequalities in personal incomes could be related to economic growth, it does so in a way different than does cross-country convergence. Therefore, that growth matters for both might, in fact, be usefully ignored in their study.

NOTES

I thank Fabio Canova, Daniel Cohen and Lucrezia Reichlin for helpful discussions, and the British Academy, ESRC and the MacArthur Foundation for financial support. All data analysis was performed using the author's econometric shell tSrF.

1 I should clarify that I am not referring here to the classical Kuznets question: what is the relation between income distributions *within* an economy and the aggregate growth path of that economy? Rather, I am interested in growth paths of many different aggregate economies and the implications those have for the dynamics of the income distribution across that same collection of economies.

2 An earlier literature (e.g. Grier and Tullock, 1989), studied a similar regression equation with growth on the left-hand side and explanatory variables on the right. I distinguish this from the later work only because that research did not show the same preoccupation with convergence. It instead only investigated, using exploratory empirical techniques, the determinants of growth – an important question, certainly, but distinct from convergence.

3 To simplify the technical exposition, I also assume that log A has bounded second moment. In neoclassical exogenous growth models, it is important that A be permitted to grow without bound, whereupon these stationary and bounded-moment assumptions would be violated. However, as should have already become clear from our earlier discussion, growth in A is not central to the current convergence discussion. At the cost of more extended exposition, everything here can be done taking deviations relative to an unboundedly growing A process. However, no additional insight obtains.

4 Leung and Quah (1996) observe that since η, the 'residual', is common across economies, a cross-section convergence regression cannot actually be estimated consistently in this model. Relaxing the commonality of η, on the other hand, means that convergence as in figure 11.1 necessarily cannot occur.

5 When $\gamma = 1$, then from (15) $\tilde{y}_j$ is always one order of integration higher than η. Thus, should the Solow residual A itself tend to an integrated order 1 sequence, $\tilde{y}_j$ will then be integrated order 2.

6 More general models with cross-sectional interaction (e.g. Bénabou, 1996 and Durlauf, 1993) could also provide other useful insights here.

7 This is a little bit of a misstatement, as we will see that in equilibrium growth turns out to be fairly mechanical, while it is patterns of convergence and divergence that are interesting and intricate.

8 This might be because ideas or memes are like viruses and thus could be dangerous – members of different coalitions are not trusted. Or members of a coalition are able to enforce intellectual property rights perfectly across

coalitions. Quah (1996d) gives a more extended discussion of this. The general idea of memes, or ideas as genes, is discussed in Dawkins (1976) and Kelly (1994).

9 Regression techniques that could potentially do so are the adaptive procedures in Ben-David (1994) and Durlauf and Johnson (1995).

10 Thus, the aim here differs from those emphasised in Canova and Marcet (1995), Forni and Reichlin (1995), Lee *et al.* (1995), Quah (1994a) and Quah and Sargent (1993).

11 The underlying data here are from Summers and Heston (1991), version 5.6. Productivity is per worker output; the normalisation is with respect to average world productivity. For simplicity, below, I refer to *per capita* income or just *income* interchangeably with average worker productivity. All densities were obtained using a gaussian kernel with bandwidth selected automatically, as suggested in Silverman (1986, 3.4.2). I used a fast fourier transform to calculate the resulting kernel estimator; a reflection method (Silverman, 1986, 2.10) took into account non-negativity in the productivity data.

12 When one is interested only in a small subset of the entire cross-section distribution, then vector time-series methods (e.g. Bernard and Durlauf, 1995) would be informative for convergence properties. Univariate time-series models, however, never are: I discuss this more below. Also, *medd* structures need not be restricted only to convergence issues, but might also be used for modelling business-cycle fluctuations across many different sectors or regions (e.g. Quah, 1994b, 1996a).

13 Note that *after* one has learnt about the dynamics of the entire distribution, it might be of interest to go back and study the underlying individual time-series representations. But, to be clear, such analysis only complements the study of distribution dynamics; it cannot be a substitute.

14 Bianchi (1995) sidesteps the dynamics in (19) and considers λ_ts in isolation. He too, however, finds the twin-peaks property of figure 11.3, as one might expect from the evidence in figure 11.4. Bianchi's work differs from those mentioned in the text as he seeks modal properties only in-sample; the others allow those properties to manifest out of sample by the extrapolation in (20). Bianchi's analysis is a statistical formalisation of precisely figure 11.4.

15 It is worth noting that similar twin-peaks features do not describe every such macro income distribution sequence. Compare what I have just said about the world cross-section of countries with, for example, US and European regional behaviour (e.g. Quah, 1996c, 1996e). Quah (1996e) has also analysed the behaviour of cross-economy income distributions, conditioning on spatial effects.

16 These variations all constitute examples of what Quah (1996d) calls *conditioning schemes.*

REFERENCES

Barro, R.J. and Sala-i-Martin, X., 1992, 'Convergence', *Journal of Political Economy*, **100**, 223–51

Baumol, W., 1986. 'Productivity Growth, Convergence, and Welfare', *American Economic Review*, **75**, 1072–85

Bénabou, R., 1996. 'Heterogeneity, Stratification, and Growth: Macroeconomic

Implications of Community Structure and School Finance', *American Economic Review*, **86**, 584–609

Ben-David, D., 1994. 'Convergence Clubs and Diverging Economies', *CEPR Working Paper*, **922**

Bernard, A.B. and Durlauf, S.N., 1995. 'Convergence in International Output', *Journal of Applied Economics*, **10**, 97–108

Bertola, G., 1995. 'Uninsurable Shocks and International Income Convergence', *American Economic Review*, **85**, 301–6

Bianchi, M., 1995. 'Testing for Convergence: A Bootstrap Test for Multi-modality', Bank of England, *Working Paper* (May)

Canova, F. and Marcet, A., 1995. 'The Poor Stay Poor: Non-convergence across Countries and Regions', *CEPR Discussion Paper*, **1265**

Dawkins, R., 1976. *The Selfish Gene* (Oxford: Oxford University Press)

den Haan, W.J., 1995. 'Convergence in Stochastic Growth Models: The Importance of Understanding Why Income Levels Differ', *Journal of Monetary Economics*, **35**, 65–82

Desdoights, A., 1994. 'Changes in the World Income Distribution: A Non-parametric Approach to Challenge the Neoclassical Convergence Argument', PhD dissertation, European University Institute, Florence

   1996. 'Determining Development Patterns and 'Club' Formation using Projection using Pursuit Techniques', ECARE, ULB, *Working Paper* (August)

Durlauf, S.N., 1993, 'Nonergodic Economic Growth', *Review of Economic Studies*, **60**, 349–66

Durlauf, S.N. and Johnson, P., 1995. 'Multiple Regimes and Cross-country Growth Behavior', *Journal of Applied Econometrics*, **10**, 365–84

Forni, M. and Reichlin, L., 1995. 'Dynamic Common Factors in Large Cross Sections', *CEPR Discussion Paper*, **1285**

Friedman, M., 1992. 'Do Old Fallacies Ever Die?', *Journal of Economic Literature*, **30**, 2129–32

Grier, K.B. and Tullock, G., 1989. 'An Empirical Analysis of Cross-national Economic Growth, 1951–80', *Journal of Monetary Economics*, **24**, 259–76

Johnson, P. and Reed, H., 1996. 'Two Nations? The Inheritance of Poverty and Affluence', *Commentary 53*, Institute for Fiscal Studies (January).

Kelly, K., 1994. *Out of Control* (New York: Addison-Wesley)

Kelly, M., 1992. 'On Endogenous Growth with Productivity Shocks', *Journal of Monetary Economics*, **30**, 47–56

Lamo, A.R., 1996. 'Cross-section Distribution Dynamics', PhD dissertation, LSE

Lee, K., Pesaran, M.H. and Smith, R., 1995. 'Growth and Convergence: a Multi-country Empirical Analysis of the Solow Growth Model', *Working Paper*, **9531**, DAE, University of Cambridge (August)

Leung, C. and Quah, D., 1996., 'Convergence, Endogenous Growth, and Productivity Disturbances', *Journal of Monetary Economics*, **38**, 535–47

Lucas, R.E., Jr., 1992. 'On Efficiency and Distribution', *Economic Journal*, **102**, 233–47

   1993. 'Making a Miracle', *Econometrica*, **61**, 251–71

Magrini, S., 1995. 'Income Disparities among European Regions', *Working Paper*, Geography Department, LSE (November)

Paap, R. and H.K. van Dijk, 1994., 'Distribution and Mobility of Wealth of Nations', *Working Paper*, Tinbergen Institute, Erasmus University (October)

Quah, D., 1993a. 'Empirical Cross-section Dynamics in Economic Growth', *European Economic Review*, **37**, 426–34

1993b. 'Galton's Fallacy and Tests of the Convergence Hypothesis', *Scandinavian Journal of Economics*, **95**, 427–43

1994a. 'Exploiting Cross-section Variation for Unit Root Inference in Dynamic Data', *Economics Letters*, **44**, 9–19

1994b. 'One Business Cycle and One Trend from (Many,) Many Disaggregates', *European Economic Review*, **38**, 605–13

1995a. 'Coarse Distribution Dynamics for Convergence, Divergence, and Polarization', *Working Paper*, Economics Department, LSE (July)

1995b. 'International Patterns of Growth: II. Persistence, Path Dependence and Sustained Take-off in Growth Transition', *Working Paper*, Economics Department, LSE (December)

1996a. 'Aggregate and Regional Disaggregate Fluctuations', *Empirical Economics*, **21**, 137–51

1996b. 'Convergence Empirics across Economies with (Some) Capital Mobility', *Journal of Economic Growth*, **1**, 95–124

1996c. 'Empirics for Economic Growth and Convergence', *European Economic Review*, **40**, 1353–75

1996d. 'Ideas Determining Convergence Clubs', *Working Paper*, Economics Department, LSE (April)

1996e. 'Regional Convergence Clusters across Europe', *European Economic Review*, **40**, 951–8

1997. 'Empirics for Growth and Distribution: Polarization, Stratification, and Convergence Clubs', *Journal of Economic Growth*, **2**, 27–59

Quah, D. and Sargent, T.J., 1993. 'A Dynamic Index Model for Large Cross Sections', in J. Stock and M. Watson (eds.), *Business Cycles, Indicators, and Forecasting* (Chicago: University of Chicago Press and NBER)

Romer, P., 1994. 'The Origins of Endogenous Growth', *Journal of Economic Perspectives*, **8**, 3–22

Sala-i-Martin, X., 1996. 'Regional Cohesion: Evidence and Theories of Regional Growth and Convergence', *European Economic Review*, **40**, 1325–52

Silverman, B., 1986. *Density Estimation for Statistics and Data Analysis* (New York: Chapman & Hall)

Summers, R. and Heston, A., 1991. 'The Penn World Table (Mark 5): An Expanded Set of International Comparisons, 1950–1988', *Quarterly Journal of Economics*, **106**, 327–68

Tapscott, D., 1996. *The Digital Economy* (New York: McGraw-Hill)

Thomas, J.P. and Worrall, T., 1990. 'Income Fluctuation and Asymmetric Information: An Example of a Repeated Principal–Agent Problem', *Journal of Economic Theory*, **51**, 367–90

Trede, M., 1995. 'The Age Profile of Earnings Mobility: Statistical Inference for Conditional Kernel Density Estimates', *Discussion Paper*, Cologne University (January)

Discussion

LUCREZIA REICHLIN

To discuss a survey chapter is always a difficult task, but an interesting one when the work being surveyed represents a challenging point of view on the way to understanding a crucial part of economics such as growth theory. What is the relevant framework – theoretical and empirical – for the analysis of whether poor countries are catching up with the rich? In a number of papers, in the last few years, Quah has developed a critique of the traditional approach and the outline of an alternative framework.

Quah's point of view in chapter 11 is that the catching-up question is a question about the evolution over time of the cross-sectional distribution of countries' *per capita* income. At the theory level, Quah argues, this question cannot be analysed by a growth model of the representative economy which has no implications for the distribution of world income; at the econometric level, neither cross-country regressions nor traditional time-series techniques are appropriate tools of analysis. As an alternative, Quah proposes a model of coalition formation where forces of consolidation and fragmentation explain the emergence of 'convergence clubs' and an econometric framework which allows us to estimate transition of groups of countries across different income brackets over time as well as to study the shape of the long-run cross-sectional distribution.

1   Can we study convergence without addressing the distribution question?

It seems to me that on this point Quah's critique against traditional growth models, deterministic or stochastic, is too severe. Although those models have no clear predictions on distributional issues, they have a clear implication on conditional convergence. Unlike what Quah claims, economies are allowed to differ since they can be indexed by their saving rates or other characteristics. Conditional on these characteristics, it can be asked whether they converge to the same level of income. This is an interesting question – it is what the literature on convergence has been about – but it is not exactly the question Quah is asking. Quah's question is not about the destiny of individual economies, but about the evolution of income groups. Unlike the traditional growth model, his model of coalition formation indeed has implications for the evolution of income distribution and this is why a companion empirical model must be constructed to address this question. I will argue that while the econometric framework being developed is a natural one to study distributional questions, it is not easily interpretable when one is interested in the conditional convergence question.

A separate issue is how to procede empirically to test for conditional convergence within the framework of traditional theory. On this, Quah has convincingly argued that, due to Galton's fallacy, cross-country static regressions of first differences of income on initial levels are non-informative. What, then, is an alternative relevant framework? Other strategies have been proposed in the literature: panel regressions, clustering, regression trees, cointegration. Quah dismisses all of these models for not being sufficiently informative about the question at hand. Let us then analyse the advantages and the limits of its proposed alternative framework.

2   The proposed empirical framework

Quah's point of view is one where the relevant economic agent is not the individual country itself, but the quantile in an income distribution; loosely, we are looking at the collective destiny of a group of countries, not at their individual performance. To this end, Quah estimates a dynamic model where the observations are not the variables themselves but the quantiles of a distribution of *per capita* income. The model is the following.

Let us define F_t as the distribution of *per capita* income (normalised with respect to world average) across countries at time t and λ_t as the quantiles relative to that distribution.

The evolution of λ_t is captured by

$$\lambda_t = M\lambda_{t-1}$$

where M is the transition matrix.

There are two goals, the estimation of M which will give us information on persistence of inequalities and the computation of the ergodic distribution. The latter will give us information on the limiting behaviour of the world income distribution.

The stochastic kernel equation can be understood as a constrained VAR where $\Sigma \lambda_t = 1$. The model being estimated is:

$$\lambda_t = M\lambda_{t-1} + \epsilon t$$

For reasons that I do not understand (it does not make the model less interesting), the author rejects this interpretation but the example used to make the point is irrelevant. What Quah claims is that if data are fixed, M cannot be identified by a constrained VAR. But this is always the case when data do not move, no matter what the model is! This is a basic principle of econometrics.

The interpretation of the coefficients of M is the following: m_{21} is the probability that country in income bracket 1 switches to bracket 2 next period. The percentage of countries in bracket 1 at t is:

$$\left(\lambda_{1,t-1}\lambda_{2,t-2}\right)\binom{m11}{m21} = \lambda_{1t}$$

The ergodic distribution can be computed as

$$\lim_{n \to \infty} m^{11}$$

which can be understood as a mean of a stationary process. Empirical estimates from Quah's various papers, on the basis of the Summers and Heston (1991) data set, show that the coefficients of M are concentrated around the principal diagonal (persistence) and that the ergodic distribution is twin-peaked (divergence) (see table D11.1a).

3   What can we potentially learn?

Inferential problems aside, this model can potentially give us information on persistence of income inequalities and on the steady-state distribution

Table D11.1a   *Ergodic distribution twin-peaked*

0.97	0.03				
0.05	0.92	0.04			
	0.04	0.92	0.04		Twin-peaked ergodic
		0.04	0.94	0.02	
			0.01	0.99	
Ergodic distribution	**0.24**	**0.18**	**0.16**	**0.16**	**0.27**

of relative income. It is the appropriate one to ask distributional questions, but it is not suitable to analyse individual countries performance and their determinants. Analysing quantiles makes us lose information on individual behaviour, and this is a problem, unless we want to focus exclusively on distributional questions. Conditioning can be handled only by chosing different normalisations. This is what Quah does for the study of regional convergence, where he normalises with respect to local averages. This exercise can be informative for the question whether geographical proximity matters, but what else can we learn about conditional convergence?

4   Convergence

Having outlined the advantages and disadvantages of Quah's framework, let me now comment on how to interpret results on the ergodic distribution in terms of divergence–convergence. Notice that the model with M constant implies that the vector of quantiles is stationary, indeed a weaker condition than stationarity of the variables themselves. This means that the world income distribution is oscillating around its steady-state twin-peaked distribution (we *have converged* to a bimodal and therefore unequal steady state) or that, having started from initial conditions far from the steady state, we *are in the process of converging* towards it.

To understand the notion of convergence–divergence implied by the model, let us first think of what the implications are of the existence of the ergodic, independently of its shape. The time-series analogue is when, for example, the difference between the income level of two countries is a stationary autoregressive process. This implies that either the two countries have converged to a situation in which the difference in their income levels is stationary or that they are converging towards such a situation. If the two series where $I(1)$ we would say that they are cointegrated. Notice that in both cases, unless the stationary process has mean zero and the cointegrating vector is $[1, -1]$ we have converged or we are converging towards a situation of stable inequality.

When we have more than two countries and a twin-peaked world average income distribution (the ergodic), the implication is that either the underlying time series are clustered in two groups whose composition does not change over time and which are each defined by having a different common trend (two cointegrated vectors if trends are stochastic) or that the two clusters are defined by a different common trend, but their composition is changing over time, preserving, however, the twin-peak shape of the distribution. The latter situation differs from the notion of cointegration since individuals may change their position while the average distribution does not change.

What we can conclude is that the notion of convergence implied by Quah's framework is closely related to that implied by cointegration. The difference is that in one case we care about groups and in the other we care about individuals.

An advantage of Quah's framework, however, is that it is better suited to handle a large number of time series than the cointegration framework is (on the limitation of cointegration for the dynamic analysis of large cross-sections, see Forni and Reichlin, 1997).

What happens, however, if we cannot find a normalisation for which the model for the quantiles is stationary? In this case, Quah's results are very difficult to interpret. From estimation of M we can compute an implied ergodic distribution, but we may be capturing a local trend and not a time-invariant average distribution. Without stating the assumptions of the model and the relation with the underlying time-series processes, it is not clear what is going on. A limitation of Quah's work is not to state the hypotheses needed clearly. The advantage of standard time-series models is that the theory is well developed and we know what the assumptions we need to make to handle inference. It seems that Quah's work is still at an early stage in this respect.

5   Inference

In all Quah's work we are confronted with estimates without standard errors. This is an obvious limitation. The twin-peaks feature of the ergodic distribution disappears if we perturb the coefficients of M by a small amount. This is shown by the examples in table D11.1b (small perturbations lead to a uniform ergodic distribution) and table D11.1c (small perturbations lead to a unimodal ergodic distribution). Once again, the framework is interesting but underdeveloped from the point of view of inference.

A further problem is the existence of the ergodic distribution. Statistically, if more than one eigenvalue of M is equal to one, the ergodic is not defined. From Quah's estimates we obtain the following eigenvalues:

$$(1, 0.9917, 0.9674, 0.9175, 0.8634)$$

which are all very close to one. Are they significantly different from one? If they are not, there is no convergence but we cannot talk of twin peaks.

Table D11.1b *Small perturbations lead to uniform ergodic distribution*

0.96	0.04				
0.04	0.92	0.04			
	0.04	0.92	0.04		Uniform ergodic
		0.04	0.94	0.02	
			0.02	0.98	

Ergodic distribution	**0.20**	**0.20**	**0.20**	**0.20**	**0.20**

Table D11.1c *Small perturbations lead to unimodal ergodic distribution*

0.95	0.05				
0.04	0.92	0.04			
	0.04	0.92	0.04		Unimodal ergodic
		0.04	0.94	0.02	
			0.02	0.98	

Ergodic distribution	**0.17**	**0.22**	**0.22**	**0.22**	**0.14**

6   An alternative framework

Let me try to clarify how some of the dynamic distributional questions that Quah asks can be analysed in a more conventional framework for which we have a better developed inference theory.

I will analyse an example of a dynamic factor model with two common shocks:

$$(1 - L)y_{it} = m + a_i(L)_{ut} + b_i(L)v_t + \epsilon_{it} \qquad i = 1, \ldots, n$$

where $(1 - L)y_{it}$ are covariance-stationary variables, u_t and v_t are orthogonal white noises with unit variance, ϵ_{it} is the idiosyncratic shock, possibly autocorrelated. We assume ϵ_{it} to be mutually orthogonal at all leads and lags and to be orthogonal to u_t and v_t.

This is the model analysed, for n large, by Quah and Sargent (1993), Forni and Reichlin (1996, 1997, 1998) and Stock and Watson (1997).

We are interested in extracting information on (1) cross-section dynamics, (2) convergence and (3) convergence clubs. On the first point, notice that we can get information on cross-sectional dynamics by looking at the distribution of the a_is and the b_is. Can we say anything about convergence? Let me give an example.

- If y_{it}s have one common trend, i.e. they are cointegrated with their cross-sectional mean, we must have:

$$b_i(1) = 0$$
$$\epsilon_{it} \sim I(0), \forall i$$

- If $a_i(1) = k \; \forall i$, variables are cointegrated with the mean, with cointegration vector $(-1, 1)$ and $(1 - L)(y_{it} - Ey_t)$ is stationary.
- If, in addition, $m_i = m \; \forall i$, we have convergence as defined in Bernard and Durlauf (1995). This can be easily tested.

We can use the same framework to try to detect convergence clubs. This can be done by looking at cointegration clusters. If u_t and v_t are both permanent and there are two groups of countries, group 1 for which $a_i(L) = k_i, b_i(1) = h_i$ and group 2 for which $a_i(1) = k_2, b_i(1) = h_2$, then each group is cointegrated with its own mean, but the two groups are not cointegrated amongst them. If we condition each group with respect to its own mean, we get a set of stationary variables, and each set is a convergence club.

These examples illustrate that most of the questions about the empirics of cross-sectional distribution dynamics can be asked within a traditional time-series framework for which we have well developed inference analysis. This framework has also the advantage of not losing information about individual behaviour through quantile aggregation and to be better suited for handling the joint dynamics of several variables (output, saving rates, etc.). On the other hand, I agree with Quah that to study distribution questions, the evolving distribution approach is potentially interesting. Theory for statistical inference, however, remains to be developed and this cannot be done without being more explicit on the assumptions on the nature of the underlying stochastic processes being studied.

REFERENCES

Bernard, A. and Durlauf, S.N., 1995. 'Convergence in International Output', *Journal of Applied Econometrics*, **10**, 97-108

Forni, M. and Reichlin, L., 1996. 'Dynamic Common Factors in Large Cross-sections', *Empirical Economics*, **21**

  1997. 'National Policies and Local Economies: Europe and the US', *CEPR Working Paper*, **1632**

  1998. 'Let's Get Real: A Dynamic Factor Analytic Approach to Disaggregated Business Cycle', *Review of Economic Studies*

Quah, D.T. and Sargent, T.J., 1993. 'A Dynamic Index Model for Large Cross-sections', in J. H. Stock and M. W. Watson (eds.), *Business Cycles, Indicators, and Forecasting*, vol. 28 (Chicago: University of Chicago Press and NBER)

Stock, J. H. and Watson, M.W., 1997. 'Diffusion Indexes' (July), mimeo
Summers, R. and Heston, A., 1991. 'The Penn World Table (Mark 5): An Expanded Set of International Comparisons, 1950–1988', *Quarterly Journal of Economics*, **106**, 327–68

Index

AFTA (Asean Free Trade Area) 36
agriculture 37–8, 257, 269
Ahn, N. 239
Alogoskoufis, G. 193
Amiti, M. 269
Anderton, R. 193
Antolin, P. 236, 238
Argentina 35, 160, 164–6
Artis, M. 218
asset market 115
Attanasio, O. 239
Austria 189, 197

Bagwell, K. 1, 19, 21–3, 53–78, 81–4
Baldwin, R. 1–4, 25, 27, 58, 251–3
Baldwin, R. and R. 114–15
Barran, F. 222
Barrell, R. 193
Barro, R. J. 277, 283, 288, 295–6, 303–4, 313
Baumol, W. 310
Bayoumi, T. 3, 187–211, 216–26
Bean, C. 194
Ben-David, D. 277
Bénabou, R. 276, 323
Benelux 189, 197
Bentolila, S. 229, 235–6
Bergsten, F. 38
Bernard, A. 334
Bertola, G. 3–4, 246, 275–93, 305
Bhagwati, J. N. 7, 30, 49, 51, 95, 183
Bini-Smaghi, L. 191–2
Blanchard, O. 189–90, 192–3, 217, 219, 229
Blanchflower, D. G. 124–5
Boden, P. 235
Bond, E. W. 12, 15–16, 19–22, 73, 75
Borjas, G. 120, 124
Bourguignon, F. 159
Bover, O. 238
Brainard, L. 114
Brock, P. 96–7

Brown, D. 128
Brulhart, M. 268
Buiter, W. 193

Cadot, O. 26
Cameron, D. 142
Campa, J. M. 20
Canada 35, 196
Canova, F. 277, 291, 317
capital
  human 282, 288, 310
  mobility 182–3, 293
Caporale, G. M. 188–9
Chamie, N. 189
Chari, V. V. 290
Chatterjee, S. 286, 288
Chile 164–6, 173
Cline, W. R. 120
Cobden–Chavalier Treaty 39
Cohen, D. 1–4, 188, 295–6
Collie, D. 14
Colombia 160, 164–6
comparative advantage 12, 14, 146
  middle-income countries 169–70, 176
  and working conditions 134, 136–7, 141
consumers vs. producers 23–4, 91
convergence
  conditional 303, 313, 318, 322
  and cross-section distribution 310–13
  definitions 298
  and growth 275, 300–4
  and market interactions 275, 289
  model 329–30; interpretation 331–2
  per capita income 275, 279
  policy impact 281
  sigma 291–2
  and technological progress 282
  without distribution 328–7
  see also globalisation; income
    distribution; integration

Costa Rica 164–6
costs
  adjustment 188
  labour 134–6, 141
  transaction 188, 217–18
  transport 13–14, 259, 263, 274
  see also trade costs
Coughlin, P. J. 97
Courgeau, D. 235
custom unions (CU) 12, 22
  free trade area (FTA) 13, 15
  optimum tariff 16–17
  preferential agreements 71–2
  reciprocity 55

Dam, K. W. 53, 63, 73
DaVanzo, J. 238
Daveri, F. 246–7
De Grauwe, P. 193, 197
de la Rica, S. 239
de Melo, J. 26, 30
Deardoff, A. W. 12
Deardorff, A. 128
Decressin, J. 190, 192–3, 229
Dehejia, V. 183
Delors Report 187, 208
demography 231, 233
den Haan, W. J. 305
Denmark 188, 189, 197
Desdoigts, A. 314, 317, 323
Desruelle, D. 27–8
Diba, B. T. 194
direct democracy model 88–90
discount rate 19, 50
disturbances
  convergence 206
  employment 190
  output movements 188
  and regional specialisation 206–7, 222,
    224–6
  supply and demand 189, 199–205, 219
  see also shocks
Dixit, A. K. 257
Dolado, J. 235–6
Durlauf, S. N. 277, 323, 334

education 147, 163
Edwards, A. C. and S. 166
EFTA 25, 34, 36
Eichengreen, B. 3, 187–211, 216–26
electoral competition model 96–7, 99
employment
  disturbances 190
  regional portfolios 191
EMU 187, 188–90, 197
endogenous growth models 246

enforcement 53, 56, 72–6
Erkel-Rousse, H. 189
Ethier, W. J. 40
European Union (EU) 20, 51
  113 Committee 32–3
  absorption of EFTA countries 25, 34
  Association Agreements 27, 29
  core–periphery 188–90, 202
  formation 73–4
  Grubel–Lloyd index 226
  MacSharry farm reforms 38
  migration 192–3, 251–3
  regional convergence or divergence
    245–6
  regional specialisation 207, 268–9
  relative prices 196–7
  Single Market 245, 248
  tariffs before and after integration 27–8
  trade policy 32–4, 35–6
  voting power 32–4; veto 31–2
Evans, P. 103
exchange rate policies 191, 196, 218–21
exports
  factor-content 158–61
  Nash policy 60
externalities 39, 55–6, 67, 69
  pecuniary 258, 265, 273, 274

factor intensity reversal 183–4
factor-endowment models 120
Faini, R. 3, 181–4, 228–49, 251–3
Fatas, A. 190, 192–3, 229
Faust, J. 190
Feeney, J. 115
Feenstra, R. C. 95, 164, 166, 182–3
Ferenczi, I. 228
Fernández, R. 79–85
Findlay, R. 30, 93
Finland 189
Fischer, B. 158
Flam, H. 86
Fontagné, L. 225–6
foreign direct investment (FDI) 40–1, 296
  working conditions 134, 137, 140–1, 141
Forni, M. 317, 332–3
France 35, 39, 86, 189, 197, 231, 234–5
Frankel, J. A. 13–17, 29
Fratianni, M. 195
free trade agreement (FTA) 22, 55, 71,
  106–8
Freeman, R. 120, 130–1
Friedman, M. 309
Fujita, M. 255
Funke, M. 189, 198

Galli, G. 240, 242

Galor, O. 288
Galton's fallacy 309, 329
games
    prisoner's dilemma 54
    repeated 21–2, 50
    sequential Nash 15–16
    static tariff 59–60
    see also international negotiation
Garber, P. M. 86
Garrett, G. 188
Gatsios, K. 31
GATT 19, 36
    Article XXIV 18, 22, 53, 71–2, 106, 108
    Article XXVIII 64
    Dillon Round 37
    Kennedy Round 37, 74
    reciprocity 55
    self-enforcement 54
    Super 301 19–20
    Tokyo Round 38, 74
    two-phase negotiations 64, 70
    Uruguay Round 27, 38, 86, 88
GATT–WTO system 53, 62–5, 80–4
geographical space 255, 256–7
Germany 35, 39, 188, 189, 190, 197,
    198–208, 234, 296
Gil, L. 243
Gindling, T. 165
Glivenko–Cantelli Theorem 309
globalisation
    external risk 141–6
    and inequality 150–1
    labour markets 117–48
    see also integration
Goldstein, M. 195
Gonzales, M. 165
Goria, A. 235
Goto, J. 16
Gottschalk, P. 122–3
government
    consumption 143, 145–6
    employment 142–3
    national fiscal stabilisation 194–5
    openness and size 142–6
    organisation 31–2
    role 119, 141–6
    welfare functions 57–8, 66–8, 80–1; joint
        60–1, 81
Greece 189, 230
Grossman, G. M. 23–6, 58, 98–9, 101–3,
    105–6, 108, 113–16, 282
growth
    convergence role 275–93
    impact of openness 296
    and income level 276–7
    and market interactions 278–81

stylised facts 276, 280
growth theory
    endogenous and exogenous 278–81
    neoclassical 278–81, 295, 300–4
    stochastic 304–10
Grubel–Lloyd index 226

Hamada, K. 16
Hamilton, C. B. 33
Hammond, G. W. 194
Hanson, G. H. 164, 166, 182–3
Harrison, A. 164, 166
Hathaway, D. E. 38
Hatton, T. 228
Heckscher–Ohlin theory 28, 88, 153–8
Heens, H. 197
Helg, R. 191
Helpman, E. 2, 23–6, 58, 86–111, 113–16,
    282
Heston, A. 330
Hillman, A. L. 86, 91, 115
Hong Kong 162–3, 173
Hufbauer, G. C. 35
Hughes, G. 238–9

Ichino, A. 235
import-penetration ratios 113–14
income 322
income differentials
    and migration 231, 233
    persistent 277–8, 280
income distribution
    and capital-deepening 286
    conditional from unconditional 318,
        322
    cross-economy 299: evolution 312–22,
        328–31
    empirics 312–22
    and integration 283–91
    traditional framework 333–4
    twin-peak 212–18, 331–2
    see also convergence
India 159, 169
industrial agglomeration 254–5
    forces for 258–9, 273
    input-output linkages 268
    trade costs 263–5
industrial linkages see input–output
    linkages
inequality
    and globalisation 150–1
    wage 118, 122
Ingco, M. D. 38
Ingram, J. 193
input–output linkages 255, 258–9, 262–8,
    273

integration 255
  economic and monetary 222–6
  full 284–7
  and growth 296
  and income distribution 283–91
  incomplete 287–9
  natural partners 72
  protectionism 19, 25–6
  and specialisation 268
  and welfare convergence 295–6
  see also convergence; globalisation
interest groups
  effect on FTAs 106–8
  internal organisation 115
  joint welfare maximisation 94–5
  and tariff-formation function 93
  see also lobbying
international interactions 36–40, 282
International Labour Organisation (ILO)
  132–3
international negotiation 18–19
  lead country 31
  Nash bargaining 108, 124–5
  time scale 19–20, 50
  see also games
Irwin, D. A. 35–6, 39
Italianer, A. 194
Italy 35, 189, 235–43

Jackson, J. H. 38, 63
Jacobson, H. 103
Jacquemin, A. 20
Jimeno, J. 229, 243
job-search 243–5
Johnson, H. G. 54, 104
Johnson, P. 277, 323
Jones, E. 194
Jones, R. W. 93

Kaldor, N. 276–7, 280
Kaplinsky, R. 171
Karp, L. 31
Katz, L. F. 120, 124, 192–3, 229
Kehoe, P. J. 290
Kelly, K. 298
Kelly, M. 305, 308
Kemp–Wan tariff reduction 20–1
Kenen, P. 187, 190
Keohane, R. O. 38
Kim, K. S. 159
Kletzer, K. 194–5
Korea 162–3, 166, 173
Kowalczyk, C. 18
Krishna, P. 24–5, 27–8
Krueger, P. 158–9
Krugman, P. 1, 11–14, 16, 49–50, 191, 206,

208, 218, 222, 245, 247, 252, 255, 257,
  260, 263, 265

labour
  costs 13–6, 141
  demand: downward slope 126–7;
    elasticity 118, 119, 121–4, 131, 151,
    157; shocks to 118, 121–2
  markets: adjustment 192–3; and
    globalisation 117–48; institutions 162,
    164
  mobility *see* migration
  standards *see* working conditions
  substitutability 118, 121, 124
  supply: from low standards 128; skilled
    and unskilled 161–2
Lambert, S. 247
Lamo, A. R. 314, 318
Lawrence, R. Z. 37, 120
Leamer, E. E. 120, 154
Lee, T. H. 159
Leeper, E. 190
Leung, C. 305, 308
Levhari, D. 247
Levine, R. 277
Levy, P. I. 27–30
Lewis, A. 246
Li, J. 97
Liang, K. S. 159
Lippi, M. 190
Livi Bacci, M. 234–5
lobbying
  micro foundations 115
  technology 102
  see also interest groups
location decision 192, 246, 255
  centre vs. periphery 259–60
  and competition 260, 261, 267–8
  formal model 269–72
  model overview 256–9
Londero, E. 159–60
Lucas, R. E. 305, 318
Ludema, R. 22

McCormick, B. 238–9
McGrattan, E. R. M. 290
McKinnon, R. 187
MacSharry, R. 38
Magee, S. 96–7
Magelby, D. B. 98
Magrini, S. 323
Malaysia 166, 173
Mankiw, N. G. 277, 281, 288, 296
manufacturing 257–9, 270
Marcet, A. 277, 291, 317
Markusen, J. 183

Masson, P. R. 191, 194–5
Mayer, W. 88, 97
Mélitz, J. 189, 194, 219
Menendez, A. 165
Mercosur 35
Messerlin, P. A. 32, 35
Mexico 30, 35, 84
migration 228–49
    and amenities 233–4
    attitudes 243–5
    barriers to 229, 245, 248
    falling 235–6
    flows 120
    gender differences 239, 241
    and income differentials 231, 233
    intentions 239–43
    internal 234–5, 236
    intra-European 230–5
    policies 230
    regional adjustment 192–3, 222
    and risk reduction 246–7
    social costs 252
    and unemployment 229, 231, 233, 236–9,
        241–2
Miller, R. 277
Minford, P. 172
model of explicit distribution dynamics
        (medd) 314, 318
Moffitt, R. 122–3
monetary integration see EMU; integration;
        optimum currency areas (OCAs)
Morrisson, C. 159
most favoured nation (MFN) 65–6, 70–1,
        81–3, 106
Muet, P. A. 193
multilateralism
    definition 8–10, 21, 41
    index 42–4
Mundell, R. A. 187–8, 190, 193, 217

NAFTA 27, 29, 30, 35, 74, 84, 86
Nambier, R. G. 159
Nelson, C. J. 98
Netherlands 188
Neumann, M. 197
Nitsch, V. 13
Nogues, J. 36
non-discrimination 53, 55, 65–71
Nordström, H. 16–17, 20
Nowell, E. 172

Obstfeld, M. 283
Olarreaga, J. 26
Olsen, M. 90
optimal import-sourcing condition 13
optimum currency area (OCA) 187–211

costs and benefits 217–18, 220
    economic effects on criteria 208
    error terms 190
    fiscal transfers 193–5
    regional specialisation 190–2
    relative prices 195–7
optimum tariff
    custom unions (CU) 16–17
    number of blocs 12–13
    political 61, 65, 70
Oswald, A. J. 124–5
Ottaviano, G. I. P. 273
Owens, T. 167
ownership distribution 90, 92, 101
Oye, K. 36, 39, 42

Paap, R. 314, 318
Padoa Schioppa, F. 239
Panagariya, A. 30, 51
Peltzman, S. 91
Perroni, C. 17
Pisani-Ferry, J. 194, 216–26
Pissarides, C. 237–8
political economy models 113–16
political equilibria 106–7
political objective function 99
political parties, contributions to 96–106
political-support function 91–2, 100, 101
politics
    domestic 18, 23–9, 30–1, 42
    internal and external 103–8
Polosz, S. 196
Portugal 188, 189, 230, 231
Prasad, E. 192, 207, 222
preferential agreements 53–78
    with CU 71–2
    with FTA 71
    market power effect 74–5
    steady state effect 75
    trade diversion effect 74–5
    transition period 73–4
preferential trading areas (PTA) 14
prices, relative 195–7
producers vs. consumers 23–4, 91
profits and trade policy 24–5
Puga, D. 273
Pumain, D. 235
Putnam, R. 87, 103

Quah, D. T. 4, 189–90, 217, 219, 277, 282,
        288, 290, 296, 298–325, 328–34
Quintanilla, R. 36

Ramey, V. 124
randomness, idiosyncratic 290–1
Rauch, J. 246

Razin, A. 228
reciprocity 53–4, 81–2
    and CUs 55
    defined 62–3
    and free trade areas 55
    in GATT–WTO system 55, 62–5
    most favoured nation 70–1
    non-discrimination 65–71
    substantially equivalent concessions 63–4
Reed, H. 323
Rees, P. 235
regional integration arrangement (RIA) 7, 49
regional trade agreement (RTA) 83–4
regionalism
    asymmetric models 15–19, 30
    benign 18
    definition 8–10
    domino 25
    effect on multilateralism 42
    political economy models 23–9, 50
    risks of catastrophe 42
    small country insurance 17–18
    symmetric models 11–15, 41
    usefulness of 22
Reichlin, L. 190, 317, 328–34
Reichlin, P. 246
Renelt, D. 277
rent-sharing bargain 118, 124–8
returns to scale, constant (CRS) 14–15, 88,
    245–6, 278, 300
Revenga, A. 164
Richardson, J. D. 120
Richardson, M. 25–8, 31, 35
Riley, J. 172
risk reduction 246–7
Robbins, D. 161–6, 173, 175
Rodrik, D. 2, 30, 102, 117–48, 150–2
Romer, P. M. 276, 280, 295, 300, 304
Rossi, F. 240, 242
Rustichini, A. 246

Sachs, J. D. 120, 193–4, 289–90, 295–6
Sadka, E. 228
Sala-i-Martin, X. 193–4, 277, 281, 288, 290,
    295–6, 303–4, 313
Salt, J. 230
Sanfey, P. 124–5
Sapir, A. 1–4, 20, 37, 49–51
Sargent, T. J. 317, 333
Scharpf, F. 32
Schattschneider, E. E. 33
Scitovszky, T. 54
Shatz, H. 120
Shepsle, K. A. 33, 88
shocks
    adjustment 228–9

asymmetric 198–9, 216, 217, 222–3
    measurement of 218–21
    origins 221–2
    policy conclusions 221–2
    symmetric 188–90
    trade 114
    see also disturbances
Sinclair, P. 12–13
Singapore 162–3, 166, 173
Sjostrom, T. 18
Slaughter, M. 120
Smith, A. 150–2, 273–4
Smith, R. 193, 207
Smoot–Hawley tariff 33, 39
Solow, R. M. 278, 307
Sorenson, T. L. 20
Spain 189, 230, 231, 235–43
specialisation
    and comparative advantage 146
    and integration 268
    patterns 255, 262
    regional 190–2, 206–7, 222, 224–6, 247,
        252
    and trade cost 268
Spilimbergo, A. 14
Spinanger, D. 158
Srinivasan, T. N. 12
Staiger, R. W. 1, 19, 21–3, 53–78, 81–4
Stark, O. 246–7
Stein, E. 13–14, 17
stepping-stone argument 28–9
Stern, R. M. 12, 128
Stigler, G. 91
Stiglitz, J. E. 257
Stillwell, J. 235
Stock, J. H. 333
Stockman, A. C. 191
Stolper–Samuelson effect 28
Stolper–Samuelson linkage 172
Summers, L. H. 8, 124
Summers, R. 330
Switzerland 88, 189
Syropoulos, C. 12, 15–16, 19–22, 73, 75

Tadas, G. 159
Taiwan 159, 162–3, 166, 173
Tapscott, D. 298
tariffs
    before and after integration 27–8
    discriminatory 75–6
    Kemp–Wan reduction 20–1
    Nash 27
    negotiated 19–23
    optimum 11–12, 12–13, 16–17, 61, 65, 70
    revenues 26
    Smoot–Hawley 33, 39

static 59–60
vs. output subsidies 102
tariff regime models 11–34
tariff-formation function 92–6, 101
Taylor, A. M. 289
Taylor, M. P. 191
technology
    and convergence 282
    and growth 278
    and wage differentials 173–5
    world-wide uniformity 281–2
Teitel, S. 159–60
terms of trade 54, 67–8
Thisse, J. 255
Thomas, A. H. 196
Thomas, J. P. 305
Torstensson, J. 268
trade
    insurance against shocks 114
    low-income exporters 169–73
    as production function 129
    skill-enhancing 174
    small gains from 117–118, 150
    and wages 120–4
trade barriers 154
trade costs 255
    defined 257–8
    and industrial agglomeration 263–5
    industrial differences 260–2
    location decision 259–60, 274
    and specialisation 268
trade policy
    cooperative 105–6
    distributional considerations 86
    efficient 60–2, 68–70, 81
    EU 32–4, 35–6
    inefficient 54–5, 56, 80
    instruments 168–9, 183–4
    international interactions 103–8
    Nash 69, 80, 82, 97
    political economy models 87–103
    and profits 24–5
    and tariff revenues 26
    unilateral 54–5, 56, 58–60, 68, 80
    and wage equality 153–79
trade protection 30
    and bureaucrats 32
    endogenous 25–6
    equilibrium rate 93–4
trade wars 103–4
transport costs 13–14, 259, 263, 274
Trede, M. 323, 328

Ugidos, S. 239
unemployment 120, 127–8
    and migration 229, 231, 233, 236–9, 241–2

policies 253
United Kingdom 189, 235, 237–8
United States 35, 37
    as currency area 190–4, 196–7, 217, 222
    labour 120, 122
    migration 229, 235, 237–8
    PACs 98
    political debate 86
    Reciprocal Trade Agreements Act 39
    regional specialisation 207
universalism 33
Uruguay 164–6

van Dijk, H.K. 314, 318
Vanhaverbeke, W. 193
Vaubel, R. 196
Venables, A. J. 1–4, 183, 207, 245, 247, 252,
    254–74
Ventura, J. 287
Verdier, T. 113–16
Vines, D. 12–13
von Hagen, J. 194–5, 197
Vorasopontaviporn, P. 159
Vori, S. 191–2, 194
voting theory
    median voter model 28–9, 90
    probabilistic 97

Wadsworth, J. 237–8
wage differentials
    capital mobility 182–3
    education 163
    industrial agglomeration 260
    low-income exporters 170–2
    migration 231
    natural resources 167–8, 176
    technical progress 173–5
    time-series evidence 166–7
    trade policy instruments 168–9
wages
    centre vs. periphery 267
    flexibility 193
    inequality 118, 122, 153–79
    minimum 166
    real 259
    skill differential 161, 164–6
    and trade 120–4
Walliamson, J. G. 289
Warner, A. 289–90, 295–6
Watson, M. W. 333
Weber, A. 188
Wei, S. J. 13–14, 17, 29
Weil 295
Weingast, B. R. 33
welfare
    convergence 295–6

welfare (*cont.*)
   government function 57–8, 66–8, 80–1;
     joint 60–1
   national 126
welfare maximising models 11–19, 30, 41,
    50
Wellisz, S. 93
Werner Report 196
Whalley, J. 17
Widgrén, M. 33–4
Willcox, W. 228
Williamson, J. 228
Winham, G. R. 38
Winters, L. A. 1, 7–45, 49–51, 73
Woglom, G. 195
Wood, A. 2, 120, 153–79, 181–4
working conditions 119, 128–32,
    151–2

   and comparative advantage 134, 136–7,
    141
   defined 132
   and FDI 134, 137, 140–1, 141
   indicators 133–4
   internationalisation 152
   and labour costs 134–6, 141
   South–North effects 130–2
   willingness to pay for 130–1
Worrall, T. 305
Wyplosz, C. 188

Yarbrough, B. V. and R. M. 9
Young, A. 296
Young, L. 96–7

Zeira, J. 288
Zhang, W. 218